Themes in Comparative History

This series of books provides concise studies on some of the major themes currently arousing academic controversy in the fields of economic and social history. Each author explores a given theme in a comparative context, drawing on material from western societies as well as those in the wider world. The books are introductory and explanatory and are designed for all those following thematic courses in history, cultural European or social studies.

Themes in Comparative History

General Editor: CLIVE EMSLEY

PUBLISHED TITLES

Clive Emsley
POLICING AND ITS CONTEXT 1750–1870
R. F. Holland
EUROPEAN DECOLONIZATION 1918–1981
Raymond Pearson
NATIONAL MINORITIES IN EASTERN EUROPE 1848–1945
Pamela Pilbeam
THE MIDDLE CLASSES IN EUROPE 1789–1914
FRANCE, GERMANY, ITALY AND RUSSIA
Jane Rendall
THE ORIGINS OF MODERN FEMINISM: WOMEN IN
BRITAIN, FRANCE AND THE UNITED STATES, 1780–1860
Ken Ward
MASS COMMUNICATIONS AND THE MODERN WORLD

FORTHCOMING

John Bohstedt
RIOTS AS POPULAR POLITICS IN THE MODERN WEST,
1750–1985
David Englander and Tony Mason
WAR AND POLITICS: THE EXPERIENCE OF THE
SERVICEMAN IN TWO WORLD WARS
Ian Inkster
SCIENCE AND TECHNOLOGY IN HISTORY c. 1750–1914
Joe Lee
PEASANT EUROPE IN THE 18th AND 19th CENTURIES
Dominic Lieven
THE EUROPEAN ARISTOCRACY 1815–1914
Rosemary O'Day
THE FAMILY IN FRANCE, ENGLAND AND THE UNITED
STATES, 1600–1850
Peter Rycraft
PEASANT REBELLIONS 1400–1600

THE MIDDLE CLASSES IN EUROPE
1789–1914
FRANCE, GERMANY, ITALY AND RUSSIA

Pamela M. Pilbeam

MACMILLAN

First published 1990

Published by
MACMILLAN EDUCATION LTD
Houndmills, Basingstoke, Hampshire RG21 2XS
and London
Companies and representatives
throughout the world

Typeset by Wessex Typesetters
(Division of The Eastern Press Ltd)
Frome, Somerset

Printed in Hong Kong

British Library Cataloguing in Publication Data
Pilbeam, Pamela M.
The middle classes in Europe 1789–1914: France,
Germany, Italy and Russia.—(Themes in comparative
history)
1. Europe. Middle classes, history
I. Title   II. Series
305.5'5'094
ISBN 0-333-38558-6
ISBN 0-333-38559-4 pbk

Contents

To Stephen, Ashha, Rhys and Llewellyn

General Editor's Preface

SINCE the Second World War there has been a massive expansion in the study of economic and social history generating, and fuelled by, new journals, new academic series and societies. The expansion of research has given rise to new debates and ferocious controversies. This series proposes to take up some of the current issues in historical debate and explore them in a comparative framework.

Historians, of course, are principally concerned with unique events, and they can be inclined to wrap themselves in the isolating greatcoats of their 'country' and their 'period'. It is at least arguable, however, that a comparison of events, or a comparison of the way in which different societies coped with a similar problem – war, industrialisation, population growth and so forth – can reveal new perspectives and new questions. The authors of the volumes in this series have each taken an issue to explore in such a comparative framework. The books are not designed to be path-breaking mono-graphs, though most will contain a degree of new research. The intention is, by exploring problems across national boundaries, to encourage students in tertiary education, in sixth-forms, and hope-fully also the more general reader, to think critically about aspects of past developments. No author can maintain strict objectivity; nor can he or she provide definitive answers to all the questions which they explore. If the authors generate discussion and increase perception, then their task is well done.

CLIVE EMSLEY

1. Who Were the Middle Classes?

IF man could have moved from rural society directly to the age of the microchip, the vast expansion of the middle classes in the nineteenth century might never have happened, indeed social structures would have been entirely different, and R.H. Tawney might never have been provoked to remark: 'The word "class" is fraught with unpleasing associations, so that to linger upon it is apt to be interpreted as a symptom of a perverted mind and a jaundiced spirit.'[1]

The aim of this book is to compare the middle classes in four of the major states in continental Europe – France, Russia, Germany and Italy – from the French Revolution of 1789 until the outbreak of the First World War. This was a period of considerable change, both in the use of the term 'middle class', and in the social groups which belonged to the category. Qualitative and quantitative changes in industry led to an expansion in the size and composition of the entrepreneurial element within the middle class. Population growth and urbanisation also contributed to the 'professionalisation' of the professions and to the vast burgeoning of the role of the state and with it the huge expansion of the bureaucracy and of all aspects of the 'white-collar' element. Generations of unsuspecting undergraduates have found the phrase 'middle class' a morass, a minefield, even a veritable Pandora's box. It is certainly a chameleon among definitions, whether flopped down vaguely to cover multifarious ignorance, used with attempted precision by social scientists searching for rigour and objectivity, or employed by political commentators as a term of praise or a weapon in an ideological armoury. Are 'middle class' and 'bourgeois' interchangeable? What do 'upper', 'middle' and 'lower' gradations of either term signify? When do 'class' definitions take over from 'orders' or 'estates'? Which of the following criteria should the historian employ in trying to explain class: financial, occupational, economic, political, status, cultural or other? How appropriate for the historian are 'models' presented by social scientists, who may be more concerned with a static analysis than with social change over a period of time? Definitions of 'middle class' are varied, ambiguous and vague, and the rapid introduction of a large element of political ideology, puritanical moralising and invective, especially by the early socialists, has certainly muddied the waters. Fervent attempts to disprove Marx's prognosis for industrial society and the numerous modifications of his ideas proposed by his followers have not helped in making definitions of class more precise, rather the reverse. The acclaimed experiences of 'bourgeois' revolutions in France in 1789 and Russia in 1917 have not facilitated the debate. In this first chapter we shall consider two aspects: first how the use of class terminology has changed through time, and secondly which groups in the four countries chosen need to be examined.

During the eighteenth and nineteenth centuries men stopped thinking of their society as split into estates or orders, in which status was based on a range of factors of which economic function was one element among many, to one of classes, where a man's job and the amount he was paid counted for much more. In the traditional structure of estates, the Church in France was the First Estate, the nobility the Second and everyone else the Third. The different estates were further distinguished by the rights and privileges of the corporate, constituent groups. By the eighteenth century these divisions gave no hint of economic function, as the 'warrior' second estate eagerly engaged in trade, nor did they illuminate social distinctions, since non-nobles could buy feudal privileges and exploit them for financial gain, with no hint of reciprocal social obligation. Within each estate were huge differences in wealth, lifestyle and occupation, to such a degree that some nobles and clergy deemed it more fitting to sit with the Third Estate than with their own in the Estates General of 1789. By the eighteenth century the existence of the obligations and, more significantly, the privileges of each estate, were often irrelevant, even harmful to social relations and the effective conduct of government.

At the end of the eighteenth century the groups we would describe as middle class were encompassed within the Third Estate, but this latter term had become vague and virtually meaningless. When the abbé Siéyès wrote his polemical pamphlet *What is the Third Estate?* on the eve of the resuscitation of the Estates General in 1789, he noted that the Third included all outside the nobility and clergy, that the vast majority of Frenchmen had no role in running their country, and that this situation must be remedied; but he was actually only interested in the political liberation of the better-off, educated element. In pursuit of this goal, he was apparently content to leave the issue of definition fudged and ambiguous. Throughout his pamphlet he used the language of 'estates' and did not probe the enormous divisions within the 'Third' Estate, for this would have revealed how narrow a sector of the estate he wanted to liberate politically, the richer bourgeoisie. Within the society of estates, 'bourgeois' was once a precise subsection: the wealthy, corporate members of an urban community. It referred to corporate status, wealth and the source of income. By 1789 it was used much more loosely, to include social and economic categories, as well as to cover various status groups and those who lived by certain standards or norms. Describing a man as 'bourgeois' told one nothing about his job; he would not be a king or labourer, but he might be a state official, a man of letters, a professional, merchant, banker, industrialist or academic. He might simply live from the income he derived from rural or urban property or from money invested, perhaps in government securities. His occupation did not mark him out as essentially distinct from some nobles, churchmen or better-off peasants. His ranking in tax obligations and privileges would help further to define him, as would his education, lifestyle, self-image and social and family relationships.

'Class' terminology was first used by the physiocrats, a section of the *philosophes*, in the mid-eighteenth century. By the late 1760s Mably was describing groups with different economic functions as classes. The British writer, Adam Smith, split society into traditional orders, and then subdivided each order into classes. His followers abandoned orders in favour of classes.[2] The groups thus described were very vague, amorphous economic entities. The use of 'middle class' rather than 'bourgeois' seems to indicate the perceived need for new categories in a time of social change. But by the nineteenth century the two terms were interchangeable, although some writers used 'bourgeois' to imply a higher financial and social rank, reserving 'middle class' for the less wealthy. The range of status, occupation and wealth encompassed led to the adoption of subdivisions, *grande*, *moyenne, petite* bourgeoisie; upper, middle and lower middle class. De Tocqueville, in describing the middle class of the *ancien régime*, concentrated on those who held public appointments, with their preference for town living, their desire to buy office and thereby to enlarge their privileges, and the resulting myriad divisions within the group. He observed that the notable citizens of one small town were split into 36 distinct sections, which were constantly trying to define their group so as to exclude some of their number. As a result some had only three or four members, and each group was made distinct by a mass of small privileges. Indeed an eighteenth-century office-holder had bought his post and was free from interference by central government. In this sense he was better off than his nineteenth-century successor.[3] This was a traditional and privileged section of the bourgeoisie, almost a pseudo-aristocracy, especially since such privileges could be handed down to sons.[4] However it was only one of many varied groups, and towards the end of the eighteenth century a bourgeois, in receipt of various privileges, might yet be at war with the concept of privilege. The term 'bourgeois' was, as a recent Marxist historian has concluded, ambiguous; the bourgeoisie was a '*classe intermédiare*' or '*classe carrefour*' which historians might try to group together, but whose constituent parts were almost infinitely varied.[5]

Before 1789 the term 'bourgeois' might help to illuminate some social, economic and cultural attitudes and functions but would mask diversity, hiding more than it revealed. The 1789 revolution fudged its meaning even more by adding a political dimension. Long-established social categories, notably 'aristocrat', 'bourgeois', and 'sans-culottes' (a term used to describe the group of Parisian artisans active in the unrest of the early 1790s), were transformed into political slogans. At times 'bourgeois' was used almost as the equivalent of '*citoyen*'. As the economic circumstances of many French families worsened in the 1790s, 'bourgeois' itself became a term of opprobrium and abuse, and the new class terminology, previously used to sketch different levels of wealth, followed suit. The attempt made in the constitutions of the 1790s to define the politically active by the tax they paid also helped to transform the new 'class' terms into political labels. In the 1790s Babeuf rated conflict between classes, which he defined in general economic terms, as more significant than the political debate. He argued that the achievement of political harmony had to be predicated upon the equalisation of wealth.[6]

Qualitative and quantitative changes taking place in industry were beginning to impinge on the consciousness of a growing number of writers. Accelerated urbanisation and the establishment of factory industry heightened the awareness of some to the gross inequalities of wealth prevailing. Praise of free competition in capitalist development was countered by criticism of new social cleavages, determined solely by money and unchecked economic exploitation.[7] The language of class seemed to echo the inadequacies of industrial society. Saint-Simon wrote of a '*classe industrielle*' and a '*classe travailleuse*' in a manner which still corresponded to traditional 'order' concepts, but he also used class terms, as did Babeuf, to describe the iniquities of the '*classe paresseuse*', the privileged who had survived the French Revolution.[8] Early socialists, anxious to eliminate the inequalities and oppression of industrial society, also effectively lumped economic and political definitions of class together, assuming a close connection between the French Revolution and social change.

It was left to Marx to attempt a scientific analysis of the development of capitalism and predict future change. He associated the concept of class wholly with labour exploitation; he defined class according to the relationship of the individual to the means of production. The basis of class rested essentially in the growth of capitalist industry and was partly economic, partly psychological and partly political. Class came into existence only when groups were aware of their conflict with others. Both financial deprivation and psychological oppression and their opposites were crucial to the existence of a working class and a middle class. But they only crystallised as classes when they united in mutually hostile political formations. Thus, Marx argued, the nineteenth-century French peasantry were not a class, because they lacked awareness of a political identity.[9] It would appear that the language of class had great historical specificity. Marx saw the revolutions of 1789, 1830 and 1848 as stages in the establishment and decline of bourgeois power. Marx himself used also class terms to describe pre-capitalist society.[10] However, he claimed that the modern bourgeoisie was uniquely a property-owning, entrepreneurial group, who exercised power entirely as a consequence of their accumulation of capital – a situation which was destined to produce unrelenting political conflict.[11] Marx also recognised the existence of other elements within the bourgeoisie, notably professional, bureaucratic groupings and the intelligentsia. Unlike later followers, he also included landowners, for instance in the wealthy bourgeoisie of the July Monarchy. Curiously, Marx's attempt to define class in the last section of *Das Kapital* was unfinished. Most of his comments on class occur in his historical works, where he sometimes refers simply to 'the bourgeoisie', or to sub-groups such as the 'financial', 'commercial', 'petty' bourgeoisie, etc., using the phrases without definition as if assuming that his readers would automatically comprehend.[12]

For Marx class was less a system of social categorisation than a prophetic war-cry. He challenged those who chose to use its terminology to express a belief in gradual or evolutionary social change, a challenge which was couched in *Das Kapital* in the language of science and objectivity, not emotion, and whose essentials seemed to be borne out in the nineteenth century by the cyclical economic crises of 1817–18, 1827–32, 1845–8, the late 1850s and the world depression of the 1870s. It appeared as if the claims made by Marx and earlier socialists such as Louis Blanc, that capitalist competition would shrink the bourgeoisie and enlarge the size and grievances of the working class, were credible.[13] Political upheaval certainly seemed to accompany these crises. The idea that class was the cornerstone of inevitable conflict was fundamental to the socialist movement which grew rapidly in the later years of the nineteenth century and seemed a real challenge to bourgeois society.

While socialist and social-reforming writers used a language of class to criticise new capitalist changes, others welcomed the new terminology and capitalism itself as elements in the liberation of society from traditional privilege. Writers and politicians like Guizot, longest-serving of Louis-Philippe's senior ministers, never ceased their praise for the freedom, equality and opportunity which existed in modern society. To Guizot the middle class typified this liberation. He argued that, since the 1789 revolution had eliminated old irrational privileges, everyone had the opportunity to make enough money to be considered middle class and qualify to vote.[14] For him class terms belonged to a world of liberty. He argued that man and society were gradually progressing, both in the realm of ideas and in man's material condition.[15] Industrial development and the accumulation of wealth benefited all. Social harmony, not conflict, was the essential precondition of such progress. 'All classes, all social forces amalgamate, combine and live in peace within the great moral unity of French society.'[16] Class was based on levels of wealth, but also on layers of moral obligation and duty. For Guizot the ability to make money and the possession of a moral conscience were inextricably linked, just as poverty was a sign of moral degradation. Thus non-socialists used an emasculated language of class, replacing inevitable conflict with moral obligation. For them morality reposed mainly in the middle class; for the socialists, in the working class.

Marx had argued that class and class conflict would only exist until the inevitable proletarian revolution cleared the way for a classless society. By the end of the nineteenth century, governments were making some effort both to improve the material condition of the poor and to persuade the latter to identify with existing society and believe that their material circumstances were actually improving. A number of social commentators rationalised persistent inequalities. The permanence of an élite based on political domination was asserted by writers like the Sicilian Mosca[17] and Pareto, the latter of whom argued that although social conflict was itself inescapable so was the existence of an élite.[18] The need for positive and conscious social harmonisation was pressed by Durkheim. Sociologists began to study society not just in historical terms; they tried to agree on objective criteria. Elements other than economic began to feature in class definition. Max Weber added the dimension of religion[19] and education, and also pointed out that the development of capitalism now put less emphasis on the individual entrepreneur than on the manager.[20] Thus he split society into four social classes: the working class; the lower middle class; the intelligentsia, which included civil servants and highly trained white-collar workers; and property-owners of all kinds, including in this group all with higher education, whether owning property or not. But he argued that groups and individuals were motivated by a myriad of factors, tradition, religion, different value attitudes, etc.[21] An increasingly significant determinant of social development was the expanding role of the state and its bureaucracy. Class interests, he suggested, were far less dominant than had been thought previously.[22] Moving even further away from economic imperatives, writers like Schumpeter stressed the social factors uniting groups. Schumpeter argued for the existence of a class spirit, which was a compound of social relationship, intermarriage etc.[23]

Views on class differentiation have always been subjective, often the product of a specific political or social-reforming ideology, sometimes imbued with messianic fervour masquerading as science, sometimes over-anxious to refute perceived 'Marxist' dogma. In this century there has been not only conflict among Marxists, deviant Marxists, non-Marxists and anti-Marxists, but also between those who take an empirical historical starting-point and those who work from an 'ideal' or 'model' stance. Until recent years historians, while utilising the tools of the social scientist, have resisted many of his concepts. Much of the work of this generation of historians illustrates the actual 'backwardness' of nineteenth-century European society, the slowness of social change, compared with the advanced industrialism described by Marx. Historians stress the resilience of landed élites, in both concrete and normative terms. Marx placed the entrepreneurial middle class centre-stage in political conflict, whereas empirical investigations demonstrate the continued role of more traditional bourgeois groups.

Having looked briefly at some of the ways in which class divisions have been described, we should note: class can have no objective reality; it was a chameleon offspring of economics and morality, later used to describe a process of social and political change which never matured according to the most famous model postulated by Marx. Marx included in his definition of class economic, political and psychological factors. We must be prepared to look at criteria such as: income levels and sources of wealth; occupational and professional links; access to political power and influence; status indicators; and the 'gorilla' factor, that is, the desire to identify with a particular group, which may include intermarriage, the acceptance of common cultural standards such as education and the degree to which such striving is reciprocated. We shall use 'bourgeois' and 'middle class' interchangeably, but accept that others may not. Whichever term is used we must be prepared for writers to subdivide either in different ways. What is the morphology of a quicksand?

Our particular area of quicksand will be the middle classes of four major European states. France is an obvious starting-point for an investigation into the role of the middle class because in 1789 and subsequent years she experienced what many near contemporary and subsequent commentators described as 'bourgeois' revolution. She was also the most important continental power in 1789 and in the following two decades conquered most of the European land mass, leaving no other major state untouched. Her influence reached far beyond the military sphere. Already French culture and ideas, most recently through the work of *philosophes* like Voltaire and Rousseau, were increasingly dominant within the ruling élites of

Europe. The wars of 1792 to 1815 gave her the opportunity to graft her own revolutionary legislation, codes of law, and political and administrative systems on to new territory, especially the German and Italian lands. It has also been suggested that French conquest allowed an alternative middle-class ruling élite to emerge, particularly in the Italian peninsula.[24] Even after the fall of Napoleon, French ideas, institutions and her own turbulent political experience continued to have reverberations on her neighbours. In recent years a whole school of revisionist historians in France has debated at length whether 1789 was indeed a bourgeois revolution and has questioned the extent of bourgeois power in the nineteenth century. By the end of our period in 1914 France had been a republic for over 40 years, theoretically a land based on equality of both rank and opportunity, apparently an advanced model of a bourgeois state. It is therefore fitting that this study should centre around her middle class and that she should be stressed as a benchmark against which other countries can be discussed.

Specialists on Italian and German history have also paid close attention to the impact of the French Revolution and conquest on social change. The conviction that the ultimate defeat of France was due to middle-class, even 'popular', patriotism, itself a reversal of earlier enthusiasm for the revolution as a liberating phenomenon, has been questioned by empirical investigations of actual responses to French rule and the institutions set up by the French.[25] Increasingly historians point out that the French Revolution, in France as elsewhere, had only a marginal impact on social change. Of far greater significance to the evolution of middle-class groups were long-term economic and demographic trends. The German states, or the German Empire as they became after Prussian military victories between 1863 and 1871, offer valuable comparisons with France. In a state which became the leading industrial power in continental Europe before 1914, with a wealthy entrepreneurial and a traditional and influential bureaucratic and professional middle class, it will be interesting to ask why aristocratic values, and indeed the aristocracy itself, continued to dominate, and actually became even more entrenched as the ruling élite. Italy, a united country in name from 1861, is a nation of contrasts, with conflict between north and south exacerbated in these years by hostility between the middle class of the south, who represented the almost feudal poorer regions, and the rapidly growing industrial and commercial middle class of the north, represented by families like Agnelli and Olivetti, standing for a world of capitalist investment, innovation, modernity and international business deals. Russia may appear to be somewhat of a maverick choice to include in a comparative investigation, as she is often designated as an empire virtually devoid of a middle class, to which absence the revolutionary disturbances of 1905 and 1917 are frequently attributed. Valuable contrasts will emerge between Russia and the rest, which will throw light on the development of each. At the onset it is clear that the autocracy – and Russia, unlike the rest of these states, remained an absolute monarchy until 1905 – tried to bolster its aristocracy, and encouraged division and dissension within the middle class in pursuit of a moribund ideal of aristocratic support for the monarchy.

Only a small minority of the bourgeoisie of early-nineteenth-century France were businessmen and industrialists, and many of them were primarily landowners. Governments were, however, responsive to their needs, and visibly so from around 1840 when the pace of economic change began to quicken.[26] Very many of those we would identify as quintessentially bourgeois were landowners and cherished this aspect of their lifestyle. The French middle class also included professional families, many different levels of officials, members of the intelligentsia as well as, at the bottom of the scale, a lower middle class of small businessmen, shopkeepers and artisans – in other words, much the same mix as before 1789. For the bulk of these groups the nineteenth century was far from being a bourgeois century in terms of the development of their influence and prestige. Revisionist historians have underlined the fact that the 1789 revolution did little to change the balance of power among the political and social forces in the country.

The élite remained a combination of wealthy nobles and bourgeois, and the neutral contemporary term 'notable' has come to be used widely to describe this element. Tudesq's monumental thesis has exhaustively explored an even smaller minority of *grands notables*, using as a yardstick all who paid 1000 fr. or more in direct taxation. The choice of whom to include was a contemporary one; in Restoration France this was the cut-off point for eligibility to the Chamber of Deputies and encompassed about 15 000 individuals. The survival of some electoral lists from the Restoration and the July Monarchy, in which amounts paid in each category of direct tax were listed, creates a comprehensible statistical basis for Tudesq's well-rounded assessment of the ruling élite.[27] One is in no doubt that landed wealth was the prime ingredient in notability. Except in a few large towns, the *foncière* or land-tax payment invariably qualified a man to vote. It should be remembered that the land tax was proportionately more onerous than the *patente* or industrial tax, for only the property, not profits, were taxed. The term 'notable' has its uses. It gets the historian off the hook of the Marxist–anti-Marxist debate, but only superficially, because in reality revisionists are often anti-Marxists, or are invariably regarded as such by offended Marxists. In other respects it is inclined to be too broad, too much of a catch-all, immediately overemployed and underdefined, needing to be subdivided into *grands notables*, the extremely wealthy families with national as well as local influence, and other *notables*, presumably less prosperous, although there is no obvious yardstick by which to measure the latter group. There is sometimes an implication that 'notable' means more than 'the very rich', and includes common political and other beliefs. Tudesq was scrupulous in delineating different political tendencies, but without further definition the term can be ambiguous. In this study 'notable' is used simply as the equivalent for the very wealthy, primarily landowners with a local power base. Tudesq used one precise financial definition, other French historians have employed different ones and historians writing on Italy and elsewhere also refer to 'notables'. There can be no statistically comparable criteria.

'Notable' is fast becoming as much of a minefield as 'bourgeois'. Let us agree that it is the equivalent of 'rich élite' and carries no implications that those discussed identified themselves as a group. Contemporaries used the word, but they also drew distinctions between its noble and bourgeois components and were aware that the hierarchical, pyramid-like social and political structures, which were perhaps overpainted by de Maistre and Marx, were in some respects intact, although nobles and wealthy non-nobles may have both been part of a landowning élite which managed its own locality and exerted a national influence. It has been suggested that land may have been even more important as a vital prerequisite of notability and for official appointments after 1789 than before.[28] The biggest divide, however, was not the possession or non-possession of a title, although the number of forgeries underlines its significance, but was political, involving attitudes to the monarchy, the Church and, later, education.

The German and Italian states fall between the extremes of France and Russia. In both areas a substantial educated professional and entrepreneurial middle class existed in 1789, and gained from the subsequent period of French rule. In the Italian peninsula there were three main divisions among the middle classes, one whose origins were historical, two which were the product of geography. The mercantile past prosperity of the city states had given rise in many regions, like Venice, to a bourgeois patriciate which governed and dominated in the manner of a nobility. In the northern provinces were professional and entrepreneurial groups whose prosperity and power were growing in the first half of the nineteenth century. They challenged both foreign rulers and the old patriciate for a say in politics, bought noble and Church lands where possible and were very interested in the extension and improvement of markets and the creation of an Italian *zollverein* or free trade area. They welcomed and profited from unification under Piedmont. Unification provided more jobs in government service, land to buy when the Church was dispossessed and opportunities when a liberalised economy was declared. In the southern provinces the entrepreneurial group was smaller, less wealthy and had fewer opportunities to exploit foreign investment than its northern counterparts. The professional middle class was also less assertive than the northern group, accustomed to living in a semi-feudal society and hostile to unification, because it brought economic exploitation and neglect by the north and the takeover of plum jobs by thrusting northerners.

Within the German states those groups who would be included in a modern definition of 'middle class' were very varied. Quite the opposite of France, where the revolutionaries proclaimed legal equality and the abolition of privileges, in 1794 the new Prussian Code reiterated the legal reality of inequality by listing the differences between the three main social groups in the state: nobles, burghers and peasants. The Prussian Code named three kinds of towndweller. There were rich patricians, who were state citizens, answerable to state jurisdictions only and exempt from local rules. Then there were the 'actual burghers', whether artisans, retailers or local merchants, who held full citizenship and took part in local political and economic life without restraint. Finally there were 'tolerated' residents who did not qualify, either by birth or by membership of a guild, for citizenship.[29] In 1789 the Holy Roman Empire, in which most Prussian land was situated, consisted of 300 states, 50 free cities and 1000 tiny territories held by imperial knights. In the free cities burghers had been left in control; but in many cities they retained only the façade of civic and guild independence. In Prussia the entrepreneurial group tended to be dependent on the state. The Prussian Code described the privileges of a traditional society of orders, but recognised that there were additional sectors. The most prominent middle-class groups were not the old-style burghers, but the bureaucrats, writers and professors, men with university training and endowed with *bildung*, a status resting on education. The Prussian Code accorded senior bureaucrats special ranking and privileges, giving them a status similar, if not superior, to that of the nobility. Senior bureaucrats thought of themselves as independent arbiters, indeed a substantial section became outspokenly critical of the king in the first half of the nineteenth century. After the revolutions of 1848 this independence disappeared, but the bureaucracy, including university professors, retained their social status at the pinnacle of the middle class. As the role and power of the centralised state and its bureaucracy grew, so the concept of city government changed and municipal autonomy of the old burghers was seen to be an anachronistic fiction. With economic development these old categories and rules ceased to have any meaning.

In his reforming programme at the beginning of the nineteenth century, Stein tried to revive elements of the old autonomy. His definition of a burgher in the City Ordinance rested on income, not birth, and was expressed in the language of the French Constitution of 1791. Stein hoped to establish modern concepts of citizenship, not based on the old idea of status acquired through birth, but gradually introducing an electoral principle, first in local and then in national affairs. According to the reform, in the free cities burghers had the right and obligation to elect their own town council and to serve on it without payment. They had exclusive rights to own urban property and engage in industry. Any adult male of substance and standing could be a burgher, with the exception of Jews and soldiers. But this attempt to revive the concept of a burgher did not succeed. While the western lands were favourable, eastern Junker society was hostile. In reality the non-noble, non-peasant and non-artisan section of society was both too large and too heterogeneous for the term 'burgher' to be more than an anachronism, applicable in a vague manner to a wealthy, urban élite. However it was again revamped, in a purely financial and functional form, as part of the three-class franchise set up by Frederick William IV of Prussia (1840–60) after the 1848 revolution. In other respects Stein's reform successfully expressed the changed relationship between nobles and the bourgeoisie. The idea that *stände*, status, was restricted to certain professions disappeared. The reform asserted that peasants and artisans could, in future, train for the professions. But there was much successful resistance to the opening up of the professions, and new educational and training conditions were imposed. There was considerable opposition to the evolution of society from one of orders to one based on class.[30] This resistance tended to make groups more rigid and more fragmented. The senior bureaucrats moved socially nearer to the aristocracy, restricting their intake to the very wealthy. The entrepreneurial and professional middle class began to identify itself more with landowners, officials and the nobility. The traditional Rhenish, often Protestant, merchant élite fulfilled the role of an aristocracy in the manner born and indeed had social relations with the small local aristocracy. The new factory entrepreneurs were equally eager to marry into the aristocracy and buy the estates of bankrupt nobles. Thus Krupp's heiress married von Böhlen und Halbach and Stümm's granddaughter wed ambassador von Kulhmann.[31] All links with the lower middle class were severed. The wealthy did not identify with a middle class. They thought of themselves as part of a privileged part of a society of orders and refused to renounce traditional notions, clinging to the idea of corporate rights and fearful that concepts of civil equality would threaten their livelihood and undermine their social position. The term *mittelstand*, which until mid-century was used for everyone from Rhenish patrician to Saxon artisan, came to be used solely for the lower middle class. The educational opportunities of this latter group were increasingly restricted, they took less and less of a role in civic affairs and were inclined ineffectually to regard more wealthy elements as ostentatious outsiders. Thus although, for neatness, historians use the term 'middle class', the wealthy, comfortably-off and poorer elements within the middling ground of German society would not have identified with each other.

Some historians of nineteenth-century Europe have observed the increasing distinctness and separation of the upper middle class, while others have paid unprecedented attention to the lower middle class. Here the question of social parameters becomes quite vexed. At the beginning of this period better-off artisans, minor public servants, clerks, etc. would fit into a category of families ever anxious to escape the epithet 'poor' and merit the description 'respectable'. By the end of the century they were joined by a vastly expanded body of shopkeepers and a huge growth of a sector with little or no independence, including state employees of all kinds and a wide range of other white-collar workers in offices, supervisory grades in industry and the service trades, embracing too the fast-expanding department stores. Such groups entirely lacked the modest independence of artisans and shopkeepers and were all the more intent on defining themselves and being accepted as middle class, through their dress, housing, social interests, education, etc., in order to insist on the differences between themselves and the working class. Sections of the lower middle class have been studied in recent years, although here because of pressure of space only brief reference will be made to them. Shopkeepers and craftsmen in particular have been the subject of detailed studies.[32]

Shopkeepers were a relatively new group; previously markets, fairs, pedlars and direct sales by craftsmen to consumers satisfied demand. Small, specialised retail shops developed, often in conflict with craftsmen because shopkeepers at this stage tended to favour free trade and the end of guild restrictions. The development of factory industry encouraged the growth of retail trade. The number of shops in Germany grew by 42 per cent from 1895 to 1907, the population by only 8 per cent.[33] Gradually the artisan-retailer gave way to shops that were purely retail outlets, except in the food trade. The prosperous shopkeeper, often trading in luxury goods, tended to stay in the same location and pass his shop on to his heirs. The less well-off were often precariously financed. In the years after 1900 20 per cent of businesses changed hands each year.[34] Shops were often started by wives of craftsmen or factory workers, sometimes women who had worked alongside their husbands in the factory and opened a shop in the front room of their house when a family kept them at home. If the shop succeeded, the husband might leave the factory to help his wife expand the business, but such shops had many problems. Their property was often rented and in poor areas where customers expected 'tick' and would go elsewhere if refused. Cash flow was thus a continual headache. Small food retail outlets, especially dairies, were often set up by a branch of a farming family, selling their own produce. The names of many shops in Paris and London still reveal these rural origins. At this poorer end of the retail business, fewer shops were passed on to children. The family would hope that through education children would 'better' themselves: perhaps a son might train as an engineer or win a scholarship to a *lycée* or *gymnasium* and become a teacher; for daughters a clerical job would offer shorter hours, more security and a better chance of meeting a well-heeled husband.

The development of department stores from the 1860s was seen as a threat by specialised small businessmen, who could not compete with the variety, price and novelty of the *Bon Marché* or the *Samaritaine*, but the numbers of both continued to grow,[35] producing yet another lower-middle-class/working-class group in the retailing staff of the department stores. Some of this staff, through commission, commanded high wages, and all of them eagerly aped a 'middle-class' lifestyle, portrayed in the stores and their ubiquitous catalogues. The phenomenon of the department store and its contribution to teaching the members, especially the female ones, of the new lower middle class how to be 'bourgeois' has thus received a fair amount of attention in the last decade. Additionally, the politicisation of the small retailers, squeezed between department stores and the even newer workers' co-operatives, who tried to defend themselves by creating political pressure groups, has been examined. The political élite was willing to exploit the grievances of shopkeepers, but drop them when inappropriate to its own objectives.[36]

Artisans are a more tricky subject because of the difficulty of assessing whether they were prosperous and independent or merely cheap 'putting out' agents for factories and department stores. Historians have noted that artisans were not solely towndwellers. The rural economy of the poor was a delicate blend of agrarian and artisan activities, laced with the product of surviving communal elements, such as wood-collecting or the use of common pasture. In addition to the substantial portion of the rural population which was neither solely artisan nor solely peasant, there were a sizeable number who were full-time craftsmen. In the Beauce, a wheat-growing region, 25 per cent of the active population were at least part-artisan, of whom one-fifth were comfortably-off, middle-class craftsmen.[37] Historians have attempted to assess the impact of industrialisation on artisans. Were they devastated by factories and the concentration of production, did ruin predate industrialisation or did industrial change actually rescue the independent craftsman? Statistics can be fielded to support both an optimistic and a pessimistic stance. Certainly guild organisations had long ceased to protect the craftsman, from either competition or the demands of merchants. The Le Chapelier law, passed during the 1789 revolution in France, underlines the loss of status of the craftsman, by obliging even master craftsmen to carry a passbook or *livret*. The Napoleonic Civil Code even rendered artisan co-operative organisations like the *compagnonnage* outside the letter of the law by permitting associations only of fewer than twenty members. In no German state around 1800 did the ratio of master to man exceed 1:1; often it was lower, and craftsmen in the food, clothing and furniture trades often had neither journeymen nor apprentices. In 1895 50 per cent of craftsmen worked alone.[38] If one is attempting a historical, not just a polemical assessment, one should probably conclude that the answer varied both between regions and between trades. Industrialisation enabled some craftsmen to become successful entrepreneurs, but some were subcontractors working for big firms and very vulnerable in times of economic crisis. Many were already struggling on a knife-edge of survival and were not helped by economic change. A revisionist view of industrialisation takes a rosy view of craft industry, but statistics reveal a decline. In Germany in 1875 two-thirds of manufacturing employees were in firms of five or less, but by 1907 it was only one-third.

In what respects were groups like shopkeepers or artisans part of the middle class? In many ways their own position was fluid, their attitudes were part working class, part middle class. The lines between artisans and shopkeepers were often blurred; some were both artisans and retailers, such as butchers and bakers. For some craftsmen and married women, shopkeeping was a semi-retirement. Both shopkeepers and artisans operated with their own limited capital, often rented their premises and employed few outside their own family, which was crucial in shaping attitudes both to the family unit and to society. For artisans and shopkeepers the family was the vital unit of work and tended to cut them off from a wider society. Their own social uncertainty led to pressure to improve the position of their children and stimulated aspirations for more recognisably 'middle-class' occupations, often as minor civil servants or elementary school teachers. Such jobs would provide the social and economic security lacking in their own field.

Thus in France, Germany and Italy the middle class ant heap, when disturbed, proves to be very diverse, indeed including groups who would have had little in common, economically, politically, socially or culturally. In the chapters which follow we shall need to consider in what respects such varied elements actually constituted a single class.

Turning to Russia we find a very different society and a proportionately much smaller and less developed middle class than in Western Europe, more fragmented and with different assumptions about status and social mobility. At the beginning of the nineteenth century, when the Russian population was reckoned to be about 41 million, 2 per cent were listed as middle class or priests. By the end of the century 10 per cent were middle class, of whom 0.5 per cent were priests. The survival of serfdom and the predominantly agrarian character of the country delayed the development of a substantial middle class. The groups which roughly corresponded to the middle class elsewhere in Europe were infinitely fragmented by privileges, some of considerable value, some honorific and some wholly sartorial, such as the provision of different uniforms to match the individual's rank. The middle classes were split into caste-like groups, with both wealth and occupation cementing divisions enforced by law and respected by social custom. There was such fundamental mutual antipathy between the intellectual and industrial and commercial elements that the Russian term to describe the middle class as a whole, *sredny klass*, is little used. The idea that they might be lumped together as a middle class along with entrepreneurs so disgusted professionals, members of the intelligentsia, better-off peasants and artisans that the merchants referred to themselves merely as the 'trade and industry class'. In many respects Russia remained a society of orders, or *sosloviia*, as established in Peter the Great's Table of Ranks, until after emancipation in the 1860s.

The Table of Ranks conferred status on the individual according to his record of service to the state. Basically society was divided into a tiny privileged section, which was exempt from the direct tax, the poll tax, and the vast unprivileged majority which was not. The former were also exempt from military service and corporal punishment. Outside these broad divisions the Table and subsequent rulings set up a myriad of shades of privilege. The Table, and unpredictable decisions of tsars to override it, made social groups, with their myopic obsession with privilege, pawns in the hands of governments. Existing nobles constantly tried to accelerate their own progress through the Table and delay that of others, especially merchants. Many social distinctions were of recent origin. It was only in 1762 that the ownership of serfs was restricted to hereditary nobles, merchants were exempted from corporal punishment in 1782, and other distinctions were not set out until the Charter of Nobility of 1785. The success of the nobility in restricting the access of merchants to the higher levels of the Table of Ranks led to the institution of a new grade of privilege. Legislation in the 1830s allowed first guild merchants of ten years' standing to be made honoured citizens, which gave them automatic, life-long guild membership. There were just over a third of a million honoured citizens, including merchants, professionals and some descendants of personal nobles. The most successful merchants were thus separated from the rest. In some respects the society of orders was demolished with the ending of serfdom in the 1860s. All individuals were personally free and land could be bought and sold without restriction. Corporal punishment was abandoned in the towns and left to the discretion of the *mir* or communal assembly in the countryside. In 1874 all exemptions from military service were withdrawn and in 1886 the poll tax was abolished. But emancipation did not end the *sosloviia*, for nervous governments preserved many legal and status distinctions despite the reform programme.[39] Old norms and institutions thus hobbled the emergence of self-conscious middle-class elements.

At the apex of the middle class were the members of the two senior merchant guilds, whose status was determined solely by their income. Members of the two senior guilds bought their membership annually, together with substantial rights and privileges. They were vulnerable; a poor year's trading would force them to apply to a lower guild. They shared some of the privileges of the nobility, but they could not own serfs and nor could they buy land until after emancipation. They were a small group, fewer than 500 000 including their families in the 1897 census, the same number as clerics and only one-third the number of nobles and officials. Senior merchants never developed the autonomous urban tradition of western Europe. Towns had tended to grow around fortresses or kremlin set up by the centralised state and the fortress aspect remained dominant. The government turned merchants into a closed caste yoked by heavy taxation. The tsars held on to lucrative trading rights, including all foreign trade, themselves, farming out the right to trade to individuals in an unpredictable manner.

It was possible to exploit the system and become extremely rich, but the individual's financial security was always at the whim of the tsar. Elsewhere entrepreneurial activity gave rise to an independent middle class, but in Russia from Peter the Great's time the state also dominated in this arena. Enterprises were created with state initiative, finance and subsidies, in villages not towns. Guilds were set up merely to facilitate the more efficient collection of tax. Despite these obstacles, successive merchant families worked themselves up from the position of trading peasants to acquire sufficient fortunes to move into the nobility. An outstandingly successful element emerged from the Old Believers, a group which grew up from a section of the Church which in the seventeenth century had refused to accept changes in the Orthodox Church designed to strengthen the power of the state. Old Believers were important in all subsequent rebellions against royal authority. They were exiled to remote rural areas until the time of Catherine II, when their entrepreneurial skills began to be appreciated. By the early nineteenth century all the main industrial and commercial activities of Moscow were in their hands. They ran the city and were its cultural leaders, forming an upper class in a way that the St Petersburg entrepreneurs, overshadowed by the nobility and the Court, were never able to do.[40] Regional differences split the wealthier merchant groups into autonomous, self-contained and mutually antagonistic fragments. When industry started to expand rapidly in the 1880s, the importance of foreign capital and the initiative of the state hindered the evolution of a native bourgeoisie. Jewish and foreign entrepreneurs predominated, which divided and weakened the native group.

Below the senior merchant guilds was the *raznochintsy*. This was an amorphous group, between merchants and peasants. It included minor officials, clergy, some teachers, doctors and the new and growing body of technically trained men, for all of whom a new term, 'intelligentsia', was used from the 1860s. There was considerable mutual hostility between them and the merchants, on a scale not encountered in Western Europe and perhaps due to the superiority accorded to the latter in law. Some of the intelligentsia were noble, men who had travelled in Western Europe and on their return entered one of the professions or became university teachers. In the West such individuals would probably have become senior clerics, but in Russia the Church was mostly a lower-middle-class preserve. Non-noble members of the intelligentsia were often journalists. The older generation tended to be romantic, the younger nihilistic, frustrated by the limited professional opportunities open to them. Partisans of modernisation, they opposed capitalism. Until the turn of the century they were associated with political opposition, but subsequently the term 'intelligentsia' tended to be used more neutrally simply to describe professions which required a high level of education. This was a period of rapid growth within the professions. New economic institutions, the judiciary, the *zemstvos* (elected local councils) and the *duma* (national assembly set up in 1905), all called for professionally trained men. There was a corresponding rise in the number of graduates, especially of economic and engineering specialists. An offshoot was the growth of professional and charitable organisations like the Writers' Union, the Pirogov Society of Russian and so on. The sense of association was strengthened by the publication of journals and the holding of conferences, significant in a country deprived of political debate and organisation. Although the intelligentsia were far less absorbed in opposition politics than past generations, they were the dominant influence in the formation of the main political parties.[41]

The *meschane* or townsmen came next in the hierarchy. They were not burghers in a Western European, privileged sense, nor were they necessarily towndwellers. Half of the 13.5 million *meschane* in the 1897 census lived outside towns. They could be tradesmen, artisans, white-collar workers, or even labourers or factory operatives. Thus this group was broader than the Western European concept of a lower middle class. Most were former peasants and their first step up the social ladder was to gain acceptance as *meschane*. Indeed many trading peasants successfully rose not only through *meschane* ranks but also to become first-grade merchants, despite the need before the 1860s to buy their freedom first.

Although these varying grades were distinct and looked on each other with rivalry and envy, movement between them was possible and indeed frequent. The senior merchant guilds were constantly renewed through the eighteenth and nineteenth centuries, and aristocratic status was both desired and achievable, despite the active jealousy of established nobles. Between 1825 and 1845 20 000 rich merchants gained ennoblement and 30 000 did so between 1875 and 1896. Social mobility could be surprisingly swift. Of the score of very wealthy merchant families in Moscow at the end of the nineteenth century, 50 per cent were only three generations away from their peasant ancestors. The rest came from families of minor artisans or merchants whose families had left the countryside for Moscow within the previous hundred years.[42]

There was movement into the middle class and within the bourgeoisie itself, but no sense of class identity or cohesion developed in the years before 1914. The merchant sector, constantly renewed by the rise of trading peasants and in the second half of the nineteenth century by the emergence of a new type of technically educated entrepreneur, might have given a lead. They were most comparable with Western European middle classes, but were a general staff with no soldiers. This was partly for cultural reasons. They were at the top of the economic hierarchy, but they had no marked impact on politics beyond the municipal level, nor did they set standards for cultural behaviour for those beneath them. They assumed that because men in their position in Western Europe were influential and respected they too should be accorded moral and political authority by those beneath them. But they were socially isolated, by the almost ghetto-like separation which still hung around the otherwise wealthy and powerful Moscow Old Believers, and by the actual foreignness of many merchants or their heavy dependence on foreign capital. By 1914 merchants were no longer a caste, but they had failed to develop into leaders of a class.[43] Warring cultural norms rather than smallness deprived Russia of a stabilising middle-class initiative. The Bolsheviks did not have to turn Russia's bourgeoisie into objects of class hatred; the potential members of that class had long been mortal enemies. The Russian middle class did not exist because its constituent elements were determined to avoid fusion and identification. The relics of serfdom and the policies of tsarist governments nurtured their mutual antipathy.

2. Economic Interests of the Middle Classes: Entrepreneurs

Time was when our baronial aristocracy was denounced by all. Now, praise be to God, it is dead and buried. But one must needs declare that the handful of new commercial aristocracies which have inherited their place are no less vain and no less tyrannical, but then they are founded on the pride born of money, and of all the family of pride there is none more despotic than this.[1]

THE capitalist, industrialist or businessman, was the pivot of the bourgeoisie as defined and detested by Marxists and, indeed, the fulcrum of the whole notion of class, predicated as it was on the assumption that European society was changed rapidly and radically as a consequence of the growth of factory industry. The entrepreneur was the central focus of the language of class, the quintessential bourgeois, a new breed typifying the demise of traditional privilege, an individual who could make his way without landed wealth or aristocratic birth. Disliked by socialists and social reformers, he was admired for his initiative and daring in challenging much more than the old forms of industrial organisation.[2] He had no recognised place in society, operating in an atmosphere of *laissez-faire*, free from restraint by governments. These last two aspects led to a schizophrenic view of the capitalist; he sometimes grasped for a traditional social identity, provided his children with a classical education, married them into the landed nobility and bought a country estate. The free competitive atmosphere in which he operated was regarded by critics as a licence for the exploitation of the weak. Thus the entrepreneur was always an ambivalent figure – a valuable, but little valued element in nineteenth-century European society.

Meshchanin, the Russian term, is used colloquially to mean vulgarity, narrow-mindedness, lack of culture,[3] and merchants in Russia were widely regarded as cheats. The term 'capital' came into common, and instantly often unfavourable use from the mid-eighteenth century. In 1780 Mirabeau, the nobleman who had an influential role in the earlier, more moderate stages of the French Revolution, wrote, 'The capitalist aims for the highest possible interest, a state of affairs which is bound up with public misery.' A *National and Anecdotal Dictionary* of 1790 stated, 'This word [capitalist] denotes a money monster, a man with a heart of stone, who is fond of nothing but cash.'[4] Later, socialists predicted the destruction of capitalism by its own competitive nature.

The term 'entrepreneur' might sound self-explanatory, but it was used in a variety of ways even in different regions of the same country. An entrepreneur might run his own industrial concern, financing it from within; he might be chiefly engaged in finance or commerce, or, as in southern Italy where the economy was poor, he might grow rich lending to the government and have almost no contact with industry or commerce. The entrepreneur might be involved in a whole range of banking, industrial and commercial activities. Thus he could be running a small-scale family business, or be an extremely wealthy man with extensive and international investments. There is an implication of modernity in the term 'capitalist' which can be misleading. In the Italian peninsula in the first half of the nineteenth century, most entrepreneurs were traditionalist and conservative. As industrial and commercial activities grew in the century, the connotations of 'entrepreneur' changed dramatically. However to some extent the perceptions of individuals altered more slowly. As in previous centuries, a successful capitalist wanted to own land and public office, and the most secure and highest percentage return on any investment was paramount. It is often assumed that profit made the entrepreneur an innovator, without whom industrial change would have been impossible. But the most successful gamblers are cautious and the example of southern Italy reminds us that the 'industrial revolution' depended as much on resources as on the investor. A recent study has shown that in Naples local entrepreneurs were an obstacle to economic development because of the very considerable profit they made from the perpetuation of poverty, for instance by lending to the Bourbon government.[5]

The nineteenth century was a time of considerable industrial change, but the rate and scale of development was geographically confined and very varied. France was the most industrialised nation in continental Europe at the beginning of the century, with traditional and prosperous artisan-based industries, mostly rural in location. Indeed three-quarters of her people lived in the countryside and followed agrarian pursuits. After the setbacks of 22 years of war, her economy grew fairly rapidly in the 1820s, with some expansion of steam power and the continued development of the modern luxury cotton industry of Alsace. The rate of economic growth was then steady, temporarily affected by cyclical recession in 1827–32 and 1845–8, but accelerating in the 1850s with the development of the national rail network. The 3 per cent annual growth rate of the 1850s was never exceeded in the rest of the century, which has afforded numerous introspective unfavourable comparisons with Great Britain, vigorously combatted by the current generation of historians, flushed with the post-1945 economic triumphs of their country.[6] France remained wealthy, with a population fairly static for 80 years from the 1850s. The pressure for rapid development was less than in Britain. The technical and structural changes which were the yardstick for the British industrial revolution were implemented in the Alsatian cotton industry, the national rail network was complete by 1871, but her metallurgical industries, for long well provided with charcoal, were consequently slow to turn to coal-smelting and grow into large-scale concerns. Throughout French industry traditional artisan techniques subsisted alongside urban factory production and there was a concentration on producing for the luxury, rather than for the mass market. By 1914, although there were some very large firms, particularly in coal and iron and steel, the norms were still the family firm, financed from within, and the artisan unit. In the present economic climate, when large firms are sometimes depicted as stultifying, the typical, small family unit of nineteenth-century France is no longer portrayed as automatically backward and unadventurous.[7]

In contrast, the economies of the Italian states, with fewer people, scant and scattered resources and very poor internal communications, turned more and more upon themselves during the eighteenth century with the continual shrinking of her maritime trade. As the previously prosperous and advanced banking, manufacturing and commercial activities of the states declined and the Atlantic trade overwhelmed that of the Mediterranean, the Italian peninsula was increasingly cut off. As the economy reverted to introspective near-subsistence, once-thriving entrepreneurial activity was replaced by obsessive concentration on landed investment. At the end of the eighteenth century new initiatives, for instance in textiles, began to emerge, to be squashed by the impact of French invasion, occupation, the blockade and Continental System.[8] The French tried to turn the peninsula into a source of cheap raw materials and a repository for French exports. Some producers of cereals, vegetables and silks benefited and her industry was basically too rural and artisanal to face any real threat from France. But traditional patterns of trade were badly disrupted, especially for those ports dealing in colonial goods.[9] Progress after 1815 was modest and gradual, even in areas with fair communications and resources like Lombardy. Even in this, Italy's most advanced industrial region, those with capital preferred to take advantage of the sale of feudal and Church lands to acquire rural property. The organisation of industry remained firmly artisanal and rural, despite the growth of both silk and cotton manufacture.[10] Adventurous, innovative capitalists were singularly lacking. Lombardy and Venetia were obliged to direct their trade to Austria, and Piedmont, when her economy began to take off in the 1850s, was mainly dependent on French money. Unification was an economic disaster for much of the peninsula. A rigorous belief in free trade was ruinous to the south and even to the north when agricultural prices fell in the 1870s. Like other countries Italy adopted tariff policies in 1878 and 1887 and these provided a positive base for industrial growth. The gulf between the poverty of the south and the prosperous, industrialising north was widened. Modern industry was effectively limited to the Milan–Turin–Genoa triangle. As in Russia, foreign capital and substantial state intervention in the build-up of heavy industry were required. From the 1890s a new generation of entrepreneurs and new industries began to emerge, including Agnelli, Pirelli, Olivetti and Fiat, and the growth of motor manufacture, rubber, cement, chemicals and electrical industries was substantial.[11] Even so, for geographical, geological and social reasons, Italy had only a very modest role in the European economy by 1914.

By 1914 Germany, on the other hand, had taken over France's continental lead and had achieved world-ranking as an industrial power. With the best European resources in iron, coal, textiles and communications, the Prussian artisan industries, cushioned by the *zollverein*, which combined a free trade association of the German states within a protectionist tariff wall, were to develop rapidly, utilising new techniques. The opportunities offered by the absorption by Prussia of all the German states except Austria into a German Empire in 1871 transformed her into the industrial giant of continental Europe. The acquisition of Alsace-Lorraine from France in 1871 was invaluable, Lorraine supplying Germany with 70 per cent of her iron ore by 1914 and Alsace incorporating an advanced cotton industry. New colonies, a vast army, a powerful navy and far-reaching mercantile and other investments made German nationalists eager for greater recognition of Germany's achievements by 1914.[12]

Russia acquired modern industrial structures and processes late. In 1800 she was the leading continental iron producer, by 1850 only fifth. It was not until the 1880s, with the building of a railway system, initially to facilitate the export of grain, that Western banks, particularly the French, intensified investment, first in the railways and then more broadly. The geographical spread of industrialisation and entrepreneurial activity was particularly limited in Russia, with concentration in three areas, St Petersburg, Moscow and the Caucasus. In 1811 there were only just over 20 000 merchants in the empire, who constituted 7.4 per cent of the urban population. In 1914 only 18 per cent of Russians were towndwellers and there were a mere three million industrial workers, out of a population of 170 million. Production was still concentrated far more in the countryside than elsewhere in Europe.[13]

Modern industrialisation therefore affected only fairly restricted areas directly and had an impact on these countries at different times and rates. The entrepreneur capitalist preceded modern industrialisation. Entrepreneurs have been enshrouded in some potent myths, the exploration of which will occupy the rest of this chapter. Marx, his followers and some non-socialists have claimed that: entrepreneurs were exclusively bourgeois; that they were 'new' men, the product of industrialisation, often barely educated; they were a fairly homogeneous group; and they exercised a powerful, almost occult influence on government.[14] We shall consider the extent to which entrepreneurs were middle class by examining these myths in relation to the origins, nature and development of entrepreneurial groups. French revisionist historians of the 1789 revolution have taken pleasure in demolishing the first of these claims in recent years, cataloguing the involvement of the nobility, especially the most wealthy and influential, in industry and commerce in the years before 1789, observing the profound obsession of the bourgeoisie itself with the acquisition of land and venal office, and finally displaying the continued resilience of the nobility throughout the nineteenth century. We are bound to ask to what extent and why was the industrial growth of the nineteenth century associated with the emergence of an industrial and commercial middle class? At the outset it was far from clear that non-nobles would predominate. In the eighteenth century, feudal customs, traditions and privileges excluded nobles from trade and restrained their involvement in industrial enterprise, but potential profits made it worthwhile for nobles suitably located to make this distinction more theoretical than real. Nobles were leading investors in mining and metallurgical concerns in France, Russia, the Rhineland and Silesia.

Nobles, some ennobled merchants, dominated Russian industry. In 1813 they held 64 per cent of mines, 78 per cent of wool cloth manufacture, 60 per cent of the papermills, 66 per cent of the glassworks and 80 per cent of the potash concerns. An outstanding example was Mal'tser, who in addition to owning 200 000 serfs had twenty factories producing metal goods, armaments, chemicals, etc. He produced the first rails, steamboats and steam engines in Russia.[15] Some noble entrepreneurs, like Mal'tser, were innovative and modern in their approach; others operated within a more traditional environment, which they seemed unable or unwilling to change. The nobles who owned the mining and metallurgical establishments of the Urals came into the latter category. Inevitably their enterprises operated within a feudal framework, but they never developed beyond the authoritarian attitudes of a serf employer. They made no attempt to incorporate modern technology or innovative methods of management. They relied on government orders and subsidies to maintain increasingly uneconomic firms. Many organisations were large and powerful, like the Demidovs, and were able to persuade the government, itself also involved in production, to maintain a high tariff on imported iron, which acted as a brake on innovation. The Demidovs preferred to diversify into platinum, copper and gold as an alternative to modernising their iron foundries. After emancipation they took on Jewish managers and later were forced to sell out to foreign capitalists.

Nobles owned most of the wool cloth industry of the Moscow district at the beginning of the century. This was another traditionally run industry. The enterprises were small scale, producing a coarse woollen cloth for domestic use. The owners struggled to maintain a Western European way of life on diminishing profits. By 1889 only 6 per cent of the 204 firms founded by nobles were still in noble hands. Most nobles, whatever their views on industry, and novels and plays of the late nineteenth century indicate that most were less than enthusiastic, were too poor to be involved. Over half the seigneurial serfs were owned by 3 per cent of the landowners, who in consequence were extremely wealthy. Some of the richest like the Sheremetevs with over 200 000 serfs, would never have entertained industrial production or investment, or indeed even the commercial exploitation of the agricultural resources of their estates. They lived royally, beyond the dreams of most European royal houses, and their concentration on conspicuous consumption of luxury items, mostly obtained abroad, was damaging to the development of the Russian economy. In contrast, the Isopovs, so wealthy that they thought nothing of hiring an entire Italian opera company to entertain them, obtained up to half of their annual income from wool cloth factories, producing military uniforms for the Russian army.[16] Nobles were not only involved in traditional industry, they initiated and ran Russia's sugar-beet industry, a modern and hugely successful development.

Noble dominance of entrepreneurial activities delayed the emergence of a substantial industrial and commercial middle class. The route to entrepreneurial wealth lay through the Court, which was monopolised by the nobility. Nobles bought, or were sometimes given, extensive rights to own serfs, to produce salt, alcohol, tobacco and tallow, to export grain and to trade with certain areas. The tsar monopolised trade in salt, vodka, grain and furs. Court power also enabled some nobles to secure army contracts for wool and iron manufacture. By the end of the eighteenth century, nobles owned 88 per cent of pig iron production and 85 per cent of copper. Their influence at Court gave them an insurmountable advantage over established merchants within the traditional guild structure. Their entrepreneurial activities did not interfere with their own noble status, on the contrary their acquired wealth enhanced their influence in Court circles. By the 1780s the traditional merchant manufacturers had been pushed out of heavy industry and for half a century they were obliged to restrict themselves purely to a trading role. The merchants resented the nobles' entrenched power at Court. In other countries, notably France, wealthy non-nobles were able to gain the ear of the monarch, to promote their own social and economic advancement and to work with nobles. In Russia competition and hostility between noble entrepreneurs and merchants was so intense that there was no possibility of such an alliance.[17]

A new breed of noble merchant emerged in nineteenth-century Russia, who not only invested in industry but had technical expertise and managed his own firm. Some noble merchants had tax-farming origins, but were not themselves tempted, as earlier noble industrialists had been, to diversify out of industry into the bureaucracy. They were enthusiastic partisans of new methods and keen Slavophils. Two central families were the Chizhovs and the Shiphovs. Chizhov came from a poor noble family. After graduating in science from St Petersburg university, he set up a model silk works and became editor of *The Messenger of Industry* in Moscow. He went on to organise a number of major enterprises, including two railroads, a bank and joint stock companies. The Shiphov brothers, from a much wealthier noble family, first held army commissions. The elder left and, via tax-farming, set up his brothers in the biggest Russian-owned machine factory in the 1850s and established textile and chemical works.[18] The commitment of tsardom to its nobility put the noble entrepreneur into a unique position. But the majority of Russian nobles were not entrepreneurs and the ethos of the caste tended to denigrate such preoccupations, which was debilitating to the vitality of Russia's industrial economy and helps to explain the demise of many noble entrepreneurs during the nineteenth century, particularly after the abolition of serfdom.

In no other country did the nobility exercise such a profound influence over industrialisation. In the German states the attitude of the nobility varied according to both the cultural norms of the area and the opportunities available. Aristocratic landowners led the way in the rapid growth of the Silesian iron and steel industry. Men like Count Reden, Henckel, Thiele-Winckler and others used local coke and iron and up-to-date technology to develop a thriving industry within the serf system. In Bavaria the nobility resisted industrial development by encouraging the innate conservatism of the local urban communities against the ruler. The government had given monopoly rights to individuals to initiate development and most of the grants went to Court favourites, who had no knowledge of industry or trade and set up weak enterprises behind tariff walls. Industrial change was resisted as the creature of 'foreign' intruders. In Saxony a thriving new sugar beet industry grew rapidly, with sixteen factories in Prussian Saxony alone by 1857. Unlike in Russia the entrepreneurs in this case were not nobles, but from the urban middle classes. They invested in factories and then often became involved in growing the beet, either directly or through less well-off tenants. In eastern Prussia also most Junker landowners disdained and opposed industrialisation, or left it to others. The landowning nobility of the Baltic coast successfully checked attempts to develop large iron-smelting plants using local materials.

In France nobles were involved both as 'sleeping partners' in commercial and industrial affairs and in direct exploitation. The leading iron manufacturers of Lorraine, the de Wendels, were a noble family. Over half the shares of the Anzin coal-mining company were owned by aristocrats such as the duc de Croy. In 1860 23 per cent of the Rouen cotton industry was in noble hands. Royal princes were also involved in industrial investment.[19] In Italy a new industrial company floated in Naples in the first half of the nineteenth century, which in fact invested in the government's indebtedness, was largely subscribed by major landowning nobles.[20] The involvement of a noble in industry was often based on the resources of his own estates. Most spare capital in Italy was in the hands of noble families and was used to buy land and for some limited entrepreneurial investment. The high profile and continued significant presence of nobles as investors in both industry and commerce make the simplistic assertion that a new industrial and commercial bourgeoisie replaced a traditional feudal nobility quite inappropriate. In conclusion we must be aware of the resilience of the nobility and their intervention in finance, industry and trade, perhaps more as sleeping partners in the eighteenth century, but later more actively, and particularly in Russia. In the transition from a predominantly feudal to a more capitalist society, it would appear that it was frequently the nobility, not the middle class who gave the lead and made the big profits, but often continued to disdain 'trade' and in doing so established cultural norms which were imitated by other groups. Industrialisation added to the wealth of some traditional noble families, accentuating the gap between wealthy and poorer elements in the nobility.

It is not only Marxists who seem to hold that the bourgeoisie were 'new men';[21] the myth of the 'self-made man' still has a potent grip on modern conservative thinking in the UK and the USA. However, recent research on the social origins of entrepreneurs in the USA and Europe has shown that most were from wealthy families. In 1865 89 per cent of British steelmasters were from well-off middle-class backgrounds, 7 per cent lower middle class and only 4 per cent had fathers who were workers.[22] The 'rags to riches' entrepreneur was the exception. A high proportion of businessmen were from business families, especially in the textile and metallurgical trades. There is no indication that the period generally termed the 'industrial revolution' was an era of enhanced upward social mobility, but it is interesting to observe that it was not the same social groups who entered industry in different countries. In Germany very few industrialists were from small or middle-sized farms, whereas in the USA farming stock yielded a number of businessmen. The explanation for the contrast seems to lie in the greater prosperity of the American family farm with a readier supply of available capital. Differences of attitude also counted: the small German farmer was far less predisposed to venture into entrepreneurial activity. Few sons of professional families in Germany went into industry, whereas boys from such backgrounds were much more likely to become entrepreneurs in France and in America. In Germany a member of the professions would look down on industry and commerce. But senior civil servants both in France and Germany launched themselves successfully into the business élite, while the corresponding group in America did not. German civil servants became involved in industrial organisation through their bureaucratic functions; indeed German public administration was seen as a model for the running of private businesses.[23] In Russia cross-pollination was more likely in the reverse direction. Links between industry and the civil service were close, especially in Moscow and St Petersburg, and senior merchants were actively involved in government commissions and bureaucratic functions from the last quarter of the nineteenth century.[24]

Links with the civil service were highly prized for contracts. Only those with money and connections, and if possible expertise combined with these, were successful in the world of industry and commerce. Very few factory workers, and only a small number of artisans or peasants, made it to the top. The only exception was the machine-tool industry, where a bright idea and job knowledge were all-important and only a very modest amount of private capital was required at the outset. In Germany there were men from farming and artisanal stock who became successful machine-tool makers, while in the USA there were several examples of factory workers graduating to become machine-tool manufacturers. Otherwise, unless an artisan or industrial worker could find himself a wealthy backer, in which case he was unlikely to be able to exert financial control over any resulting enterprise, he would not have access to the capital needed to go into business. A German artisan, Dinnedahl, tried to set himself up in a firm making steam engines, but lacking sufficient capital went bankrupt. The educative experience of repeated cyclical depressions in the business and industrial world – in 1817–18, 1826–32, 1845–8, the late 1850s and, most dramatically, the world depression which began in the late 1870s – graphically illustrated the dangers of entrepreneurial ventures. All of these crises brought catastrophic increases in the number of bankruptcies. Even at the end of the century 40 per cent of all German firms went bankrupt. Occasionally a government would provide capital for a project. A Swiss cotton merchant, Hotho, was given 10 000 thälers by the Prussian government to develop a factory near Berlin, but such funding was rare and exclusively for those already wealthy, with an ear to government. In the first half of the nineteenth century industrial investment was unusual. Government securities paid 6 per cent in Prussia and were secure. Private banks and stock exchanges concentrated on government securities, commodity and currency speculation, and business and commercial deals, not industry.[25] Even in 1880 only 35 per cent of the members of the Bank of France were from industry; the rest were merchants or merchant bankers.

However, statistics can be proferred to show that a high proportion of employers were former employees. In France in 1872 80 per cent of employers were former workers and 15 per cent sons of workers, but statistically the vast majority of 'firms' in France were small, family, artisanal enterprises. In the early nineteenth century there were 3000 mills in the cotton industry of Normandy, many started by local foremen or clerks, apparently an example of how industrial development encouraged social mobility. However, a hundred were derelict and the 'artisan' industry was dominated by two main groups: ten Protestant families from Bolbec who entered the cotton industry in the 1750s, and a group of merchants and bankers from

Rouen. These merchants either put up the money for mills actually established by English experts in the 1780s or set up their own firms after the French Revolution. By the 1840s the ten largest of these firms employed over 60 per cent of all workers, and their hold gradually increased with the escalating cost and complexity of new machinery.[26] Small, apparently independent firms were actually mere putting-out depots. Statistics on the gross number of small enterprises can be misleading. It has been calculated that fewer than 5 per cent of the master craftsmen in Prussia in the second half of the nineteenth century were actually independent. In France in 1913 there were two bosses for every five workers and 90 per cent of firms had fewer than ten workers, while in Germany 90 per cent had fewer than five and in Russia 96 per cent of enterprises were small. But, put another way, over half of Russian workers were employed by the remaining 4 per cent.[27] Major German industries like capital goods and coal were large scale, 9000 of them employing 50 or more workers each. Thus the trend towards concentration, technical innovation and the establishment of factories pushed out the small businessman who did not have the capital to compete with more prosperous and thrusting fellows. Small retail outlets were sometimes crushed by the convenience and cheapness of the new large department stores, although the gloomy picture portrayed by Zola of the collapse of small shops was too extreme.[28] Very many small concerns were ephemeral, but more were always being launched. Very few firms in Germany or Britain were headed by a man from a working-class family at the end of the nineteenth century, rather more in the USA. Nevertheless estimates that have been attempted of rates of upward mobility in the business élite of France, Germany, Britain and America show a marked overall similarity, not at all what one would imagine of the USA where the image of the self-made millionaire is strongest.[29]

The capitalist-entrepreneur evolved gradually. Many new firms were the result of the extension of the role of the merchant in traditional craft industries, the triumph of merchant over craftsman and the gradual whittling away of the craftsman's independence. The merchant was better able to survive in times of insecurity such as the French Revolution and the period of revolutionary wars which followed.[30] Previously, groups of master craftsmen had been able to negotiate a 'just' set price for their goods, which was respected by most merchants. Typical was the silk industry of Lyons, where increasingly in the eighteenth century merchants were able to ignore the masters' requests for a set price and where masters gradually came under the financial control of the merchant. Technical developments in this traditional craft industry, such as the introduction of the Jacquard loom, were beyond the financial resources of most masters, once more leaving them vulnerable to the increasingly 'capitalist' merchants. In the early decades of the nineteenth century an occasional silk merchant actually set up large, technically innovative workshops, but the more successful concentrated on controlling the existing masters, not unlike the activities of the Rouen merchants in their cotton industry. Thus many 'new' entrepreneurs were merchants, adapting their role to the opportunities offered by technical change. As the middle men, they were in a stronger position to do this than the masters themselves, who in the 1830s began to band together to try to protect their livelihood but did not embark on joint enterprises.[31]

Curiously, in Russia the notion of 'new men' was far more of a reality. In the late eighteenth and early nineteenth centuries a substantial number of peasants successfully transformed themselves into businessmen and industrialists. In the dislocation of the Napoleonic Wars there were fortunes to be made and some serfs became wealthy and free. Merchant groups were constantly renewed by the influx of small craftsmen and trading peasants, encouraged by tsarist governments anxious to check the pretensions of established merchants. In Moscow province such peasants made their mark, not only in textiles but also in furniture, clock-making and the manufacture of scientific and musical instruments, all trades which grew out of small-scale craft production and were initially heavily dependent on highly skilled manpower. In Vladimir province trading peasants gained control of the metallurgical industry. Their role increased rapidly in the topsy-turvy world of the Napoleonic Wars and by 1815 they were setting up more firms than merchants or nobles. In 1824, along with nobles, trading peasants were permitted the same commercial and industrial rights as merchants, if they could put up the money for guild membership. The old, almost 'caste' structure was no more. Peasants were allowed officially to settle in the towns. From peasant to trader to free man became simply a matter of cash as governments relaxed rules. In 1825 fifteen Ivanovo industrialists bought their freedom and turned Ivanovo into a Russian Manchester. One of Count Sheremetev's serfs, a multi-millionaire hat-maker, bought his freedom for 800 000 roubles. Statistics on this enormously important aspect of social change and the evolution of Russia's industrial bourgeoisie are lacking, but the indications are that the old merchant groups were swamped. Moscow's old merchant population fell from 70 000 to just under 36 000 between 1827 and 1840. In the 1830s 27 000 freed peasants went to live in the towns and between 1834 and 1836 alone over 2500 transferred into the merchant class by buying guild membership. Thus Russia's merchant class was dramatically altered in the first half of the nineteenth century, with the collapse of many old families. By the mid-1850s the vast majority of the 175 000 merchants in Moscow had worked their way up from the peasantry.[32]

A typical such family were the Morozovs. The founder of what became a powerful and ubiquitous dynasty was Savv, a serf, who began making and trading in ribbons in 1797, and found a ready market because the Continental System cut Russia off from British imports. In 1820 he bought his own and his family's freedom. An entrepreneurial dynasty was founded. In his portrait, Timothy Morozov, Savv's youngest and most innovative son, looks a peasant, but he built up a staff of competent engineers, many of them from Britain, and invested large sums in training native talent. He endowed scholarships to train engineers at the Imperial Technical College. In 1880, 110 years after his father's birth, Timothy was the leading industrialist in Russia, with a net annual profit of 2 million roubles from textiles, railways and banking interests. One son married the daughter of the Transport Minister in the 1890s; another, Savva, married a peasant operative in one of Morozov's factories and was himself very close to his peasant origins, although he had a fashionable palace built in Moscow. He helped to found the Moscow Arts' Theatre, designing the building himself using the most modern techniques. Unlike his more autocratic predecessors, he was a humane employer. Women had a strong influence in these peasant-industrialist dynasties. Savva's mother headed the family firm when his father died, and when Savva proposed a profit-sharing scheme in April 1905 she dismissed him. Other members of the family, women as well as men, made a name for themselves in business or the arts. Varvara not only ran the Tver factory very successfully after her husband's death, she also established a factory school which was imitated by others.

The Morozovs typified many aspects of the entrepreneurial middle class, with their serf, Old Believer origins and their ethic of hard work and tough policies, so reminiscent of the Protestant entrepreneur of Western Europe. They were also typical of similar Moscow families in the interest shown by the third generation both in the arts and in revolutionary ideas. None of these peasant Old Believer families were established in industry significantly before the middle of the eighteenth century. In 1765 they owned a mere 2 per cent of the industrial undertakings in the Moscow area, but by 1850 they constituted 90 per cent of the first-grade merchants in Moscow, controlling not only the textile industry but also the banking, commerce and government of the province.[33] The rise of a whole group, sharing the same peasant and religious origins, had been meteoric and total. It would seem that this important group of entrepreneurs were to a large extent 'self-made', more so than in the other areas we are considering.

The 'self-made man' myth also encapsulates the notion that entrepreneurs were rough and ready with little schooling. In reality not only were most from comfortably-off backgrounds as we have seen, but they were also often well educated. Although only 2 per cent of the population in general went on to higher education, almost half of the business élite in France and over a quarter in Germany, compared with 33 per cent in Britain and 27 per cent in the USA received a higher education. Koechlin, Dollfus and Schneider sent their sons to the Conservatoire des Arts et Métiers, and higher education, rather than an apprenticeship within the firm, quickly caught on in France. Two-thirds of the top industrial families of Alsace opted for the Ecole Centrale in the years before 1860 and their sons followed them a generation later.[34] Many top families chose the Ecole Polytechnique and the Ecole des Mines. Thus a large number of France's leading industrialists had a classical baccalaureate, without which higher education would have been denied to them until late in the century. This was followed by scientific and mathematical training if possible, or scientific and technical. Parents chose a form of education regarded as appropriate for an élite, one which would be shared by many not destined for industry. But the training was more relevant than that accorded the sons of British entrepreneurs, who for preference after public school would go on to Oxbridge, followed by a profession, the civil service or politics. In Britain the son destined for the business usually had no specific training after school. In France each entrepreneurial generation was better trained and more professional. Unfortunately the *polytechnicien*, which every businessman's son most wanted to be, was a theoretician, taught by the school to despise industry. He had been educated in a hot-house, élitist environment, which tended to make him a distant and difficult boss. If the firm were large enough, by the end of the century he would hire a more vocationally trained engineer to work under him. In Germany the son of an entrepreneur would usually study business affairs not science and would routinely hire an engineer to work for him.[35] In Russia Moscow merchants resisted education as a limitation on their patriarchal authority, as a diminution of their role in educating their sons for business. When it became clear that such a strategy was disadvantageous, they tended to opt for a classical rather than a business education. It was in St Petersburg and the new industries of the Ukraine that scientific and technical education made rapid strides under the leadership of the Mining Institute in the later decades of the nineteenth century. Such engineers were employed, either as managers by foreign owners or by Russian merchants who had been classically educated.[36] Some also became factory-owners. Thus all entrepreneurs saw the benefits of education, but the type of education they favoured varied from country to country, and, in the case of Russia, within the country. Whether the type of training they received had a material effect on their success as businessmen is another matter. The marked and growing interest in classical education among successful entrepreneurial families seems to denote in some cases a sense of social insecurity. In the 1860s a survey was made in France of the career expectations of boys taking the baccalaureate. Very few boys whose fathers were in an entrepreneurial job wanted to do the same sort of work and no other boys contemplated such a career.[37]

On the other hand the development of technical and technical higher education indicated the increasing need for specialists and the emergence of a new type of 'middle-class' career in industry, which offered opportunities to sons of artisans and so on.[38] In some respects these were 'new men', but promotion prospects for those who attended the lower-level engineering schools were modest. Experienced engineers were at a premium in the first half of the century. For most training was 'on the job', and the successful engineers operated Europe-wide and often progressed to ownership.

Guppy, Brunel's partner in the GWR, later managed the Pietrarsa engineering works near Naples and then owned his own firm in Naples.[39] Many of the next generation of senior engineers were trained in higher technical institutes or universities. This new species of university-trained engineer, required to cope with the increasing size and technical complexity of industrial production in the later decades of the century, was less likely to be from humble beginnings. In this case the job specification was 'new', but most university-trained engineers came from prosperous families, sometimes noble ones. St Petersburg university and its specialised institutes led the way in providing highly trained personnel for the new oil and mining and metallurgical industries of southern Russia. From managerial posts in foreign-owned firms, some progressed to ownership themselves. They brought with them new attitudes, which extended beyond technical competence. They held American and West European management as their ideal and introduced into Russia a modern business culture and more humane man-management techniques.

Thus to describe entrepreneurs as 'new men' is not very helpful. They were an old species which evolved in a variety of ways from traditional backgrounds in response to the challenge of industrialisation. Noble families, through their landholdings and capital resources, made a substantial impact. Many entrepreneurs came from merchant families and turned traditional rural artisanal craft industries into dependent capitalist structures. Old attitudes and structures were slow to change; in mid-century only 20 per cent of the Lombard silk industry was using the technically advanced Jacquard loom and, as in France, small-scale artisanal silk production still prevailed. Even those entrepreneurs working in the newer cotton industry were exceedingly cautious and resistant to innovation.[40] It was only in the later decades of the century that a more modern type of entrepreneur began to emerge; on the one hand the specialist engineer, manager or owner, and on the other the capitalist whose entrepreneurial investment involved no personal contact with the firm. While emphasising the gradualness of change, however, one should note that the impact of prolonged war between 1792 and 1815, commercial experimentation during that war and repeated cyclical depressions during the century made entrepreneurial investment more risky than usual. All the prominent entrepreneurial families in Russia in 1914 postdated the Napoleonic Wars.[41] In

Naples, although the same names dominated the Chamber of Commerce from 1815 to the 1860s, none of them predate the Napoleonic Wars and some leading eighteenth century families such as the da Leva and the Basile disappeared completely. Neapolitan merchants were very dependent on Court contracts and the temporary removal of the Bourbons was a disaster.[42] Although the nineteenth-century merchants were new families, their attitudes were identical with those of their predecessors. Thus, although there was considerable continuity among entrepreneurs, sudden political change might well lead to a more dramatic alteration in personnel than did the apparently more radical process of industrialisation. However cautious, there were risks in war, and particularly in political upheaval, for which an entrepreneur could not prepare.

Marx categorised the nineteenth-century capitalist bourgeoisie as if entrepreneurs constituted a cohesive, distinct and united entity, destined to dominate the new industrial world before themselves facing destruction. However his own thesis revealed the fallacy behind the notion of a class 'identity', for within his own terms the economic imperatives of capitalism demanded that entrepreneurs were always in a state of mutual antagonism and competition. On the occasions where groups of entrepreneurs formed close communities, this was often for religious reasons, not because of their economic role. Entrepreneurs were apparently often outsiders in their own community. The bulk of the traditional merchant group in Moscow were Old Believers. They had excluded themselves when the Orthodox Church changed itself, and had initially been banished from the cities. Later, when many had transformed themselves from itinerant serf hawkers of ribbons etc. into prosperous textile manufacturers, they had been encouraged back to settle in Moscow. There, despite their enormous economic influence, they set themselves apart, living in almost 'ghetto' seclusion a very private, domestic existence, mixing socially and in marriage only with their own kind, retaining old habits of dress, diet and home furnishings – a peasant-like existence despite the very considerable wealth of many families. In France the Protestant cotton manufacturers of Alsace lived in a close-knit community,[43] although they were active in politics.[44] Jewish businessmen were even more distinct and separate, with not only a different culture and religion, but also a different language. There is no doubting the importance of these 'outsiders' and that to some extent their isolation had a bearing on their career choices. Religion was not the only determining factor. The cotton manufacturers of Roubaix-Tourcoing lived like 'outsiders', while to all appearances being 'insiders'. They were Catholics, like the rest of the population, and they were rich and locally powerful. But their large families were careful to marry within the group, they functioned with almost a 'Protestant' ethic and they had a strong sense of being different and needing to try harder. It appears that they felt underdogs in comparison with their fellow cotton magnates of Lille.[45] For different, but not for economic reasons, some entrepreneurial communities shared close, common interests. But this unity did not make them leaders of bourgeois society in a broad sense; rather it cut them off from the rest of the country, including other members of the industrial and commercial bourgeoisie.

There are numerous examples to demonstrate the close, indeed closed communities formed by groups of entrepreneurs in the same industry – the Moscow merchants, the Alsatian cotton magnates, etc. – but how socially cohesive was the industrial bourgeoisie? When one studies a single country, or even one industry in one country, a more profound impression is one of a diversity that is a matter partly of geography, partly of the needs of different industries. A metal worker had a slim chance of getting into business on his own, but a textile worker had almost no chance of owning the mill. Most first-generation mill-owners moved from commerce to absorb the production side of the business. Often individuals started iron foundries attracted by the combination of iron and timber for smelting on their own land. This was true of the noble iron masters in eastern France, in Silesia and in the Urals. But the noble owners of iron deposits and forests in the Rhineland did not follow these examples. Cultural as well as geological and geographical imperatives were clearly at work. French ironmasters came from a wide range of backgrounds. Schneider moved from small-scale trading via banking; Wendel was a noble landowner with the lucky coincidence of the essential raw materials; Talabot was a *polytechnicien*.[46]

In the German states there were marked contrasts between the origins of Saxon entrepreneurs and those in western Germany, particularly the Rhineland. In the Saxon linen industry, entrepreneurs grew out of the artisan class, with men setting up their own firms in close proximity to those of their former employers. In the Rhineland the commercial and banking families provided the entrepreneurs, who set up family businesses employing successive generations of workers. Differences of origin may help to explain other contrasts. The Saxon textile industry declined towards the end of the nineteenth century; industrialists were cautious and limited in their horizons, unwilling to risk the major innovations essential for growth and development. The heavy industries of the Rhineland expanded rapidly in the later years of the century, always responding to technical change. Clearly in part this was related to the origins of the owners, those in the Rhineland having more capital for development, and obviously too the heavy industries had greater scope for growth than a basically artisanal linen industry. Other factors help to illuminate the attitudes of the owners. The Saxon governments consistently encouraged the independent producer in opposition first to the guilds and then to the restrictions imposed by the local community. The industrial classes were thus thrown into conflict, but the local community retained vitality and a sense of purpose. Prussian government strategies were heartily detested in the Rhineland, providing a common grievance which united the different social groups, but which facilitated the decline of the local community.

In the Rhineland–Westphalia the strong entrepreneurial group consisted of local notables throughout the first half of the nineteenth century. Around 1840 a new type of industrialist began to appear from among the existing workforce. Such men were tougher employers but soon intermarried with the older families. In the early years of the century the industrial élite saw itself as part of the local community, considering, for example, that a limited suffrage would be adequate for proposed elected assemblies because they would be able legitimately to represent the interests of the working class. With the emergence of men like Lassalle in the early 1860s, who encouraged the working class to separate its interests from those of the employers, the industrial bourgeoisie, cut off and isolating itself from the local community, began to ape the aristocracy. Such behaviour was typified by extravagant living, by the quest for noble marriages, especially for daughters, by reserve officer commissions for the adult males in the family, and above all by a preference for investing spare capital in country estates rather than continuing to plough everything back into the firm.[47]

Many rich businessmen and industrialists could not wait to break free from the rest of the middle class and kick away the entrepreneurial ladder by imitating groups they considered to be more prestigious. There was nothing new in a successful businessman marrying his children into the nobility, but it spoiled the notion of the rich bourgeois as the leader of a new social order, for when wealthy industrialists like those of Milan wed into the local patriciate, they adopted their attitudes along with their titles.[48] Interestingly, there were limits to such social climbing: in Naples rich entrepreneurs married into the families of nobles like the S. Angelo and the Bellelli, but not into the inner circles of the top aristocrats like the Caracciolo and the Pignatelli.[49] Rich merchants might want to disguise themselves as nobles, and nobles were more than willing to make an entrepreneurial killing and an astute marriage, but social distinctions were always maintained.

The diversity and divided nature of the entrepreneurial bourgeoisie were underlined by the role played by foreign engineers, foreign capital and foreign firms in industrialisation. There had been a notable presence in Russia since Peter the Great's positive encouragement of foreign technology. In 1811 Russians controlled only 11 per cent of their foreign trade. Russian merchants felt threatened both by foreign counterparts, who were encouraged by the tsarist governments to develop newly acquired territory, and by ethnic groups within the empire such as Poles, Germans, Jews, Greeks, Armenians and Tatars. These were permanent residents, but they lived very separate existences and their close ties with corresponding communities abroad gave them advantages over Russian merchants, who were often ignorant of conditions abroad. Russian governments were eager to exploit their talents, according them special privileges. Ethnic merchants worked together with actual foreign ones, thus circumventing a rule that foreign merchants could not trade in the interior. The endemic rivalries of the different ethnic groups served further to fragment the merchant class. Foreign merchants often became permanent residents, like Knoop, a German-born cotton millionaire who became a Russian subject. Foreign capital began to enter Russia on a large scale during the Napoleonic Wars and by 1914 there was colossal dependence. British and German firms dominated the foreign trade of St Petersburg at the beginning of the nineteenth century; control of its industry followed. St Petersburg was the industrial capital of the empire but by the middle of the nineteenth century almost half of its factories were in foreign hands. English and Scottish firms employed 70 per cent of machine-making operatives.[50] Foreigners supplied roughly four times the total capital provided by natives for Russian industrial growth, especially in new industries. Nearly one-third of the largest cotton factories were entirely foreign controlled. Also in foreign hands were the oil industry of the Caucasus and the coal and metallurgical industries of the Ukraine. The most modern industries, electrical, chemical, and machine-tools, were in a similar position. Foreign firms were generally larger than Russian-owned ones and used the most modern production techniques. French banks entered the Russian market in a big way, especially after the signing of the Franco-Russian alliance of 1894. They favoured mining and metallurgical concerns, investing chiefly in southern Russia in the Urals. In 1913 firms dependent on French capital contributed just over half the coal production and nearly 80 per cent of the smelted iron of south Russia. French owners organised and ran syndicates in both industries to create powerful pressure groups to protect producers and keep up price levels. Germans predominated in the Baltic provinces; Jews in the former Polish lands. The latter's role in the Ukraine also grew.

Russian-born merchants complained about the foreigners, but tsarist bureaucrats blamed the Russians for lack of initiative. Russia's traditional merchant class tended to live within the old borders of the empire: in 1851 75 per cent lived in the territory which had constituted Peter the Great's Russia and nearly all lived in European provinces. This proved an insuperable barrier to success in foreign trade. In addition industries were moving out from the centre, especially from Moscow, and the traditional merchant class failed to follow, let alone lead. In 1814 99 per cent of textile firms were in the Moscow area, by 1859 the figure was 54 per cent of firms and 75 per cent of workers. Eighty per cent of the sugar-refining plant was in the Ukraine where the beet was grown. Non-Russians tended to respond rapidly to opportunities, regardless of geography, and were able to supply the necessary capital.

Resentment at the very high profile of foreigners caused serious rifts in Russia, but foreign participation was not inconsiderable elsewhere. In Naples names like Close, Rogers and Valentine traditionally represented commercial houses with broad international interests; the Rothschilds helped to shore up the Bourbons, but many other foreigners arrived with the French occupation and became permanent residents. Egg, a Swiss, founded the local textile industry in an ex-convent provided rent-free by Murat as a factory. The Bourbons gave him the factory buildings, allowed him to import cotton duty-free and banned all manufactured cotton imports, thus giving him a monopoly in the local market. His advantageous position was not unique. In 1841 only four out of the ten local textile factories were run by Neapolitans. The Swiss predominated, wooed by the Bourbons for the capital they brought with them. Some north Italian capital was also invested, but the textile entrepreneurs often brought their workers with them too, so providing little stimulus to the local economy.[51] Foreign bankers were even more significant. A Frenchman, Degas, was used by Joseph Bonaparte to float a National Debt. Engineering, the only other innovative industrial development in Naples in the first half of the nineteenth century, also owed much to foreign money and engineers. The first steamship company was founded in 1818 by a French engineer, and French entrepreneurs and bankers were among the main shareholders. Englishmen also ran steam packets, and the largest steamship venture, Sicard-Viollier, obtained most of its capital from France. Only a few Neapolitans could afford to subscribe and these were mainly noble landowners, such as the Prince of Ottaino and the dukes of Bovina. Naples had the first railway on the peninsula, largely financed by foreign capital.[52] Under the minister responsible in the first two decades of the Restoration, de' Medici, foreign capital was sought out in order to conserve meagre domestic reserves, and all manner of schemes were encouraged, including one proposal 'for importing camels for transporting goods to places where there are no roads'.[53] The less backward north of the peninsula was equally dependent on foreign capital, predominantly French, for schemes from the construction of a unified railway system to the expansion of textile and metallurgical firms.[54] Of the four big railway companies, only one could attract any capital investment at all within Italy, the rest initially came exclusively from abroad. By 1878 only 39 of the 64 locomotives operated by Alta Italia were home built. Railway construction did not act as a catalyst for industrial growth as it did elsewhere. In 1865 only one in four of the railway companies made a profit. The textile and shipping industries were mostly foreign owned, and foreign investment alone provided Italy with a gas industry. Much of Sicilian industry was financed from Britain, including sulphur and wine and oil. Even the Venetian glass industry was sustained by British investment. To a lesser extent foreign experts and capital contributed to the industrialisation of France and Germany. Almost 40 per cent of the capital for the Prussian mining industry came from abroad, mainly from France and Belgium, although governments insisted that the majority of the board of directors and the president of the company should be German.[55] The presence of foreign experts, investment, bankers and actual firms was often crucial for modern development, especially in the more backward Russia and Italy, but their presence meant that native entrepreneurs would be divided, perhaps ultra-nationalist, resentful of government favours to foreigners and of the fact that foreigners were better able to survive political upheaval. The most prosperous native entrepreneurs were likely to have foreign investments themselves and therefore divided loyalties.

In evaluating the degree to which entrepreneurial groups shared common interests, the issue of capital is crucial. One is immediately aware of the different ways in which industry was financed and of the widespread separation between financial and industrial interests. Many industrial concerns were financed from within. The provision of capital unquestionably made the entrepreneurial family at least as important as the entrepreneur himself. In France, in Moscow and initially in Germany most firms were family owned and run, finding their capital from economies and profits.[56] All members of a family enterprise were expected to contribute, men and women. Wives often helped in the running of the firm, especially bookkeeping, and widows were expected to manage the whole organisation. Families were usually large, professional managers rare. The most astute male offspring took over the business. Nicholas Koechlin, son of the founder of one of the most dynamic Alsatian cotton enterprises, was succeeded by his nephew, André, and his four brothers-in-law. André married into another cotton family, the Dollfus, while yet another Dollfus, great-grandson of the founder of Dollfus-Mieg, wed into another big cotton family, the Schlumbergers. Children were vital, not just as a comfort for one's old age but to infiltrate a neighbour's factory. This was the age of wise matrimony, not takeover. Family connections were important both to reduce rivalry and for investment. Daughters made their contribution by marrying into a neighbouring firm. Often the new partnership would then set up in business, the two surnames being hyphenated in its title. Thus the number of firms grew, not the individual enterprise. Inappropriate offspring were pruned, hived off into the Church or possibly the bureaucracy. Patriarchal authority was paramount and unquestioned, backed by a strong religious faith and a paternalistic, if exacting, attitude to employees who were regarded, perhaps somewhat hypocritically, as very junior members of the extended industrial family. Thus family firms, whether in textiles or in other branches of industry, usually survived and maintained their place in the hierarchy. In St Denis in the second half of the nineteenth century only 134 of 496 firms were reorganised under a new trade name.[57] If the family firm ensured stability, it may have hindered innovation. There is some indication that this was so in Moscow, but present-day commentators are no longer convinced that the larger and more impersonal the organisation, the more successful it will be.

Moscow merchants, whose patriarchal firms were not unlike those of the Alsatian cotton magnates in some respects, were anxious to maintain personal control over their empires, although it appears that none believed himself truly financially secure until he diversified out of business. Each year he had to find the set sum to belong to the guild and was therefore disinclined to take risks or join in partnerships. Legislation on the setting up of joint stock and limited liability companies was fiercely resisted, the merchants preferring to shelter behind a wall of state tariffs and subsidies. Departure from the privately owned firm was slow and successive governments discouraged change, fearful for the security of the regime. Moscow tended to develop share partnerships, St Petersburg joint stock companies. In 1890 out of 667 factories in Moscow, 534 were privately owned, 75 were trading firms, 46 were share partnerships and only 12 were joint stock companies. The tsar's signature was needed on the charters of joint stock companies and share partnerships.[58] In France also authorisation was needed for both share partnerships, *sociétés en commandite*, which permitted limited liability, and *sociétés anonymes*, which offered similar facilities. In 1867 all restrictions on limited liability were lifted and this form of structure became common in mining and metallurgical firms.

If entrepreneurial activity often grew out of the profits of merchants and if family firms were auto-financed, what role had the banks? In Russia banking was slow to develop. Individuals resisted formal institutions because the record of the government was poor. Currency depreciation was common. Attempts at stabilisation from the first issue of paper money in 1768 were notoriously unsuccessful even a century or more later. Entrepreneurial fortunes were fragile and transient. Hence Russian entrepreneurs were even more anxious than their French and German counterparts to buy land. The State Commercial Bank of 1817 was designed to help commerce not industry and in reality lent mostly to landlords. Most of the few private banks were agents of foreign institutions. The biggest private bank, Stieglitz, was a German foundation and lent to the government. The State Bank had the right to sanction the first private banks. The big Moscow banks, run by the merchants, remained partnerships, not joint stock companies, and at the beginning of the twentieth century were still predominantly controlled, as earlier, by tightly woven family networks. In contrast St Petersburg banks were more cosmopolitan, innovative and willing to invest in industry. Foreign investors preferred bank shares to direct industrial investment. In 1916 foreigners owned 45 per cent of the shares in the ten largest joint stock commercial banks. Russian banks preferred to trade in foreign industrial shares, partly because of the technical complications of the Russian share market, partly because overseas profits were higher. But by 1914 Russian banks were much involved in industrial enterprise in Russia itself, playing a more direct role in industrial development than in other states, utilising foreign capital, government investment and private resources.[59]

French banks were so little committed to industrial enterprise that at the end of the century only 35 per cent of the members of the Bank of France were industrialists; the rest were merchants and bankers. Banks invested in government securities, later in foreign industry, notably initially in Germany, Italy and Russia, through the aegis of other banks. In 1914 France had the highest level of foreign investment after Britain: 50 billion gold francs, which was equivalent to between one-quarter and one-third of her wealth other than land and consumer capital.[60] Where major capital outlay was called for in France it was usually supplied by merchant associations, for instance in the iron industry and sugar-refining. *Notaires* often acted as money-lenders, but not to industry – their interest rates, often 24 per cent were unattractive to businessmen.[61] In both Russia and Germany banks were the intermediaries for such investment; Moscow merchants were often major bankers too, though links between business and industry were less developed than in St Petersburg. In Germany investment changed as industrialisation proceeded more rapidly. A new type of capitalist entrepreneur emerged. Gustav von Mevisson was the president of the Darmstädter Bank and the Luxembourg International Bank, the chairman of three others, on the board of two more, as well as of six mining companies, and the head of two industrial firms. Typical of Germany, and very unlike France, was the close association between banks and industry. In Rhineland–Westphalia many private bankers began their careers as wholesale merchants, helping to cement the close links with commerce and industry. New names on the board of directors of more than one bank included Thyssen, Stümm, Bocking, Hoesch and Siemens. Quite modest civil servants, who earlier in Prussia had been involved in industrial investment, were pushed out by the scale of the operation. Investment was only for the rich, partly for organisational reasons, partly because of the high level of risk in the formative period, when companies tended to overextend their credit and collapse in large numbers in crisis years. Industrial investment gained a wider appeal in the 1870s and forged a strong link between the landowning aristocracy and the middle class. Industrial investment became fashionable, no longer something to be indulged in clandestinely. German family firms were transformed into joint stock companies in order to expand. Silesian industrialists, previously able to finance themselves, now became dependent on the Berlin money market, as did the rapidly growing Ruhr area.[62] Once this degree of anonymity was reached, capitalism had moved into quite a different phase, but it should be noted that this was a feature only of the last quarter of the century and was geographically limited.

Did industrialisation bring political dominance to the bourgeoisie, as Marx and his followers predicted? Before the 'industrial revolution' entrepreneurs were traditionally close to government. In Naples the two were mutually dependent: the Bourbons on the capital which could be advanced to finance a near-bankrupt state, the entrepreneurs on the fat contracts and monopolies they could obtain to run state institutions, such as tax collecting, which the Bourbons could not afford to do themselves. Of course such privatisation did not constitute modern entrepreneurial activity, at least not until the 1980s, but smacked of *ancien régime* decadence. The nineteenth century brought with it elected assemblies, in which entrepreneurs took a fairly modest direct role, even by 1914. However the power of the industrial bourgeoisie rests not in democratic majorities, but in the size of the industrial undertaking. It was the big combine, the cartel, which carried clout. In France ironmasters exerted the most visible pressure on governments, textile manufacturers generally less, although the Alsatian cotton magnates were active in local politics and in the liberal opposition to the Bourbons. Pressure groups were often a feature of the size of a firm and associates. The French iron industry in the nineteenth century rapidly became concentrated. By 1869 the ten largest firms accounted for over two-thirds of the industry's capital and 44 per cent of production; de Wendel's alone produced over 11 per cent of France's iron. In 1864 the main producers set up the Comité des Forges to be a pressure group on government in favour of protectionism. In the First World War its power was such that it had almost complete control over war contracts and purchases from abroad. But the Comité had its opponents and in reality the iron industry was less significant than the textile industries, accounting for only 2.2 per cent of the country's national product in 1910, compared with textiles' 16.5 per cent. The German iron industry was far more concentrated. In 1913 twelve French firms were responsible for 80 per cent of production, whereas in Germany seven firms accounted for 88 per cent. The influence of French ironmasters came not just from iron. Many were nobles who, unlike many middle-class entrepreneurs, actually ran their own businesses. Ironmasters were a powerful political pressure group long before the setting up of the Comité des Forges. During the Orleanist regime the richest men in fourteen departments were ironmasters, and their wealth of all kinds, including land, made sure that they had representatives in parliament. Eugene Schneider was president of the legislative assembly for the last six years of the Second Empire. Subsequently his son-in-law was a minister and his grandson a member of parliament.[63]

In Germany there were close links between leading politicians and economic interests, particularly in the case of Miquel and Kardoff, the leaders of respectively the National Liberals and the Free Conservatives, the two main parties behind Bismarck. Kardoff was closely associated with the Bleichröder Bank and with a group of Upper Silesian industrialists was prominent in railway development. He was a founder of the Central Association of German Industrialists, set up in 1876, and was subsequently on various significant pressure groups. Previously close links between government and industry had been rather schoolmasterly, now the government tried to maintain a favourable climate for development. Some successful businessmen accepted official posts, but the reverse was more usual because of pay differentials. The world depression witnessed an acceleration of pressure. The Association of German Steel and Iron Industrialists successfully obtained protective tariffs in 1879 and the crisis years helped to formalise cartels.[64] The Rhine–Westphalian coal syndicate formed in 1893 had an enormous impact, for instance in the Dortmund area it represented nearly 87 per cent of production and nationally it approached near-monopoly. It was found that price-fixing cartels were as efficacious in prosperity as in depression. By 1908 the whole of the coal industry was grouped into regional sydicates. Cartels grew up in associated trades, such as wholesale coal merchants. By 1905 there were 385 cartels, but no total monopolies. They encouraged greater industrial concentration. Between 1873 and 1900 40 per cent of mining companies disappeared as independent organisations. Trusts were set up through joint stock banks. The very big families and the Silesian noble mining magnates stayed aloof to some degree. A Thyssen could judge individual cartels empirically, but on the whole the structures they created were lasting and ubiquitous, forming the basis for government management of industry during the First World War.

Russian entrepreneurs formed many pressure groups, but all regional in their appeal and sometimes mutually contradictory. St Petersburg entrepreneurs maintained close links with government, but did not have the upper hand because of their dependence on government contracts. They were also weakened as a pressure group partly because many were foreigners and even more because merchants and manufacturers were not one and the same as in Moscow, but often held opposing views. In 1903 only one of the 78 electors and candidates of the St Petersburg Exchange was also a member of the Society for the Assistance, Improvement and Development of Factory Industry. They were overshadowed locally by the Court and nobility. Unlike their Moscow counterparts they ran no newspapers, salons, theatres or museums. Moscow merchants kept clear of the government, siting most of their factories in the countryside to side-step bureaucratic regulations. Three issues stirred a younger generation of Moscow entrepreneurs. The Crimean War and the Polish revolt of 1863 awakened them to Panslavism and more active loyalty to the person of the tsar. But more specifically they began to organise themselves, first to oppose a low-tariff policy with Germany and secondly to promote industrial progress. The Moscow group were a minority clustered around a newspaper which ran for five years from 1860 and itself generated a Society for the Assistance and Development of National Industry. They attacked the high profile of foreigners in Russian industry. They gained representation on the government's tariff committee. In the 1880s an increase in tariffs came as a direct consequence of merchant pressure, exerted through the Moscow Exchange Association which this group had formed. A Society for the Encouragement of Russian Industry and Trade attracted a broader membership of five hundred from 65 towns, which held national congresses and secured the backing of noble as well as merchant entrepreneurs. Merchants supported government plans for colonial expansion and formed companies to that end.

The engineer-capitalists of the Ukraine, encouraged by French owners, formed an Association of Southern Coal and Steel Producers, which became the most powerful pressure group in the southern industries. The coal and metallurgical industries themselves joined to form large trusts at the turn of the century and took central roles in the Permanent Advisory Office of Metallurgists in St Petersburg and the council of the Association of the Representatives of Trade and Industry. Several were elected to the State Council and the Special Council on Defence in the First World War. A substantial number were foreigners or Jews. The only Russian in the top group was Avdakov, a graduate of the Mining Institute, who, having established himself as a successful factory-owner, served on every relevant government commission, culminating in his election to the State Council. The southern group was robbed of influence because of the preponderance of foreigners, who were detested by local landowners and failed to gain the confidence of the local technical and professional élite clustered around the Technological Institute of Kiev, where the sugar beet and railroad interests held sway. Nonetheless they were instrumental in obtaining high tariffs on imported coal and pig iron and in determining the route of the new railway.

It was not until the years of the Great Depression that Italian industrialists in the emerging modern complexes of the Po valley began to exert positive pressure on liberal governments, leading to the introduction of protective tariffs and an increasingly close relationship between major industrialists and government. As in

Russia, the poverty of the internal market meant that the government was the main purchaser of manufactured goods. Thus angling for fat military contracts encouraged the emergence of pressure groups.

In conclusion we must note the great diversity in the social origins of entrepreneurs and the major role played by nobles, especially in Russia. We are now aware that the self-made man was a rarity; most success stories were built on wealth, not luck and native cunning. We should also take account of the fact that, although entrepreneurs did not often become politicians, through pressure groups they adequately represented their own interests. One is struck by the apparent lack of social confidence in their own way of life: many gave their sons a classical education and encouraged them to enter the professions. British capitalists were not alone in seeking to make enough money to lift their families out of business. Presumably one great imperative in this drive to acquire land, or some other means to a comfortable life, was economic. Repeated industrial and commercial crises in the nineteenth century encouraged the pursuit of a more secure investment, which for much of this period seemed to be land. The Russian merchant was particularly vulnerable and could not diversify into land until the 1860s. Entrepreneurs were not always in the van of modernity and innovation. In more backward regions like Naples, where the highest returns could be made by propping up the ramshackle Bourbon regime, they were, in many respects, the biggest obstacle to economic change because of the control they had over credit.[65] We have also traced the stratification and divisions within what might have been assumed to be a single group. Entrepreneurs did not constitute a monolithic pressure group regardless of industry and region. Conflicts were most pronounced in Russia. It is clear that the great fragmentation of this section of society in Russia contributed substantially to the collapse of the tsarist system. Divisions were significant elsewhere too. It is questionable whether what united entrepreneurial elements, where they were linked, was the identity of class which Marx and many others have claimed. The examples we have considered indicate that religious, racial, cultural and educational affinities were important and that geographical and specific economic factors were vital. It is hard to equate these with a broad sense of class identity, since the groups thus formed were small. Russia is an extreme example of division, but it is clear from our discussion of the origins and assumptions of the industrial bourgeoisie elsewhere that a sense of common purpose, which Marx thought distinguished them, was lacking. The very economic interests which Marx believed they shared tended rather to divide them. In France ironmasters and metallurgical interests were intent on maintaining a high-tariff system to smother foreign competition in the first half of the century, a preoccupation they shared with grain producers. Silk and wine manufacturers, on the other hand, were aware that France's commercial policy was reducing their own export market. The free-trade policies of the late 1850s and renewed protectionism in the 1870s and 1880s similarly split entrepreneurs according to the imperatives of their particular product. A similar phenomenon can be observed in other states. Factory industry remained very localised and limited, even in Germany, well into the later decades of the century, which meant that the bulk of industry was still fragmented, rural and small scale, stimulating only a tiny 'capitalist' class in a Marxist sense. Only after 1870 in Germany, somewhat later in France and a generation later in Italy and Russia did specific regions begin to develop large-scale factory industry and a noticeable body of entrepreneurs.

3. Economic Interests of the Middle Classes: Bourgeois Landowners

In the great revolution, France swept feudalism away and established the hegemony of the bourgeoisie, doing this with an exemplary completeness not achieved in any other European country.[1]

THUS Engels summarised the traditional Marxist thesis that the 1789 revolution had been the instrument of immutable social change in which the aristocratic, feudal and landed élite was replaced by the entrepreneurial bourgeoisie, the symbol of capitalist industrialisation. As we have already noted, some rich nobles were entrepreneurs. We have observed that many middle-class entrepreneurs demonstrated an un-Marxist preoccupation with the acquisition of landed estates. Bureaucratic and professional elements in the bourgeoisie were equally active in the property market. While the middle class were eager to buy land, European aristocracies were far more resilient than Marx had expected. In this chapter we shall consider the impact of the bourgeois quest for landed respectability. Why did the bourgeois want to become the squire and what were the consequences for social and economic development in the nineteenth century?

The bourgeoisie were not newcomers to the land market on the eve of the French Revolution. The proportion of land they owned varied from the Russian Empire, where eighteenth-century legislation had forbidden merchants ownership of populated (i.e. serf) estates and the royal family and nobles monopolised landowning, to France, where in 1789 the bourgeoisie owned 25 per cent of the land, about the same proportion as did the nobility, the Church owned about 20 per cent and the peasantry the rest. In the Italian and German lands a growing minority of landowners were middle class. In Bologna, 18 per cent of the land was owned by the bourgeoisie.[2] Only 40 per cent of the land of Prussia was retained by nobles in the early nineteenth century, but the estates they held were large. There were 15000 such estates of 375 acres or more in Prussia in 1850, although there were few to match British large aristocratic holdings of 10000 acres and much more. In Britain at the end of the eighteenth century the aristocracy held 55 per cent of the land, or 69 per cent if estates of 300–1000 acres are included, as they would in France. There were far fewer large estates in France than in England.[3]

The wealthy bourgeois, whether entrepreneur, professional, or state bureaucrat, uniformly and traditionally nourished the ambition to acquire land. Land was regarded as the most secure, profitable and prestigious investment. Its ownership conveyed a myriad of benefits, sometimes including the status of feudal privilege early in this period. The rules of the new nineteenth-century electoral game were always bent towards the landowner. During the constitutional monarchy in France (1814–48), the *foncière*, or land tax, was the main element which qualified both voters and parliamentary candidates, and after 1848, and even after 1871 when universal suffrage operated, constituencies were drawn up to give greater weight to rural areas. Piedmont and later united Italy adopted a suffrage similar to that of Louis-Philippe's reign in France, where the land tax counted for most. In Prussia after 1848, and in Russia in *zemstva* (local assembly) elections after 1864 and *duma* (national assembly) elections after 1905, the franchise was heavily weighted in favour of the aristocratic, landed vote. Thus the reality of nineteenth-century political systems encouraged the politically active to place particular value on the possession of land. While feudal institutions persisted the social and economic advantages of the acquisition of land were inseparable. The eighteenth-century expansion of the land market was partly in response to the opportunities offered by the feudal system, partly an aspect of its decline. In France the wealthy urban bourgeoisie acquired estates carrying feudal privileges both for status and in order to exploit their added commercial possibilities, as Arthur Young noted in his journeyings through France in 1789 and the following years.[4]

In the Italian states governmental attacks on feudal noble and clerical privileged landowning were supported by contemporary physiocratic enlightened ideas, but in actuality during the century the proportion of the most desirable land in noble, clerical and rich bourgeois hands increased as the decline in commercial activities made land by far the most rewarding investment.[5] If attempts to curb feudal privilege were opposed by the strength of the market in such estates, other aspects of traditional agriculture had fewer defenders. The communal system, which traditionally protected the rural poor by providing common grazing, the opportunity to collect timber etc., was actively undermined in the modern period by the ambitions of the better-off in the rural community. Desirable common land was enclosed, in southern Italy on such a scale that a rural bourgeoisie or *galantuomini* thus emerged.[6] The spur to the land market was thus governmental and individual ambition, with the support of modern economic theory, but interest in land was also a response to the growth of a larger, more accessible urban market. There were constant changes in land use. The rivalry between the *galantuomini* and other peasants in southern Italy was not a simple issue of burgeoning rural capitalism versus traditional farmers but the rivalry between settled grain producers and transhumance graziers. To complicate the situation, the grazier who wanted to preserve traditional communal rights was often the employee of, and protected by, a wealthy local baron. Pressure for better government had an inevitable impact on those who paid the bill. Greater efficiency in the collection of taxes in Lombardy, Piedmont and Naples, and the introduction of land tax surveys, pushed landowners to raise rents and encouraged production for the market. Land purchase by middle-class office-holders, professionals and businessmen was not necessarily linked to a generalised decline in feudalism and intensification of capitalist agriculture. Bourgeois purchasers consciously bought status with their acres and feudal privileges were socially desirable. The new owner did not necessarily radically alter the way the land was used.

Thus on the eve of the 1789 revolution a range of factors was stimulating the land market. The revolution itself had a very visible impact, with the dramatic abolition of feudal rights by the National Assembly on the night of 4 August 1789 and the confiscation and sale by the government of both Church land and the property of those who followed members of the royal family into exile. Marxist historians were quick to describe this process as a major element in the decline of the landed aristocracy and the advance of the capitalist bourgeoisie, and the novels of Balzac and others indicate that rural France underwent consequent changes in the nineteenth century. The French conquest of much of Europe was accompanied by similar policies. Russia was the last to pursue rural 'modernisation'. Serfdom was not abolished until the 1860s. To what extent did such changes serve the interests and appetites of the bourgeoisie?

Making more than general polemical or literary statements about changes in landownership is a difficult and onerous affair. The nature of surviving records does not facilitate easy calculations as the example of France shows. In France there are three basic types of document. The cadastral surveys made in the nineteenth century present evidence of how the boundaries of parcels of land altered, but they do not reveal who owned which parcel or how much he owned.[7] Secondly, there are tax records, which tell us the amount of *foncière*, or land tax, paid by each individual, but give no details of his land.[8] Last there are wills, registrations, *mutations par décès*, records deposited with a *notaire*, detailing the whole of a man's estate, including his land. Such records are not uniformly well preserved and in many cases have entirely disappeared. Hence the opportunity to go beyond fairly general statements about changes in landownership is slight and one is bound to resort to a broadly delineated sketch.[9]

Until recently it was assumed that the French Revolution was a major watershed in landowning, that it marked the decline of an aristocratic landowning class, that a new, larger group of peasant proprietors emerged and that the aristocratic, landowning interest gave way to that of entrepreneurial capitalism. The decisions of the revolutionaries, motivated by political rivalries interlaced with physiocratic concepts of reform and economic imperatives, affected landholding in several different ways. Firstly, the sale of Church lands put an unprecedented amount of land on the market at one time. The property of *emigrés*, who fled France to join the royal family, was also liable to confiscation. Both categories were declared *biens nationaux* and sold by the government. Secondly, in an emotional outburst against privilege feudal rights were abolished. Thirdly, revolutionary governments reinforced the onslaught of the better-off against communal rights. Finally, the Napoleonic Civil Code ordered the subdivision of land among all surviving heirs. As a consequence of the publication of the Civil Constitution of the Clergy in 1790 all

Church lands were nationalised and sold, and land belonging to families where the head of the family followed the deposed Bourbons into exile as an *emigré* was expropriated and sold. Initially an attempt was made to divide this land into small lots to allow the less well-off to acquire property, but because of the huge amount of land on the market and the collapse in value of the new *assignats*, the paper money issued to ease such transactions, most of the land sold went to existing property holders. Church lands in particular were sold off in large lots to middle-class or rich peasant purchasers. These were often sited on rich alluvial land near to towns and could be used for cash crops. *Emigré* lands were sold in smaller lots, but the Convention, alarmed by the effect of land subdivision, would not allow peasants to group together to buy a plot and subsequently divide it among themselves. Purchasers were allowed twelve years to pay; later this was reduced to four because of the disastrous collapse in the value of the *assignats*. In total up to 29 000 noble estates and 60 000 religious holdings were sold to 2 million purchasers. Although the richer middle-class buyers did best, there were many peasants among the customers and some of the poorer land bought by the urban bourgeoisie was sold later to peasants.[10] *Emigrés* were often noble and the confiscation and sale of their land might have had a destructive effect on their estates and on the social composition of the landholding groups. However, other members of an *emigré* family, acting through agents, sometimes bought the land. Woodland often went unsold and *emigrés* who returned under Napoleon, or even with the Bourbons in 1814, were able to repossess such property.[11] In areas where large, aristocratic estates had been the norm before the revolution, such as the south and west, these survived in the nineteenth century. In the Cher large noble holdings remained intact and this was pretty well the same in Maine, Anjou, Vendée and Loire-Inférieure. Bourgeois property-owning increased markedly in areas where they were already well established as landowners, like Normandy and Alsace.[12] The proportion of the land of France in noble hands fell by no more than 5 per cent as the result of revolutionary land sales.[13] The nobility remained the richest group in French society at least until mid-century.[14]

Most of the land sold went to existing bourgeois property-owners, especially the former venal office-holders compensated by the revolutionaries. Other urban groups such as professional men joined in the scramble. Some entrepreneurs in Alsace found the property of religious orders suitable for new factories. Some peasants benefited. In the Nord the peasants' share of the land went up from 30 per cent to 62 per cent, but the revolution did not enrich and enlarge the peasant landowning class in general, indeed the impact of revolution and civil and foreign wars added to the misery of the poorer sections of the peasantry.

The abolition of feudal dues, despite its egalitarian and radical ring, brought little comfort to peasants, although it did bring a temporary cease-fire between the peasantry and their oppressors in the rural areas. Nor was the abolition a 'bourgeois' measure, for members of the bourgeoisie had been keen to buy feudal rights. Owners were initially promised compensation, but this was not forthcoming. Many simply rewrote tenancy agreements to incorporate feudal obligations into ordinary rents.[15] Even more disastrous for poorer peasants was the decision of the revolutionaries to accelerate the dismemberment of the communal system, ostensibly a progressive reform, in reality the product of pressure from the richer members of rural communities. Communes were allowed to partition common land in response to local initiative in a series of laws published between 1790 and 1792. Although further division was halted in 1796, subsequent legislation in 1827 undermined the local community's control over commonly held forests, etc. Common land left tended to be marginal. In France as a whole 10 per cent of the land in 33 departments was held in common in 1863, but the highest proportions were in the poorest departments. In the Hautes-Alpes 51 per cent of the land was common, in Savoie 42 per cent.[16] The attack on communal traditions can be interpreted as a 'modernising capitalist' trend, facilitating the development of a market economy, but it was far from new. The revolutionaries did not initiate the process. Ironically, peasant attempts to defend communal traditions ensured that poorer peasants would be involved in repeated clashes with governmental authority, of all political hues, in the nineteenth century.

The revolutionaries of the 1790s officially supported the small farmer and opposed privilege. As part of such a strategy the Civil Code published in the Napoleonic period ordered the subdivision of land among all surviving heirs. In the nineteenth century France had a very much larger number of landowners than anywhere else in Europe, but so had it before the publication of the Civil Code. In 1862 there were reckoned to be 6 200 000 landowners in France.

Most held only very small parcels; 75 per cent of the total number of properties were of less than 5 hectares, too little to provide for the needs of a family. Only 46 000 owned land taxed at over 500 frs. a year. Some commentators argued that subdivision had been exacerbated by the Napoleonic Code and popular novelists joined in the criticism. But recent research has shown that the legislation was often ignored, especially by the wealthy, so that large estates were maintained. Varied local inheritance customs prevailed, actively supported by the *notaires* who drew up legal settlements. However the result was a great increase in litigation and the less well-off preferred to observe the law.[17] In reality the degree of subdivision or concentration depended less on the Code than on the prosperity of the family and the profitability of the soil. Sixty thousand landowners owned 25 per cent of the land. But large estates were chiefly concentrated in the north, especially in the Paris Basin, and many were accumulated by wealthy bourgeois whose tenants engaged in advanced capitalist farming, notably for the Paris market. Subdivision was most prevalent in the poorer areas of the south. Small peasant farms still occupied 40 per cent of the cultivated land at the end of the century. The average plot was just under 9 hectares and in mid-century 40 per cent of land was held in parcels of between 10 and 100 hectares. Towards the end of the century only 15 per cent of agricultural workers had no land of their own. But sharecropping persisted in the less productive areas of the south.

The bourgeois landowner bought land as a safe investment and rarely farmed. The owners, and indeed the prosperous tenants, of the large farms of the Paris Basin might be seen as typical examples of the impact of middle-class land purchase, in their development of capitalist agriculture. But the type of bourgeois owner varied according to the locality. He leased his estate for a fixed term and for a money rent, but in areas where land was poorer, especially in the south and west, he practised traditional *métayage*, or sharecropping, providing tools and seed and sharing the harvest. However, there was a marked reduction in the proportion of land under *métayage*. In the 1830s between one-third and one-half of France was share-cropped; by the 1890s only 11 per cent.[18] At this latter date just over half of the land was farmed by owner-occupiers, most of the rest by tenants.[19] Only a tiny proportion were producing on a large scale for the market; most were operating within a semi-subsistence local economy. The coming of the railways expanded the market possibilities. In France alterations in the pattern of ownership and exploitation were gradual and the most marked impact of the revolution ˌwas to speed up the acquisition of land by wealthy middle-class and peasant groups through the sale of Church lands. In the nineteenth century the urban bourgeoisie continued to set their sights on land purchase, but themselves continued an urban lifestyle, perhaps retiring to their country house for holidays and to impress guests. Their main preoccupations were still urban. The consolidation of large holdings producing for the market created a resident rural bourgeoisie with specific rural interests. But capitalist agriculture was not uniquely the concern of the bourgeoisie. Indeed bourgeois land acquisition was still, in part, a laundering process to make a bourgeois seem like a member of the traditional landed élite, perhaps quietly inventing a title to go with the estate.

In conquered territories French revolutionary governments pursued similar policies of selling Church land and attacking feudal and communal traditions, giving succour to the rich with capital and, it was hoped, loyalty to spare. The impact of French policies was necessarily limited by the short and stormy period of her rule and most success was achieved in areas where there was some basis and sympathy for the revolutionary strategies. The Italian land market had been active in the eighteenth century as those with spare capital moved away from the declining profits of industry and particularly trade. Nobles, the Church, wealthy bourgeois and new nobles increased their holdings. As in France, the proportion of land owned by the nobility and the Church varied between regions. By the mid-eighteenth century the nobility owned between 42 and 47 per cent of the land of Lombardy and the Church had also increased its holdings to 21–3 per cent. The Papal States were held almost exclusively by privileged groups; nobles owned 70 per cent of the plains in Bologna. Some of the land thus acquired was former common land and noble holdings thus became noticeably more consolidated. Fewer and fewer noble families held more and more of Italy as the application of mortmain and entail legislation limited the sale of land to non-nobles. However, in some provinces the amount of privileged land remained small. In Piedmont nobles held only 10 per cent, the Church 15 per cent. In common with most of Europe nobles were non-resident landowners, being themselves towndwellers. Estates were managed by middle-class agents or *gabelloti*. Many families were ruined by the shrinking Italian economy and their own lack of attention to their economic interests. The bourgeoisie seized some of the opportunities thus offered. The *gabelloti* were often in a favourable position to buy up such bankrupt noble estates, creating in northern and central Italy the nucleus of a rural bourgeoisie. They were also well placed to do battle with the peasantry for possession of common land. More illustrious bourgeois land purchasers came from the wealthy merchant caste of cities like Florence and Venice, eager to turn their backs on deteriorating commercial investments, and if possible buy feudal titles with their estates, most likely in Naples and Piedmont. Merchants and bankers from Lombardy, Venetia and Genoa were notably active in the southern land market.[20] The contribution of the French was to fuel ambitions to buy land by selling Church and communal property and by trying to dismember feudal tenancies. In Naples active defeudalisation was attempted from 1806 accompanied by the sale of common lands, but the main consequence was the creation not of loyal subjects but of thousands of litigants as communities and individuals sought to protect their interests.[21] Church lands went principally to existing estate-owners, both noble and rich bourgeois families. Landownership was thus concentrated even more in the hands of a small group of notables. In Piedmont it was in these years that the main political families of the period of unification, Cavour, Balbo, d'Azeglio, created their economic power bases. In the kingdom of Italy Napoleon's senior bureaucrats were able to amass huge estates. In Naples Church lands went to Court nobles, senior military and civil officials, and rich merchants. Big estates became vast territories but, as elsewhere, the land sales also encouraged the build-up of smaller, though still substantial holdings by the prosperous rural middle class.[22] De-feudalisation superficially benefited the peasantry, but in reality, as in France, the chief consequence was the vastly accelerated demise of common land and rights, the backbone of the economy of the poor. De-feudalisation was a complete 'catch-22' for the peasant; the community suffered and the feudal lord was able to acquire common land in the name of modernity and progress, for himself or suitably quiescent *galantuomini*. The French, and the restored Bourbons after 1814, hoped that de-feudalisation would bring in more revenue. Their legacy was the undisputed power of the big landlord and constant rural unrest by rebellious peasants determined to regain lost communal lands and rights.[23] Statistics for changes in ownership are striking. In Bologna in 1789 the Church owned 19 per cent of the land, nobles 55 per cent and the bourgeoisie 18 per cent. By 1804 these proportions had changed to 4 per cent, 50 per cent and 34 per cent.[24] In the Veneto nobles lost half their land between 1740 and 1839, and land was bought by wealthy, long-established banking and commercial families and others who had profited from the French occupation.[25]

The removal of the French had no more of a unique impact on the pattern of land ownership in Italy than had the French conquest itself. In Naples the desperate need of the Bourbons for money led to the sale of demesne land at bargain rates to the same groups who had prospered under the French. Whether noble or bourgeois the new owners were traditional in their attitudes. They managed their land through bailiffs and continued to lease it in small parcels as before. Constantino Volpicello, a leading Neapolitan merchant who died in 1850, left a substantial fortune, D. 100 000, to his son, most of which consisted of small, individual blocks of land let out to tenants in the traditional manner. Entrepreneurs bought land for respectability, not capitalist adventuring. Indeed there was more profit for an entrepreneur to lend capital at high rates to the government, or to other landowners, than to invest it to try to make his own land more productive.[26] Sometimes an attack on common rights was linked to 'progressive' agriculture. After 1815 the Austrian rulers launched a major scheme of land reclamation in the Po valley, which threatened the livelihood of those who lived in the marshy terrain. By 1839, when the Austrians insisted on the sale of surviving common land, only poor quality land such as that in the Alpine valleys and the lower Po valley was still owned by local communities. Peasants put up considerable resistance, but found the revolutionaries of 1848 no more sympathetic; many had themselves bought common land and were afraid of peasant demands and violence. In Naples the Bourbons were habitually hostile to the peasants until 1848 when the big landowners ungratefully sided with the revolutionaries. In Sicily the big barons formed a consolidated front, despite repeated attempts by peasants in favour of beleaguered communal traditions. But the primacy of noble and supporting bourgeois landownership was not universal in the peninsula. In Piedmont peasants had also gained from the sale of Church and demesne land and there were more peasant owners than elsewhere in Italy.[27]

Unification brought the next main developments in landownership in Italy. Remaining Church lands were sold off in the south, and the main purchasers were northern, particularly Piedmontese, wealthy property-owners, both noble and non-noble. These became absentee landowners. They ran their farms through local agents, as was the norm, but preferred to lease to tenants rather than to sharecroppers or poor peasants. As in France, the least well-off suffered from the extension of bourgeois ownership. Northern owners were less desirable than any species of the southern brand, whether clerical, noble or bourgeois, for they treated the south as a colony. While the rich agricultural areas of the north, particularly the Po valley, produced for the market, the south grew even poorer;[28] peasant unrest and violence continued.

The increase in bourgeois ownership did not, automatically, lead to a more commercial exploitation of the land, and this was particularly true in the south, where the poverty of the soil and the difficulties of communication in mountainous terrain did not favour production for a market. In Sicily the sickle continued in common use and there were few cattle.[29] For peasants the change in ownership was a double blow. Clerical landowners had been more accessible and had provided a skeleton social service in return for the monopoly of the land. The Catholic Church had offered a little in the way of health care, primary education and employment in religious houses. After unification the only recourse for many peasants in the south was emigration to the north or abroad. Even by 1914 it was reckoned that, although 55 per cent of the Italian population lived off the land and 25 per cent owned some or all of the land they farmed, only 1 per cent was owned by those who farmed it and an average plot was only 1 hectare. The process of unification and its political, social and economic implications led to guerrilla warfare in which more men died than in all of the earlier wars and revolts linked to the Risorgimento. Southerners, both peasants and nobles, rejected, and in the case of the latter scorned, the northern, mainly bourgeois, control of their region.

By the end of the century there were about 200 000 men with private incomes from land. Many were not particularly well-off and could almost be categorised as an unemployed upper class. The economic position of landowners, especially noble ones, deteriorated through the nineteenth century, with estates heavily mortgaged as a result of the Napoleonic Wars and the depression which followed. The governments in Turin and Naples tried to help by restoring entails and primogeniture in 1815, but to no avail. Southern nobles in particular stuck to their estates, leasing out the land to others. It has been calculated that between 1820 and 1860 the number of landowning families in Sicily rose from 2000 to 20 000, with estates becoming progressively smaller. The south did not offer the potential for an obvious alternative to agriculture, but even in the most industrialised province, Lombardy, there was five times as much investment in agriculture as in industry in 1850. Landownership carried social status, the 40-lire voter of post-unification Italy qualified mainly on his land tax and Italy lacked a wealth of industrial resources to exploit.

In Prussia feudal customs were still in force at the end of the eighteenth century and the Code of 1794 reiterated the ban on the sale to non-nobles of lands carrying feudal privileges. The bourgeoisie coud buy non-feudal land and found ways of acquiring noble estates. By 1800 10 per cent of noble estates had been sold to non-nobles. The impetus to sell was heightened by a sharp rise in land prices. Between 1740 and 1801–4, the average price of a manor rose by 394 per cent in Brandenberg. But during the nineteenth century the Junker aristocracy remained the dominant landowning group. Feudal institutions were eliminated on royal estates in Prussia following the French Revolution; neighbouring Westphalia and the Grand Duchy of Warsaw also abolished serfdom during the Napoleonic Wars; the Prussian king decreed its abolition in 1810. Peasants who had traditionally worked land as hereditary tenancies were asked to renounce one-third in return for their freedom. Those who did not have such rights were obliged to give up 50 per cent of the land they farmed. The aristocracy protested at the generosity of these terms[30] and an edict of 1816 declared that they could not be applied to peasant smallholdings or to property acquired by peasants since the reign of Frederick II. For the majority of peasants serfdom remained a reality until after the revolution of 1848, indeed total abolition was only completed in 1865.

The abolition of serfdom was accompanied by the consolidation of estates by the major aristocratic owners. About 45 per cent of land farmed by peasants, 2.5 million acres, was acquired by the big landowners as a direct result of the elimination of serf institutions. It was often quickly resold to middle-class purchasers, no longer debarred from ownership. Their purchases increased, facilitated by substantial noble sales during a prolonged depression from 1806 to

1857. Prussia did not follow the tariff policies of most other states after the wars and food prices slumped in the years of bumper harvests. Junker mortgage debts more than doubled in the first half of the nineteenth century. They alone were able to obtain cheap credit from *landschaften*, banks specialising in loans to large landowners, but they foreclosed on 40 per cent of mortgages. Between 1824 and 1834 230 estates went bankrupt in the Junker lands east of the Elbe. They were bought as large units by wealthy middle-class purchasers; some were sons of former tenants, some agriculturalists from western Germany, but some again had made their fortunes in trade, finance and industry. They introduced modern management and intensified the trend towards agrarian capitalism, assisted by a rise in world grain prices from the 1830s to the 1870s. The amount of land under cultivation in Prussia doubled between 1816 and 1866, and the productivity more than kept pace with population increase, thanks to technical developments.

The new owners sought acceptance by the Junkers, who held them at arm's length but imitated their farming methods. Despite the sales Junker power remained unchallenged. Although there had been over 14 000 sales among 12 000 *rittergüter*, or privileged estates, in Prussia between 1835 and 1864, this was less disastrous for the noble landowner than it sounds. Less than one-third of the large estates were of this privileged *rittergüter* category.[31] But in the last quarter of the century grain from the USA and Russia began to undermine the prosperity of the great estates. In the 1860s Germany provided 60 per cent of Britain's wheat imports; by the 1880s this had fallen to 4 per cent. Bad harvests in the late 1870s pared profit margins almost to nothing. Even before the world depression hit, 40 per cent of large landowners were in debt to 60 per cent or more of the total value of their property. More and more businessmen, like Bismarck's Jewish banker, Bleichröder, bought Junker estates to try to gain social acceptance in a country where, despite the lessening of Junker economic pre-eminence, their social and political dominance remained intact. Bleichröder, the first and only Jew to be made a hereditary noble in the reign of William I, bought a seigneurial estate from Von Roon who was moving into bigger premises in 1873. Von Roon was exceptional. He was influential in national politics and not wholly dependent on his land.[32] From the late 1870s the 25 000 big estate-owners, of whom 50 per cent were still Junkers, depended on a stiff protective tariff to keep them afloat, enabling the landowners, 50 per cent of them still Junker aristocrats, to assert their power.[33]

Outside Prussia the situation varied. The French abolished serfdom without compensation in the Rhineland and Westphalia, although Westphalia retracted for a time after the defeat of France. The example of the Rhineland illustrates the reception given to French 'liberal' reforms. The French set up a military occupation, confiscating the land of local princes, *emigrés*, guilds and ecclesiastical institutions. Over half of it was bought by the established middle-class business élite, but the occupation did not add to the prosperity of this group. During the occupation 1.25 million soldiers were billeted on 1.5 million Rhinelanders. Levies, requisitions and blatant plundering added to the economic disaster. The French promised benefits in the abolition of tithes and feudal dues, but this process had been started before the French arrived and their main contribution was to permit extra rents to replace the old dues. The French held on to some of the confiscated land; in Clermont-Tonnère only 6.8 per cent was actually sold. The government then offered land to rent on impracticable three-year leases. Schleswig and Holstein both abolished feudal rights with the approval of large landowners. Some aspects of serfdom were eliminated in Bavaria in 1808, some remained until 1848 but, as in parts of north-west Germany and Thuringia, serfdom was never of great account. Elsewhere, even when serfdom was abolished, feudal jurisdiction remained. The expansion and consolidation of estates eliminated the small farms which had been part of the feudal structure in areas like Silesia, Pomerania and the Mecklenbergs, and the independent farmers were reduced to labourers. Two and a half million acres of peasant land thus came under Junker control. Peasants were helpless to prevent big landowners acquiring old common lands, equivalent to 12 per cent of the land formerly cultivated by them. In western and southern Germany feudal dues were commuted to a cash payment and there smallholdings predominated, but population growth led to land-hunger and poverty. Elsewhere, in southern Holstein, Oldenburg and Hanover, peasants were prosperous.

In Russia the pattern of landownership was very different from the rest of Europe, partly because of a high level of state ownership: in 1877 448 million acres in European Russia out of 1200 million acres. Nobles owned 14 per cent of the total, a proportion similar to that owned by French nobles but considerably less than that of

British aristocrats.[34] In addition, although the nobility and royal family had a monopoly of private landownership in the eighteenth century, the nobility never considered itself primarily a landed, but rather a service, nobility. Hence the term for noble, *dvorianstvo*, means 'the people of the ruler's Court'.[35] He did not even assess his wealth in land but by the number of his serfs. A commercially negligent attitude to the land meant that the main landowners were non-resident and increasingly indebted. In 1858 one-third of all nobles were towndwellers; by 1893 nearly 57 per cent. By 1859 two-thirds of all serfs were mortgaged and the emancipation of the serfs had become at least as vital to the noble landlords as to the serfs. Emancipation laws allowed nobles to sell land to the peasants who had previously farmed it and considered it theirs by right, without need of purchase. Initially middle-class purchasers bought twice as much of the available land as did peasants, but peasant purchases increased with the setting up of the Peasant Loan Bank in 1883. In 1877 nobles owned 177 million acres while peasants owned 313 million acres. By 1905 peasants were the largest group of private landowners, in possession of 63 per cent of the privately owned land of European Russia, compared with 22 per cent held by nobles and 7 per cent by the bourgeoisie.[36] They also of course continued to lease land owned by the nobility and the middle classes. In 1889 35 per cent of the land in the Black Earth region owned by nobles was leased to peasants. Successive governments tried, fruitlessly, to protect the noble landowner. Peasants liberated in the 1860s were obliged, unless they accepted a very small parcel of land about 25 per cent of the minimum size listed in the statutes of emancipation, to buy their land over a 49-year period and to own it only as members of the commune, not as individuals. Nobles received a lump sum less their mortgage debt from the government for the land, and purchasers paid their debt to the state. The extent of noble indebtedness continued to increase and further measures were taken to try to preserve the nobility as landowners.[37] In 1885 a Land Bank for the nobility was established with interest rates of 4–4.5 per cent, well below normal, and a very soft policy towards foreclosure. But although nobles retained forest land and sold the timber at a good price, and although there were examples of spectacular wealth and conspicuous consumption, the general economic decline of the nobility continued. The urban middle class were not allowed to buy land until after emancipation. By 1905 they owned 15 per cent of the privately owned land of European Russia. More significantly, groups of wealthy peasants, kulaks, were emerging into an embryonic rural bourgeoisie. The terms of emancipation had tried to avoid social stratification among the peasants, but such divisions had occurred long before emancipation, as we have seen in our discussion of entrepreneurs. At emancipation some peasants were far better able to buy available land than others. The emancipation decrees tried to mask this and retain what was seen as the traditional social structure of Russia, in the hope of strengthening the autocratic political framework and avoiding the social and political dislocation observed in western Europe in mid-century. Thus the emancipation decrees insisted, somewhat unrealistically, that the commune through its assembly, the *mir*, actually owned the land. The terms of emancipation satisfied no one, and the check on the emergence of a group of wealthy peasant owners was damaging to the regime. Repeated unrest from the landless, whose position was made worse by the doubling of Russia's population in the half-century after emancipation, and from others discontented with redemption payments and unsatisfactory communal ownership, culminated in a substantial peasant contribution to the revolution of 1905. As a consequence in 1907 the tsar's minister, Stolypin, legalised the irresistible fact that those who had paid for the land owned it as individuals. By 1917 over half of the peasant land was held in full hereditary tenure and a peasant élite, or rural bourgeoisie, was firmly established.[38]

Thus middle-class ownership of and attitudes to land varied. In general land was bought by members of the middle class with money acquired elsewhere, in trade, industry, finance, government service or the professions, in order to acquire privileges or social status, to 'lift' themselves socially and live 'nobly' on rents, sometimes retiring from their previous occupation. The purchase was designed to make a qualitative change in the family and its style of life. Rarely did a member of the bourgeoisie buy land to live on it permanently and farm it, although in France, Germany and Russia he would use the 'big house' for a summer residence while leasing out the rest, normally to tenants who were in a position to exploit the land commercially. Land was a safe investment, particularly in times of political upheaval. Middle-class land purchase was not always followed by more commercial exploitation. Production for the market depended not only on the social status of the owner but on the observed potential of the land itself. In buying an estate the bourgeois was imitating the noble; in using the land he often continued to copy his aristocratic model. The obvious commercial potential of rich arable land, for instance in the Paris Basin, in the wheat lands east of the Elbe, in the Po valley and in the rich Black Earth region, was developed by its owners, whatever their social origin. Increasingly these were likely to be bourgeois. The railway extended their opportunities by permitting rapid access to large towns for perishable goods. In Russia it was the wealthy peasant who turned the country into a grain exporter, providing, by 1914, 25 per cent of western Europe's grain needs. Commercial exploitation was not, however, the work of the owner in all cases. In France the consolidated holdings in the Île de France were leased; the lease-holder was the real rural entrepreneur. Thus bourgeois land purchase might diversify the interests of the middle class at two levels: the owner, who in France would continue his basically urban existence, and the farmer, who was the actual rural bourgeois. Lack of commercial exploitation sometimes persisted among the nobility as a traditional prejudice against commerce, and might be imitated by the bourgeoisie. This did not necessarily constitute negligence, especially in poor agrarian regions. Southern Italian entrepreneurs competed to buy rural estates, but did not then invest capital in them, modernise and eliminate feudal structures. Ownership was enough. Investment opportunities were far more important in perpetuating the old ways, buying monopolies, privileges etc. from the government, or maybe lending capital to others to buy land, a not altogether unfamiliar sequence in today's financial world.

Bourgeois fascination with the land had little to do with romance in the nineteenth century. Snobbery plus 5 per cent might be an adequate summary. Marx may have told European society that the age of the feudal landed aristocrat was over, but the bourgeois apparently yearned more for times past than did the researcher in the British Museum Reading Room. Respect for hierarchical social structures, more akin to the notions of Bonald and de Maistre than Marx, meant that in common parlance the owner of a landed estate was nearer the top of the social ladder than a mere lawyer or entrepreneur. These social norms were reinforced by the electoral systems and political power structures created in the nineteenth century. Confidence in land was practical too. The economic opportunities were palpable and irresistible. Europe did not become one big factory overnight. The agrarian sector was dominant for most of the century; even in Germany, it was only in the last quarter of the century that industry took over from agriculture in the national economy. In France the landed interest, led by the aristocracy, may not have escaped the revolutionary decades at the beginning of the century totally unscathed, but it was by far the richest and most influential sector until well after 1850. The exigencies of the Revolutionary Wars ruined some entrepreneurial, but no agrarian, endeavour. Population increase and urbanisation offered a guaranteed market for grain and other products until the 1870s when foreign competition altered the situation. Additionally, a well-located estate contained the raw material for entrepreneurial gain in the resources under or grown on its soil: iron, wood, wool, wine, etc. The cascading bankruptcies of repeated commercial and industrial crises in the century underlined the prosperity and security inherent in the possession of land.

Accelerated to a lesser degree by political revolution and upheaval than has sometimes been suggested, the decline of traditional social structures, communal, feudal and clerical ownership, created excellent opportunities for the investor. As we have noted, these were seized, to an extent which would have surprised Marx, by the nobility itself in some areas; typically, though, they laid the basis for urban bourgeois acquisition and the creation of a rural bourgeoisie, sometimes owners, like the kulaks in Russia, sometimes tenants. The bourgeoisie profited from the sale of Church lands and the inability of poor peasants to preserve communal rights and traditions. The ascendency of the urban bourgeois was predicated less on noble than on communal collapse. As the pace of economic change increased in the century and railway construction made a market economy possible, less prosperous noble families were also obliged to sell. Areas like parts of southern France and southern Italy, with little apparent potential for exploiting the market, suffered the most in terms of an increase in poverty, though noble families tended to try to hold on to their land in default of alternatives. The decline in aristocratic ownership was marked in Russia after emancipation and in Germany. But the largest and wealthiest noble estates survived, through size and capital resources, and the bourgeois owner could not rival them. Middle-class participation in the landed interest was very varied. Universally land was expected to yield independence and social progress for the family. But the *galantuomini* of southern

Italy, though dominant in the local community, were predictably the clients of traditional aristocrats, thus merely adding a rung to the social ladder. Bourgeois purchase nearly always signified the decline of traditional practices, sharecropping and the communal system. Bourgeois cultivation, often by wealthy tenants, signified modernisation and capital investment. But rural capitalism could develop under noble or bourgeois direction. Its determinants were a fertile soil and accessible markets.

The interests of the landowner and the industrial entrepreneur were not necessarily different and the problems of the world depression of the 1870s cemented a common interest in protectionism among many. The success of Russian arable farmers, and even more the spectacular development of Prairie wheat, caused such a drop in the price of grain that, for a time, western European arable land lost some of its attraction. But social standing and reputation survived the economic setbacks of the later years of the nineteenth century. In Germany the standards and norms of the old landed nobility continued to dominate the behaviour and attitudes of the wealthy bourgeoisie and to command their respect, for the basis of the fortune of the wealthier element in that élite was never eclipsed. Indeed the landed interest continued to exercise a powerful influence on governments, today indicated by the Common Agricultural Policy of the Economic Community.

4. The Middle Classes and the Professions

ASIDE from the entrepreneur, the most telling and the more traditional image of the bourgeois is the professional – educated, technically competent and secure. The older professions like law and medicine were well established in 1789, but the period saw many changes and a conscious 'professionalisation' process. At the beginning of the nineteenth century perhaps the most distinguishing feature of a member of the professions was that he was paid fees, rather than a salary, and thus could claim a special independence. Professionals saw themselves as a sort of service élite, with a particular sensitivity to social duty and honour.[1] With population increase, urbanisation, industrialisation and above all the growing role of the state, the size and character of existing professions altered and new jobs jostled for professional recognition. It became imperative to establish parameters and definitions for characteristics previously assumed and understood without question. The need for definition became acute as salaried sectors emerged, the first being bureaucrats, who led the way in defining a new professional ideal in which public esteem rather than independence was the prime feature.[2] Members of recognised groups, notably law, medicine, engineering, academics etc., began to demand certain educational prerequisites from acolytes, to establish more or less of a consensus on skills to be acquired before employment, and to set conditions for membership. Thus a profession became an increasingly closed corporation, similar to a successful medieval guild or a species of secret society, limiting membership by various means to protect 'standards', but also to defend the income enjoyed by those who belonged to the particular organisation, which could be seriously eroded if non-members were allowed to practise or the size of the group allowed to grow unchecked. Acute problems, political as well as professional, were presented by uncontrolled expansion. Italy produced far more lawyers and doctors than could ever find employment. Many turned to politics and it was widely believed that such a phenomenon could be dangerous to the political fabric, particularly since, by the end of the century, many who trained were without independent means. In the first half of the century in Prussia concern over the political consequences of the overproduction of graduates, given the reduction of senior posts in the civil service, led to university entry being restricted to those who had passed the secondary school leaving certificate, the *abitur*.

Professional associations and conferences grew apace in the second half of the nineteenth century, especially within groups whose role was changing rapidly, for example engineering, or among occupations with a low ranking who were anxious to assert their status. Professions were exceedingly hierarchical, not only within themselves but in their jealous regard for other groups. There was a recognised progression, with law at the head and organisations like veterinary surgeons towards the rear. Within professions the lines were just as clear-cut. In France engineers who worked for the state basically in an administrative capacity had status and prestige. Those who actually worked in manufacturing industry, an increasing number towards the end of the century, were disdained by their fellows, although their pecuniary rewards might be much greater. It should be noted that there was an assumption in most professions that members should not be dependent on the income gained from their calling, but should have independent resources. From about 1860, however, as professions were no longer likely to be mainly staffed by sons succeeding fathers, fewer individuals were financially independent, especially in the lower status professions and the subsidiary ranks of the senior ones.

Unprecedented population increase, urbanisation and the consequent mushrooming both of the size of the existing professions and the off-shoots of new ones, dictated that informal links between colleagues, the ability to make recommendations based on close, personal knowledge of a man's probity and skill, were inevitably reduced. Increased specialisation was another consequence of growth. When there was an adequate, but finite, supply of patients, and the likelihood of competition from other practitioners, a doctor was less likely to pull teeth or perform other functions for fear of being thought a quack. Specialisation led to far more precise definitions than before of what constituted the parameters of the profession, the educational and other preconditions for entry and the training necessary before a man could reasonably claim, before colleagues and clients, to be qualified. In part these educational and professional qualifications, which increasingly were tested by formal oral, written and occasionally practical examinations, were a product of the need to assess much larger numbers of aspirants. They also correspond to a more widespread belief that all things were subject to rational measurement, that in medicine, for example, there was a definable and unprecedentedly rapidly expanding body of knowledge and expertise that anyone who called himself a doctor should acquire. Hence the development of professional journals, filled with learned articles. Medicine is, in fact, somewhat of a maverick, for even by the end of the century there was no real consensus, either on the essential body of knowledge or on the best means to train and test hopeful aspirants to the profession, the latter problem leading to serious dissension and unrest within the Paris faculty.

In other specialisms the task was easier. The codification of laws, such as that undertaken and completed in France by the Directory and Consulate and imitated elsewhere, ensured that there was a distinct and tangible mass of information, which ought to be at the disposal of a skilled lawyer; concurrently the French also undertook a standardisation of judicial practice, which was followed by other states at later stages of the century. Hence, in theory, there should have been no difficulty in defining and determining the qualifications needed for different types of lawyer. To a considerable degree such standardisation was achieved, though in reality legal practice differed markedly even in the various regions of France. Difficulties arose because the body of required knowledge *was* accessible; in France *notaires* were constantly undercut by cheaper legal agents, unencumbered by the *notaire*'s obligation to collect a tax for the government on each legal document in addition to his own fee. A *notaire* was a professional man, but the parameters of his profession were extremely vague. There was no stipulation that a would-be *notaire* should have any previous knowledge of the law, merely that he should have enough cash to buy his *étude*. Court prosecutors, judges, etc. were expected both to have university legal training and effectively to have served an apprenticeship in the judicial hierarchy. But their appointments were essentially personal and political, influential patrons being far more significant than the level of their own professional skill. Their own political affiliations were absolutely crucial to their survival and success. It would be naive to labour this point by elaborating on the destitutions effected in the judiciary at every swing of the political pendulum in France or elsewhere. What is perhaps curious is that educated opinion never questioned that a man appointed to uphold the law, and thus, apparently, to be an independent arbiter, should be wholly subject to the whims of individual governments.

The erection of educational fences around a profession protected members against encroachments by state bureaucracy. If members established their own ground rules, they would forestall intervention. The determination to maintain a fee structure rather than accept a salaried status, a feature of most professions, was certainly intended to protect independence and autonomy. But the obedience of German academics to government wishes, despite their ability to earn a high proportion of their income from independent fees, makes such a distinction itself rather arid. Certainly the fact that university dons in France received only a token 'salary' may have helped them to survive the vicissitudes of repeated faculty closures and staff dismissals in the nineteenth century, but probably less because of their professional status than because academics were men of independent financial, as well as ideological, means. The belief that a profession guaranteed certain standards and offered protection to members was based, in the final analysis, not on objective criteria, but on the continuance of traditional patterns of personal experience, family connections, 'old boy networks' and on the tacit agreement of governments not to put the illusions of autonomy to the test. There was a fair degree of consensus between most governments and the professions; both feared what was perceived as the ultimate triumph of democracy, the replacement of the influence of the upper and middle classes by that of the working class. Thus governments did not challenge professions as they constructed walls around their trade to limit its practice to themselves and those they perceived to be their own kind. But mutual suspicion, rivalry, snobbery and self-protection caused most professions to become very fragmented. An excellent example is the teaching profession, where university dons and primary school staff were light-years apart, the latter striving for professional recognition, which other professions, including branches of teaching itself, were reluctant to concede. It may be that in the later years of the twentieth century we are beginning, at last, to realise that the professions, apparently so carefully defined in the nineteenth century, are like the emperor whose vanity allowed him to walk the streets naked.

Four leading professions will be examined in the following pages: law, medicine, engineering and teaching. It is only in the last few years that historians have begun to study the history of professions systematically and in depth, and, as a consequence, the current state of knowledge on the subject is very patchy. Historians of France have been in the van. We shall need to consider the extent to which professions changed as membership swelled, whether the influx in the second half of the century of an increased number of participants whose fathers had not practised, either in the same or in any profession, had an impact on attitudes. Did the emergence of new professions, or the total transformation of others, produce radical change? We will need to ask whether there was a distinct ethos which made professions the preserve of a section of the middle class, or whether different callings in fact encompassed a broad spectrum of middle-class groups. Finally we ought to try to approach the issue of whether the old élites retained control, continuing to sustain the norms of the old-style professions.

The legal profession ranked high in terms of antiquity, fee income and prestige. There was an enormous social and often educational gap between the magistracy and other elements in the legal system. In 1850 the marquis Alfieri reported to Nassau Senior that 'The Revolution has given great importance to advocates; they are almost the only members of the Chamber who can speak, but their social position is not high. The bar is not the road to the magistracy.'[3] In France *notaires* trained on the job; those aiming at the magistracy followed a totally separate route, involving secondary and higher education. Law faculties never lacked students, for their graduates could practise privately, enter either the judicial or administrative branch of the civil service and often become politicians. The cost and length of legal education meant that few lawyers came from humble backgrounds. A successful lawyer needed connections to obtain work and many men were following a family tradition. Modern bureaucratic, parliamentary states increased employment, but the popularity of legal studies, and the determination of the profession to maintain its exclusiveness, led to a surplus of law graduates in most countries during the century.

Magistrates were university-trained. Traditionally they came from higher social groups within the bourgeoisie. In France in the 1860s it was calculated that 80 per cent of law students were upper middle class and 60 per cent were sons of established lawyers, big landowners or *rentiers*. Another 16 per cent of students came from families of senior professionals, or from the industrial or commercial middle classes.[4] This latter group saw legal training as social advancement for their offspring. In 1864, of the 187 pupils at the *lycée* in Douai only twelve planned industrial careers, while 54 hoped to train as lawyers. In Lille nearly a quarter of the pupils from entrepreneurial families who were studying for the classical baccalaureate were destined for law.[5] In Germany too the wealthy industrial middle classes sometimes preferred the status of legal qualifications for their sons, and their numbers were perceptibly increasing in Leipzig by 1870.[6] But the largest proportion of German law graduates were sons of lawyers. In both France and Germany the profession was regarded as a closed shop. Sons of senior officials, themselves lawyers by training, dominated law schools. In the first half of the century in both countries more than half of all law students were sons of lawyers. Italian law students also came primarily from the middle class, but from more varied backgrounds. There was so little suitable employment for the middle class in southern Italy that governments found it expedient to encourage boys to continue their education, and a high proportion completed their studies with a law degree.[7] In Russia, after the reforms of 1864, professional legal training was attractive to the sons of middle-class officials, schoolteachers, etc.

In France law students constituted the largest group at university along with medics. In 1908, of 39 000 undergraduates two-thirds were studying these two subjects. Two years later 17 000 were enrolled in law departments. Law was the only active, organised university faculty.[8] In Italy 40 per cent of students were in law faculties in 1877. By 1914, when the university enrolments had reached 30 000, one-third were still lawyers. Professional unemployment was a serious problem.[9] Each year about 1700 graduates were unleashed, many of whom could not find jobs. Yet the legal profession in Italy was vastly overstocked. In 1901 she had 24 196 trained lawyers, compared with 4273 in Prussia. This figure only includes lawyers in full-time legal employment; the number of law graduates was much higher. In addition there were over 6000 *notaires*, compared with about 8000 in France, which had roughly 15 million more inhabitants. In both countries the number of *notaires* fell in these years; in Italy from nearly 8000 in 1882, in France from over 10 000 in 1834. But in Italy between 1882 and 1901 20 000 new law graduates and 2000 men with notarial diplomas had entered the job market.[10] In France most law graduates proceeded to a career in law, probably in conjunction with politics. In 1867, of 4895 law students in France just over 2000 were aiming at the bar or the magistracy, just over 1000 at other legal jobs. In addition some 659 planned to enter the civil service, 136 commerce or industry and just under 500 were enrolled simply to complete their education.[11] In Germany all bureaucrats had to be trained in the law. In the years 1830–60 nearly a third of all students were lawyers, although this fell to 20 per cent in 1911, as other subjects became attractive and pay in a judicial career somewhat less rewarding.[12]

Legal training was kept socially exclusive partly by cost. Fees were 1500 frs. a year in mid-century in Paris, 1000 frs. in the provinces. German fee levels were comparatively low but the prospective magistrate had to complete a ten-year unpaid stint before he could apply for an official post. Prussian universities produced far more prospective magistrates than were needed in the first half of the nineteenth century, with a consequent crisis both in the profession and in Prussian politics as junior magistrates took a lead in the political opposition to Frederick William IV (1840–60). Universities restricted entry to law schools for nearly twenty years, urged by the government. University entry was limited to candidates who had passed the *abitur*. The subsequent rise in numbers followed an expansion of the judiciary. Despite the prolonged period of training for magistrates, they ranked below other civil servants, and there was a noticeable decrease towards 1900 in the number of sons following fathers as magistrates. In Italy, despite, or perhaps because of, the backwardness of her economy and the lack of future job prospects, it was made easy for students to complete a university training. In the later years of the nineteenth century, a much higher proportion of the age cohort attended universities than in France or Germany. Fees in both secondary schools and universities were deliberately kept low; at the end of the century, a budding Italian lawyer paid less than a third the university fees paid by undergraduates in most other countries. Successive governments were aware that low fees encouraged the lower middle class to send their sons to university and created expectations which could not be realised.

Italy at the end of the century had a large unemployed intellectual proletariat, especially in the south; this was politically explosive for the regime, for a large proportion were law graduates, who quickly turned to politics to express their professional frustration. As in Prussia earlier in the century, the answer finally arrived at, after much parliamentary debate over nearly a decade, was to raise university fees for law students by 50 per cent to 860 lire a year and for notarial students to 200 lire.[13]

Russia was unique among this group of countries in that she had no separate judicial system until emancipation of the serfs made its creation unavoidable. Previously the administration of justice had been subsumed within the bureaucracy and, despite the codification of laws finally achieved in 1835, the tsar had total autocratic jurisdiction. Most judges had no legal training and more than half were totally illiterate. This was a considerable drawback to the fair and impartial administration of justice since, before 1864, all inquisitorial proceedings, which formed the entire investigation into a case, were written, judgment then being delivered by the judges after consideration of the portfolio of written evidence. The court secretary, who naturally had to be literate, thus exerted considerable influence, as did the police, and both were notoriously subject to bribery. Courts passed cases on to other courts in a random and confusing manner. To obtain judgment was thus enormously time-consuming and expensive, as well as being quite unreliable and unpredictable. Every feature of Russia's pre-emancipation legal system, if one can use the term, favoured the wealthy noble. His evidence would be believed in preference to any other, even discounting the way he could use his financial resources to bribe different courts. In 1864 a recognisably modern system of legal administration was established. Judges were to be appointed for life by the tsar from a panel suggested by the judiciary. Trials were held in public with the participation of juries, which immediately improved the speed, impartiality and general professional character of the courts. A rational hierarchy of courts replaced the previous confusing array.[14] But despite the professionalism and the appeal of a legal career to sons of the middle class like Lenin, much of the unpredictability of autocracy remained. Unquestionably in other countries too the dice were heavily loaded against a totally independent magistracy. Governmental and bureaucratic influence could be considerable in denying promotion to an opponent, or moving him to an undesirable part of the country. In Russia special military and other courts were retained, and any case, particularly those concerning political opponents, could be removed from the jurisdiction of the normal system; the government could also declare martial law, removing sensitive political cases from the ordinary courts.[15] In this way the Russian system lacked the independence which was treasured by professional lawyers elsewhere.

One cannot doubt that law was an honoured and ancient profession, but if the definition of a profession is that members are highly educated, have specific and specialised knowledge, and organise to protect their interests, where exactly did the *notaire*, especially in France, fit? He was often regarded as the supreme representation of the bourgeoisie in many communes and the main interpreter of the law for most Frenchmen. Yet he had rarely completed the baccalaureate and almost never studied law at university. A prospective *notaire* simply needed an exorbitant sum of money to buy an *étude*. It was an old profession and one which benefited from reorganisation at the time of Napoleon. But it was a most unprofessionalised and unspecialised profession, yet one requiring deep specialisation and knowledge to perform the very wide range of functions. The *notaire* drew up legal documents for individuals, registered wills and collected a tax on them for the government. In addition to negotiating agreements of all kinds, *notaires* were often money-lenders or financial middlemen. The growing status of the profession is noted in the term used for the *notaire*'s place of work: a *boutique* until the 1730s, subsequently an *étude*. In theory a *notaire* was inferior to a magistrate in education, status and income, but there were huge variations in both professions. Theoretically, a *notaire* could rise from humble beginnings, but poor notarial clerks, like solicitor's clerks, usually stayed that way, unless they were lucky enough to have a boss with a peculiarly ugly daughter. In the middle of the nineteenth century the least desirable *étude* would cost 20 000 frs. and one in central Paris was priced at 700 000 frs. His licence to practise cost up to 50 000 frs. and a tax of 2 per cent had to be paid when an *étude* was sold. A *notaire* had also to pay the *patente* tax, even though he was specifically enjoined not to engage in business or industrial ventures.

Hence it is apparent that prospective purchasers needed a rich family or wife, or the skill to persuade someone else that he and the *étude* were credible investments. Many went bankrupt. This ancient profession had no specific parameters and in the nineteenth century, unlike other professions, created none. But the temptations were great; some took off with their clients' cash, a practice which increased dramatically. In 1875 there were 28 cases of absconding *notaires*; in 1889 103. Between 1880 and 1886 *notaires* 'lost' 62 million frs. of other people's cash. The problem was that there were too many of them, chasing insufficient work. Between 1895 and 1909 over 400 unproductive *études* were abolished. Some produced very rich pickings, 100 000 frs. and more in Paris, and the job thus had a glittering image. But in the 1850s average earnings were 2000–3000 frs., and even in 1913 some earned under 2000 frs., with only 1000 over 30 000 frs. Thus some earned fifty times as much as others. Some were really artisans, with their wives keeping shops, perhaps neighbouring cafés.

The role of the *notaire* and the fees he could earn varied enormously from region to region. In some parts of the country they were required to draft proportionately far more legal documents than elsewhere and in some provinces legal matters were dealt with in court, providing more work for the *notaires*, which in other provinces were settled with no court appearance. In addition fees were not uniform and much undercutting occurred, for there was no obligation, and little incentive, to employ a fully-fledged *notaire* when cheaper agencies, which mushroomed at the end of the century, were available. *Notaires* had no professional mechanism for controlling this phenomenon. In addition to his own fee, a *notaire* had also to charge a state tax on every transaction. He took eight times as much in taxes as in his own fee income. Thus a peasant who had very little to bequeath would know that over half the value of the inheritance could be swallowed up in fees and taxes. *Notaires* were also resented because they were the local money-lender; in 1912 to the tune of 748 million francs, compared with the *Crédit Foncier*'s total of 124 million.[16] In all the French *notaire* was a jack-of-all-trades, whose profession changed apparently reluctantly and slowly to match the growing specialisation of the time.

Indisputably the legal profession was predominantly attractive to the middle class. Its upper reaches, the magistracy, was almost a closed, hereditary corporation, staffed in France by notables, the upper middle class and the nobility, in Prussia mainly by wealthy, educated members of the bourgeoisie, many of whom were ennobled in office. In examining the members of the French appeal courts in the constitutional monarchy, one is struck by how often their personal dossiers refer to the fact that their ancestors had been members of the *parlements*, the appeal courts of pre-revolutionary France. Detailed studies of the magistracy reveal the high degree of continuity (32 per cent), between *ancien régime* and Napoleonic magistrates, despite the sustained upheaval of the 1790s.[17] The legal profession was predictably very hierarchical and those in more modest posts tended to come from correspondingly less wealthy middle-class backgrounds, but often also from legal families.

How independent was the legal profession? This question can be considered on two somewhat mutually contradictory levels: the degree to which lawyers remained aloof from the infighting of parliamentary politics; and the extent to which lawyers in official posts in the judiciary were really appointed for life, according to the principle enunciated by Montesquieu, and were therefore able to give judgment free from party-political considerations. Lawyers were closely linked with politics. In France and Italy there were large numbers of trained lawyers in parliament. In Prussia magistrates lost their taste for politics after 1848, successive generations preferring to exercise influence through their profession. In Russia when a bar of professional lawyers was introduced for the first time in 1864, lawyers quickly assumed the fairly predictable role of critics of the autocratic system, opposition leaders in the duma and revolutionaries. Except in Germany then, lawyer–politicians were usually government critics. However, the élite of the profession, the magistrates, always spoke of the separation of powers and the need for an independent judiciary. As the power of the state and the intervention of elected assemblies grew in the nineteenth century, the ideal was increasingly compromised. *Ancien régime parlements* were able to defy eighteenth-century French kings and Prussian magistrates in the eighteenth century believed they exercised a role as independent arbiters in the state, but their nineteenth-century successors were made to feel the advancing power of the state. At the Restoration in France in 1814 the magistracy was purged of political opponents no less than other branches of the administration, despite the fact that article 58 of the constitutional charter said that judicial appointments were permanent. Fifty-five presidents, 41 *procureurs généraux* and *avocats généraux*, 202 *conseillers* and 1400 judges were dismissed.[18] Magistrates, along with other officials, were asked to take oaths of allegiance to successive regimes. In 1830 the purge was even more extensive, including 156 magistrates who actually refused the oath of allegiance to Louis-Philippe.[19] Additionally the *procureur*, the government's representative in the tribunals and courts of appeal, would simply freeze promotion for a recalcitrant member. In post-unification Italy 80 magistrates were retired, 23 transferred to less attractive posts. There were ways around life-long appointments. In Prussia, judicial reform in the early nineteenth century seriously reduced the number of senior posts, causing promotion log-jams and a conflict with the government that the magistrates ultimately lost. Most junior magistrates in Italy, the *prétori*, who were responsible for 70 per cent of all civil and criminal cases, had no job security, almost no chance of promotion and their pay was as low as that of policemen. What shred of independence remained was obliterated by their subservience to the local prefect. Nineteenth-century professions often made themselves sound like independent corporations, but in reality, for lawyers at least, the prospect of and need for state employment made the separation of powers a mirage.

At the beginning of the period medicine was a profession, but there was no recognised, standardised training, an enormous range of philosophies of medicine and even greater disparity in the financial rewards to be gained. Some doctors also practised as dentists. There was also a great disparity in the status of doctors in different countries, high in France, Germany and Italy, low in Russia, a tradition which still persists. Like law, it was predominantly a bourgeois calling. In 1850 the marquis Alfieri commented in rather Nancy Mitford-like tones to Nassau Senior, 'Nor would a member of the aristocracy readily make his son a physician. It is looked upon as a sort of trade.'[20] By 1914 universities ran universally accepted courses, the profession itself had a corporate sense and the vast expansion in the role of the state had transformed many doctors virtually into civil servants.

In France medical training was in the hands of the medical faculties and the Academy of Medicine. In principle students needed the baccalaureate, a first degree in science, and four years of medical instruction during which five levels of examinations and a thesis were undertaken. Hospitals had no role in medical education, unlike Britain. There were three faculties of medicine, Paris, Strasbourg and Montpellier, and an additional 22 towns with preparatory medical schools. In 1865 there were just over 3000 students in all of these.[21] By 1910 this had grown to 10 000, making it still the second largest faculty subject after law. In 1902 regulations demanding that students understand Latin were abolished, to the disgust of doctors fearful that their profession woud be overrun by incompetents. More theoretical science was added to the syllabus, but student unrest at the lack of practical instruction and the dominance of a tiny wealthy élite within the profession led to riots in Paris. Between 1905 and 1913 the faculty had to be closed annually because of the hostility of students to the system and their superiors. They were supported by doctors' associations, which by 1910 included over 50 per cent of the profession. Pressure grew for hospital-based training. In 1907 a parliamentary reform commission recommended major changes, but these were only partially applied before the war. It should be noted that Britain and the USA were experiencing similar difficulties in these years.[22]

The need for a consensus was all the more acute since training was both a long and expensive process, one of the most costly exercises in tertiary education. Fees ran at 1500 frs. a year in Paris, 1000 frs. in the provinces. When Raspail, the famous republican democrat and doctor of the Parisian poor, left the seminary in his native Vaucluse to embark upon the study of medicine and law in Paris, the major constraint upon him was not the need to acquire a very specific body of information, but the need to finance his studies. He tried to obtain a teaching post; he had studied for the priesthood and was tolerably qualified. He then turned to tutoring, following a variety of university science courses, and like many pursued his own concept of what constituted medical education.[23] Many different philosophies of medicine abounded. Medicine did not attract those who stayed at school to complete a baccalaureate. In a survey of 1865 very few students expressed a preference for a medical career.[24] In 1864 only eleven of the 187 pupils at the lycée in Douai hoped to become doctors.

There were 2505 medical students in Germany in 1831. Fears of professional overcrowding generally led to a tightening of abitur regulations and by 1848 there were only 1610. But by 1882 numbers had risen to just over 5000, comparable with the law faculties. In Germany doctors' sons were increasingly likely to follow their fathers' career. In 1850 32.7 per cent of Halle medics were in the same trade as their father and by 1880 this figure was 50 per cent.[25] The same was true in France. Raspail, always a rebel in his profession, was nonetheless followed by one son and two grandsons who became doctors, another son who was an *officier de santé* and several descendants, including his third son, who were pharmacists. In Italy medicine was the most popular course after law in the universities. In 1901 Italy had over 22 000 qualified doctors, compared with 17 616 in Prussia. A decade previously the General Office of Statistics estimated that Italy needed 600 new doctors annually, whereas 900 qualified. The problem was part of the same phenomenon experienced in the legal profession and the lean years of the great depression reduced even further alternative jobs. Reluctantly and belatedly, medical fees were also raised, but less than legal fees, to 450 lire a year. Whereas unemployed lawyers berated the government in parliament, new doctors, without the family money or connections to survive at home, emigrated. In the years between 1901 and 1911 the number of doctors in Italy increased by 1200, yet 7000 had graduated in this period. Over half of these new graduates emigrated to find work.[26]

A doctor was always seen as a bastion of the middle class, though not necessarily politically conservative like the *notaire*. Indeed France had a tradition of socialist doctors, like Raspail, who worked among the Paris poor. Doctors were not particularly well paid and most had private means. In the days before a state-run social security system was developed, the doctor relied on fee income; he therefore needed well-heeled, open-pocketed patients, and unfortunately the two tended to be a contradiction in terms. As mutual benefit societies developed, doctors content with a less illustrious clientele began to have a tolerably secure income, with some loss of independence. For the average doctor, pay was scarcely commensurate with the cost of training. In 1842 it was reckoned that a doctor would rarely command an income above 3000 frs. He might add to it fees as consultant to a hospital, as a police surgeon etc. Even by the turn of the century only about half a dozen earned between 200 000 and 300 000 frs. a year; about a hundred got over 40 000 frs., while 80 per cent had less than 8000 frs. Thus the lowliest paid might only rank with a labourer. Doctors needed a private income, a good marriage or to embark on a political career, which many did. A medical journal of the 1880s calculated that a doctor in one of the prosperous districts of Paris needed 12 000 frs. to keep up appearances. In the provinces many practitioners asked only 1.5–2 frs. a visit. In 1879 a new association of medics, Concours Médical, was formed to press for uniform fees. They suggested a three-class structure of between 1 and 10 frs. Although many resisted established scales of fees, the increasing need to negotiate with insurance companies and local authorities urged on the case for standardisation.[27]

Doctors were anxious about the identity of their profession and its composition. In 1822 a Society of German doctors was formed[28] and in Paris in 1845 over a thousand doctors and pharmacists and a few vets held a professional conference to discuss the perennial problem of standards, training, overcrowding and relatively low pay. A Union Médicale was set up to represent the interests of doctors. Napoleon had instituted an inferior grade of *officier de santé* to serve poorer areas, but the category became permanent and by the 1840s these far less qualified men were often calling themselves doctors and threatening the livelihood of fully qualified men. By 1847 there were 7500 *officiers de santé* and 11 000 doctors. In addition there were about 800 practitioners with no qualifications, pharmacists, army doctors and midwives, all keen for a slice of the action. The conference urged the government to abolish the grade of *officier de santé* and allow existing ones to complete a full training. Although the government was sympathetic, it was many years before the problem was solved.[29] In the 1840s 2850 men, mostly from humble origins, secured diplomas to work as *officiers de santé*, while 3045 qualified as doctors. Pressure for higher standards began to have an impact. By the 1870s the number of *officiers* who qualified had fallen to just over 1000, while 5344 became doctors. By the 1890s very few men were training as *officiers*. The original idea, to provide men with some basic skills to work in the poorer areas, had very obviously failed. In 1891 the very poor department of Lozère had only one *officier* and 24 doctors, while the Nord, a centre of industrialisation and new wealth, had 201 *officiers* and 353 doctors.

The evidence of fee scales indicates a profession high on status, but low on material rewards. Could the indication of fee levels have been a fudge by doctors to fool the tax inspector? Or were doctors universally in receipt of a sufficient private income, or possessed of enough altruism, to work for almost nothing? Professionals tended to praise their own disregard of money compared with the industrial and commercial middle classes, but it is difficult to believe that sons would have been so keen to follow their fathers' careers in order to live in penury. Both the legal and medical professions, long established and with an accepted role as a service élite, were relatively free to define their own standards and entry qualifications in the nineteenth century, and to some degree they succeeded in excluding partially qualified interlopers. The major changes were in terms of numbers in each profession and in the creation of a more positively defined job function. There was little change in the social origins of members of each profession. Indeed, lower status and lower-class practitioners like the *officier de santé* were removed. The establishment of educational hurdles to commence training, in the form of the baccalaureate, *abitur*, etc., and more rigorous standards of professional qualifications, served to make the professions more positively jobs for well-heeled sons of the bourgeoisie.

The engineering profession, in response to accelerated industrialisation, was, in contrast, a profession which underwent radical change in the type of work undertaken and the social origins of members. It was one of the few professions whose social basis expanded, creating opportunities for the lower middle class. In eighteenth-century France an engineer was a man specially trained by the state in the corps of army engineers, the corps of naval engineers or the corps of bridges and roads, and then employed therein. There were only about 300 of them and they had a strong corporate sense. The Ecole Polytechnique continued the tradition, while the school of roads and bridges added railways to its orbit in mid-century. It was only in the 1850s that private industrial concerns became large enough to create a demand for engineers beyond those trained within the family by the firm itself. Once launched the private sector expanded rapidly and by 1914 was predominant, with the formation of many new industrial engineering schools. In the early part of the nineteenth century military engineers were paramount, while those employed in the civilian bureaucracy had considerable power as administrators with the right to grant or refuse permission for projects. The profession had a high status; engineers were reckoned to be above material or monetary considerations. They attracted the wealthy, upper middle class, which accounted for over half the profession up to the 1880s. Officials were particularly fond of turning their sons into state-employed engineers, as were large landowners and professional men. Only about a fifth of the profession were from lower-middle-class origins, middle-grade officials and entrepreneurs especially. A mere 5 per cent were sons of artisans or shopkeepers and a bare 1 per cent were of lower-class origins.[30]

The nineteenth-century engineer came predominantly from a

notable family, partly because of the financial outlay needed to train him. He was required to complete the baccalaureate before applying to the Polytechnique, and after his two-year course he would be expected to undertake at least three years' further training. The Ecole Polytechnique was founded in 1794 by a friend of Saint-Simon to provide scientific education and training to civil and military engineers and to be a spearhead of industrial progress. The latter was lost sight of in the immediate pressing need for military engineers. The school was run by the Ministry of War. Maths and descriptive geometry were the basis of the curriculum of the two-year course which prepared students for the specialised schools, particularly for the Artillery School of Metz and for the army engineering schools.[31] The former was a boarding school and a sense of corporate identity was actively created. Students lived and did their private study in dormitories of eight. Up to 1836 the chance of getting in was one in three, subsequently one in six. In 1820 sixty were enrolled, after 1870 this was more than doubled. The school prided itself on selecting students entirely on ability. Napoleon established thirty scholarships; in 1850 the number was unlimited but means-tested. By 1881 half of the students received a grant. Fees were 1600 frs. Despite the school's ideal, 70 per cent were from wealthy upper-middle-class backgrounds in 1815. More than a third were sons of officers or officials, nearly 30 per cent sons of large landowners and 14 per cent sons of the industrial and commercial middle class. In the first half of the century this pattern remained fairly constant, with only an occasional student from the 'popular' classes. Apparently it was not entirely a question of cost; families in the retail trade sent their sons to other costly educational establishments, but not to the Polytechnique.[32] Graduates earned respect, but army salaries were not generous. The lower middle class looked for a good return on their investment in fees. Later in the century, the social composition of the school changed, with up to 35 per cent of students coming from less well-off families and gaining scholarships. In the 1890s many of the scholarship holders were sons of enlisted soldiers and minor civil servants. Some groups within the lower middle class began to treat the school as a social ladder. An increasing number entered with the 'modern', rather than the classical baccalaureate.

After graduation students would proceed to one of the applied schools. The Ecole des Mines, founded before the revolution, provided a two-year course, the Ecole des Ponts et Chaussées three years. These would be the most obvious routes for those who were joining the army or the civil administration as engineers. In the years after Waterloo 56 per cent joined the army; towards the end of the century the proportion had risen to 74 per cent. Very few went into private employment: only nine of the 120 graduates in the mid-thirties did not enter public service.[33] The Polytechnique expected certain cultural norms to be observed by applicants. They were tested in riding, fencing, gymnastics and art history, skills which only a notable would acquire as a matter of course. It was also assumed that the *polytechnicien* would enter state service; it was constantly emphasised that private industry was undesirably materialist. The taboo was very real, as was the concentration on theory during training. The industrial application of that theory was regarded as beneath the notice of a *polytechnicien*. Interestingly, for all its status and influence an engineering career did not offer material rewards commensurate with the outlay in training. It was assumed that such a professional would have a private income.

In the early years of the nineteenth century most family firms used and trained their own offspring to work in the organisation, adding a period in Paris or abroad if appropriate. Likewise Rhenish manufacturers made a point of placing their sons with foreign firms in order to acquire new techniques more cheaply and reliably than importing foreign technical experts. In Russia the close-knit family firms run by the Old Believer textile magnates in the Moscow area educated their sons exclusively in their own firms and failed to pick up the up-to-date expertise that a period abroad gave to their competitors in Mulhouse. Before 1840 only a few very wealthy families in the most advanced industries in France valued formal education for their heirs. The Conservatoire des Arts et Metiers, founded during the revolution, was in the forefront of new technology. Future famous French industrialists, like the silk-loom inventor Jacquart, studied here. It led the world in chemistry teaching in the first half of the nineteenth century and in 1853 set up the first engineering teaching laboratory.[34] The famous Alsatian cotton magnates, Koechlin and Dollfus, sent their sons there, as did the Schneiders.

Interest in practical engineering expanded along with economic growth. The Ecole Centrale was set up in 1829 to provide the training for future leaders of industry which the Polytechnique despised. It was a private foundation and initially its best applicants were upper-middle-class Polytechnique rejects. Prejudice against practical learning died hard. Thus the Centrale accepted only baccalaureate graduates and taught a curriculum of which only one-third was practical. The typical *centralien* came from a well-heeled family, somewhat less prosperous than the *polytechnicien*, and unlike the *polytechnicien* his father was often in manufacturing or business. By the 1860s 80 per cent were from rich industrial families[35] and by the end of the century 25 per cent of *centraliens* were second-generation students. Lower-middle-class families were increasingly attracted as the practical emphasis grew, but senior civil servants and professionals never patronised the Centrale as they did the Polytechnique. The school cultivated a strong corporate identity. Emile Thomas, a former student and director of the National Workshops after the 1848 revolution, used former fellow students as assistants on the project and tried to inculcate the same *esprit de corps* among the unemployed as had existed at the school.[36] In mid-century the Centrale was taken over by the Ministry of Commerce, which expanded the three-year course to an intake of about 100 students.

In 1848 *centraliens* tried to set up a professional body for engineers to raise their status in comparison with *polytechniciens* and the status of their profession in general. Their society of civil engineers was the first and remained a pioneer for a long period.[37] They published a journal which, like both the Polytechnique and Centrale, was somewhat left-leaning and Saint-Simonist in sympathy. The journal stressed the need for more industrialisation and the joys of increasing man's control over nature. They were anxious to point out that *centraliens* were the real engineers, *polytechniciens* mere administrators. They gave publicity to engineering achievements and developments. But it was an uphill struggle for recognition, even amongst *centraliens* themselves apparently, for only 600 had joined by 1868. Membership was small when one considers that there were 3000 engineering graduates from the Centrale in circulation by 1880 and another 7000 in the state corps.

Before 1870 the market for engineers with higher education was limited, but there was an increasing need for more middle-range technical training. In France the more modest training of the Ecoles des Arts et Métiers produced men with sufficient skill and experience for supervisory jobs, which was the most that the majority of firms needed. The first Ecole des Arts et Métiers was set up on the eve of the French Revolution by the duc de Rochefoucauld-Liancourt to train the sons of his regiment to be skilled artisans and foremen. Napoleon added centres in Chalons and Angers to provide opportunities for boys from poor families.[38] Abandoned in the Restoration, the schools were re-opened in 1830, providing 200 places to train boys in practical and applied science. By 1840 there were 800 candidates for the 200 places available each year and a third school was opened in Aix-en-Provence. Boys were enrolled from fifteen to nineteen and by 1860 there were 5000 of them employed in industry, providing 40 per cent of France's trained engineers and middle-level technicians. Three more schools were opened. Fees were low and bursaries were available. In addition the schools helped their graduates find jobs. Up to 1830 42 per cent were sons of employees and soldiers, but subsequently the schools began to appeal to a more prosperous clientele. Between 1830 and 1860 50 per cent were sons of owners or managers of firms, master artisans or small shopkeepers, businessmen or independent farmers. During the latter years of the century sons of industrialists, businessmen, company engineers and managers predominated, this last group going up from 3 to 12 per cent, presumably a reflection of the growing size of firms and resulting changes in structure. Former pupils usually began their working life as skilled manual workers, but their training put them in line for early promotion. Within five years 44 per cent had middle-ranking supervisory jobs and two-thirds became senior supervisors or owners. Those who stuck to private industry did better than those who opted for the railways or public service. Three-quarters stayed in the same field as their fathers.[39]

During the second half of the nineteenth century the engineering profession gradually became recognised as an essential component of modern industry, and in France, Italy, Russia and Germany the number of technical institutes expanded. 'Modern' curricula were devised in schools, with far less or no concentration on the classics, to prepare students for careers like engineering. But the assumption that a practically trained engineer was inferior to a classically educated man persisted, causing the universities to disdain technical subjects and graduate engineers to treasure a classical high school certificate as a prerequisite to further training. In Germany separate technical universities were founded, the first of which was set up in Karlsrühe by Tulla, a former student at the Ecole Polytechnique. Others began, but their growth was modest up to 1840. By 1875, however, they had almost a third as many students as the universities, 5449. In the great depression they shrank to 2549, but this was only a temporary setback and by 1914 enrolment was 11 451. By 1910 there were ten technical institutes, admitting students from 'modern' schools, who had not studied the classical *abitur*. The profession itself, with the universities and the bureaucracy behind it, fought this 'dilution' of their job, but from 1899 the institutes were allowed to confer doctorates. By the end of the century 20 per cent of all tertiary-level students were enrolled in technical institutes studying applied science and engineering. Research and development were funded by both government and private sources. Engineers were one of the few groups of Italian professionals who did not suffer chronic unemployment. The number of engineering graduates more than trebled in the decade and a half to 1913, reaching 3227. The growth of Italian industry in the period after 1906 provided jobs in the building industry and railways, but civil engineering was not so buoyant; the number of trainees fell and many were forced to emigrate to find work.[40]

In Russia the Mining Institute of St Petersburg initiated the reorganisation of research and science teaching in higher education. The St Petersburg technical institutes promoted engineering education, attracting the sons of nobles, often those who had done well in tax-farming, sons of foreign industrialists and some Russian-born. But traditional merchant families, especially those of Moscow, were slow to see any benefit in schooling.[41] The institute's graduates went on to spearhead the technically advanced mining and metallurgical industries of southern Russia. Such engineers began as managers, but often progressed into partnership or outright ownership of industrial concerns, challenging the many foreign engineers then managing the largely foreign-owned firms in the Donbas area. The Russian engineer's route to ownership often meant a move from a modern factory into the mining area, where profits were larger and where he was within easy reach of foreign capitalists eager to incorporate his expertise into a new enterprise. Industrial training schools were set up and run by the Minister of Finance. Legislation in 1888 recognised four categories of schools: Higher Institutions, for graduates of the seven-year *realgymnasia*; Middle Technical schools, which took students from the fifth year of the *realgymnasia* and gave them four years of training to qualify them as assistant engineers; Lower Technical Schools, whose intake was from the sixth year of urban schools and which trained future foremen in a three-year course; and Craft Schools, available for elementary pupils who had completed three years of education, providing a programme which lasted three years and turned a boy into a skilled workman.[42] Thus, the Russians too were providing both middle-level and highly skilled training programmes.

In France there was a rapid expansion of engineering training towards the end of the century, with the setting up of colleges midway between the very practical approach of the *gadzarts* (Ecole des Arts et Métiers graduates) and the level of the Centrale. Establishments like the Ecole Supérieure de Physique et Chimie demanded a high standard of secondary education from applicants, the baccalaureate or a pass in their own entrance examination, and attracted principally sons of middle-level managers (22 per cent) and senior managers (15 per cent). Minor officials and members of the lower bourgeoisie were also keen to see their sons as engineers. Most of the graduates of these new engineering schools went into industry and did well. The expansion of industry and the creation of these schools made the engineering profession accessible to sections of the middling ranks of the middle class who had previously sent their sons into the army or into primary or secondary school teaching. Teaching was becoming overcrowded, while army pay and status were deteriorating in comparison with other jobs. The status of the engineer was enhanced by the pace of industrial growth and the job was depicted as the key to industrial and technical progress. Traditional engineering schools began to appeal to a wider social market too, placing greater emphasis on qualifications and less on family connections. By 1872 nearly 39 per cent of *polytechniciens* were from less well-off families and by 1900 45 per cent. On the eve of the First World War 45 per cent of the students at the Ecole des Mines and 41 per cent of those at the Ponts et Chaussées came from poorer backgrounds. Thus even the élite establishments were beginning to attract sons of minor civil servants, employees, artisans, shopkeepers and schoolteachers, aided by a more generous provision of scholarships. Theoretically all this might have indicated both social mobility and the emergence of a new type of industrial leader, but in reality only just under 2 per cent of *polytechniciens* went into industry in the years after 1900. Few firms could make use of their skills, which were still far more theoretical then practical. Students at other engineering schools also tended to feel frustrated and useless, which may explain their radical associations. The railways could offer some engineering opportunities. By 1870 there were 575 *polytechniciens* working in the private sector. The first car factory was set up by two Centrale graduates, while two aviation pioneers were from the same stable. Engineering offered more social mobility than any other profession,[43] but the route to the top still lay with the Old Guard.[44]

Teaching is another profession where nineteenth-century developments necessitated major changes. As governing élites saw fit to provide schooling for a larger and larger proportion of children, so the social and educational range of the profession itself expanded. One cannot speak of a teaching profession, but of professions, because those engaged in teaching in the different branches of education were worlds apart in levels of pay, preliminary training and, above all, status. Those involved in higher education, whether at a university or higher institutes, together with the staff of *lycées* or *gymnasia*, were regarded as members of a profession, while primary school teachers emphatically were not. University professors in Germany often received a title, while the doctorate earned by a teacher in a *gymnasium* permitted him to marry above himself, so socially appealing was the appellation *frau doktor* for a prospective wife's family. Teachers in higher education often came from wealthy families and could supplement any salary from the state, which might be minimal, with substantial private fees. Secondary school teachers tended to come from comfortably-off middle-class families and were well regarded in their local community. Primary school teachers received a pittance for their teaching and had to supplement their income with a variety of lowly and equally poorly paid functions, which often interfered with their teaching. They came from lower-middle- or lower-class families, often artisan or peasant. There was no point of contact between the primary school teacher and his prosperous colleagues, either social or professional. The only link that might exist would be the determination of a primary school teacher to obtain a scholarship for his son to train as a secondary school teacher. When the different teaching groups began to form professional associations to assert their claims for recognition, the various groups formed entirely separate organisations. This internal social stratification, visible in the other professions we have touched on, was particularly damaging in education because the nineteenth-century trend towards state education meant increasing bureaucratic intervention. The issue of professional independence, most marked in the universities, was crucial in a number of stages throughout the period.

In France professors were esteemed but there were no universities in the sense of corporate institutions for teaching and research until the end of the century. The separate faculties were skeletons. The regional academies employed only a handful of professors, whose lectures at best were pieces of theatre to entertain the fashionable élite. In Paris professors frequently taught at the specialised *grandes écoles* in addition to their duties in the faculty. They often moved into politics, leaving a substitute to do their teaching, which consisted exclusively of lectures.[45] The University of Paris was headed by a Grand Master, the academies by rectors. They and the staff were all appointed by the government, and were consequently vulnerable. They lacked research facilities and finance. In 1855 the Faculty of Letters at Clermont-Ferrand had five professors and seven students, and used its budget of 22 286 frs. (£891) to pay its staff 4000 frs. each. Their main income came from the fees they charged for conducting examinations. Students were few. In 1864–6 the academy of Poitiers had only 300 students, fewer than most *lycées*. Those who enrolled received their instruction elsewhere in the *grandes écoles*. They were not obliged to attend the large university courses in order to sit their examinations. Only when the faculties were grouped into actual university institutions at the end of the century did they begin to function effectively. The adoption of smaller group teaching and the introduction of student grants also began to make university teaching more meaningful, but the dominant lead taken by the *grandes écoles* in both research and teaching was hard to challenge, especially as faculty professors themselves taught in both institutions and had a vested interest in the survival of both.

Thus the research of university professors was conducted in institutions like the Collège de France, the Paris Observatory and the Musée d'Histoire Naturelle, and the Ecole Pratique des Hautes Etudes founded by Duruy in the 1860s when the faculties were unresponsive to his concern about the backwardness of French scientific research compared with Germany. The Academy of Science was dominant in scientific research. For the bulk of the nineteenth century scientific research was in the hands of notables. The Academy was an elected body, in 1840 of sixty-three members, men well advanced in their careers; they were all forty or more years of age, had annual incomes in excess of 100 000 frs. and were a close-knit group who knew each other well and whose families intermarried. They were close to government circles. This situation was to change towards the end of the century when the Ecole Normale Supérieure took the lead. Founded initially in 1795 and restarted by Napoleon in 1808, the school was closed between 1822 and 1826 because of the liberalism of its staff. Established to train staff for the *lycées*, under Louis-Philippe its reputation in both teaching science and scientific research grew and it became a rival to the initially more prestigious Polytechnique. It became a centre of academic excellence. Its former students, spectacularly successful in the *agrégation* (final examination), dominated the *lycées*, the faculties and eventually the ministries. Duruy was a *normalien*. In the early years of the century a student would complete his *agrégation* and was then assigned to a *lycée*, those with the best examination results receiving the more desirable postings. He would then progress through the various grades of *lycée*, with little opportunity to pursue scientific research. By the end of the century the career of an ENS student had become far more research-oriented. His first posting was likely to be as a research assistant, where he would be expected to complete his doctorate and would then proceed to a provincial faculty of science, and, if successful, Paris. The *agrégation* had become far less significant. *Normaliens* formed a very closed society. Like the Polytechnique, the school built up an intense corporate spirit. Students lived in residences run by the school and were taught in small seminar groups, a method of instruction pioneered in France by ENS. By 1890 there were ten times as many applicants as places, and the school had become so successful that it was partly absorbed by the University. As a consequence of the achievements of the ENS the faculty of science in Paris now dominated scientific research. The top men were no longer notables, for whom scientific research was a serious hobby, but career scientists, whose salaries at their peak were no more than 20 000 frs. The intake of the ENS was predominantly middle class, but by 1880 only 35 per cent came from very prosperous families. A high proportion of fathers were themselves teachers, or in a public-service post related to teaching. Integration into the University of Paris lowered the social tone. Up to 1903 18 per cent of students' fathers were landowners, businessmen or industrialists, but by the war this had dropped to 4 per cent. In 1914 nearly 40 per cent were lower middle class, a quarter were sons of *instituteurs*. Almost another quarter were from working-class families. In great contrast to the Polytechnique where the notables retained a strong, though declining position, the ENS made scientific research and associated university teaching an affair of more social opportunity for the lower middle class than any other career. Parents who were intent on upward social mobility chose ENS in preference to other establishments.[46]

To what degree was a member of a profession independent when he received a salary? How can one square professional independence with the growing role of the state? Universities and most institutions of higher learning were state-owned and although their staff might be well regarded socially, as state employees they were expected to toe the political line. No university had private funds to maintain even a pretence of political neutrality. Professors like Guizot and Cousin were dismissed for their liberalism in the 1820s and whole faculties, considered disruptively liberal, were closed for lengthy periods.[47] The Second Empire was equally sensitive to the political opposition of many academics. German universities were self-governing, the professors defined their own syllabus. Fees were low and universities owned very little property, so they were almost entirely dependent on the state for financial support, a dependence which increased markedly towards the end of the century. Effectively universities were part of the state bureaucracy. Professors were state officials, taking an oath of allegiance to the regime. The government could and did exercise considerable 'moral' influence over staff. Towards the end of the century, when a junior lecturer openly joined the SPD (German Socialist Party), legislation was introduced to ensure his dismissal. His daring was apparently almost unique. Professors with full tenure were few in number and were mostly eager members of the conservative establishment. They thought of themselves, and were regarded by others, as a special and separate élite, a 'professorial' class within the middle class. They were recruited from an already wealthy group: 65 per cent were sons of senior officials and professors, only 5.8 per cent from the industrial middle class. Senior professors were equal in status to counsellors of state, were almost on a level with government ministers. They received a government salary and fees from 'private' lectures. Some were paid as much as 40 000 marks; an ordinary professor earned 6000 marks. Thus a senior academic would rate with a successful lawyer, doctor or businessman,[48] but apparently accepted gratefully his quiescent role as a civil servant. In France the situation was less straightforward as we have noted, but the most dangerous exposition of the problems of salaried professionals was that in Russian universities.

The statute of 1804 gave Russian universities autonomy in their administration and in the appointment of staff, a radical experiment for an autocracy. Nicholas I regarded this as a challenge to the centralised state. He considered the university a branch of the state bureaucracy and expected that his officials would supervise both appointments and curriculum. In 1835 government-appointed curators were installed to oversee each university. The curator now hired and fired staff although the elected councils of professors remained. Inspectors, under the direction of the curator, were responsible for student discipline. The faculties were remodelled on German lines. For thirty years from 1830 there were no chairs of philosophy in any university. The government also ordered that lectures on psychology and logic were to be given by the professors of orthodox theology. But the authorities were only partially successful in keeping out dangerous foreign ideas. Moscow University remained fairly open in its thinking, with a high proportion of German staff. In general there was a serious deterioration in morale. The status and salaries of academics fell so low that many vacancies remained unfilled and teaching was poor. In the early 1860s some measure of university self-government was reintroduced. The electoral principle was restored. The faculties recovered their right to elect their rector and professors and the number of chairs was increased. Professors regained their control over syllabus, but the ministry continued to administer the examination system and the general lines of the curriculum. The number of universities was increased to eight. Salaries of staff were improved and the number of state studentships increased to cover 40 per cent of undergraduates. Careful note was made of the progress of foreign universities. But despite these new liberal arrangements for higher education, student unrest continued unabated and St Petersburg University was closed for a time. In 1866 a student attempted to assassinate the tsar and it was suggested that he was a member of a student revolutionary circle. Student societies were banned and police supervision of students restored. Staff were similarly harassed. The persistence of unrest led to a commission of enquiry in 1878. The commission blamed harsh police supervision and in 1879 universities were allowed to appoint their own inspectors. Student unrest continued and government opinion hardened in favour of a return to government control. A new university statute of 1884 abolished the right of staff to elect their own officers. The powers of the government-appointed curator were restored and he was allowed both to supervise teaching and stop law-breaking. Rectors and professors were to be appointed by the Minister of Public Instruction, deans by the curator with the approval of the minister. The inspectors of students were once again government-appointed and under the control of the curator. All students' associations were banned and undergraduates were once more ordered to wear uniforms, in order to be easily distinguishable to the police. Fees were multiplied by five to exclude any remaining poor students. The proportion of Jews in the student body was limited to 10 per cent. Women students were banned and their numbers fell from 2000 to 144.

Student protest understandably grew worse. In 1887 another student tried to assassinate the tsar. Five universities and two higher institutes were closed. Universities became the main centres of opposition to the autocracy and unrest was endemic. Typical student associations of natives of each province originally grouped together for self-help and friendship, like the Ukrainians and Poles, turned to resistance and opposition to police repression. They organised strikes, which led to up to 1000 expulsions. The Moscow Commission of students reckoned that over 2000 students were expelled, arrested or banished in the last twenty years of the century from Moscow University alone. A universal strike in all universities was sustained throughout the spring of 1899. A commission of enquiry blamed student poverty for unrest, but plans to increase governmental financial support were not realised. Expelled students were to be enlisted in the army as private soldiers. Serious disruption at Kiev University was followed by harsh repressive, measures. A year later, in 1901, the Minister of Public Instruction was assassinated. An enquiry at Moscow University again blamed government repression and urged the restoration of university self-government. Once more policy swung briefly in a more liberal direction, but the Minister of the Interior retained the right to ban students and was himself murdered by one. The universities were in ferment during and after the 1905 revolution. In 1907 21 Moscow professors and 80 lecturers resigned, and protestors sprayed lecture rooms with poison gas to deter police spies disguised as students. Thus unlike Germany, where professors, critical of governments in the early part of the century, became bastions of conservatism later, retaining through their privileged social status only the shadow of former autonomy, the Russian academics were in the forefront of criticism of the autocracy throughout these years.[49]

Universities and specialised institutes like the *grandes écoles* jealously guarded their privileged position in research and teaching. Convinced that it was in their interests to preserve élitism in higher education, they set high standards for entry, insisted on a classical secondary school curriculum, and fiercely resisted the growth of higher technical institutions which were willing to enrol students who had followed a 'modern', in the view of the universities 'inferior', school curriculum. Because the universities themselves denigrated practical, vocational education, and even in some cases applied science, they attempted to relegate such teaching and research as substandard. Although the battle was lost in the last quarter of the century, the assumption that a classical education was the best and that only pure science was really desirable is thought to have held back technical developments and scientific research, particularly in France, although some recent historians claim that this conclusion is the product of myopic concentration on work being done in Paris and that research, especially in applied science, was valuable and innovative.[50] The prejudice was ubiquitous however. In secondary education, schools offering practical, vocational curricula were considered suitable only for the lower classes.

If teachers of technical subjects tended to rate poorly in the pedagogical pecking order, primary school teachers were beneath notice. Many were priests, trained in seminaries where educational standards were often low and faith was far more important than scientific awareness, which was generally deplored. It was only late in the century that a determined effort was made to replace clerical with lay primary teachers, both in France and in Russia. The Guizot law of 1833 obliged each commune to set up a training college for teachers. Teachers had to be certificated or members of religious orders. The number of *écoles normales* rose from twelve to forty-seven during the July Monarchy. *Instituteurs* were usually from humble backgrounds. In St Lo in 1880 over half were children of peasants and forty years later almost the same number were from workers' families. Generally they attended only primary schools before training and had an uphill struggle to gain recognition as professionals. In the 1830s communes were ordered to pay a minimum salary of 200 frs., which although less than a subsistence wage for a working man was often more than the total communal budget. Teachers could be little more than assistants to the priest. They worked as grave-diggers, bell-ringers, were the clerks to the municipal council, kept the registers of births and deaths and usually lived with their family in the room which also served as a schoolroom. The higher primary schools founded in accordance with the law were rarely popular except as a preliminary to teacher training. In 1848 some republicans hoped to broaden the scope of the system but when new legislation was enacted in the Falloux law of 1850 the *écoles normales* came under fire, accused of being hotbeds of radicalism. Local authorities were empowered to close them if they wished; three were abolished and the religious content of the syllabus of the rest increased. *Instituteurs* were not intended to hold independent political views. Low pay and public esteem kept primary school teachers on a par with manual workers. There was little expectation that they would be recognised as members of a profession. After all, could there be a professional woman?

The way in which different professions are measured rests only in part on their own standards of entry, membership, etc. How they are regarded by others is crucial. Interestingly, assessments have remained fairly constant over the last century. A recent survey listed individuals according to their earnings, arranging them in a long march, ranging from those negative earners, portrayed as upside down underground, many of whom were in fact wealthy businessmen with clever accountants, to the odd financial giant whose chin would scrape the aerials on top of New York's World Trade Centre. Teachers are above the height they measured in 1970, university teachers have shrunk nearly a foot since 1970, but are still tall, average 10′ 9″, in relation to all wage-earners. Other professionals follow, with many lawyers and doctors 15′ and more. Merchant bankers are as big as skyscrapers and the richest landowner, the Duke of Westminster, tops the lot, 20 miles above most people.[51] It is apparent that the relative profile has changed only modestly for those in the professions since 1914, although exclusive concentration on earning power underlines the reduced stature of professions where pecuniary rewards are modest.

In some respects the increase in numbers in the professions, the growing specialisation and the redefinition of some jobs previously regarded as artisanal rather than professional had very little impact on the pecking order. Law and medicine were as pre-eminent in western Europe in 1914 as in 1789, although both remained absent as jobs carrying real status in Russia. Both continued to be widely regarded as closed shops, restricted in practice to family members or sons of the traditionally wealthy élite. Very few sons of industrial or commercial middle-class families were launched into such careers, where connections and family money were indispensable for success. The dominance of traditional élites in the legal profession is easy to understand. Such a trade kept them close to the seat of power. The *parlementaires* had challenged royal authority before 1789; the magistracy conferred status and was a route to ennoblement, both in Prussia and France. The growth in the power of the state and the development of industry in the nineteenth century changed this balance. Gradually magistrates found themselves more circumscribed, their traditional autonomy being replaced by a role which conveyed respect, but less room for initiative. This was reflected in Germany by the decreasing attractiveness of the profession for families who traditionally had staffed it. Where industrial growth was more limited, particularly Italy, legal training remained the prime target for an ambitious young man.

The degree of change within the professions was circumscribed most by the best established of them. The combination of professional and government initiatives led to severe cutbacks in the numbers training for both law and medicine in mid-nineteenth-century Prussia. The introduction of educational hurdles for entrants, the high cost and length of training and the very modest immediate financial rewards kept the senior professions for the élite, with the exception of a small minority of determined individuals, or poor men with wealthy patrons. The assumption that a profession was an indicator of status or, put more subtly, a mantle of service, rather than a route to riches, left fee structures which could be unrealistic and a thoroughly unprofessional lack of protection from charlatans for those who had undergone a proper training. The development of professional organisations and associations was beginning to alter this 'gentlemanly amateur' approach, but old assumptions were slow to die.

If the most senior professions remained under the control of their traditional élites, this was not so with others. Change was most marked in areas like engineering, which, with the growth of industry and new technical institutes, began to offer unheard-of opportunities to lower-middle-class boys. Boys from poorer families remained excluded by the need for primary education before training and the need to defer earning for a number of years. However, even in this, the most open profession, it was noticeable that better-off families began to take up an increasing number of training places later in the century and that, at the peak of the profession, the old notables, who traditionally dominated the Ecole Polytechnique, continued to hold sway, not merely by their physical occupancy of the plum roles but in professional attitudes and the continued deference to classical, theoretical education.

To what extent was the concept of a profession revolutionised in the nineteenth century? It was certainly more formalised, with school-leaving certificates being required before training could begin. The idea of what constituted a profession was also more systematised, training was more standardised, but there were notable exceptions, for instance the position of the *notaire* in France. Engineering is probably the best example of such change. Industrial growth began to turn France's prime professional training school, the Ecole Polytechnique, into a species of dinosaur, leaving the way open for the development of institutions with a more practical approach, both to training and the job itself.

When one considers the entrants to the professions, one is struck by the increasing range in the social origins of new members, embracing the old élites, including nobles, in the well-established occupations where sons succeeded fathers and families intermarried, but also including sons of artisans who trained as technicians and engineers. Newer professions, veterinary science, pharmacology, primary school teaching, etc., brought in sons of peasants as well as artisans. A profession ceased to involve a classical secondary education followed by a spell at university or a *grande école*. Acceptance by traditionalists of these new occupations as professions was slowly and reluctantly given. Many considered that professional status was being eroded, from a classical, post-university base to a post-primary-school, relatively brief training. There was criticism of the decline in standards, but in occupations like engineering there was a great deal to be gained from engineers with practical and managerial skills. If lesser jobs came to be accepted as junior professions, lower salaries maintained the old hierarchy and access to senior levels was severely restricted. Thus the old élites survived to an extent, to lead the new professions and infiltrate their base with traditional philosophies. The ideal of the independence of professional men compared with wage-earners persisted, unrecognised as myth or mirage until the 1980s. The overwhelming impression, from this brief investigation of a range of professions, is one of diversity, that the various occupations attracted very different social groups from within the middle classes and had very little in common. A *notaire* could not recommend industrial investment to his clients because industrial France was another world. The entrepreneurial middle class rarely sent their sons for legal or medical training because they, equally, knew nothing about such professions.

5. The Middle Classes and the Bureaucracy

WHILST for Marx the middle-class entrepreneur was the dominant element in the bourgeoisie and the professional a minor subsection, the fastest-growing and most numerous element, the bureaucrat, was quite unnoticed by him; perhaps a not unreasonable attitude in a thinker who confidently expected that the centralised state would wither away! The unprecedented expansion of the role of the state and the consequent employment provided at all levels is the subject of this chapter. The rapid growth of state administration and its transformation into a recognisable modern bureaucracy was closely related to the demographic explosion, subsequent urbanisation, and economic and social development. The rationalising ideas of the eighteenth-century *philosophes* added respectability to the attempts of 'reforming' autocrats to exercise greater control of traditional sources of independent authority within the state, feudal, communal or clerical. In this formative stage in the development of the modern state, bureaucratic structures crystallised. Governments sought to transform their administrators, who might have local loyalties and a degree of autonomous authority, into obedient civil servants committed to furthering the power of the centralised state, in other words bureaucrats. An administrator might, because of the strength of his regional power base and the size of his own fortune, or as in Prussia because of traditional respect for *bildung*, culture and education, seek to shape or openly to criticise royal policy. A bureaucrat would be far more likely, even at the most senior levels, to be dependent upon his salary and psychologically, as well as financially, tied to a hierarchical promotion ladder.

The transition from an administration to a bureaucracy was a compound of greater professionalism in recruitment and training of officials, specialisation within recognised hierarchies and, of course, size and financial dependence. Demographic and economic change dramatically altered the concept of state power. Previously modest administrative structures were radically reworked to take on totally new functions, notably in the second half of the nineteenth century as industrialisation proceeded and *laissez-faire* attitudes were forced to give way to interventionism. Employment mushroomed at all levels, but was numerically greatest for the middling and lower ranges of the bourgeoisie. The state assumed a new role in education, the social services in the broadest sense, medicine, transport, etc. Concern with law and order at home, the successful conduct of war with foreign nations and the collection of sufficient revenue to maintain itself were joined by new functions for governments, organising and supervising aspects of the life of the individual and community, which previously had not been within the brief of the state.

When is it appropriate to designate the machinery of a state bureaucratic? For our purposes it is perhaps enough to refer to two characteristics: size, and professional, regular, directed structure. The term 'bureaucracy' was first applied to France, in a dictionary of 1802. Max Weber, still accepted by social scientists as a prime authority, held that an administration became a bureaucracy when it operated in a rational and legal framework in response to a superior will. Views already expressed on the continuing power of the old élites may cause one to question whether the second half of this definition became applicable anywhere except in Germany itself before the end of the nineteenth century. However, it has been suggested that for France the decisive change came with the revolution, particularly with the Directory (1794–9),[1] although de Tocqueville stressed the similarities between the administration of the *ancien régime* and that of post-revolutionary France.[2] There could be no question that France was possessed of a complex and highly developed bureaucracy in the second half of the nineteenth century, but the changes of these years were mainly quantitative, with the addition of 80 000 primary school teachers and 50 000 new postmen.[3] For Prussia the period of the Stein reforms (c. 1807) was perhaps most decisive in changing an already sophisticated administrative framework into an organisation uncritically committed to the state,[4] although the process extended well before and after these dates. In the Italian peninsula likewise administrative reforms were launched in several provinces in the second half of the eighteenth century. The period of French rule accelerated the pace of change in some cases, but the transformation to modern bureaucratic structures was patchy and regional, and was finally fudged into a thoroughly unsatisfactory imposition of the Piedmontese system after unification.[5] Russia cannot be said to have had a professional civil service until after emancipation and the reforming legislation of the 1860s. She had very few civil servants, in 1800 38 000 and in 1855 114 000, a much lower proportion than in other European states, and many were former army officers, in receipt of ludicrously low salaries.[6] The lines between military, civil and judicial administration were quite blurred and successive autocrats showed little inclination towards rationalisation. A professional and distinct bureaucracy began to emerge only slowly after the 1860s.

This chapter sets out to explore the position of the middle classes in the burgeoning state bureaucracies, addressing, in particular, the question of the changing socio-economic origins of civil servants, the contribution the bourgeoisie made in the different ranks of bureaucratic hierarchies, and the extent to which senior state servants adopted the attitudes of the old nobility. We shall consider the extent to which bureaucracies became more professional in their entry requirements and educational and training standards. It is necessary to stress at the outset the enormous diversity of ranks within these state bureaucracies; from ambassador and permanent ministerial secretaries to postmen and policemen; some historians and social scientists would object to the classification of the latter positions as middle class, but nineteenth-century statistics lump the different social ranks of the bureaucracy together. In 1789 the most highly regarded and most influential role to which a wealthy non-noble could aspire was that of public servant. In the century which followed, two main trends emerged: the power, standing and social isolation of the élite sector increased; and there was an explosion in the number of minor bureaucrats as the scope and range of central and local government and of other institutions expanded. Increased professionalism at the top only served to widen the unbridgeable chasm between the senior and lesser administrator. The actions of successive governments everywhere intensified the separation of the mandarin element, which was made up of the rich, both titled and bourgeois.

In France on the eve of the revolution, when administrative posts were venal, 39 000 of the 51 000 most desirable offices were in middle-class hands. Families whose fortunes were often made in trade or the professions moved into state service as the route to marriage into the nobility, or to the direct acquisition of a noble title. There was lively competition for the most lucrative and prestigious senior posts; in some areas prices rose beyond the reach of most professional men and became one factor in the frustrations and resentments of this section of the middle class in 1789. Office-holders were personally thrusting, ambitious and politically aware. Over 40 per cent of the members of the Third Estate group elected to the Estates General in 1789 fell into this category.[7] The social insecurity and ambition of the non-noble rich was utilised by autocratic rulers to curb the demands of the established nobility. In Russia Peter the Great tried to make state service, rather than a previously acquired title, the criterion for social standing and advancement, although subsequent amendments of the Table of Ranks, successfully urged on by the nobility, restricted access by commoners. The attempt by rulers to bring the wealthy non-noble into government, typified by the appointment of men like Colbert by Louis XIV, was pursued with considerable success by Prussian kings, eager to both control their powerful nobles and centralise their scattered lands. A virtually autonomous, self-recruiting bureaucracy emerged in eighteenth-century Prussia. Senior posts went not to landed nobles but primarily to commoners, who within the century emerged as a service nobility. They imitated the nobility, however, married their daughters into noble families and bought noble estates where possible. A cultured, educated mind and a civilised lifestyle or *bildung* became more important than privilege of birth for senior posts in the administration. Frederick the Great, conscious of the dilution of independent royal initiative, reversed the trend, restricting senior posts to landed nobles. He appointed only one non-noble to the General Directory and gave senior posts to Junkers with no administrative experience. Frederick hoped that noble civil servants would be more tractable, but to no avail.[8]

The bureaucracy was to become even more independent in Prussia before monarchical control was fully re-established. A new General Code of 1794, which was to serve effectively as Prussia's constitution until after the 1848 revolution, exalted the status of the senior civil servants and formalised their separation from the rest of society. The bureaucracy was recognised as a corporate body, a distinct estate, different from both nobles and the bourgeoisie. Its privileges included exemption from local taxes, but there was a corresponding attempt to exclude them from the local estates. This rule, which successive kings tried to enforce, intensified the isolation of senior bureaucrats. Civil servants identified themselves by their profession much more than by their origins; whether landed (*landadel*) or service (*dienstadel*) nobility, social relations between the two groups and intermarriage blurred the social distinctions just as they did in France. The service nobles, whose titles were their reward for their contribution to the administration, were originally seen as a counter-balance to the ambitions of landed nobles. Between 1794 and 1806 one-third of senior posts were held by service nobles and their 1100 occupants considered themselves superior to the landed nobles. The feeling was apparently mutual. The bureaucracy was bounded by powerful hierarchical and family traditions and at the turn of the century held little appeal or opportunity for the sons of the landed nobility who, at this time anyway, generally lacked the educational qualifications for appointment or promotion. In the 1820s only 8 per cent of the students in the law faculty at Halle University, the main nursery for promising bureaucrats, were sons of landowners.[9] Military defeat by Napoleon facilitated the attempt of the senior career bureaucrats to establish their control through Stein's reforming programme after 1807. Thus at the beginning of the century the Prussian bureaucracy was dominated by service nobles.

At this time the less well-off were not excluded, as they were to be later in the century. Family connections helped an aspirant, but merit and talent played a not inconsiderable part in entrance and promotion. At that time, the absence of formal entrance or promotion criteria allowed the clever sons of even peasants and artisans to join like the rest, at the bottom, and compete for the top posts. The service could quickly mould a man, whatever his social origins. Thus, although in important respects the bureaucracy was closed, it was not a totally socially exclusive caste. In the first half of the century, one-third of the law students at Halle were from the peasantry or artisanry, or were sons of elementary school teachers or junior officials. It was reckoned that, of the senior men recruited from the universities in the 1820s, 70 per cent were from the 'cultivated' classes. The fathers of more than half of these were either bureaucrats or professionals. Sons of businessmen numbered 11 per cent, sons of big landowners 9 per cent, and sons of peasants and artisans 12 per cent. Between 25 and 30 per cent of those who entered from the universities in the 1830s were lower middle class, sons of minor officials, peasants, artisans, etc.[10] But during the rest of the nineteenth century opportunities for men from these social groups declined markedly. Although the Stein reforms had declared that official appointments were to be made on talent, the number of senior jobs was halved and subsequently held firmly in check, despite the increase in population. Fierce competition in the second half of the century excluded men from modest backgrounds. Universities began to demand an *abitur* pass from entrants in the 1830s and the numbers of lower-class children at university in the second half of the century dropped in consequence. Official appointments were restricted to those who had attended university. This was a deliberate attempt to exclude the lower classes from all bureaucratic posts except the most menial. Boys from poorer families who persisted in trying to 'better themselves' were not admitted to student societies and military groups, whose accolade they needed if they were to be considered for the bureaucracy. Thus the social base of the bureaucracy was consciously narrowed in the name of social conservatism and security. By the turn of the century there were no candidates for senior posts from lower-middle-class families or below.

During the century the Prussian bureaucracy was gradually transformed from a privileged, self-recruiting corporation into simply one manifestation of a new, more consolidated upper class. In the early years a high proportion of civil servants were following a family tradition. In 1820 370 out of 893 senior men were from noble, mostly service backgrounds. Up to around 1850 over half of the law students destined for the service were from bureaucrat families. By 1900 this dynastic tradition was fading. This was partly because existing officials either did not marry or had fewer children because of financial or professional constraints. At Halle in the 1850s 51 per cent of the students in the law faculty were sons of officials, by 1870 only 36 per cent. Sons of officials were beginning to choose other jobs, in business, industry and the army, occupations which earlier were thought inferior. Up to 1848 the bureaucracy had been hostile to the army, but by 1860 their sons were second only to the sons of army officers in their preference for a military career. By 1900 they actually headed the lists. An army career was now often the prelude to a successful later period in the bureaucracy. By 1900 nearly 70 per cent of the senior officials in the Rhineland had military links, which encouraged conformity, uniformity and authoritarianism. The same tendency can be traced in marriage arrangements. Officials had been inclined to marry daughters of colleagues, but by 1900 only 34 per cent of the wives of senior Rhenish men had officials for fathers, 48 per cent of fathers were in business or industry. Among the officials themselves only 37 per cent of the senior men in the Rhineland had fathers with a civil service background, 17 per cent were landowners, 30 per cent were in business or industry, 6 per cent were military and 10 per cent from other groups.[11] In 1903 only 4 per cent of the candidates for senior posts were from middle-ranking service backgrounds and only 30 per cent had fathers who were senior officials, whereas 15 per cent had fathers who were senior army officers.[12] Landed families supplied 22 per cent, business 16 per cent. Between 1794 and 1806 60 per cent of all senior officials were nobles, of whom 36 per cent held new, and therefore probably service, titles. In 1820 the figure was 42 per cent; by 1916 it had risen to 50 per cent.[13] An increasing number of nobles sought state service because of the impoverishment of their family estates. In 1801, when there were 20 000 noble families, the proportion of families to noble estates was 2:1. By 1880 it was 6:1. At first their main refuge was the army, lacking the education necessary to qualify for the civil service. Later in the century sons of nobles were more prepared to complete the required university training. In 1820 24 per cent of bureaucrats were nobles, by 1852 32 per cent. Between 1850 and 1870 an increasing number of sons of landed aristocrats and also sons of the wealthy industrial middle class wanted to be officials. The proportion of landowners' sons at Halle rose from 10 to 14.5 per cent and of businessmen's sons from 9 to 17 per cent. It is true that, although the numbers of landowners' sons in the bureaucracy rose, in the long-term they formed a smaller proportion of the whole, down from 46 per cent of senior men in 1839 to 25 per cent in 1914, but they continued to hold an increasing number of the top posts. They came from wealthier families, indicating that their career choice was no longer a bolt hole from economic deprivation. The more traditional senior officials, accustomed to the process of ennoblement for state service, resented the intrusion of landed nobles and disliked even more an increasing tendency of the ruler to ennoble large landowners in preference to office-holders. In 1840 the royal cabinet complained to Frederick William IV:

The officials' place in civil society, the orientation of their education and way of life, as well as the nature of their wealth would prevent them from owning even a modest piece of land and therefore preclude their entry into the nobility.

After 1850, although the proportion of civil servants from noble families did not grow, bureaucrats were recruited from increasingly wealthy families. The impact of rapid industrialisation began to make its mark on the social composition of the bureaucracy, for the richer civil servants were mostly from business families. In 1850 38 per cent of the senior men in the Rhineland were noble and by 1905 this was 13 per cent, but in 1850 47 per cent had an independent income, whereas by 1905 this had risen to 64 per cent. Money, not *bildung*, had become the chief qualification. Over the century the social composition of the German bureaucracy had undergone a major transformation. At the outset its members had seen themselves, and had been regarded by others, as a sort of platonic guardian class, recruiting from all social groups, although chiefly from the wealthy commoners and nobles, and representing not a class interest but the whole of society. Gradually they came to represent the upper class only, and to be not only separate from the rest of society, but isolated from and apprehensive of large sections of the community, particularly the new factory working class. By 1900 they were the staunch defenders of the established social and political order, inextricably enmeshed in conservative politics, very different from their colleagues half a century earlier. There was no longer a civil service ethos, rapidly absorbed by recruits from a wide social spectrum who therefore contributed collectively a broad knowledge of society, but a wealthy, upper-middle-class stance, which excluded consideration of other groups and increasingly excluded profound social ignorance and fear.

The 'golden age' image of the earlier civil service should not be overdone, but, even when leavened with a pinch of scepticism, one cannot doubt that the administration had undergone real change. How can this be explained? A new concept of the role of the bureaucracy emerged, partly the product of internal pressures, partly a response to broader political innovation – such as the development of elected assemblies to replace the old estates – and partly due to the impact of industrialisation. Faced with the need for reform after defeat by Napoleon, the number of senior administrative posts was halved in 1808. Subsequent population growth and the rapid expansion of numbers of qualified graduates in peacetime Prussia, created bottlenecks in the bureaucracy, both of men seeking initial appointments and of others striving for promotion. By the 1830s government officials were convinced that the universities were accepting too many students and restrictions were imposed. Senior administrators, eager to preserve their own social and economic status, were opposed to expansion. Entrance examinations became stiffer and were restricted to graduates. Even so, by the 1850s there were five times more applicants qualified for entry to the judiciary than earlier in the century. The social basis of recruitment was deliberately and substantially narrowed. Previously, when the unpaid ten-year apprenticeship for prospective bureaucrats in the judiciary had followed secondary school, it had been difficult for lower-class applicants; now it was virtually impossible to consider such a career without a rich family. Generational conflict also grew up, undermining the traditional homogeneity of the civil service. Pensions were small, there was no retiring age and increasingly men preferred to die in office. Thus those who gained the initial foothold found promotion blocked.

Younger officials were inclined to take a new view of the ethos of their calling, showing less respect for corporate honour than for the specific skills and efficiency of the individual professional. Such attitudes were held to be more appropriate to the new industrial society and to correspond to changes in the education experienced by younger officials. Early in the century the ideal education was reckoned to be one which contributed to a man's *bildung*, or general culture and civilisation. Later more specialised training was required for specific jobs, which made transfer and contact between departments more difficult and also led to a cultural gap between the older and younger generations of officials. Bureaucrats were becoming more like businessmen, as concerned with the amount they were paid as with status and titles, and more inclined to identify themselves with groups outside the service than with their own superiors.[14]

In the Italian peninsula also there were attempts by Restoration rulers to economise by reducing the size of the civil service which the French had enlarged. In Austrian-ruled Lombardy a higher standard of education was demanded of recruits, in particular a longer university course, which as in Prussia excluded lower-middle-class families. Blocks on promotion at all levels were even more

annoying for the bourgeoisie than a similar policy in Prussia, for
Italians were specifically denied access to senior posts. As in Prussia
there were complaints about the financial rewards, even of senior
office. In his biography, written in retirement in the early 1900s, a
former royal procurator claimed that a young magistrate could look
forward to:

> fifteen years of almost intolerable and often absolutely intolerable
> residence in the provinces, and at least 6–7 transfers before
> attaining the grade of judge or assistant procurator, while a
> junior Assize Court judge might thereafter hope to become a
> supplementary judge after another 5–6 years, and then allow
> himself the luxury of an occasional meal in a restaurant and a
> few new shirts: yet there is still another 8–10 years before he dons
> the full judge's robes.[15]

The lack of recruitment and stifling of career prospects for junior
officials turned sections of the professional middle class in Italy and
Prussia into active critics of their governments and into supporters
of constitutional reform.[16] In mid-century Prussia, political activism
replaced loyalty to a corporate identity, particularly among younger
members of the judiciary. Young men began to talk in terms of
civic responsibility and an unprecedented conflict with the crown
developed. Younger members of the judiciary took a decisive lead
in opposition groups, despite the attempts of Frederick William IV
to muzzle them. The king tried to use the new United Diet against
them in the 1840s, but found that the leaders of the opposition in the
assembly of 1847 were four senior bureaucrats. Younger colleagues
joined artisans in 1848 in forming organisations like the Democratic
League in Trier and the Political Club in Berlin to promote the
democratic cause. Others joined Constitutional Clubs, which pressed
for representative institutions, but with a limited suffrage. In the
elections for the Prussian assembly in 1848 older officials stood as
liberals, younger as democrats. The social standing of bureaucrats
and the absence of alternative leaders contributed to their considerable success. The liberals were supported by better-off members of
the industrial and business communities. The democrats appealed
to artisans and poorer groups, who hated the bureaucracy as such.
They were clearly motivated to a large degree by their sense of
personal grievance and deprivation, sometimes referring to them-

selves as 'proletarians'. In Berlin a third of those elected were university-trained bureaucrats; nearly a quarter were members of the judiciary. The eastern provinces chose more conservative older-generation administrators than the west, where younger candidates were preferred. Even more striking was the difference between the radical men elected in the towns, a high proportion of whom were officials, and the more conservative choice of the rural areas. Before the revolution there had seldom been a civil servant in the city council, now they constituted 50 per cent of the body and all were liberals or democrats. Forty-two per cent of the new national assembly were bureaucrats: 26 per cent from the judiciary, 16 per cent administrators. Hausemann and Camphausen, who had directed the opposition in the old United Diet, now led the right as champions of limited suffrage and were the king's choice to head the new government. Some junior members of the judiciary, operating as leaders of the left and left-centre defied the king and tried to prevent the closure of the assembly in November 1848.

When a new assembly was called by the king in 1849 to discuss his proposed constitution, civil servants were given the right to participate in politics, but another change of direction was percep-tible. Extensive judicial reform, abolishing surviving feudal regu-lations and using the French-style Rhenish system as a model, necessitated new courts and thus greatly extended employment opportunities. The new assembly still contained 42.2 per cent bureaucrats, but 16 per cent were now conservative. Of the 140 left-wing deputies, 53 were in the judiciary and they continued to lead the democratic movement outside parliament too. The introduction in May 1849 of a three-class franchise, with resulting gains for the propertied classes, increased the number of senior conservative bureaucrats from 40 to 113. The 'constitutional' bureaucrat was being superseded by the supporter of autocracy. New regulations tried to stop civil servants entering politics. Politics itself was moving on from being a pursuit of local notables, in which administrators were natural leaders, to become the concern of political parties and interest groups.[17] Although civil servants continued to be elected to the Prussian parliament, by 1855 the vast majority of administrative members were pro-government, as were 55 per cent of elected magistrates. When William I as regent in 1858 relaxed the new regulations, old opponents re-emerged. But they were the same men, older, cautious, liberal, no longer radical, and concerned, above all, to hold on to their official posts and take no risks. There were no new, younger men. Subsequently bureaucratic involvement in parliamentary politics waned rapidly, in sharp contrast to most other countries. In 1855 bureaucrats constituted 50 per cent of the assembly, but between 1873 and 1912 only 24 per cent and in 1904 only 17 per cent. This was so exceptional in comparison with other European states that it is worthy of further examination.

The year 1848 was a disappointment for some bureaucrats because of the degree of radicalism which sprang up, for others because the radical movement failed. The establishment by the king of a *landtag* or parliament in Prussia was likewise disillusioning for some because it proved to be ineffective in limiting royal power, while a growing conservative element wanted to control parliamentarianism for the opposite reason. In other countries election to parliament brought tangible material and professional rewards for civil servants, notably in France, Italy and Britain, but the opposite was true in Prussia. After 1848 some leading democrats like Temme and Stieber were tempted away from opposition by attractive job offers; others were threatened into submission. Bureaucratic independence was gone. In addition professional frustrations were substantially alleviated by salary increases and a 75 per cent growth in the size of the bureaucracy in the second half of the century. In assessing the contribution of broad demographic, economic and political issues to the changing attitudes and role of civil servants, it would appear that the events of 1848 were crucial in determining the pace of change.

The increasingly professional bureaucracy was also more socially exclusive and more authoritarian. It was not only that less well-off recruits were excluded – so also were Jews and Catholics. Elsewhere, as the civil service became more professional, so its close links with the aristocracy were loosened. Great Britain developed both a strong, independent bureaucracy and full representative institutions. In Prussia the 1848 revolution gave conservative bureaucrats the opportunity to challenge reforming colleagues and consolidate and entrench a reactionary bias. The emasculation of parliamentary institutions after 1848 left officials with little alternative but to become unquestioning champions of royal authority. A further key to the attitude of the bureaucrats lies in the absence in Prussia, and later in Germany, of an independent judiciary. As in Russia, all judicial appointments emanated from the Crown once patrimonial justice had been abolished. The attempt by younger members of the Prussian judiciary to challenge royal authority did not survive 1848. There was no concept of the separation of powers, a factor which in France proved so unsettling for the Crown. There was no parallel to the battle which raged in the second half of the eighteenth century between the Bourbons and their *parlements*, or courts of appeal.

If the 1848 revolution had a major influence on the development of the psyche of the Prussian civil service, what of the impact of the 1789 revolution on the French bureaucracy? Historians of all political persuasions used to be convinced that the revolution not only set up the institutional form of the modern French state, but also introduced a new bourgeois administrative élite. In the last generation revisionist historians have taken up the theme of continuity between the *ancien régime* and the revolution, which was first popularised by de Tocqueville, and have quantified the impressive survival, or rather re-emergence, rate of eighteenth-century bureaucrats. The bureaucracy occupied a different place in the hearts of the French than it did in Germany. In public the French tended to regard their civil servants with suspicion and scorn, not awe and admiration as in Germany: 'Le français est donc publiquement anti-fonctionnaire. Ceci-dit, il faut également savoir que la plupart des français désirent que leurs enfants soient des fonctionnaires, parceque le fonctionnaire est tout-puissant.'[18] There was considerable structural similarity between the centralised administrative system of the *ancien régime*, when the traditional provinces were run by *intendants* appointed by the king, and the highly centralised structures which emerged from the upheaval of the revolutionary and imperial years, when the country was split into much smaller units, departments, each run by a prefect appointed by the Minister of the Interior. The Napoleonic Council of State was reminiscent of its predecessor under the Bourbons.

But there were also fundamental differences. *Ancien régime* appointments were venal and could be inherited. Incumbents thus had an independence lacking in salaried personnel, especially as financial difficulties obliged successive rulers to launch new sales of office. The revolution abolished venality and compensated the office-holders. Subsequent officials were all salaried and held their job at the pleasure of the government. At the more senior level of *fonctionnaire*, political loyalty was paramount and frequent changes of personnel accompanied both the upheavals of the revolutionary years and the turbulent and even the quieter years of the nineteenth century. At the more junior level of the *employés*, those in work took care to keep out of politics for the sake of their jobs. Offices were no longer bought, but a man was expected to possess a level of fortune and public standing commensurate with the role to which he aspired, since salaries were rarely adequate to sustain the lifestyle of a notable. A suitable family background was indispensable and many successful nineteenth-century bureaucrats could date their lineage back to a robe noble, *parlementaire* past. (Initially a robe noble's title was a reward for judicial service.) One of the main differences between the *ancien régime* official and his nineteenth-century successor was a greater emphasis on a certain level of education and eventually professional training. One area where there was little change, either in the short- or long-term, was in the social origins of the more responsible bureaucrats, who in the nineteenth century were uniformly notables, drawn from a wealthy, usually landed background, some titled, many bourgeois. Curiously, although offices could no longer be inherited, a dynastic tradition developed very rapidly after the revolution.

The Directory may be seen as the turning point in the development of the French bureaucracy, given the enormous expansion and extension of the authority of the administration. The Directory was equipped with a quarter of a million civil servants, five times as many as before the revolution. The central core had grown 850 per cent, from 700 to 16 000.[19] The revolutionary years offered real career opportunities to experienced men who could navigate political rapids. Most officials at all levels were of middle-class origin and 8 per cent had received some higher education. Within the junior ranks of *employés*, 20 per cent of those working in the central administration before 1789 had a father or other relative in the ministry, but this figure fell to half during the Empire. There was no chance of promotion from the junior grade of clerk, or *employé*, to become a *fonctionnaire*. A clerk could hope to rise only within the grades set out for *employés*.[20] Among the more senior *fonctionnaires* the issue of the relationship with their superior authority, which was to divide the Prussian bureaucracy until the 1850s, was speedily resolved in revolutionary France. A *fonctionnaire* either conformed enthusiastically with the politics of the government and conducted himself with total discretion, or accepted inevitable dismissal. After ten years of foreign and civil war, Napoleon was careful to involve both revolutionaries and members of the pre-1789 élites in his service. In recent years French historians have made exhaustive local studies of Napoleon's officials, to assess the degrees of continuity and innovation within the élites. There was a high level of continuity: in central government 27 per cent of officials had begun their careers before 1789, in local administration 34 per cent, in the judiciary 32 per cent and in the financial administration 20 per cent. Those whose appointment had been mainly honorific rarely survived and senility and death had taken their toll.[21] Ironically then, one must assume that many upper-middle-class *ancien régime* officials had pocketed their compensation, bought themselves a nice estate with the proceeds and, when the main upheaval of the revolution was over, re-established themselves in the bureaucracy. Of course there were new names and new families. The long duration and scope of the Revolutionary Wars, a fair level of wastage among officers and consequent rapid promotion, coupled with Napoleon's tendency to reward senior military officers with important administrative posts, ensured that new blood was injected into the notable group who governed in the Emperor's name. But there was no takeover by a new 'upper middle class', for many senior officials, with *ancien régime* as well as revolutionary and imperial experience, already belonged to a well-established bourgeoisie. Many who accepted the new Napoleonic titles already had *ancien régime* ones. By the end of the Empire 21 per cent of prefects were of noble origin.

After Napoleon's defeat in 1814, and even more after his return from Elba and second defeat, there were extensive changes within the bureaucracy, reducing middle-class participation in favour of pre-1789 nobles or families well on the way to acquiring noble status on the eve of the revolution. By 1830 45 per cent of prefects were noble. Seventy per cent of prefects appointed during the Restoration were noble, many were *emigrés*,[22] and the service looked increasingly like that of the *ancien régime*. Indeed Restoration prefects were noticeably older than those who had served Napoleon and their approach was patrician rather than professional. Quite a number were writers, some were deputies or peers, who spent the parliamentary session away from their department. Administering a department was often treated as a part-time job, to be left to subordinates. Some were professional idlers. Casteja, prefect of the Haut-Rhin in 1819, came from a family whose title of nobility dated back to the fifteenth-century. But it was said of him, 'Il ne passe son temps qu'à table, au jeu et au lit, jamais il ne se leve qu'à midi et souvent plus tard.'[23]

The Restoration quest for noble officials did not mean that there were sweeping changes in 1814 on either political or social grounds. Two-thirds of the new Bourbon prefects had also served Napoleon in the same capacity. But twelve of the new faces were *emigré* nobles, whose status was treated as a qualification, present attitudes being guaranteed by the past loyalty of the family. The number of nobles employed as prefects almost doubled, from 30 to 58 in March 1815. After Napoleon's escape from Elba, Carnot instituted another bureaucratic revolution, in which the proportion of nobles in the prefectures dropped dramatically, from one in three to one in nine. It is interesting to note that the restoration of the upper middle class to the prefectures was no more a clean sweep than the changes of the First Restoration. It was considered expedient to adjust the social composition of the bureaucratic corps, but equally important to maintain the highest level of experience. Sixty of the new prefects of the Hundred Days were old hands, the pool of talent of those deposed at the First Restoration being trawled. Similarly after Waterloo, Louis XVIII (1814–24) on his second time around, was careful to stem the ultra-royalist backlash of revenge and seek compromise and conciliation within and from his bureaucrats. Only one of the new prefects appointed had not served Napoleon. However loyalty to the Emperor in the Hundred Days was a different matter and was normally followed by a prolonged period of enforced leisure. Out of one hundred prefects who served the emperor during the Hundred Days, only ten secured an official post of any kind again before 1830. The middle-class official with prefectoral ambitions found the Second Restoration a desert. Of 164 men appointed as prefects, 118 or 70 per cent were nobles whose titles predated the revolution. Eleven had had fathers or grandfathers in the *parlements* and a number of others had links with the *ancien régime* magistracy. The Restoration asserted the concept of service over professional training in the bureaucracy. Candidates stressed their family tradition of state service and would list genealogy. Napoleon's attempt to insist on a degree in law or science for the post of *auditeur* in the Council of State, a common starting-point for a future prefect, was long forgotten. For sub-prefects the local influence of their family was qualification enough. A prefecture was often a second choice for an *ancien régime* soldier who had not joined the imperial army, sometimes because of his age. None of this was strikingly out-of-line with the composition of the imperial bureaucracy. The difference lay in the initial and sustained preference given to those with noble titles, 75.6 per cent by 1816.[24] There is no doubt that the exclusion of upper-middle-class candidates was based on political calculation and the assumption that nobles, especially those with an *emigré* background, were likely to be more sympathetic and loyal to the monarchy. No one expected a prefect to be an impartial platonic guardian. His main job was to win elections. But the experience of the Restoration, and particularly that of Charles X (1824–30), showed that an impeccable pedigree was not enough. Charles, committed to ultra politics, lost the elections of 1827 and 1830 partly because his prefects lacked the professional knowledge and training to act both as agents of the government and as the co-ordinators of the views of local notables. The revolution of 1830 showed that if a prefect was to be a successful electoral agent, a task never required of an *ancien régime intendant*, professional competence and experience were vital attributes.

There was a complete reconstitution of the bureaucracy after the July Days. Only seven of the old prefects survived, all of the generals commanding the nineteen military districts were dismissed and 400 members of the Restoration magistracy were replaced. The purge descended even to the administration of forests and the postal service. At the pinnacle of the bureaucracy only ten of the 34 Restoration councillors of state were maintained.[25] It was the most thorough administrative revolution of the nineteenth-century. To some extent nobles gave way to middle-class appointees; although titles were still valued, they were likely to be of Napoleonic origin. The basis of the purge was political: to eliminate those sympathetic to the Bourbons who refused to take an oath of allegiance to the new king, Louis-Philippe (1830–48). Since the new men were themselves professionals, whether senior generals or members of the judiciary, experience was a vital prerequisite and thus the pool of new men was to a large extent composed of Napoleonic servants unemployed since 1815 or after the more liberal phase of the Restoration. Typical was Choppin d'Arnouville, an *auditeur* in the Council of State in 1813, made prefect of the Isère by Decazes, transferred to the Doubs in 1820, but dismissed by the new, more right-wing government before he could take up his post and subsequently out of office until 1830, when Guizot made him prefect of the Doubs.[26] The Orleanists respected Bonapartist antecedents, sometimes a little too much, for men out of office since the Second Restoration could prove too radical for them. A number, including Fargues and Viefville de Essarts, prefects respectively of the Haute-Marne and Côte-d'Or, still smarting under the injustice of their dismissal by the Bourbons, were too anti-clerical and radical and were dismissed by Casimir Périer in March 1831 when the Orleanist regime settled for *résistance*, not *mouvement* (terms used for the two tendencies within Orleanism) in its politics.[27] Dynastic traditions were, however, unswervingly respected. Old, pre-revolutionary robe families continued to prosper. The first two prefects of the Vosges after the revolution of 1830, Nau de Champlouis and Siméon, came out of this stable. De Champlouis's family had held public office, it appears, since the fifteenth century and his grandfather and father had been *avocats* in the *parlement* of Paris.[28] Siméon's grandfather was an imperial, Hundred Days and royal deputy (from 1825–31), as well as being a First Restoration prefect, subsequently *conseiller d'état* and Minister of the Interior under Richelieu.[29] When one studies bureaucratic careers and family links, continuity is more in evidence than change. That more new men were untitled compared with Polignac's men did not constitute a 'bourgeois' revolution, although the Orleanists were not totally displeased when left-wing critics made the allegation. Rather the Bourbons had tried to turn back the social clock by their promotion of an unprecedented number of nobles. Pursuit of an ultra-royalist myth had begun to distort the role of the middle class in the bureaucracy. The Orleanist regime set the tone for the rest of the century, with the consolidation of a bureaucracy recruited at the higher levels from the notables. The only break from tradition lasted for a few months after the February Revolution, 1848, when *commissaires* replaced prefects. Men of more modest middle-class status were appointed and officials were enjoined to be totally impartial, a recipe which proved disastrous for the government in the elections of April 1848. Subsequently the old notables rapidly resumed their accustomed role.

A glance at the bureaucracy of the Second Empire (1852–70) reveals with what success the notables had sidestepped the brief democratic stampede of 1848 and indeed had come to terms with the restitution of universal suffrage by Louis-Napoleon. In Louis-Philippe's reign bureaucrats and politicians were indistinguishable; habitually over 40 per cent of the Chamber of Deputies were office-holders, a practice which political opponents decried as corrupt. The obligation of a deputy to seek re-election when he received an official appointment did nothing to lessen this criticism. In the Second Empire the ties remained close, but the prefect-deputy was a much rarer bird. Prefectoral dynasties were well developed. Of the 220 prefects appointed during the Empire, only ten had fathers who were deputies, while a total of 159 had held an official post, mostly a senior one. Thirty were close relatives of generals. Only three bankers' sons and ten sons of industrialists became prefects. Politicians put their sons in the Council of State or the treasury. Wealth and family connections were all. Only three (1 per cent) of Second Empire prefects were from modest backgrounds, 38 (17 per cent) were lower middle class, while 91 (42 per cent) were from better-off, including very wealthy, middle-class families and 88 (40 per cent) were nobles. By 1870 the proportion of noble prefects had fallen to 33 per cent. The prefectoral service remained the third most noble of the branches of the bureaucracy. Sixty per cent of the titles were First Empire creations and many married into other illustrious First Empire families,[30] but the emperor was less haunted by his great-uncle when appointing prefects than was Louis-Philippe a generation earlier.

In both France and Prussia the traditional administrative élites proved very resilient and assumed their perpetuation in senior ranks. Historians have noted some degree of 'democratisation' in France, but junior officials have to be included in the tally to produce such a profile. Only one-quarter of Directory officials had a lower-middle-class background, whereas by the 1860s over 40 per cent were sons of shopkeepers, artisans, clerks, peasants or other workers. Indeed if junior grades are included the figure actually reaches 66 per cent. Likewise in the 1860s one-third of the secondary school graduates who opted for the civil service had upper-middle-class fathers and only 25 per cent had bureaucrat fathers, compared with 33 per cent during the Directory. One has to take into account when considering these comparisons that the civil service was not generally a first choice for boys, apart from the ones whose fathers' position guaranteed a prime posting, for promotion was slow and pay levels relatively modest. The size of the bureaucracy had grown, but so had alternative attractive professions. Thus the conditions of the 1860s were rather different from those of the Directory.[31] On the other hand, if the huge number of new junior posts is excluded from calculations, the notables clearly remained firmly entrenched.

If genealogy, wealth and political adaptability counted for so much in French bureaucratic dynasties, in what ways can it be claimed that the French civil service was becoming more professional in the nineteenth century? This is another slightly ambiguous question on which it is not easy to arrive at precise information. Historians disagree over whether Napoleon's bureaucrats, after the infusion of returned *emigrés*, were better educated than earlier ones, a view propounded by Whitcomb, or inferior in training, an opinion adhered to by Church.[32] Education was valued by bureaucrats when grooming their sons for succession, but so had it been a century earlier. In both periods officials generally expected their sons to follow them and, in the absence of specific educational or professional hurdles or entrance examinations similar to those in Prussia, a good general classical education was regarded as the best preparation. Officials patronised secondary schools out of all proportion to their numbers, just as they did in Prussia. In the eighteenth century the college at Avallon had an intake 45 per cent of whose fathers were officials or professionals. When the *lycées* and municipal colleges replaced the old royal colleges under Napoleon, 6000 *lycée* scholarships were offered, the bulk of them going to sons of officials and officers as a reward for the loyalty of their parents. Even in 1911 over half of the awards went to sons of officials. Senior men were more likely to patronise the exclusive *lycées*: 151 of the Second Empire prefects went to secondary schools, 90 of them to Parisian schools. Minor officials sent their sons to municipal colleges as day-boys. These less prestigious schools offered a route to a minor official post for the sons of lower-middle-class parents, including artisans and peasants.[33] A law degree was increasingly regarded as the best training for a bureaucrat. Over half of Louis-Napoleon's prefects, 130, studied at the law faculty in Paris, 36 at provincial universities,[34] and 84 were called to the bar with a view to improving their administrative prospects. In 1867 nearly 700 of the 5000 undergraduates were planning to go directly into the civil service. The élitist educational system and increasing emphasis on educational qualifications may have enhanced professionalism within the civil service, but the cost and time factors intensified the hold of the notables. Indeed letters of recommendation and information collated on candidates for bureaucratic posts placed far more emphasis on genealogy, good connections and family prosperity and prestige than on education, which seemed to be passed over as an incidental.[35] Bureaucratic service brought rich rewards for those at the top. An ambassador might earn 150000 frs. a year, just over a hundred civil servants were paid 20000 frs. or more. A few prefects netted 60000 frs., but 228 of the 277 prefects and sub-prefects earned only 3000 frs. There were substantial variations between ministries. In total contradiction of the notion that professional qualifications were more significant, those with most training earned least. An engineer at the top of his profession could expect the far from princely salary of 4500 frs. and juniors received a very modest stipend. Some posts were regarded as part-time, and in many cases not only did salary levels presuppose a private income, but parents also often had to promise to support their son during training, as in Germany. Financial administrators were expected to provide a sum as a deposit, or caution money, when they took a post. Until the end of the century foreign service recruits had to prove that they had a private income of at least 6000 frs. a year. The bureaucracy was indeed, as Zeldin put it, almost a corporation similar to the *ancien régime* Church, and like the Church the salary differentials were huge.[36]

The growing army of middling and junior officials diluted this corporatism and consequently felt most deeply the need to make the service more professional, by trying to introduce a charter of rights and duties, rules for appointment and promotion. In the 1840s a journal, *La France Administrative*, was started to promote the cause of unity and professionalism in this hierarchical organisation. The revolutionaries of 1848 took up the cause and founded an ephemeral national school of public administration, but some bureaucrats were so hostile that it was not until 1945 that the Ecole Nationale d'Administration was finally launched.[37] Concern over the lack of specific training was sharpened by the military defeat of 1871 and another attempt was made to impose an entrance examination (the first had proved abortive in Napoleon's time). However, patronage still remained crucial. A more striking achievement was the founding of the Ecole Libre des Sciences Politiques, a private college to train a new generation of leaders. It was successful, almost beyond reason, in providing a bureaucratic élite. Between 1900 and 1937 116 of the 120 *conseillers d'état* were graduates, 209 of the 218 *inspecteurs des finances*, 249 of the 284 members of the diplomatic corps, and 83 of 94 *conseillers* in the *cours des comptes*. Since the school's recruitment was largely from notable families, the institution of specific professional training reinforced the hold of the traditional élite on senior bureaucratic posts.[38]

The administrative service in France was highly stratified and hierarchical. At the senior level, progression was typically from a junior post in the central bureaucracy, a tradition established by Napoleon, to a prefecture. The prefectures themselves were graded, with wealthier departments nearer to Paris being more attractive, better paid and obviously more prestigious than those in remote mountainous areas. Sub-prefectures formed a separate group, the pre-revolutionary tradition of leaving local administration to local notables orchestrated by an outsider as *intendant*, later as prefect, being maintained throughout the nineteenth century. The sub-prefect was typically the member of the regional élite most acceptable to his peers. Following the news of the 1830 revolution, liberal notables appointed each other as sub-prefects, a process normally rubber-stamped by Guizot, the new Minister of the Interior. Sub-prefects were often well advanced in a career, usually legal, sometimes both legal and bureaucratic, when they were appointed. Demesmay, a well-established *notaire* who became sub-prefect of Pontarlier, Doubs in August 1830, was a member of a powerful local clan. The comment made of him typified the assumed criteria for a good local official: 'Demesmay appartient à une des plus honorables familles du pays.' He was a member of the general council of the department, the *arrondissement* council and was the sitting member of parliament. He had the area sewn up, a state of affairs comforting and satisfactory for his superior. One can also see the effects of the dynastic tradition at close quarters here. When appointed in 1830 he set to work to turn his locality into even more of a family fief.[39] One of his sons succeeded him as sub-prefect, another as deputy.

The absence of local prestige and fortune was often disastrous. It could occur when a local powerful patron overreached himself in promoting his supporters. The duc de Choiseul, a leading local liberal, made Laurent, the son of a local miller, sub-prefect of Neufchateau in August 1830 as a reward for his indefatigable labours as secretary of the liberal electoral committee. Laurent, though an *avocat*, barely qualified as an elector and lacked the usual prefectoral graces. Even his noble protector had to admit that 'the local nobility find him lacking in manners'.[40] For a prefect at the *chef-lieu* of a department, a rich family was even more important since elaborate entertainments were expected of him and salaries and allowances were meagre. One individual lost all credibility with the local élite when he tried to hold receptions with an orchestra consisting of one violin. A prefect needed to be accepted as a notable in order to understand and translate the wishes of the local élite to Paris, but it was important that he was not of the locality, in order to referee inevitable local rivalries. A successful prefect needed wide-ranging influence and affiliations if his career was to progress. The baron de Trémont, made prefect of Dijon by Casimir Périer in March 1831, was one of Louis-Philippe's godsons and his case was urged by the dukes Choiseul, Praslin, Plaisance and Marmier and comte Alexandre de Rochefoucauld. High recommendations could be no guarantee of competence, and de Trémont's tenure of the prefecture was brief and stormy.[41] The personal files of nineteenth-century prefects make it clear that good connections, formed through lineage, the right lycée and marriage, were vital. Intermarriage among bureaucratic families was common and provided excellent dynastic cement. The dynastic tradition was unbroken by the institution of a democratic republic in 1870 and remained intact at the outbreak of the First World War.

Within the service, however, changes were taking place. There was a notable increase in the numbers of French civil servants in the second half of the nineteenth century, but they were such lowly categories with appalling scales of pay that more senior groups were concerned about their status. At the turn of the century there were many complaints that the bureaucrats were the new proletariat, a description used for different motives by senior Prussian radical bureaucrats in 1848. French officials in 1900 were mainly worried about money. Average pay of just under 1500 frs. put them on a par with a labourer. Meanwhile the big department stores in Paris were paying their 250 best salesmen between 20 000 and 25 000 frs., as much as a prefect earned. At the top, civil servants could quadruple their pay by going into the private sector. What they lost in salary, civil servants made up, to a modest degree, in greater security. The political and administrative merry-go-round which traditionally accompanied even major governmental shifts, never mind revolutions, was slowed down to some extent during the century. Officials successfully pressed for a recognised and permanent career structure and for acceptance as impartial, professional administrators. Pensions increased the sense of security. At first they were limited to the army, offering 1200 frs. to a captain with 30 years' service. A law of 1790 provided for half pay after 30 years for civil servants, but only a small number actually received what was due. Only after 1853 did such pensions become the norm.[42] Thus in a variety of ways the French bureaucracy was substantially transformed during the nineteenth century. In social terms, as in Prussia, the control of the wealthy was actually enhanced by emphasis on education and qualifications. The dossiers of individual officials show that factors which affected employment and promotion had changed very little and still restricted senior posts to the notables. The 1789 revolution had a marked impact on size and in rationalising the structure – in this sense Weber's thesis is applicable to France – but the retention of power by the notables diluted the effect of change, even after 1850 when the vast increase in junior posts began to challenge corporate attitudes.

It has been argued that French rule in the Italian peninsula during the Revolution and Empire stimulated the development of a new bourgeois administrative élite, which was then pushed to the sidelines by former officials at the Restoration. Consequent resentment helped to turn the Risorgimento into a class war, with the dispossessed Napoleonic office-holders and their families struggling to regain power.[43] In this thesis the French Revolution is of prime importance, in the evolution of both the middle class and the bureaucracy itself. However, recent detailed studies of social change suggest that the Italian experience was more complex, that structural reform preceded the revolutionary years and that, as in France, the old élites had considerable tenacity. The Austrian-ruled lands of northern and central Italy experienced the benefits of 'enlightened' ideas on administration with the centralising policies of Joseph II, but the ruling élites of Lombardy and Tuscany blocked significant progress. Venice tried to come to terms with its economic decline by instituting more centralised administration, but conflict within its élite proved self-destructive. In other areas, Genoa, Piedmont, Parma etc., no reforms were attempted.

The French takeover[44] was a matter of military opportunism and opportunity, since the fragmentation of the Italian states left them vulnerable. The initial reaction of local élites to the French presence was hostile, while bourgeois elements tended to be more adaptable, but the degree to which French rule offered opportunities in administration depended on two factors: direct absorption into the

French Empire meant French, not local, officials at senior levels; and financial constraints, everywhere paramount since the French were conquerors, severely cramped administrative reform. In addition political fluctuations in France affected the pace and scale of administrative reorganisation in Italy. Areas where reform had already been attempted were more responsive to French proposals. In such confusion, it was often easier for the French, once the radical Jacobin phase was behind them, to follow the direction of Napoleonic France, by encouraging the survival of the old landed élites.[45] This was particularly true in Piedmont and Naples, where old families were tempted by administrative and military posts. They quickly took over the new prefectoral system in Lombardy, Emilia and the Kingdom of Italy.[46] The propertied classes proved far less hostile to reform than in the previous period, appreciating that, although de-feudalisation might work against their interests (though not necessarily), they could profit handsomely from the accompanying sale of communal land and disposal by the French of clerical estates. However, because the French also vastly expanded the number of civil servants, there were more opportunities for the bourgeoisie, and promotion was somewhat less tied to noble birth than in the past. There was a blending of long-established and newly rich families whose fortunes were made in the revolutionary decades, such as the Cavours and the Pignatellis. The introduction of imperial titles, primogeniture and the setting up of French-led freemasonry lodges all helped to consolidate a 'merged' administrative élite. In Naples Murat tried to encourage the growth in numbers of middle-class administrators at the local level by making it possible for them to acquire some of the land that went on the market. But he found that Naples lacked a large, educated, alternative bourgeois élite to run the courts and local government, and he was unable to challenge the power of baronial courts and feudal administration. The local barons were thus able to re-establish their traditional role.[47] Given the long-term decline in the Italian economy, it is not surprising that, even where French rulers tried to encourage the local bourgeoisie, they met with most success in the more prosperous regions. However a very recent account suggests that even in Naples Murat put together a new bureaucratic élite which later figured in the liberal movement.[48]

Structural reform of the administration was modelled on that of France. Central government was rationalised, departments were set up with prefects appointed from Paris, and consultative councils were created which had very little to do. Internal customs barriers were abolished, weights, measures and money were standardised, taxation was re-organised and roads, bridges and canals were built. The French civil, penal and commercial codes were introduced. Hospitals and schools were revamped on French lines. This programme would suggest a total reworking of all aspects of administration. Detailed information on its effectiveness is lacking, but there were considerable regional variations; central government reform was more likely to be implemented than local proposals, which were often forgotten. The nearer to Paris, the deeper the impression made. It was not simply a matter of propinquity, but of cost. Cash was a major factor in Naples, along with endemic corruption, unashamed stealing and relentless opposition to bureaucratic reform, especially of the tax system. The personal greed of the Neapolitan élite was reinforced by proclaimed patriotism; everyone knew that the French Empire was designed to benefit France.[49]

In assessing the impact of the revolutionary decades on bureaucratic development and the role of the middle class, it is clear that a range of factors have to be considered. In the current state of research, it no longer seems appropriate to claim that French conquest permitted a new élite, bourgeois or otherwise, to take the floor. It seems more likely that military and financial expediency was paramount and that, as in France, Napoleon compromised with old élites, either noble or part noble, part bourgeois, to survive. Regional differences and the varying forms of French rule, direct from Paris, through a French-appointed puppet, or allowing a measure of autonomy, also had a decisive influence on the degree to which structural reform of the administration was acceptable and long lasting.

After the defeat of Napoleon, the Austrians and other restored rulers were initially cautious in their attitude to French institutions and bureaucrats. Lombardy and Venetia, absorbed within the Austrian Empire, enjoyed a pause before senior posts were handed out to Austrians and the local élite were left to fill the minor roles, with the sop of rather ineffectual consultative assemblies.[50] Often the cost of a large, French-style bureaucracy was resented, and in Naples, for instance, supporters of the restored Bourbons were clamouring for jobs, which added to the insecurity of the French-appointed officials. An attempt to slim the bureaucracy was a major factor in the revolution of 1820. The attempt the French had made to create a rational framework collapsed as financial expediency obliged the Bourbons to resort to traditional stratagems. Distinctions between the public and private sector were rapidly blurred. As in the past the need for cash forced the government to farm out tax collection, communications, public services, even the payment of the salaries of officials. A new joint stock company, supposedly formed to promote much-needed industrial development, found it more profitable to use its capital to advance salaries and pensions at 4 per cent. All the concerns relevant to a modern bureaucracy were once again put in the hands of private contractors.[51] Nor can it be said that this resounding return to the *ancien régime* brought rebellious protests from an emergent bourgeoisie, for Neapolitan merchants as well as landed aristocrats invested in the joint stock company. Meanwhile the Bourbons were forced to work with a skeleton administration, which was poorly and intermittently paid and lacked central direction and authority. In truth the shuffle back to traditional methods in the Kingdom of the Two Sicilies was somewhat exceptional and most provinces retained and developed aspects of administrative modernisation before unification. This was notably the case in Piedmont, where the total abandonment of French institutions in 1815 was reversed after the 1848 revolution, with the establishment of a hierarchical prefectoral system staffed exclusively by the political élite.[52]

Unification in the 1860s may not have meant the military conquest of 'colonial' Italian provinces by Piedmont, but the introduction of Piedmontese bureaucratic institutions certainly made the south at least regard the unitary state as a foreign yoke rather than as liberation. France, via Piedmont, was used as a model for the creation of a highly centralised, and at the top levels highly politicised, civil service, but the mechanism for training and promotion was embryonic. This is vividly illustrated by the continued dominance of Piedmontese or other northerners within the bureaucracy. In 1875 of 198 employees in the Ministry of the Interior, 73 were born in Piedmont or Liguria, and 38 in Lombardy and the Veneto. This geographical imbalance persisted. At the end of the century 65 per cent of prefects, finance inspectors and generals were from the north, as were more than half of all higher civil servants. Movement between politics and administration was easy. Giolitti, after a spell in the treasury, five years as secretary of the court of accounts, went on to become a deputy and Prime Minister. Below the very top levels, little work has been done on the 30 000 civil servants. Most bureaucrats were trained lawyers, but not because this was an actual prerequisite. There was no formal structure of promotion, transfer, guarantees of tenure, rules for dismissal or pensions. Each ministry recruited its own men, who were poorly paid, dependent for basic survival on responsibility allowances etc., and so were totally at the mercy of their superiors. There was no concept of a career structure, or of independent initiative, which made the transfer of all decisions to the capital even more pronounced than elsewhere.

Despite the apparent unattractiveness of a job in the civil service, there was a plethora of candidates at all levels. Local resentment and the very visible backwardness of the southern economy after unification made it politically necessary for the state to make up the deficiency. In the south it was assumed in this period that senior posts would be reserved for aristocrats, who otherwise, as a contemporary observed, would be unemployable. These top jobs offered far more than a salary and status, they were regarded as heritable fiefs.[53] Unification brought a rapid expansion in the number of posts, both in civil administration and the magistracy, with a consequent 50 per cent rise in costs. The number of magistrates employed was the same as in France, with half the number of courts.[54] Between 1882 and 1911 the size of Italy's public administration grew from 98 000 to 260 000. But it should be remembered that this figure by 1911 included 117 000 posts which could not have existed in 1882, notably jobs in the rail and telephone services.[55] Apart from the judiciary, growth in numbers reflected a genuine expansion in the role of the state in the later years of the century. As in France, most new recruits were in very lowly paid positions; before 1870 primary school teachers received less than labourers. But in many of the poorer provinces lower-middle-class adults would have been totally unemployed apart from the cornucopia provided by the state. A civil service posting gave status and security, but the worst pay in Europe.[56] By 1907 there were 139 216 established civil service posts, by 1914 165 996. In 1882 there were 103 heads of division, in 1914 314. The colonial ministry employed twice as many officials as its British counterpart, despite its more modest responsibilities. Even so demand could not be satisfied and the promotion bias in favour of northerners remained. Hence in Italy the growth in numbers and in the role of the service exacerbated regional social tensions within the middle class.[57] Although aspects of professionalism developed in the Italian bureaucracy, the idea that civil service posts were within the gift of leading notables and local politicians remained entrenched, and indeed underwent embellishment, as the range and number of actual jobs expanded.

Russia did not even begin to develop a recognisably modern civil service until after emancipation. Well into the century military, civil and judicial functions were indistinguishable. Senior posts were totally reserved for the nobility, and retired military men were preferred for civil postings. Until very recently the Russian bureaucracy has been regarded by historians as a 'hidden third estate'. It has been treated not as an organisation to be studied as an entity, but as part of the function of a noble, a way up the social ladder for the ambitious son of a priest, a way of life despised and rejected by some nobles, especially by the nineteenth-century intelligentsia, many of who were noble.[58] Superficially there were similarities between the development of the role of the middle class in the Russian bureaucracy in the nineteenth century and that of France and Germany, in that the number of middle-class civil servants rose as the service expanded, while nobles retained the top posts, as they did in Germany, though not in France. But the contrasts are still greater. Peter the Great created the administrative system of Russia which lasted until the 1917 revolutions. Using both Sweden and Prussia as models, he set up an administrative Senate and five 'colleges' or government departments. Inspectors, vividly depicted later by Gogol, were appointed as checks on the bureaucracy. Peter's aim was to establish the concept of service to the state as supremely meritorious, overriding the privileges and pretensions of the nobility. He failed and the nobility managed to use his system to intensify their own power, gradually unravelling elements of his arrangements. In the nineteenth century they strove to preserve bureaucratic posts for themselves, trying to exclude the growing number of middle-class aspirants and resisting the increasing professionalism of the corps, asserting, ironically, the principle of service over specific training for a particular job.

As an essential corollary to his bureaucracy, Peter set up a Table of Ranks for Civil and Military Service, with fourteen ranks or *chin*, designed to make civil and military posts equally desirable, to compel all well-born men to serve him and to reward all according to their bureaucratic achievements. The non-noble could gain a noble title through the system. In the lower grades the title was non-hereditary, but from the eighth rank, hereditary. By the end of the eighteenth century, however, the nobility had carved a privileged position for itself and from the mid-nineteenth century nobles gained the right to more rapid promotion than non-nobles. They tried unsuccessfully to persuade the tsar to make the nobility a closed group, but it did become more difficult for merchants and descendants of personal nobles to acquire noble status. As Peter's rules were relaxed, so standards for promotion were no longer based on the quality of work or intellectual attainment. Alexander I attempted to set new standards with examinations for entry into the eighth *chin*, but noble resistance was so great that Nicholas I had to abandon these in 1834. Nicholas distrusted his bureaucrats, titled and untitled, and preferred to import Germans from the Baltic provinces, despite the protests of his subjects.[59] Foreign advisers and experts were no novelty; Peter the Great had included nearly 200 among his most senior officials. The trend had continued as the only effective way of countering noble pretensions, given the small size of the native middle class. The exact dimensions are hard to quantify, as place of birth was not recorded. However religion was noted and this is a reliable guide. It is reckoned that up to 20 per cent of central government bureaucrats were foreign-born, but none in the provinces.[60] Later in the nineteenth century the number of foreigners increased as more technical and engineering experts were needed to service the progress of industrialisation. In France and Germany such posts were filled by highly educated members of the upwardly mobile and ambitious middle class, but, significantly, in Russia bureaucratic service was less attractive, less of a guaranteed route to social improvement. The nobility clung on to the privileges they had carved out within the bureaucracy. Indeed, noble pressure on official posts increased with the diminishing economic position of many nobles. They fought off the development of professional standards and criteria, such as emerged in France and Germany, and helped to turn jobs needed by impoverished nobles into jobs disdained by the noble office-holders themselves.

In general the *chinovnik* was relatively lowly paid: although ambassadors earned 50 000 roubles a year and ministers 18–23 000, directors of departments were paid only 7000 roubles and some senior bureaucrats as little as 1500. Only about 20 per cent of senior men were paid more than 1000 roubles, although 700–1000 roubles was considered the absolute minimum to maintain a middle-class lifestyle. Junior civil servants were notoriously badly paid, which encouraged ubiquitous corruption. Despite the pay, the service had its attractions because, in a state where movement from one social group to another was difficult, the bureaucracy offered the chance to advance through the Table of Ranks and gain some social prestige. However promotion was entirely a matter of seniority. The social status of the civil servant was very visible, since elaborate uniforms, different for each grade, were worn. But the bureaucrat had no security of tenure. The term used to denote a civil servant, *chinovnik*, was employed by Turgenev to describe a fair-weather friend. Whereas in Germany the bureaucracy was respected, in Russia the institution was treated with some social and intellectual condescension. Turgenev described a typical senior official, Panshin, in his *Home of the Gentry*. The son of a retired cavalry captain and notorious gambler, Panshin received from his father no money but a cultivated education and recommendations into the most illustrious aristocratic circles:

> The promised land of high society spread out before him. Panshin soon learned the secret of such a life; he learned how to imbue himself with real respect for its rules, how to talk nonsense with quasi-facetious importance and give the appearance of considering everything important to be nonsense, how to dance to perfection and dress in the English style . . . He was only in his 28th year and already the holder of a post at court with an exceptionally high rank in the civil service.[61]

In short, as a bureaucrat on course for the top, Panshin was determined to promote his career in a manner guaranteed to succeed, by being so dazzlingly negative that no one noticed the absence of decision. With senior men like Panshin the problems of the Russian autocracy are easy to understand, but with eloquent intellectuals like Turgenev against them, as so many were, one almost feels sympathy for the bureaucrats.

In the middle of the eighteenth century most Russian bureaucrats, at all levels, were sons of men who had also served the state. In the upper reaches 90 per cent were from noble families. In theory, the Table of Ranks might have reduced noble dominance, since any civil servant could aspire to noble status with promotion, but a law of 1727 excluded peasants from bureaucratic service and successive legislation tried to keep out non-nobles, or at least limit their chances of promotion. Such legislation had only partial success and the social composition of the bureaucracy, at all grades, changed very little up to 1850, when 25-33 per cent of senior officials had non-noble fathers. There was some change in the type of noble at the top of the service. In 1755 40 per cent of senior central government officials owned 500 or more serfs; by 1850 40 per cent owned none, but 20 per cent still owned large numbers. Thus the civil service was becoming less the preserve of a landowning élite, but the transformation was very gradual.[62] A fair number of commoners achieved hereditary nobility in this century. In 1755 25 per cent of men in the 8th rank, where hereditary nobility was conferred, were from non-noble families. The nervousness of traditional landed nobles at the inroads being made by the bourgeoisie led to a change in the rank which secured hereditary nobility, from eight to five. By the 1850s there were about as many commoners at the 5th rank (33 per cent) as in 1755, but between the 8th and the 6th nearly 50 per cent were commoners, denied noble status by the legal change. It has been calculated that between 1825 and 1845 20000 men were ennobled by state service, not a large proportion of the male noble population of 113093 in 1858, but the result of steady growth.

In mid-century 40 per cent of Russian bureaucrats came from a background not dissimilar to that of Turgenev's hero. They were sons of nobles, mostly of modest means, but adequate to provide the higher education necessary for advancement. A further third were sons of minor bureaucrats or army officers, while 20 per cent were sons of priests, anxious to rise in the world. Only 2 per cent were sons of merchants. Senior posts mostly went to the noble-born (70-80 per cent), 42 per cent of whom were from bureaucratic noble families with no serfs or land.[63] The real social divide between bureaucrats turned more on wealth than birth. In studying their social origins, the relevant question is not whether bureaucrats were noble or non-noble, but what sort of noble they were. The noble who worked as a clerk in the provinces had little in common with the big serf-owner who ruled the roost as a minister in St Petersburg, and, however hard the former worked, he would never challenge the minister for his job. The very successful senior men often owned large numbers of serfs, but by the 1850s 21 per cent of ministers owned none, and the high-fliers did not consider the purchase of land or serfs an advantage for themselves or their careers. Nor did they try to marry their children into serf-owning families. There was no intermarriage between bureaucrat nobles who were big estate-owners and those who were not. There was a distinct élite of career officials, another of officials whose families owned large estates. Money was a different matter. Senior officials habitually came from wealthy families. Wealthy landed nobles however tended to prefer an army career for their sons and it is noticeable that civil servants who had migrated from the army were more likely to be serf-owners. Poor pay and lack of real respect and authority left most bureaucratic posts by 1900 in the hands of low-ranking nobles or the middle class. In the second half of the century the number of officials quadrupled and between half and two-thirds were middle class. In 1897 78 per cent of officials in the bottom five ranks were middle class. The need for some professional skill and training at this level made it unlikely that sons of impoverished nobles would either apply or qualify for such jobs, hence the preponderance of sons of merchants, professionals and minor civil servants. As in Germany, there were groups within the middle class who would not be considered for official appointments, notably Catholics and Jews. It was assumed that senior posts would be filled by nobles but by 1900 a substantial number of provincial civil servants came from lower-middle-class and peasant backgrounds via the universities.

The access of non-nobles to the senior levels of the Russian bureaucracy did not change dramatically; the nature of the service itself altered, but very gradually. We have used the term 'bureaucracy' to describe the administration of the empire, but it lacked rational structure before the 1860s and what existed conformed to a Weberian definition only in the theoretical assumption that the service possessed some sort of single direction. Slowly the bureaucracy became recognised as a career involving certain educational prerequisites, thus conforming to the situation in the rest of Europe. In 1755 half of the central administrators were retired soldiers, and in the provinces the proportions were even higher, which is a clear indication of just how indigent the poorer nobles were, for the pecuniary rewards were very small in the provinces. During the nineteenth century the numbers of ex-soldiers fell, though in the senior ranks (5 and above) 35 per cent of officials remained military in origin. By the middle of the century most minor provincial officials were life-long bureaucrats, but top jobs were even more well endowed with ex-officers than in central government. From 1827 higher educational standards, involving basic literacy and numeracy, acted as a filter. As the numbers of noble, virtually untrainable ex-officers fell, professional skills also improved. It was in this respect that the first half of the century was a real turning-point. In 1755 67 per cent of those in senior posts had received no formal education and only 9 per cent (six men) had attended university, abroad because there were no native universities at this time. Consequently the educational attainments of civil servants were few; overall, 75 per cent had no formal education and anyone whose father could afford a private tutor would not consider such a job.

Aware of the ignorance of their public servants, tsars tried to remedy the situation. Peter the Great had tried to provide on-the-job training for noble bureaucrats and to exclude commoners, but neither objective was successful. The age at which young men became apprentices rose from 14 in the eighteenth century to 17 around 1800 and 22 by the 1840s, presumably with beneficial results for the level of literacy, although boys began to enter the service at a later age before educational standards were introduced. In 1828 graduates of district schools were given preferential entry, *gymnasium* graduates even more so, while a man who knew Greek was employed immediately at the 14th rank. Those who graduated from a *lycée* or a university were offered even more preferential terms. High-fliers began their careers at the Tsarskoe Selo *lycée*, the School of Jurisprudence or, less desirably, a university. The first two were restricted to nobles, and universities also tried to exclude commoners. Thus in the first half of the century, there was an unprecedented development of an educated élite. Noble recruits were always promoted one rank faster than commoners, so that the latter never overcame the disadvantages of their birth, even if they were well educated. Despite this, commoners who succeeded in embarking on an administrative career would do well. More nobles were high achievers simply because more nobles entered the service initially. Graduates of Tsarskoe Selo and the School of Jurisprudence occupied up to 28 per cent of senior jobs by the mid-century, while a further 30 per cent were held by former military men, of whom 80 per cent were nobles. Commoners could enter the bureaucracy as apprentices, as graduates of a university or technical institute, or from another career, especially teaching or medicine; 37 per cent of non-nobles in top posts entered by this last route. Thus the civil servant became positively more educated, but the service itself was no more democratic or open. Education did not run deep. If specific training was increasingly required for some posts and a university education for senior appointments, very much as in France and Germany, the vast expansion in the number of bureaucrats meant that education standards of recruits were not universally high. In 1894–5 over half of the more than 4000 new men had neither university nor secondary education.

Compared with France and Germany the Russian bureaucracy had very little sense of corporate identity. It was heterogeneous, very divided and never threatened to challenge the ruler on political issues in the way that bureaucrats in Prussia did up to 1848. The gulf between central and local government was immense, both in pay and in prospects. There were very few senior posts in the provinces, only 1–2 per cent at rank 5 or above: a governor, his deputy and at the most two or three other jobs. But in St Petersburg, 15 per cent of officials were at rank 5 or above. Except at the top, provincial salaries were much lower; officials would be five or six years older than comparable men at the centre. Only 13 per cent of provincials had advanced education, compared with 50 per cent at the centre. In St Petersburg many middle-grade officials were well educated and confident of further promotion, whereas in the provinces 92 per cent of middle-grade men had received secondary education at the most, and had no prospect whatsoever of promotion. The provinces were another world, usually staffed by local men who did not move to other areas. Senior provincial posts went to men shipped in from St Petersburg or the army; 60 per cent of upper-middle-ranking jobs went the same way. A provincial bureaucrat could expect only a truncated career in his region. A few might move into central government, but only 20 per cent of central government jobs went to provincials. Thus an ambitious man would not begin his career out of the capital. There were also social cleavages between the centre and the localities. There were up to 20 per cent more non-nobles in the lower reaches of provincial administration.[64]

The concept of career structures was slower to emerge in Russia than elsewhere. In 1800 most senior posts still went to retired army officers, whereas by mid-century 60 per cent of top jobs were held by men who had spent their whole career in the service. The bureaucracy grew rapidly, from 10 500 in 1755, of whom 2500 were in rank 14 or higher, to 38 000 in 1800 and 113 990 in 1856, of whom 25 per cent were in rank 14 or above.[65] Despite Gogol's accusations in *The Inspector General*, Russia actually had comparatively few bureaucrats. It was reckoned in 1910 that there were 176 official posts for every 10 000 inhabitants of France, 126 in Germany, but only 62 in European Russia and only 40 if the whole empire was included. Of these just under 64 000 were *chinovniks* and just over 160 000 of lower status. Such figures are tantalisingly inconclusive of course because there is no way of knowing whether like was being compared with like. Were all of those paid by the public purse included and, if not, were those excluded the same in each country? Indeed until 1897 one could only guess the size of the Russian bureaucracy. In 1897 the state administration employed 260 000, of whom 105 000 were in the police.[66]

Our conclusion on this theme of the relationship between the bureaucracy and the middle classes must be a statement of diversity, diversity based less on the job the bureaucrat was being asked to do than on the general conditions in each state. Everywhere the role of the state expanded in an unprecedented manner. There were armies of officials, fulfilling a growing range of functions. The expansion in numbers swelled the lower and middling reaches even more than the senior levels, but the likelihood of promotion outside a man's 'natural' station in life actually decreased. The hold of regional notables was tenacious, particularly in France and Italy. In Italy the compliance of regional élites after unification was customarily won through 'favours'; public institutions and private patronage were therefore closely interwoven. This phenomenon was beginning to weaken towards the end of the century as the electorate expanded, and it was far less influential in more economically advanced areas like the Po valley. In the more backward south, local fiefs remained intact in 1914. Thus centralised bureaucracies were often far less powerful than they looked or desired to be.

It is clear that the nineteenth-century emphasis on educational qualifications did not open up opportunities to the talented poor, even to the ambitious son of an industrialist, although more sons of entrepreneurial families were gaining senior posts in Germany by the end of the century and in Italy it was politically essential for the state to provide for the educated and otherwise unemployable lower middle class. More education did not mean either the democratisation of education or increased social mobility, as we shall see later.[67] Indeed the increased demand for educational qualifications excluded men from humble families, who, in Prussia in particular, had previously made headway as civil servants. More years spent without an income was a luxury affordable only to the rich. Hence, as bureaucrats became more professional, the senior levels of bureaucracies became totally and exclusively the preserve of the élite. In Russia the level of education, especially higher education, rose dramatically, but it had little impact on the social composition of the bureaucracy. Rather it produced a political crisis later in the century, when radical university students expressed violent hostility to the narrow, rigid, civil service career for which their education supposedly prepared them. In Russia senior posts were still dominated by nobles, but fewer were military men and high officials were far more likely to be divorced from the land and totally dependent on the state for both their job and their social prestige. Elsewhere access to the most senior posts generally became more rigid, more likely to go to a member of an established noble family in Germany, to remain firmly in the hands of the wealthy notables in France and to go to a northerner in Italy. On the other hand a vastly expanded spectrum of middle-range and technical posts were filled by bourgeois applicants, some of whom had been classically educated, some in more modern or technical subjects. Opportunities for the lower middle class also grew rapidly, but were strictly confined to clerical and other lowly functions. As bureaucracies expanded, they became far more hierarchical, emphasising the impassable ravines between different groups whom we, for convenience, lump together as middle class. Access to the middle class may have been open to all, from the standpoint of a notable like Guizot,[68] but access to the glittering prizes of power and influence became, if anything, even more limited.

6. Professional Armies and Civilian Militias

I had no choice . . . every career was barred to the future Marquis de Claviers-Granchamps. Yes, barred. Foreign affairs? Barred. My father, at least, would have been accepted by the Empire. Today we are no longer desired. The Council of State? Barred. The Administration? Barred. Can you see a noble acting as a Prefect of a Department? . . . The Army alone was left me.

It might be assumed that the officer corps of the European armies became increasingly middle class during the nineteenth century, but, as this quotation shows, there were pressing practical reasons, in France at least, which directed the nobility into the republican army. Common to all of these states by 1914 was the presupposition that an army would be completely committed to the regime which it served, and willing to repress domestic riot as well as fight foreign enemies, but this was far from axiomatic earlier in the century. All of these countries had standing, professional armies, recruited partly by conscription, with officer corps drawn from the élite and serving as privileged volunteers. Technical competence was needed more and more, particularly in the artillery, and specific technical and scientific training was increasingly required. The technical corps attracted not aristocratic officers, like Claviers-Granchamps, but men from middle-class backgrounds who had followed a 'modern' syllabus at secondary school and received a specific scientific and technical training subsequently. They were often patronised by their aristocratic fellows and were themselves inclined to overplay an 'aristo' role, but they were always inferior in the military hierarchy to the traditional officers. Thus by the end of the century European armies had two officer corps, divided on class lines.

The way in which the army was regarded was crucial to its social composition. Such norms were strongly influenced by political developments in each country. In Prussia a central conflict in the century was essentially between the aristocracy and the middle classes both to control the army and to determine its character and role. The army had close ties with the monarchy, while maintaining an almost semi-autonomous position in the state. In the nineteenth century the reserve force, or *landwehr*, became the bastion of middle-class liberalism. The creation of an elected *landtag* after 1848 posed a challenge to the independence of the army. The battle for control of both the regular army and the reserve dominated the 1850s and early 1860s. In France the needs of war in the 1790s created a conscript 'citizens' army', while the fear of popular disorder at home prompted the setting up of a citizens' militia, or national guard. The guard became a symbol of the 1789 revolution, precious to the bourgeoisie, but embarrassing to the wealthier, politically dominant groups, due to the propensity of some members to rehearse their traditional political radicalism by supporting popular unrest rather than suppressing it during the nineteenth century. In Italy rivalry between the concept of a professional army and the notion of a volunteer citizens' formation was played out dramatically in the risings and wars of the Risorgimento. Everywhere the gap between officers and men was immense, but equally great was the divide between senior and junior officers. This was particularly marked in Russia, where the ordinary soldier was never more of a serf than when he was also a soldier and where the block on promotion for junior officers became more, not less, immovable during the nineteenth century.

The attempt to maintain the aristocratic character of the officer corps was pronounced, and nowhere more so than in Prussia. The participation of non-nobles was specifically discouraged in the Prussian officer corps in the eighteenth century, both by Frederick William I and Frederick II. Both tried to consolidate the support of the Junker nobility by making the army their preserve. But comprehensive defeat by Napoleon convinced later governments of the need for change. Many noble serving officers were well past their prime. In 1806 four generals were over eighty. In 1808 a War Ministry was formed under Scharnhorst, himself the son of a peasant. In future, promotion was to be by merit and a new military structure was introduced. After 1813 universal conscription was the norm. Men served for three years in the regular army, then two in the active reserve, followed by seven years in a *landwehr* or reserve army. Finally they would spend another seven years in a second levy of the *landwehr*. The reserve was independent of the regular army and rapidly became the cornerstone of bourgeois liberal hopes, and later myths, to the chagrin of regular officers. Opportunities for middle-class promotion in the regular army dried up after 1815 when the nobility resumed control.[1] But the *landwehr* remained the pride of middle-class liberals, a bulwark against the overweening influence of the professional soldier in Prussian society. Being a *landwehr* officer became a pinnacle of bourgeois ambition and the institution was treasured by the middle classes as the personification of civilian domination of the military. The lengthy period of peace prevented the regular officers asserting their power over that of the *landwehr*, as they would have done in war. The increasing social gulf between middle-class *landwehr* officers and noble regular army officers was accentuated by the political divide between the liberalism of the former and the reactionary attitudes of the latter. The year 1848 both brought the rivalry to a head and exposed the tendentious and fallacious character of middle-class liberalism. When property rights and middle-class privileges seemed to be under siege, as in the latter days of the Frankfurt Parliament and the radical fag-end of the Prussian assembly, the better-off middle classes welcomed the use of troops to terminate both assemblies, leaving them on shifting sands, both intellectually and in practical politics. Middle-class fears of popular unrest lent an air of unreality to the final struggle over the role of the army. William I battled with the majority liberals in the assembly, striving to eliminate the semi-autonomous status of the *landwehr* and promote the standing and power of the regular army, still somewhat shaken by his predecessor's refusal to let it fight against the revolutionaries in 1848. Although the liberals successfully blocked the growth of the army and its attempt to gain control over the *landwehr*, the fragile and illusory nature of their triumph was exposed by the tactics of Bismarck after 1862. The military victories of the regular army in 1863, 1866 and 1870 made its revived dominance unassailable. The period of regular service was extended, the autonomy of the officer corps strengthened, officer selection became rigidly aristocratic and the new elected assembly lost virtually all control of military budgets and planning. The status of the *landwehr* officer ironically grew as the actual power he exercised plummeted. It was said of many a well-heeled and influential bourgeois that his reserve officer's commission was more precious to him than anything, certainly more precious than his political rights. But the middle-class reserve officer had effectively become a servile pawn and noisy champion of the regular army, a conservative nationalist, poles apart from his predecessor early in the century.

The German officer corps became increasingly aristocratic and predictably and predominantly Prussian, both in its composition and tone. The Military Cabinet, at the peak of power through its close contact with the Emperor, was almost exclusively noble in membership. The General Staff, an élite group of about 240 in 1888 to which ambitious officers aspired, was mainly noble and nearly 200 of its members were Prussian. Entry was via examination to the War Academy. There was a positive preference for cavalrymen, the branch of the service more attractive to the nobility. In 1906 60 per cent of the General Staff were noble and their numbers were growing. However, it should be noted that a few outstanding officers, like Ludendorff and Groener, were able to rise through merit. Furthermore within the officer corps as a whole the proportion of noble entrants was much lower than their overwhelming presence in senior posts might indicate. In 1867 49 per cent of Prussian officer cadets taking ensigns' examinations were noble. Of the rest, most were from the upper reaches of the middle class, primarily from the old educated, professional and bureaucratic families. Of those who actually passed the ensigns' examination in that year 33 per cent were sons of army officers, 20 per cent of landowners, 26 per cent of senior officials, 7 per cent of clergy and teachers, 6 per cent of minor officials and only 5 per cent from merchant and manufacturing backgrounds. In 1912–13 the proportion of merchants' and manufacturers' sons had risen to 15 per cent, while the number of landowners' and army officers' sons had fallen. Higher officials, academics, doctors and clergy still totalled 40 per cent.[2] The actual proportion of aristocratic officers had fallen from 65 per cent in the Prussian army in 1860 to 30 per cent in the German army on the eve of the First World War.

The fall in the proportion of officers who were noble and the rise of the middle-class officer was deplored by contemporaries, who feared that it would weaken the army. There were complaints that sons of traditional officers' families were preferring more lucrative business careers and sons of wealthy industrialists were replacing them, but less out of a desire to serve than through vanity. However the proportion of nobles remained much higher than their actual numbers in the population would justify, and unquestionably nobles were promoted faster to higher ranks than their middle-class contemporaries. Even in the infantry regiments, considered less desirable to the best families, only 39 of the 190 generals were bourgeois in 1909. Four years later 53 per cent of officers with the rank of colonel and above were aristocrats. Cavalry and guards regiments were almost entirely aristocratic. However, regiments where special skills and technical training were required attracted very different personnel. Artillery regiments, growing in numbers and importance with the development of new types of warfare, were staffed entirely by bourgeois officers.

A speech of the kaiser's in 1890 was suggestive of the poor reception that the increase in the number of bourgeois officers received within the military hierarchy. He urged social solidarity among the better-off groups to counter the spread of social democracy:

> I look for men who will build the future of Germany not only among the offspring of the aristocratic families of the country and the sons of my gallant officers and civil servants who have formed the keystone of the Officer Corps, but also among the sons of honourable bourgeois houses in which love for King and Country and a heartfelt devotion to the profession of arms and Christian culture are planted and cherished.

But the wealthy bourgeois was expected to assume aristocratic attitudes. Many sons of industrialists were turned down by regiments because of their background. Their exclusion was facilitated by the process of election of new officers by the other regimental officers. Middle-class aspirants were heartily despised. They were under suspicion for their advanced education. 'Character' was reckoned to be more important than cleverness in a soldier.[3] Educated officers must have seemed a real threat to the Old Guard. In 1890 only 35 per cent of officers had the *abitur*; by 1912 this figure had risen to 65 per cent. Some were technically qualified artillery officers, but many were graduates from the *gymnasium*, who hoped that their classical education would be accepted as some form of substitute for noble birth. Criticism of middle-class officers was so pronounced that the top brass actually opposed further expansion of the size of the army to match population growth because the number of aristocratic candidates for officer grades was too low to fuel a larger army. Schlieffen, Moltke and Ludendorff were in a minority in their attempt to counter a view which clearly placed social issues above the military viability of the army. Their opponents were convinced that an army with a high proportion of middle-class officers would be politically unreliable. Shortly before the outbreak of war the 'aristocratic' case was succinctly put by Bethmann-Hollweg:

> We would not be able to meet these greatly increased requirements without lowering our standards by using men from unsuitable classes to increase the officer corps and this, quite apart from other dangers, would expose the army to democratisation.[4]

There was also increasing resistance to the appointment of middle-class Jewish officers. At the time of the Franco-Prussian War, there had been a number of Jewish serving officers in the army, but by 1910 there were none. The general tone of German nationalist ideas nurtured anti-Semitism and Jewish officers were attacked on the grounds of racial incapacity. A Jew would not even be elected to the mess, and thus did not even reach first base for a commission. In contrast, despite the Dreyfus Affair, France had 720 Jewish officers, the Austrian army 2179 and even in Italy, with a much smaller Jewish population, there were 500. All manner of excuses were used to justify their exclusion, including lack of 'social tact'. Some were offered the prospect of a commisson if they accepted Christian baptism. Serving Jewish soldiers were persecuted in petty ways too. They were not allowed to obtain kosher food and some were prevented from attending the synagogue. Prejudice extended to the reserve too. Albert Goldschmidt-Rothschild, welcome at Court, with a fortune of 80 million marks and a generous benefactor to charitable causes, was refused the rank of a reserve officer despite the intervention of Chancellor Bülow. Opposition to middle-class Jewish officers was only abandoned with the outbreak of the First World War. Bavaria, with its separate army in peacetime, was more tolerant. There were 46 reserve officers and 42 other *landwehr* officers who were Jewish, some of whom were from other parts of Germany and had entered the Bavarian army because there was the chance of officer status.[5]

In Germany the assumption that fundamentally the army was

more a 'service' institution than a professional one intensified the idea that only officers of noble birth were intrinsically qualified for the most senior ranks. The growth of industrial society and accompanying working-class political aspirations exacerbated the perceived need of the wealthy, whatever the source of their fortune, to cling to traditional, even anachronistic, social norms. Middle-class officers enthusiastically accepted the aristocratic model and tolerated antediluvian derision of engineers and professionally quali-fied officers. The performance of the German army in the First World War reflected a profound acceptance of the ways in which the technical developments of industrialisation had transformed warfare. However, the unwillingness to expand the size of the army, because of the consequent need to dilute the aristocratic character of the officer corps, might have had even more dangerous military results than the feared political repercussions, had not technical changes and the imperatives of the First World War forced rapid expansion. In Germany the aristocratic ethos was sustained, but bourgeois professional and technical expertise prevailed:

> It was almost impossible to make a career except by serving in the armed forces; all the senior officers of state–ministers, senators, governors, were given over to military men, who were more prominent in the sovereign's eye than officials of civilian agencies.[6]

Russia's senior military men certainly had a role in civilian government quite beyond that in the other states looked at here. During the reign of Nicholas I, 61.5 per cent of ministers were generals or admirals (32 out of 52). Only ten had never served as army officers. The Senate was comparable; 83 per cent were senior officers in the 1820s, although the proportion had fallen by 20 per cent by 1846. The need to colonise and defend territory in the eighteenth century helps to explain the preponderance of military titles among provincial governors. Nearly all of the 77 incumbents after 1775 were army officers. Border provinces, predictably, were governed by army men, but in 1816 both Moscow and St Petersburg were assigned a new official, a military governor-general, and both remained under military rule for the rest of the reign of Alexander I.[7] In 1853 only twelve of the provinces of European Russia were under civilian governors. In fourteen others governors were either subordinate to a military superior, or under a military governor-general with responsibility for several provinces. A typical military governor was a noble of about 50, who had entered the army from a prestigious military academy, had seen some action, had personal links with the tsar or a top general, and had some experience of police work after transferring to the civil service. During the first half of the century, the role of the military in civil administration declined as the bureaucracy became increasingly a lifetime career. However, they retained a significant role and, in the more outlying provinces, a preponderant one. The civil and military bureaucracies remained more closely intertwined in Russia than elsewhere, although traditionally richer, landed, noble families sent their sons initially into the army, rather than the civil service.

The army was also dominant in terms of sheer numbers and cost. In 1808 it consumed 56 per cent of state expenditure.[8] Russia amassed an army of one million in the nineteenth century. Between 1 and 2 per cent of the eligible unprivileged payers of poll tax were conscripted, bringing in about 80 000 men each year. Wealthy middle-class merchants, like nobles, were exempt, and most members of the middle class and better-off peasants could bribe their way out, or buy a substitute. 'Awkward' serfs and convicted criminals would find no escape. It was a virtual life sentence of twenty-five years for the ordinary conscript, who might be enlisted at any age between 20 and 35. In contrast, officers were volunteers. The officers prided themselves on parades and conformism, and despised intelligence, education and any innovation. Most were nobles, who entered initially in the ranks, after little or no education, and would receive their first commission after a couple of years. An embarrassingly large number of very poor sons of gentry joined the army, for the sake of the family finances. For them, promotion from the ranks would be slow, but a well-connected fellow might be a major in his early twenties. Not uniquely, in Russia officers were obsessed with rank, in particular with the jump from captain to major, after which promotions were in the direct gift of the tsar. The privileges of senior officers were considerable. Provision of leave was more generous and they were better placed to obtain transfers. Their pay was much higher than that of subordinate officers. However, officers had to pay for their own horses, clothes and equipment, the totals being deducted at source. In the most desirable and privileged regiments expenses could easily outstrip pay. Those who had to live on their salary could be very poor and dependent on the charity of their colleagues. Some were as poor as their men. General Zakrevsky told how, as a junior serving in Lithuania in 1802, he had had to lodge in a henhouse and live off the eggs. Allowing for poetic as well as culinary licence, the gap between officers and men could be narrower than outside the services. Getting out of the henhouse was quicker if your father had held a commission. It has been calculated that a non-noble NCO would be promoted within four years if his father was an officer, but would have to wait for twelve if he was a civilian. The law thus provided for promotion according to social rank.

In 1800 most officers were noble, but there were huge differences within this category. Only a small proportion were from the wealthy élite of big landowners. In 1864 only 16 per cent of officers stationed in Moscow owned land. It is not easy to calculate the number of non-noble officers. In the 1850s about 50 per cent were from hereditary noble families, 35 per cent were sons of personal nobles, while 15 per cent were from non-noble backgrounds.[9] Promotion conveyed nobility on to the serving officer, whatever his background. Nicholas I was determined to restrict state service to the nobility and a decree of 1845 was designed to eliminate men of lower-class origins and poor education from all branches of state service. The decree was potentially very significant. Hereditary noble status was only to be conferred on staff officers, men with the rank of major and above, whereas previously ensigns qualified for a noble title. However the needs of the Crimean War nullified the long-term impact of this law. The officer corps was not a closed caste, but being a noble conveyed distinct advantages and most officers accepted the discrimination. Only sons of nobles could enrol in the élite Tsarskoe Selo *lyceum*, founded in 1811 to prepare boys for military or civil state service. The cadet schools and other military academies also restricted their intake to the nobility. During the century the attraction of the army for the sons of poor nobles decreased. Nicholas I, so intent on preserving the dominance of the nobility in the officer corps, was also keen to develop military education, which tended to torpedo his efforts to maintain the social exclusiveness of the officer corps, for the poorer nobles, who were the most willing recruits, had little or no formal education.

A positive attempt was made to improve the educational standards of the officer corps, or rather to introduce education standards. Nicholas I founded nine new cadet schools, which, during his reign, educated nearly 18 000 men of whom over 14 000 went on to become officers. But the cadet schools could not fill the 2000 vacancies in the officer corps each year, indeed they could only provide about 600 potential officers. Their graduates took up just under 40 per cent of the vacancies in the guards or the engineers, but line regiments could satisfy only one-sixth of their needs from the schools. Thus Nicholas' attempts to introduce examinations for commissions were impeded by a serious lack of basically educated officers. Many officers were promoted NCOs, most of whom were sons of very poor nobles. Defeat in the Crimea led to major changes. Non-nobles were allowed to enter officer-training schools and by 1871 12 per cent of their intake were commoners. Military service for the ranks was reduced in theory to fifteen years followed by ten in the reserve, while in reality the periods actually served dropped to between seven and thirteen years. The annual intake was set at 100 000 men. More significantly, noble and upper-middle-class exemption from conscription was withdrawn in 1875. Preference was to be given to educated and qualified candidates for commissions, nobility alone was no longer to be treated as the only real qualification for an officer. University graduates who volunteered were automatically made officers and served for only three months. Other educated volunteers would also qualify for exemptions, depending on the level of their education. Those conscripted, from whatever social class, would no longer be able to purchase a replacement.[10]

As in Germany, the increased emphasis on educational standards reflected the demands of modern warfare. The army itself grew to 4 million men by 1905 and the officer corps expanded from 27 000 in 1876 to 41 000 in 1897. By this date 50 per cent of officers were noble, 40 per cent in the infantry, 96 per cent in the cavalry. Guards officers represented a noble, landowning, hereditary caste. As in Germany, the officer corps of the artillery and engineers were very different from the more traditional regiments, where technical training was minimal. In the navy the line officers remained noble, but a separate corps of naval engineers and technical officers was recruited and these were almost exclusively middle class. They were trained in special naval engineering and shipbuilding schools, and the distinction between them and the traditional aristocratic officers was emphasised by the titles they received, which for many years were military rather than naval. Only the appellation of a naval officer was needed for his colleagues to know his social origins. In the army, guards officers, as in Germany, were noble, but a title alone was insufficient to sustain a commission, for salaries were meagre. There were traditional cadet schools, whose intake was restricted to the nobility. Russia had military training establishments, with titles similar to those specialised *grandes écoles* in Paris which educated the élite of France's army. There was a Mining Institute and Institute of Engineers of Ways and Communications, the former originally set up by Peter the Great, the latter in 1800. But like the School of Navigation and the various engineering schools these were, in the nineteenth century, chiefly fashionable finishing schools for the nobility, more concerned with social polish than technical expertise, as likely to turn out actors as engineers. The cadet schools began to admit any one with the necessary educational qualifications only in 1913. But outside the guards regiments, middle-class penetration of the officers corps was more rapid. In the 1860s 81 per cent of the students in the Moscow military schools were sons of hereditary nobles and 9 per cent were sons of personal nobles. By the late 1870s 45 per cent were hereditary nobles, 33 per cent sons of men with personal titles only, 13 per cent were middle class and 11 per cent sons of clergy. The collapse of the noble monopoly was then very rapid. Within ten years only 12 per cent were noble and there was even a 5 per cent peasant intake. By the outbreak of the First World War, nobles constituted only a minority of students in the military schools. In 1913 only 9 per cent were sons of hereditary nobles and a further 28 per cent were sons of personal nobles. An additional 28 per cent were middle class and 19 per cent were from peasant families, which would have been quite inconceivable 50 years earlier.[11]

The effect of this very rapid social transformation of the Russian army, unprecedented in any other European state we are studying, was to create massive areas of internal social tension. The senior command was even more socially distinct from the rest of the officers and men in Russia than elsewhere. The officer corps continued to describe itself as noble because there were no non-nobles with the rank of colonel or above, but there were few nobles among the junior officers. Although in theory educational attainments had replaced social status in decisions on promotion, the reality was very different. Non-nobles could qualify in the military schools, but their progress was very limited. There was no change in the social composition of the senior officer corps before 1914. Engineering regiments were looked down on and the cadet corps encouraged a caste spirit, especially in the guards, despite the reduction in their tangible privileges. Pay differentials remained huge, both between senior and junior officers and between officers and men. In 1905 the 1673 general officers cost the state 10.8 million roubles, while men received only 3–4 roubles a year. The social gulf between junior and senior officers was growing and in some ways was greater than that between officers and men. Officers, especially the more senior, were even more isolated from civil society than in the past, while their men were closer to civilian life, serving only for an average of four years. Conflict between senior and junior officers is vividly depicted in Solzhenitsyn's *August 1914*.[12] The massive social divide in the army was to contribute to the disasters of the war effort and even more was to be a major factor in the mutiny of officers and men, first in February and then in October 1917. Whereas in Germany middle-class officers often aped the senior noble leadership, in Russia the total block on promotion to senior posts for the middle class contributed to profound personal and professional frustration. Given these circumstances, it is perhaps not at all surprising that Trotsky had so little difficulty in constituting an officer corps for the Red Army from former Tsarist officers.

Prussia had its *landwehr*, which in the first half of the nineteenth century fulfilled for the middle classes the psychological needs of a citizens' militia, although it was in reality merely the reserve of the standing army. In France a militia, or national guard, grew out of the concern of middle-class property-owners with the degree of popular unrest which developed on the eve of the French Revolution. The Bourbon army was transformed into a national, partly conscript army from 1792, and the concept of a reserve was abortively attempted during the Restoration. The attitude of the French towards the civil militia depended on the favour with which the individual regarded the revolution. The national guard was a two-headed revolutionary ogre or patriotic symbol, according to one's politics. One head was the quintessential revolutionary, on guard, whether in Paris or small commune, against any manifestation of counter-revolutionary, religious or monarchist activity. The second head looked to preserve order and protect private property. The first head might be sans-culotte or it might be the representative of the poor Protestants of Nîmes hitting out at the old notables.[13] The second head was almost universally well-off and the owner of the property, blusteringly attentive to service in the guard only when civil disorder was in the air. The schizophrenic nature of the beast was echoed by its duties. The guard was expected to act as a reserve army; the Parisian guard tried to stem the Allied advance on Paris in 1814 and was ready to resist a Prussian attack on the city during the siege of 1870–1. In this sense it typified the revolutionary concept of the 'nation-in-arms', a classless, patriotic notion. Additionally the guard was used to maintain order; the Parisian guard was used in joint patrols with Allied troops in 1814 to hold the local population in check. The middle-class guardsman who dominated the officer corps tolerated his role as an auxiliary policeman when times were hazardous. In quiet times he was less willing to turn out for his twice-weekly patrol and it was noticeable that the Parisian shopkeeper-guardsman began to send his shop assistant as a substitute when the Restoration seemed secure. The Rennes guard was rapidly transformed into 50 former Napoleonic soldiers, 'substituting' for a daily fee of 26 sous. In wartime or during periods of social disorder, middle-class guardsmen were reassured and patriotic in their 130-franc pants and 60-franc helmets and the weapons they had also to provide for themselves, but the frequent banquets and subscriptions of peacetime were costly and Restoration government demands that the guard should participate in religious festivals were resented. When the middle-class property-owner could see no further purpose in the guard it faded away, but he kept his uniform and weapons in case of future need. Thus after 1821 there was no guard except in larger towns, and the same was true during the July Monarchy from the mid-1830s onward. But the guard remained a potent patriotic memory and also a symbol of perceived local rights and grievances.

In the July Days of 1830 the guard was speedily and spontaneously reorganised, having been dissolved by Charles X, humiliated after a revue of the Parisian batallions in 1827. Both in Paris and the provinces the resurrected institution was less in the van of revolution than anxious to control the riotous inclinations of the less well-off, suffering from the combined effects of high food prices and industrial recession.[14] The new Orleanist monarchy, far less fearful than the Bourbons of the civil militia, restored to the guard its old revolution-ary right to elect its officers by universal male suffrage. The main consequence of this decision was to ensure that, as patriotic enthusiasm waned, the guard became the province of the lower-middle-class urban radical. February 1848 saw the revived guard occupy its old role, part insurgent, part policeman, but in June 1848 it was apparent that the Parisian guard represented very different interests from its provincial counterpart. The artisans of the Parisian guard often joined with the insurgents in the June Days, desperate for the measures of social reform and economic regeneration which the newly elected Constituent Assembly, filled with old notables, was determined to smother. The provincial middle-class guardsmen, on the other hand, horrified at the cost of Parisian public assistance, enthusiastically supported the Assembly in crushing the June Days. The contradiction between the insurgent role and the policeman function had turned into a conflict between Paris and the provinces. Louis-Napoleon cautiously licensed only selected bourgeois guards and did not even permit them to elect their own officers.[15] Finally in 1870 the Parisian guard was stretched to a peak of patriotic endeavour during the siege and collapsed to a nadir of frustrated radical nationalism when faced by Thiers' peace terms and conditions for the return of normality in the capital. The result was that the central committee of the Parisian guard called for the election of a Commune for Paris, reminiscent of the 1790s. But in 1871 the by now predominantly artisan guard was even more out-of-tune with the rest of France than in 1848 and Thiers unhesitatingly used the army to destroy the Communard rebellion and subsequently dissolve the guard.[16] From its inception the guard had been ambivalent and ambiguous in its attitude to law and order, in civil disturbances not infrequently on the opposite site to the standing army. More than any other institution the guard symbolised the aspirations and disappointments of elements within the lower middle class; viticulturalists, silk weavers and Parisian artisans. It became an embarrassing champion of perceived revolutionary tradition in a country where, even when democratic principles were adopted, the attitudes of a wealthy minority continued to dominate.

The regular army was not without its schizophrenic image too. Public gardens displayed notices saying 'No dogs, no whores, no servants and no soldiers',[17] yet the most prestigious of the *grandes écoles*, the Polytechnique, specifically prepared men for a military career. On the eve of the 1789 revolution the royal army was 60 per cent artisan in the ranks, but noble dominance of the officer corps increased during the century and was a contentious issue. By the mid-eighteenth century only 5–10 per cent of officers directly commissioned were non-nobles and this minority were pariahs. Even more beyond the pale were the up to 10 per cent who were promoted from the ranks. The posts of captain and colonel were venal and a cavalry regiment could set a man back up to 120 000 frs. Officers' salaries, on the other hand, were far from princely and a private income was essential to keep up appearances. Poorer nobles often had to enlist in the ranks. Only a noble who had been presented at Court qualified to proceed beyond the grade of colonel. In 1789 only nine of 196 lieutenant-generals were not noble and of the other generals only 20 per cent lacked a title, and they had aristocratic pedigrees. Only six of the infantry colonels were in a similar category. The increased determination to exclude commoners was resented and a source of considerable acrimonious debate after defeat in the Seven Years' War. The Choiseul Ministry began a programme of army reform in 1761. Attempts to reduce the disproportionate number of officers displeased poorer provincial noble families who depended upon the army to provide a career for their sons. Venality was gradually reduced so that by 1790, when actually abolished, it survived only in a few cavalry regiments. The Segur decree of 1781 restricted direct entry at an officer grade to men with four generations of nobility behind them, which lessened the complaints of poorer noble families. Twelve provincial military schools were founded, offering 600 scholarships to such families. One man thus attracted was Napoleon Bonaparte. Attempts to make the officer corps not only the preserve of the nobility but of one particular section were resented both by more recently ennobled families and by commoners. The *cahiers de doléances* of 1789 demanded that officers be chosen by merit and not because of their family background.

Many officers and men resented their use as police to suppress popular unrest in 1788 and the number of desertions grew. In 1789 soldiers deserted to join the newly formed national guard and on 14 July only one of the six batallions of the French Guards remained loyal to the king; the others took part in the storming of the Bastille. Between August 1789 and 1791 possibly half of the capital's 4000 national guardsmen were army deserters, eager both to earn a better wage and also to demonstrate their enthusiasm for the revolution. Relations between noble officers and men deteriorated; there were demands for the expulsion of certain officers. In 1790 men of the garrison in Nancy became convinced that some sort of aristocratic plot was afoot and arrested their officers, raided the arsenal and handed over weapons to the national guards. The National Assembly, anxious to keep the army together, authorised a military attack on the mutineers in which a hundred were killed. At this stage, criticism of the attitude of noble officers was increasing, but few officers had emigrated, although many took prolonged leave in the autumn and winter of 1789–90. The Flight to Varennes clarified the king's hostility to the revolutionary assembly and by August 1791 1500 officers had refused to take the new oath to the assembly, their departure leaving some units with no senior staff. By the end of 1791 60 per cent of officers had emigrated. Unprecedented promotion opened up for NCOs who had risen from the ranks after many years' service. In 1792 over 2000 soldiers became officers and the new officers, unlike the old, knew their men well. The initial effect of such promotion was to halve the number of middle-class soldiers, because such individuals, literate and reasonably articulate, were raised from the ranks much faster than in previous years. The social composition of the army became more representative of the nation as a whole, although the numbers from industrial or commercial middle-class families continued to be very small. Noble numbers fell fast. The declaration of war in 1792 provoked more noble resignations. To cope with the pressure of foreign invasion and civil war the revolutionaries encouraged the formation of volunteer units, the idea of the *levée en masse*, the nation-in-arms as opposed to the professional army of the Bourbons.[18]

It quickly became apparent that the professional corps was vital and the volunteers and line regiments were merged. Each department had to provide a certain number of volunteers each year, or select men by lot if necessary, which it was. The unlucky could pay a substitute, often a former soldier. There was no more enthusiasm for service in the ranks than before the revolution. In 1798 only 25 per cent of the target number was reached and in 1811 alone 66 000 deserters were arrested. The idea of conscription gradually came to be accepted. By 1830 only 2 per cent were defaulting. In 1848 25 per cent of the army were conscripts and another 25 per cent substitutes, often former soldiers, while 50 per cent remained volunteers. Conscription often brought in more men than were needed. Among the volunteers 50 per cent were middle class, one-third were working men and one-fifth peasants. After defeat in 1870–1 and the disbanding of the national guard, full universal conscription was introduced, with a five-year period of service. The scheme was not, however, egalitarian. A man could volunteer shortly before he was due to be called up, and as long as he could afford the 1500 frs. needed for uniform and equipment he would be released after one year. This system, which made the middle classes more equal than others, was abandoned in 1905 when all exemptions, for instance for priests and teachers, were brought to an end and everyone was obliged to serve for two years.[19]

The revolution challenged, but did not eliminate, the privileged position of the nobility within the officer corps. Two principles dominated promotion: election and seniority. All corporals were to be elected by the men and two-thirds of all officers between sergeant and lieutenant-colonel were also elected. The rest were promoted on seniority. By 1793 70 per cent of the officers were enlisted men, but in the more senior grades the proportion was still small. The officer corps was still predominantly upper class. In 1793 up to 20 per cent of captains and lieutenants were still of noble birth. But in general the wealthy middle class had replaced the nobles. Among the field-grade officers 40 per cent were sons of professional men, officials, etc. and 20 per cent of regimental officers had fathers in the liberal professions. Before the revolution these men would have remained in the very junior officer grades. Lower-middle-class and lower-class soldiers also secured undreamed-of advancement, although it should be emphasised that all were career soldiers whose army service was well advanced and that very few were uneducated. Clearly the unprecedented activity of the army during 22 years of war made promotion, even by seniority, fairly rapid. The army came to be seen as the way up the social ladder, a route which inevitably was blocked by peace, the end of the Empire and the return of the Bourbons. The military tunic gave way to the black cassock for a young man like Julien Sorel, ambitious to make his way in the world.

The imperial military traditions were effaced as far as was possible. Imperial regiments were replaced by infantry regiments recruited and organised on a departmental basis. The continuity of cavalry, artillery and other regiments was likewise deliberately broken. Military considerations were replaced by social and political dictates. Wherever possible *emigrés* who wanted to join the army were engaged and promoted. A commission was set up to examine the imperial officer corps, in which the smoothest talkers with the most influential patrons survived.[20] Chaos was averted by the appointment of

Gouvion St Cyr as Minister of War in 1817. One of Napoleon's marshals and a known liberal, he introduced a working compromise and a framework of organisation and promotion which was to survive with minor modifications until after the 1871 war. France was to have a professional, national army, not just the king's army. Officers were not to be appointed just on the whim of the monarch. A soldier had to serve for two years before he was eligible for promotion to officer status or he had to have attended military college and passed the required examinations. Two-thirds of officers were to come from the colleges, one-third were to be promoted from the ranks. The king could still dismiss a man without an explanation and some leapfrogged the system. Many Bonapartist officers who had been retired on half-pay at the Restoration were brought back because of acute shortages, and rivalry between them and more royalist appointees was rife. Some tried to have it both ways, like the batallion commander who sported an eagle under his fleur-de-lis emblem and those officers who organised Carbonari units in some regiments in the early twenties.

Initially a reserve was planned, but this was abandoned in the mid-1820s. Subsequently men were required to serve for eight years and the army became increasingly separated from civil society, although the need to lodge a proportion of each departmental contingent with local families in fact retained links, not always of a harmonious nature. In the early years of the Restoration the army was regarded by élite society with a mixture of suspicion and disdain, but the Spanish campaign was a success and the army was transformed into the king's army. Military uniform became fashionable at Court; even the duchesse d'Angoulême acquired a military boyfriend. Links were established with the Church. Louis XVIII consecrated regimental flags at Notre-Dame. Chaplains were appointed with the rank of captain, although they were not well received. The royal family associated themselves closely with the military college at St Cyr and right-wing generals spoke of the Algerian expedition as a crusade. The symbol of the nation became a privileged minority with a distinctly aristocratic, anti-bourgeois, anti-civilian ethos, even though the officer corps contained Napoleonic veterans and career soldiers from the middle classes.[21]

The aristocratic image of the officer corps gave way to a more bourgeois one for the duration of the July Monarchy, but with the aristocratic tinge re-emerging in the 1860s. In reality a far higher proportion of officers were promoted from the ranks than St Cyr originally intended. In 1824 75 per cent were Napoleonic veterans, mostly from very modest origins, and this tradition of promotion from the ranks remained potent. Between 1821 and 1831, of just under 4500 promotions to sub-lieutenant nearly 2000 were college graduates and 2500 were from the ranks.[22] In cavalry regiments, which were seen as the most 'aristocratic' sectors, the number of men promoted from the ranks was sometimes higher than in the infantry. In 1854 the first cavalry regiment included ten officers who were college graduates, 34 from the ranks. Such figures do not, however, indicate that the army offered limitless opportunities to the son of a minor official, artisan or peasant. Although the majority of officers were from very modest backgrounds, their actual movement through the military hierarchy was equally modest. It took about twelve years' service to reach the officer grade and few rose above the rank of captain and chevalier in the legion of honour. It was not the career for an ambitious lad with no connections. Stendhal's Lucien Leuwen, *polytechnicien* and son of a rich businessman, chose the army as a protest against the materialism of his times: 'I will only make war over cigars . . . I will be a pillar of the military cafe in a miserable garrison of a little, ill-paved town.' The army did not offer either monetary rewards or an exciting career. Poor pay and boredom help to explain the rash of support for the Carbonari in the early 1820s. In the mid-century a sergeant received only about 1 franc a day, a captain up to 2760 frs. a year. A sub-lieutenant earned about the same as a primary school teacher. A man had to serve a minimum of four years in each grade before he could be considered for promotion, and two-thirds were promoted on age not merit. A man would probably be in his mid-forties before he reached the rank of captain. Few could afford to marry. Until the end of the nineteenth century an NCO could not marry unless his wife had a dowry of at least 5000 frs. An officer had to submit to a lengthy investigation of his wife's family and income before he married.

There was an impassable divide between the man who rose from the ranks and the college-educated officer. The former remained close to the soldiers and had little social contact with the other officers. Money, not birth alone, made the difference. In France there was no officer tradition like that of the Junkers in Prussia. The majority of officers were not following a family tradition. Only one-sixth of those trained at the artillery school in Metz between 1830 and 1836 were from military families. There are examples of some famous noble families whose representatives served the Bourbons and in which a later generation was attracted to the army in the 1860s, notably Rohan-Chabot and Clermont-Tonnère, but the numbers are not substantial. There was a definite increase in the number of nobles entering the army from the 1870s, when St Cyr, the military college named after the reformer of the Restoration period, experienced a trebling in the number of its applicants. Unlike in the 1820s these nobles looked to the army to provide a career for life. But as in the 1820s their presence created an additional split in the officer corps between the aristocratic, clericalist and rather anti-republican section, which was also anti-Dreyfus, and the non-noble, anti-clerical and Dreyfusard group. The army became a repository of patriotism, stress was placed on its moral role while its public order function increased with the increasing unrest of the decades before 1914, but the French officers never formed a single caste as they appeared to do in Germany. The college-trained minority set themselves apart, and were the high-fliers. Some reward was needed to compensate for the outlay of about 12 000 frs. in training and equipment. There was a much higher proportion of them in the more technical regiments.

The Ecole Polytechnique provided the most sought-after initial training in mathematical and engineering technique. In the first half of the nineteenth century the majority of students came from noble or rich middle-class families. Later the social composition changed and up to 35 per cent of students came from less well-off families, entering the school with the help of state studentships to cover the high fees. By the 1890s many scholarship holders were sons of enlisted soldiers and minor civil servants. After two years of essentially theoretical training, a man would undertake further, more specific, military education at the Ecole des Mines, the Ecole des Ponts et Chaussées or the Artillery School at Metz. In the years after Waterloo 56 per cent of *polytechniciens* joined the army; towards the end of the century the proportion had risen to 74 per cent. All except the training school at Metz charged high fees. In the 1830s St Cyr began to offer up to 25 scholarships and in 1848 this was increased to 75, specifically for men whose families could not afford the fees. Even so, those who won scholarships were middle class. For others the cost was 1500 frs. a year and an additional 750 frs.

for equipment. In the Restoration St Cyr attracted the aristocracy and the landowning, wealthy middle class. In 1830 the students hastened to St Cloud to defend Charles X. However half of St Cyr's students were from very modest backgrounds, similar to the men who enlisted. Over half the intake at the artillery school in Metz between 1830 and 1836 were from middle- or lower-middle-class families, particularly from the professions.

The way in which the French army was regarded by middle-class groups changed during the nineteenth century, in response to internal political upheaval, social unrest and the likelihood of foreign and colonial war. In 1814 the army was thought of as a radical organisation and was purged as far as possible by the returning Bourbons, but the Bonapartist element remained strong. Gradually during the century the politicisation of the army declined; legitimist officers resigned in 1830 rather than take an oath to Louis-Philippe. In 1870 only one officer wrote to Louis-Napoleon asking him to absolve him from his oath in order to serve the republic.[23] During the Third Republic, although a substantial section of the officer corps was monarchist, clericalist and anti-Semitic in attitude, its loyalty to the state meant that the regime was not under threat. The response of the army to social unrest also changed during the century. During the 1830 revolution soldiers deserted Marmont in Paris in large numbers, and in February 1848 also there were desertions to the insurgent national guard. However the perceived threat to property produced a more conservative reaction in the June Days and the regular army was used to crush the Paris Commune in May 1871 and subsequently to break strikes. Disaffection in the first half of the century has been associated with the low status of the army after Waterloo and poor pay and prospects for the junior officers who led the desertions. It has also been suggested that, later, soldiers became more separated from the civilian population and thus less likely to identify with rioters from a similar social background to themselves, although evidence here is ambiguous given the continued billeting of troops with private families. Success in colonial war and limited European victories under Napoleon III restored the self-confidence of troops, though this must have been shattered by the Franco-Prussian War. There seems general agreement that the army declined in attractiveness as a career for the élite during the nineteenth century, despite the status of the Polytechnique. As in Germany there were complaints that intelligence and expertise did not bring advancement. General Thomas, clearly a man with a grudge, commented in 1870:

> What one needs most of all for promotion is a handsome body, good health and a correct uniform; on top of that in the infantry ... to place one's hand correctly on the seam of one's trousers, to fix one's eyes fifteen paces in front of one while paying attention to the colonel ... in the artillery, to appear to despise technical expertise ... but above all to have a patron.[24]

These may be the complaints the world over, but there is no doubt that the army did not have the allure for the middle classes in France that it had in Germany.

The fragmentation of the Italian lands before unification under mainly non-Italian rulers meant that the professional military experience of most Italians was in foreign armies. Napoleon regarded the Italian peninsula like all conquered territory as a ready source of raw material for his armies. Where they could be relied on, the local notables organised the recruitment, but resistance was considerable. Men recruited in Rome in 1809 rioted and the residue deserted at the first opportunity. Murat held out against trying to enlist southerners and in 1809, when pressure from the Emperor became irresistible, the reaction of the recruits was so violent that a system of summary execution for deserters had to be implemented.[25] However some recruits received meteoric promotion, and overall the Napoleonic years witnessed an unprecedented number of Italians trained for the military life at all levels. But the experience did not endear the concept of a Jacobin-style conscript army to Italians. After Napoleon's fall, the restored rulers, including the Austrians, were obliged to use the nucleus of Napoleon's armies for their own protection, as well as quickly introducing their own form of conscription. In Lombardy and Venetia, the Austrians enlisted adult males in their imperial army for eight years, during which time they were unlikely to see service in the peninsula. The experience of Napoleonic veterans was invaluable, but men and officers were inevitably in an ambiguous position. They were reviled by the local gentry as collaborators, but were essential to the newly restored traditional rulers. In 1814 Victor Emmanuel of Piedmont conscripted the veterans, but the stigma of Napoleonic service never left them. In the Kingdom of the Two Sicilies Napoleonic officers were all downgraded one rank when incorporated into the Bourbon armies. Whether the suspicion they encountered was wholly political or partly because they came from middle-class rather than noble society is not recorded. But the experience of the post-imperial years justified official caution. Army units in Naples, Turin and elsewhere were the nucleus for secret societies and conspiracies, with the aim of obliging autocratic rulers to introduce constitutions. Frequently disappointed hopes of promotion and professional frustrations figured high as motives for unrest. The Carbonari risings of 1820-1 were all military putsches. In Piedmont they centred on a group of aristocratic officers who laboured under the misapprehension that the heir to the throne, Charles Albert, would agree to be a constitutional monarch.

These abortive risings thoroughly discredited the notion that a military mutiny could challenge returned rulers, but they provoked princes to institute military reorganisation. It was commonly believed by established rulers that their rebels were primarily educated, urban middle-class officers and intellectuals, despite the evidence that noble officers often took a lead. As in Prussia, prejudice against bourgeois officers needed little encouragement. There was a positive attempt to exclude them, at some considerable cost as technical experts were needed in increasing numbers. The Piedmontese army was reorganised, partly on the French, partly on the Prussian model. A period of conscription was followed by service in a reserve reminiscent of the *landwehr*. Each year 8000 conscripts were chosen by lot. After one year's service, they spent fifteen years in the reserve. The rest of the army of 16 000 men were volunteer professional soldiers.[26] Despite the restructuring, the contribution of the Piedmontese army in 1848-9 was singularly unimpressive. In default of other protection, restored rulers had to fall back on Austrian troops or encourage the formation of voluntary militia, normally composed of members of the urban middle class. An extreme right-wing Neapolitan royalist, the prince di Canosa organised a civilian militia in Modena and in Rome in 1830. Such militias, particularly concerned with the protection of urban property against marauding peasants, were important in 1848. The Bourbons used them in Naples to control peasant disorder. The urban poor were mobilised into city militias, very illiberal in inspiration. Unlike the *landwehr* in Prussia, they were the bane of the liberal middle class, especially in the 1860s.[27] In Venice in 1848 Manin was keen to protect the republican revolution with a defensive volunteer force. There was no shortage of men with military experience. It was calculated that there were 60 000 men in the province who had served in the Austrian army. Like the rest of the local urban bourgeoisie, Manin preferred to evoke the élitist traditions of the old republic and shun a new democratic and popular image. He refused to consider conscription and hoped to rely on *corpi franchi*, volunteers from each province, fighting to defend their own territory. The formation of a civic guard of 6000 men was announced in Venice towards the end of March, but by mid-April only 3600 had enrolled and lack of weapons suspended further recruitment. The volunteers were a worrying mixture for the new republican leaders. Alongside sons of patriotic middle-class families were local criminals, presumably hoping for easy pickings.

Venice was opposed to the creation of rural detachments, refused to provide them with financial support, ignored their existence and branded them as lawless brigands, which, to property-owning Venetian notables anxious for the security of their rural estates, they probably were. The decision of rural areas to recruit volunteers was warmly received in mountainous districts, where local peasants had been conducting a guerrilla campaign in defence of communal forests and communal rights since the Napoleonic Empire had sided with wealthy landowners eager to buy up such valuable property. Numbers were swelled by the promise of up to 2 lire a day in pay, a sum granted for each man to the commander of the guard in Lonigo. The promise of pay encouraged landless labourers in the districts on the plain to join. Poorer parish priests were eager propagandists and bishops and priests encouraged men to participate in a 'holy war' against Austria. The better-off inhabitants of the countryside were confident that the peasant volunteers would remain under their influence but the Venetian authorities turned their face against such patriotism, which in reality might have proved too localised to sustain a campaign against the Austrians.[28] Thus the idea of a volunteer force foundered upon rivalries between town and country, the unwillingness of the bourgeoisie to yoke itself to peasants whose economic interests were diametrically opposed to their own, and their fear that the rural guards might turn on the urban élite itself. In the event the main combatants in the campaigns of 1848–9 in northern Italy were the professional armies of Austria and Piedmont, but the volunteer militia tradition was to be revived by Garibaldi in the 1850s.

The political and military élites were closely interlinked. It was customary to send one son into the army and another into politics. Carlo Cardorno became a minister, his brother, Raffaele, a general. Raffaele was also a member of parliament from 1849 to 1872 and then entered the Senate. In 1861 there were forty officers in the chamber of deputies and this tradition was sustained in both houses of parliament throughout the century. Until 1907 the Minister of War was always a serving officer.[29] The military did not aspire to direct political control; they were already close enough to the seat of power. Military service was the norm for Piedmont's landed élite. La Marmora, who became Minister of War after the 1848 revolutions, had two brothers who had fought with Napoleon. But up to 1848 promotion depended entirely on seniority and most senior officers were very elderly. La Marmora set up new infantry and cavalry schools and an academy in Turin for engineers and artillery officers. The debate over military legislation in 1854 involved a typical conflict, between a parliament which preferred the concept of a national militia and feared the power of a professional army and the determination of the military leaders to forge a reliable fighting force. The assembly was always aware of its limited control over the army, which, although scrupulously loyal, always maintained a distance, almost a semi-autonomy, reminiscent of the army in Germany. In 1854 La Marmora won the tussle with parliament and the period of conscription was raised from just over a year to between four and five years, followed by a period in the reserve. As in France the system of drawing lots with substitutes and exemptions allowed the better-off to escape the service at a price. The retention of non-Piedmontese who had joined during the 1848 campaign made the army appear less narrowly provincial. Despite the very limited participation of the Piedmontese army in the Crimean War, the event raised morale and helped to contribute to a growing professionalism. In 1856 a military journal, the *Rivista Militare*, was started, a sure sign of this trend. However, despite the fact that the army was consuming up to 28 per cent of the national budget, in 1859 Piedmont was able to field only 65 per cent of her promised contingent in the campaign against Austria. Her officer corps was more professional, her soldiers better paid and supplied, but it was still France's victory.

Garibaldi's 20 000 volunteers were treated as an embarrassment by the regular army and disregarded in the Austrian campaign but, in the rest of the struggle for the peninsula after Austria's defeat in the north, the volunteer and professional traditions were to some degree merged. Tuscan troops deserted to the rebels and one of their officers joined the provisional government. They formed the basis for a central Italian army under General Fanti, a Modenan officer who, exiled after the conspiracy of 1831, had served with the Spanish army until the revolutions of 1848 brought him to Lombardy to lead the rebel troops. His conspiratorial and Spanish past took a lot of living down, a perpetual problem for Italian officers of the period. La Marmora gave him a chance in the Crimean War and he fought at Magenta. By 1859 he was politically conservative, quarrelling with the choice of Garibaldi as head of the Tuscan division. He set to work to forge a professional body, actively preparing for its incorporation into the Piedmontese army. He even numbered the units as if they were already merged. His forces soon numbered 50 000 and made it quite impossible for the old princes to return. Following the plebiscite in March 1860, his forces officially became part of Piedmont's army and Fanti was rewarded by the gift of the war ministry.

He worked to create a national professional force out of the armies of Piedmont and the remnants of those of the other states. There was little enthusiasm for the incorporation of the 50 000 Garibaldian volunteers and their 7300 officers, for their loyalty to the House of Savoy and the Piedmontese notables was considered doubtful. Garibaldi was angry that only 2000 of his officers were allowed to join the new Italian army, along with a mere 20 000 of the men. Fanti, patron of the opposing concept of a professional army, offered only a two-year engagement or demobilisation with six months' pay. The latter option was generally preferred. The former Bourbon army in the south received much more generous terms and a warmer welcome. Its officers could join the Italian army with no loss of status and 2000 accepted, though many chose to retire. Many ordinary soldiers from the old Bourbon army simply disappeared, to re-emerge among the brigands, and this tendency increased dramatically in 1860 when conscription was introduced into the south, making the guerrilla struggle a sort of class war. Brigands fought for traditional causes, such as the defence of the communal system, and against new ones, notably the imposition of the Piedmontese regime. Captured brigands were simply shot. Ironically guerrilla warfare was now a threat to united Italy. The civil war in the south was a testing and unpopular engagement for the new national army. More men were lost than in all the previous wars to liberate Italy. By the end of 1861 50 000 were fighting in the south, against difficult odds since there were no topographical maps of the province in existence, a matter irrelevant to the rebels. By 1863 40 per cent of the army, twice as many as two years earlier, were visibly losing to 25 000 guerrillas, despite the concentration of 40 per cent of Italy's budget on the campaign. A modicum of control was achieved only when local volunteers were found to fight the rebels and the southern élite agreed to mobilise units. But brigandage remained a serious problem,[30] for in some districts brigands had powerful backers. The guerrilla activity of groups like the mafia proved indestructible. The army thus became a very visible means of maintaining public order. Large garrisons existed in all sizeable towns and confrontations with strikers, including women, were not infrequently bloody. Martial law was declared ten times up to 1919. While the use of an army for such purposes was considered unavoidable by all European ruling élites, the Italian experience was particularly violent, reflecting a high level of social tension.

The policy of trying to mould a positively national force continued. Gradually, through the absorption of trained men from the old armies and universal conscription, the army grew to 250 000. The officers were predominantly Piedmontese, two-thirds initially, or Savoyard, though there were quite a few from Lombardy, the central areas and the south. The concept of the professional army gained total sway. The army was far too important a weapon in combatting civil disorder for the tradition of volunteer formations to survive. Soldiers did not serve in their own locality and were moved every four years to prevent the growth of local links and loyalties. Garibaldi was keen to model the national guard on the Prussian *landwehr*, but the army officer corps and the notables were convinced that civilian militias were stiff with dangerous urban democrats. The national guard was treated with the same embarrassed neglect it received in France. In 1876 a programme was begun to replace it with a territorial militia under the control of the army, and this was completed in 1885. Meanwhile the regular army was revamped, this time entirely on the German model. More emphasis was given to military education. A new war school was founded, teaching was improved in the military academies and exams became more of a decisive factor in promotions. Technical training remained embryonic, however, held back by the unpopularity of a military career with that section of the middle class who in Germany were increasingly eager to serve in the army. Earlier prejudices against bourgeois officers were not dead. Officers' pay was poor and the career did not have the standing of its German equivalent. The northern middle class preferred industry to the army. However the bourgeoisie were ready volunteers; one year of such service avoided a much longer spell as a conscript. Few stayed beyond the year. In 1910 it was assessed that of 19 000 who had volunteered since 1900 only 622 remained when the first year was up. Thus in 1914 only 50 per cent of the officer corps was bourgeois, compared to 67 per cent in Germany and 60 per cent in Great Britain. In addition the army appealed to a less well-off group in Italy; most officers were from small provincial towns, often from the south or from the lower middle class. The recruitment of the officer corps was always difficult, and numbers in the military schools fell constantly until 1909. As in other countries promotion from the ranks was possible, but prospects were limited. An enlisted man would almost never rise above captain and his promotion would be constantly checked by graduates from the military academies who rose faster and further.[31]

By 1910, the Italian army consisted of 1 393 000 men and 14 000 officers, with 16 000 reserve officers. Pay and armaments were gradually improved, though this always meant imports, despite the existence of enormous arms factories. Social and regional rivalries were exacerbated within the army. In the First World War most soldiers were peasants, fighting for one-third the wage of industrial workers in munitions factories. Northern industrial workers were exempt from conscription or, if they fought, were enlisted into the artillery and were therefore never in the front line. Hostility to such 'shirkers', or *imboscati*, became pronounced. Within the middle class there was a similar north–south divide. The southern middle-class recruit fought in the front line; the northerner was put into the artillery and left at the rear, too precious to be risked. The southern bourgeoisie thus also built up a profound resentment against their colleagues.[32]

Thus in Italy middle-class participation in the army was always limited and traditionally the bourgeoisie had been more inclined to favour a volunteer than a conscript army. The volunteer tradition was successfully stifled in the later decades of the century, but the army never managed to attract the middle class into the technical branches of the service as was done in Germany, and never tried to imbue bourgeois officers with a 'copy-cat' respect for aristocratic military traditions. Regional differences and rivalries among bourgeois officers remained potent and divisive.

The status of middle-class officers in all of the armies we have considered was comparable to the way in which the bourgeoisie was regarded in society in general. Irrespective of whether they came from wealthy professional families or were sons of lower-middle-class artisans, bourgeois officers were valued for their adaptability, technical education and expertise. They were commissioned into the engineers or the artillery, regiments which would be central to the type of warfare experienced in the First World War but nevertheless sections of the army which were undervalued and somewhat despised by the traditional officer corps. Throughout the First World War the aristocratic cavalry waited behind the trenches for the moment of glory when the artillery were routed and a mounted attack would be possible. They waited in vain. Warfare had moved into the age of the industrialised economy, but social attitudes and norms had not. The ideal of the aristocratic mounted warrior, loyal, courageous, but not particularly bright, continued to dominate the thinking of those who ran the armies. The result was that, effectively, each of these countries was possessed of divided armies, exemplified to some degree by the schism in the French army stimulated by the Dreyfus Affair. The aristocratic, Catholic, right-wing officers who had come to the fore in the French army since the time of the Second Empire were apprehensive and suspicious of intelligent, educated, technically aware bourgeois officers, particularly the Jewish ones, like Alfred Dreyfus. The arguments about his guilt and innocence, and it was finally accepted that he was no spy, also reflected the cleavages between the claims of socially élitist and technically literate conceptions of an army. The French officer corps remained split between Dreyfusards and anti-Dreyfusards during the exigencies of the First World War. Yet more damaging to their wartime operations were the social tensions in the Italian and Russian armies. Even in Germany, where the army was so successful for much of the war, and where bourgeois officers were recruited in increasing numbers, their visible presence was considered politically inexpedient and attention was still paid to inculcating respect for traditional aristocratic values.

7. Education and the Middle Classes

As professions, bureaucracies and armies became more 'professional-ised' and the pace of technical change demanded better educated engineers, foremen and workers, formal education itself became a prime concern for the various groups within the middle classes. For these reasons alone a comparative investigation of education in these four countries would be apposite. But education meant more than the acquisition of special skills. The state education systems evolved by the political élites both reflected and contributed to social and political norms. Constant reference has been made in earlier chapters to the fragmentation of middle-class elements in society along lines of occupation and income. We have observed that, far from being a single *class*, the different components had very separate and distinct identities, interests and concerns, although it remains to be considered whether such divisions had an impact on politics. The development of the professions, of the civil service, the army, etc., intensified stratification, making the wealthy bourgeoisie an almost impenetrable caste, with far more in common with the nobility than with the rest of the middle class. Conversely a huge lower middle class emerged whose members might anticipate some lateral, but no vertical, social mobility. Thus the middle classes consisted of a number of layers which were increasingly watertight. The layers themselves grew larger, but an individual would be held like a fly in amber. What contributed to this rigidity? One of the main explanations seems to lie in the education systems which evolved during the century, with their underlying assumptions that education ought to fit a child better to occupy the social position into which he was born. Formal education might nurture technical skills and play a part in the development of the economy, but this was almost by chance rather than design. The struggle for recognition of technical education would support this view. On the other hand the use of literacy, for all groups within the middle class and especially for the poor, was to inculcate an acceptance of social and political order and stability. Education was a double-headed animal: it might promote 'progress' in an advancing industrial state, yet also guard a cul-de-sac of political and social security for the ruling élite. To this end primary schooling was deliberately limited in scope and offered almost no access to further learning. Concepts like nationalism were driven home.

In this chapter the pursuit of social and political objectives in education will emerge as paramount. Such aims, assumed or overt, lay behind the increasing élitism of secondary and higher education and the emphasis on classical learning. Indeed the relegation of technical and 'modern' subjects to an inferior status indicated, that far from being a component of economic progress for the élite who directed the state systems, education was fundamentally an instrument of social control and stratification, particularly as parliamentary regimes expanded to become democratic. In Russia there were repeated attempts to restrict secondary and higher education to the nobility through higher fees and scholarships. In Italy, on the other hand, secondary and higher education was made more accessible to all groups within the middle class than in any other country, not to satisfy the demands of an expanding economy, but because Italy so obviously lacked such development yet possessed a growing population whose need for jobs could not be satisfied. Both regimes were conscious of their economic backwardness and sought to preserve social and political stability by manipulating education as a carrot before different sets of donkeys. In the past historians have assumed that the development of state educational systems in the nineteenth century was an aspect of 'progress', comparable with the construction of efficient drains, railways, etc. Education was depicted as a response to economic, social and demographic change. With examples such as those of Russia and Italy, the issue of social and political manipulation cannot be ignored.

The comparison we have already noted between the objectives of governments in Russia and Italy is revealing, but very few educational historians have attempted historical comparisons between the educational systems and especially the consumers of education in a range of countries. There is a lack of genuinely comparable statistical data, despite similarities between countries in terms of both educational norms and institutions. There are also problems of ambiguous definitions, to which reference has already been made. We shall discuss contemporary surveys used by recent historians, which divided school pupils or university students according to their social origins. However, interstate comparisons have their dangers. What was meant by the designation of particular social groups in one country may not be comparable across national boundaries, as, hopefully, is present-day information. In Germany, because official appointments carried most prestige, there was a tendency to claim 'official' status, even when unmerited. Thus assertions about the proportions of different social groups preferring certain types of education and pursuing specific subsequent careers in different countries have to be guarded. Secondly, the position of the Church, clergy and clerical education complicates comparisons. In France and Italy the Catholic clergy were educated totally separately, completely outside the state system. Their non-appearance in university statistics exaggerates the élitism of education, particularly tertiary education, in both countries, since most priests were from humble origins. In Germany and Russia the Protestant and Orthodox clergy were educated within the state system, thus swelling substantially the proportion of boys from modest families on secondary school and university rolls, for there too most clergy came from less well-off backgrounds and indeed in Germany could obtain a government loan to cover their university training.

Whereas an assessment of the interests of the present-day middle class could bristle with statistics about social classes 2 to 5 and so on, an attempt to consider the same subject for the nineteenth century has to be far more impressionistic. In recent years historians have begun to produce detailed and specific studies of different aspects of nineteenth-century education, but for limited periods and single countries. France has been well served, as will be obvious from what follows, with investigations published by French, British and American scholars. A reasonable impression of aspects of German education can be gauged from literature available in English, but for Russia Nicholas Hans' account of that country's educational system, published in 1931, is still well regarded by comparative educationalists. Barbagli's study of Italy is invaluable, but otherwise there is very little in English on Italian education and apparently no detailed attempts have been made to examine the social composition of different schools and the university population even in Italian. In this account we shall attempt to make comparisons between the four states where valid and appropriate, as well as looking at each country in turn.

Education was crucial to the growth, definition and development of middle-class groups in the nineteenth century. The countries studied here shared certain assumptions about the aims of education, the ideal school and the types of structure needed. All were convinced that children from different social groups should be educated separately to preserve the fabric of society. All admitted the need to provide basic schooling for the poor, including artisans, and supported a secondary system for the better-off middle class and those members of the nobility not educated by private tutors. Differences occurred in the precise role the state should play, although by 1914 the end result everywhere was a state-run system. The central institution was the secondary school. It provided a common cultural core, the route to university or professional training and a meeting place for children of similar backgrounds. Educational institutions were the stuff of social cohesion and definition, and offered some measured modest horizontal social mobility for those who could afford the fees. Classical education was the norm, vocational training was regarded as inferior. The names of the schools proclaimed their character: *lycée* in France, *lyceum* in Italy and Russia, *gymnasium* in Germany, Russia and Italy. The avowed aim of a syllabus which was almost 50 per cent Latin and Greek was to provide a good general education. The final leaving certificate, which was devised at the beginning of the century and became a basic qualification for university entry, was rigorous and exacting. In France habitually only 60 per cent of the candidates, roughly 0.5 per cent of the age cohort, passed the baccalaureate; in Germany where students were tested annually, leading to the *abitur*, there was a high drop-out rate, up to 75 per cent in the 1880s. Those who completed the nine years or so of secondary education normally went on to further education. In France this usually took the form of professional training, if the student was lucky enough to gain a place in one of the specialised higher institutes, or *grandes écoles*. In Germany, Russia and Italy, he would normally proceed to a university. The *abitur* qualified a boy for a job in the middling grades of the civil service, afforded him the opportunity to take higher state examinations, or guaranteed him a university place. In Russia also the leaving certificate conferred positive privileges and job opportunities.

Until the later years of the nineteenth century, a classical curriculum was regarded as the best in secondary schools. The specialist technical *grandes écoles* in France and universities everywhere demanded a classical secondary leaving certificate of their applicants. Secondary and higher educational institutions were committed to what was seen as the traditional transference of a common western culture and the concept of the education of the 'whole' man, not only as an individual but as a constituent element in society. Classical education was meant to produce a 'gentleman', a man of civilisation and culture or *bildung*. It was an education originally designed for a senior public servant or professional man and bore little apparent relation to the needs of the growing industrial and commercial middle class. But the better-off within this group often seized on a classical education for their offspring, perhaps to confirm and proclaim their middle-class status to the world. Enrolment in the classical stream of a *gymnasium* or *lycée* would presumably announce that the family business was going well enough to allow the son several years of leisure before joining the firm, and that it was sufficiently prosperous to tempt him back afterwards.

A classical education also taught the son the ways of thought and behaviour of the aristocracy, which were eagerly aped by the bourgeoisie and were skills that the parents might not possess. Hence an education which might at first sight seem inappropriate was regarded as desirable almost because of its remoteness from modern capitalism and its association with an aristocratic tradition of cultivated leisure. It has been argued that industrial and business families were schizophrenic in rejecting modernity in their choice of education and thus contributed to a fundamental disharmony in the social system.[1] But it is more likely that social disharmony was the result of restricting educational provision to an increasingly narrow élite. The educational institution was seen to confer status upon an individual whose family lacked that quality. Attendance at a secondary school conveyed certain tangible privileges, in Russia exemption from military service, the attainment of a position in the Table of Ranks and so on. Education was attractive not only to families striving for acceptance, but also to those anxious to maintain their position in a fast-changing society. In 1879 civil engineers in Germany objected to the proposal that graduates of non-classical secondary schools should be allowed to enter their branch of the civil service, not because Latin was really needed to do their job but because they considered that the classics, through their character-building ethos, gave their profession a status that would disappear if traditional educational prerequisites were eliminated. During the century, alternative 'modern', technical and scientific curricula emerged, often giving rise to new secondary schools. For many years these were treated as second-rate by traditionalists, appropriate only for the socially inferior and less able pupils. In Germany and Russia in the 1840s there were fears expressed that such educational programmes were politically dangerous, both in their content and in their candidates. Only towards the end of the century were leaving certificates in non-classical subjects recognised as a qualification for university entry.

Education was designed to justify and reinforce a ruling élite based not on birth or inherited privilege, it was asserted, but on the acceptance of certain standards of culture and civilisation, which were claimed to be inaccessible to those without wealth and education. Since education had to be bought through fees, and since it was assumed that those of superior merit could always earn sufficient money to purchase education for their children, the poor were arguably excluded justifiably, yet the system could still be defined as open to all. A man's personal qualities, which included his educational achievements, marked him as a member of the governing classes.[2] The assumption that education was vital to the individual's complete personality and his cultural maturity was essentially linked to the associated view that only those with a certain wealth ought to qualify as participants in what was essentially a closed and élitist system. Entry to higher education was similarly restricted, on the grounds that the real hurdles were intellectual; the exceptionally gifted child of poor parents would not be denied access.

The élitism of the system was also justified on very pragmatic grounds. There were only a limited number of public service and professional jobs available, therefore secondary places should be restricted to avoid a surplus of educated men. Otherwise there was the danger of the emergence of an unemployed educated group, which might be discontented and subversive. Commentators in France and Germany were concerned about this perceived threat and took steps to avoid it. The events of 1848 were interpreted in both the west and in Russia as a consequence of acting too late to avoid the problem. Secondly, since the number of professional opportunities was limited, it would be foolish to attract sons of peasants and artisans. Middle-class politicians and educationalists waxed lyrical on the dangers of educating a boy so that he was an alien in his natural environment. Nineteenth-century ministers of education were convinced that education should match social class, except for the odd ragged genius. Otherwise there was the risk that an educated proletariat would emerge, unemployable, rootless and socially disruptive. It was recognised that some basic education was necessary for the poor, and that practical, technical or commercial training was increasingly required by lower-middle-class groups, but systems of elementary, vocational and technical, and secondary education were universally designed to be parallel but separate. Transfer from elementary to secondary school was deliberately made increasingly difficult in the name of social harmony. In some cases secondary and university fees were successively raised to discourage the overambitious poor. In both Russia and Germany education became even more a privilege of the rich. The institution of an educational hurdle, the leaving certificate, for entry into the civil service, as in Germany, and for access to tertiary education, may sound pedagogically justified and more professional, or even fairer, but in effect it excluded poorer candidates and made some jobs and education itself increasingly socially exclusive. Thus standardisation and systematisation made social élitism more rigid, cementing the privileged yet further in a place of dominance. In reality exceptions occurred, sometimes in most unexpected quarters. Italy educated a broad spectrum of its lower middle class to try to preserve social harmony. Recent historical research has suggested that, although the members of the existing élite may have wanted to limit upward social mobility, in reality in France upwards of 40 per cent of secondary school graduates were from lower-middle-class or poorer families.[3]

In the 1790s in France the revolutionaries tried to make fundamental changes in France's system of education, partly for pedagogical, partly for philosophical reasons. They revered education as a vital prerequisite of individual and social progress. Condorcet stressed that educational opportunities would reduce the inequalities between men.[4] New subjects as well as new ideals were urged, especially scientific disciplines. The anti-clericalism of the revolutionaries ensured that the Church would be dispossessed of its land and its educational role, but the upheavals of the 1790s meant that no coherent alternative emerged. Napoleon reached a concordat with the Pope and a compromise over education that led to state and Church sharing the role of educator during the nineteenth century. In many respects the principles of Napoleonic reform established in France and to some degree in the Italian lands were similar to those enacted in Prussia and Russia. French education, especially her *lycées* and *grandes écoles*, was often copied. In the 1790s the revolutionaries had tried to decentralise secondary education, but this experiment was abandoned and a state secondary system emerged. There were two types of publicly run schools, *lycées* and *collèges municipaux*, both of which owed much to eighteenth-century schools, indeed they were often virtually the same establishments. In addition there were many privately run schools, mostly secular until mid-century when the role of the Church was allowed to expand. The law of 1802 replaced the revolutionary *écoles centrales* with *lycées*, semi-military boarding schools for boys from the age of twelve. By 1808 37 of the planned 45 *lycées* had opened.[5] The curriculum was a blend of classical and scientific subjects and was crowned by a universal oral leaving examination, the baccalaureate, introduced in 1808. In that same year the education provided in secondary schools and institutions of higher learning was put under the centralising control of the rather misnamed University of Paris, under a Grand Master nominated by the Emperor, organised hierarchically to serve as an examining body. In addition municipalities were empowered to run *collèges municipaux*. But, in the nineteenth century, only one provincial city could boast a choice of state secondary school. The curriculum itself often reverted to that taught by the Jesuits in the middle of the previous century, with just enough maths and science to scrape a qualification for the *grandes écoles*. The baccalaureate became more and more an oral test at the end of a boy's school career. There was always a high failure rate. In the 1840s only 3000 of the 5000 candidates passed each year. Of the successful, 47 per cent were from the *lycées* and 26 per cent from *collèges municipaux*.

Despite their examination successes, the state schools accounted for fewer than half of secondary establishments in 1815 and for half a century numbers fell. In a survey of 1843, the Minister of Education, Villemain, estimated that in 1789 there had been between 50 000 and 70 000 boys in secondary schools, roughly 2 per 1000 of the population. In 1843 this number was no more than 1.8 per thousand; the 46 *lycées* had 18 697 boys, the 312 *collèges municipaux* had 26 584, and 1016 private schools accounted for 43 195. Thus secondary education was catering for a tiny and shrinking minority of the population.

Primary schools offered a different syllabus and deliberately catered for poorer social groups. The provision of a basic education for the masses was increasingly perceived as vital for social stability. In 1816 Guizot wrote, 'Ignorance renders the masses turbulent and ferocious.'[6] Napoleon, like his predecessors, had left the literacy of the poor to the Church, which had an interest in offering a basic education to those sons of peasants who were willing to train for the priesthood. There were *petits séminaires*, started in 1814 by the Christian Brothers to train boys for the priesthood, but which provided basic education for others. Bishops ran diocesan colleges. In 1816 it was decreed that each commune should run a school and that education should be free for poor families. By 1820 24 000 out of 44 000 communes had primary schools, but by 1828 4 million of the 5.5 million 8–15-year-olds never went to school. Half of army recruits were illiterate, far more from the south and west than the north and east.

The Guizot law of 1833 obliged each commune to provide a school and free education for the poor. Each department, or region, was obliged to found a training college for teachers and each *chef-lieu* and town with more than 6000 inhabitants was to set up a higher primary school. Teachers had to be certificated or members of religious orders. By 1846 33 000 children were attending school but most had left by ten or eleven. In 1848 some republicans hoped to broaden the scope of the system, but when new legislation was enacted in the Falloux law of 1850 the drafting commission chaired by Thiers was mainly motivated by memories of the June Days and a determination to crush radicalism. Pressure to replace the Church as the main educator at primary level no longer seemed urgent. The Church seemed an ally. The new law basically re-enacted the Guizot legislation but by its terms permitted Church-run schools to expand. Any qualified person could open a school. Jesuits could resume a teaching role, the *petits séminaires* could openly teach those not intended for the priesthood and restrictions on what private schools could teach were not renewed. Although the apex of the system remained the baccalaureate, run by the University, the Church opened more schools than the state in the 1850s. Seventy-five of the 307 *collèges*, mostly in the west, came under clerical control, the number of *petits séminaires* grew to 137, and diocesan colleges, run by the bishops, increased to 70. Schools run by religious orders, often funded by individual bequests, became increasingly popular, accounting for 47 per cent of all new boys' schools in the 1850s. There was also a marked expansion in Church-run schools for girls. The proportion of children thus educated rose by 7 per cent for boys to 22 per cent and by 9 per cent for girls to 54 per cent in the years 1850 to 1863.

The Church provided a variety of schools to appeal to different social groups. The legitimist aristocracy and those members of the upper middle class who rejected *lycée* education utilised the costly and exclusive schools run by the Jesuits, Marists and Assumptionists, which were the nearest equivalent to the English public school. They stressed corporate, élitist ideals and provided an education even more classical than the *lycée*. Their teachers, untrained in science, associated such subjects with immoral materialism. The Jesuits, however, concentrated on preparing the sons of the legitimist aristocracy for the *grandes écoles* and military careers, and taught science and other modern subjects. Such schools were expensive boarding establishments in rural settings. The less well-heeled, but still prosperous middle classes favoured the Christian Brothers, who ran some fairly costly boarding schools. They already had a well-established reputation in the larger towns, were adaptable, modern and efficient, and provided courses in technical subjects. They steered clear of polemic and were discreet and moderate. In 1850 they had eight *pensionnats*, by 1860 sixteen. In 1855 their school at Passy had 600 pupils. Theoretically, to side-step the University, the education was deemed primary, but they also provided modern secondary schooling with no Latin, very acceptable to the middle class. The order also had a commercial school in Paris, an agricultural institute and two technical schools. In addition, like lay teachers, they put on evening classes for adults and young workers. For the less well-off there were the *petits séminaires*, diocesan colleges and other small Catholic schools, which were attractive to peasants and townspeople for their cheapness. The level of teaching in the Church schools, particularly at the poorer end, often reflected the price, lacked any spirit of enquiry, rejected modernity of all kinds, was increasingly authoritarian and was even more committed to the notion that men should be educated for the place in society to which they had been born than were the state schools. However the view of society provided by state and Church schools was very different and there was growing concern in mid-century that educational developments in the two types of schools were tending to produce two societies in France. The numbers in secondary schools doubled in the twenty years after the Villemain report, in the 1850s the Church taking a lead, in the 1860s the state. The 1860s witnessed developments in two directions: the standardisation of a modern or 'special' alternative to the classical baccalaureate, and increased provision for women.

Alternative practical, technical and more scientific curricula were introduced, but the drawback was that only the full classical baccalaureate qualified a boy for the *grandes écoles* and the senior professions. The alternatives therefore lacked status and authority. In the early 1860s a standardised four-year course in technical subjects was devised and a similar programme was introduced by Duruy in 1865. Although it proved popular with peasants, small shopkeepers and workers, the middle class rejected the new 'special' programme. The effect was therefore further to increase the class stratification of education. The special programme pupils were often referred to as 'grocers' and some municipalities hestitated to introduce it for fear of losing better-off families to the Jesuit schools. In 1869 19 per cent of pupils in the *lycées* but just over one-third in the *collèges municipaux* were enrolled on 'modern' courses. The drop-out rate was high in both types of school. In 1876 there were 2599 in the preparatory classes of the *lycées*, but only 263 by the fourth year. The special programme was most successful in smallish towns, least so in large towns where the secondary school was a *lycée* and the new alternative was regarded as a poor second choice. The new course was also more acceptable in towns with a substantial industrial and commercial middle class, like Mulhouse, Nancy and Nantes, where *écoles professionnelles* already existed. In towns like Grenoble and Orléans, where the middle classes were predominantly legal and professional, the traditional classical curriculum continued to hold sway.

Until the 1860s there were no secondary courses for girls. Duruy introduced courses similar to the 'special' programme, but the opposition of the Church limited participants to daughters of Protestants and university teachers. Some middle-class girls took the higher level teachers' certificate in pursuit of a more advanced education. The first female candidate to pass the baccalaureate succeeded in 1862, but had only 49 imitators by 1882. The first *lycées* for girls were founded in the 1880s. Most middle-class parents preferred to send their daughters to Church-run schools, which often left a cultural divide between lay-educated husbands and their wives. Late nineteenth-century Catholic education for girls provided them with the right social ambience in which to meet an acceptable husband and the social and domestic graces to remain entombed in the family home for the rest of their lives. 'The wife belongs to the seventeenth century, the husband to the end of the eighteenth.'[7] The cultural isolation of the bourgeois wife can be exaggerated;[8] despite their apparent lacking of technical or managerial education, widows often took over and ran family businesses, most visibly in the textile trades. It should also be remembered that only the richer bourgeois ladies were of the 'leisure class'. In lower-middle-class commercial and industrial families it would be the norm for the wife to take an active role.

It used to be assumed that nineteenth-century French schooling was only for an élite, given social norms and high fees. Recently some historians have pointed to the appeal of secondary schools for less affluent parents. As we have seen schools were tailor-made to cope with the perceived needs, illusions and vanities of different sectors of society. It would appear that schools moulded children for a rigidly defined social role. In recent years historians have investigated the extent to which secondary schools achieved the expectations of contemporaries in their socio-economic orientation. Were schools actually instruments of social stability?

Research on the families using different schools in the eighteenth and nineteenth centuries would seem to indicate a high level of stability. Studies of eighteenth-century *collèges* revealed that at Avallon over 45 per cent of students' fathers were professionals or office-holders, whereas 33 per cent were merchants of varying degrees of wealth and better-off artisans. Seven per cent were merely described as bourgeois, which is assumed to indicate wealth, 10 per cent were nobles and 4 per cent substantial farmers. There were no sons of peasants or the urban lower classes. At Gisors and Auch, where the *collèges* had less of an academic reputation, and were really lower secondary schools, there were more sons of artisans. Superficially the nineteenth-century records seem to complement this picture. The level of fees and the nature of the curriculum tended to dictate the social composition of the school. Most of the pupils of both *lycées* and *collèges municipaux* belonged to the middle classes, cost, curriculum and location being the determinants. Both types of secondary school were fee-paying. A top-rank Parisian *lycée* would cost 1500 frs. a year for a boarder, less in the provinces, which would seem to restrict pupils to a narrow range of the wealthy upper middle class. From the outset 6000 scholarships were offered, but these were rewards for the offspring of loyal officers and officials, not designed to test and nurture the talents of the poor. Napoleon had hoped for a democratic intake and the *lycées* prided themselves on trying to encourage the able, regardless of wealth. However by 1842 only 13 per cent of secondary school pupils were exempt from all fees, compared with 46 per cent in pre-revolutionary *collèges* in 1789. The numbers of scholarship holders continued to fall during the century. There were only 1588 by 1865, at which time 300 awards were made annually, from about 1600 applicants. In 1911 51 per cent of awards went to the sons of officials; only 20 per cent went to sons of peasants, workers or artisans.

Despite the appearance of strict social stratification between schools, in effect 44 per cent of *lycée* pupils were day-boys, paying 110 frs. Sixty-two per cent of boys in *collèges municipaux* were day-pupils, paying half that fee. Recent research has revealed that the *lycées* took substantial numbers of boys from poor families. Nearly 50 per cent of the graduates of provincial *lycées* and *collèges* between 1860 and 1866 were sons of peasants, shopkeepers and lesser civil servants, and the proportion would be much higher if boys in younger age groups were included in the totals, for many boys from poorer families were forced to leave before the end of the course to take jobs.[9] In 1864 the fashionable *lycée* Condorcet in Paris included 250 small tradesmen among the 1200 parents. The *lycée* Charlemagne included 17 sons of small tradesmen, 18 clerks and 15 artisans, and in all at least 82 out of 305 boys came from families of modest means. The larger provincial *lycées* were mostly filled with sons of professionals, officials and the industrial and commercial middle classes. In Angers 9 out of 51 boys were of humble origins. In Besançon alongside the 12 sons of officials were 9 boys from poor families, and in Dijon the total of less well-off boys was 13 out of 77. The *collèges* had a substantial lower-middle-class presence. Indeed upper-class parents would opt for a *lycée* or a select Catholic secondary school instead of a *collège* to preserve their social exclusivity. Around 1850 the Assumptionist college in Nîmes had an intake which was

27 per cent noble. *Lycées* in the larger towns were kept socially select by the cost of boarding and the impossibility of travelling long distances on a daily basis. *Collèges municipaux* tended to have a broader social base in the larger towns; in smaller towns peasant pupils would have weekly lodgings with local shopkeepers, often taking their week's food with them to cut costs. In 1865 67 per cent of the pupils at the *collège municipal* of Le Quesnoy in a mainly rural area were boarders, while in the industrial town of Armentières only 13 per cent boarded. Looked at overall, in 1865 state secondary schools were comprised of 27.7 per cent pupils from lower-middle-class families and another 12.3 per cent sons of peasants. Thus a total of 40 per cent came from families for whom education was a sacrifice. On the other hand, officials sent their sons to secondary school ten times more frequently than one would expect from their actual numbers. There was no examination for civil service entry until the 1870s and a secondary school education was considered the best preliminary training. A similar phenomenon has been observed in Germany, where a disproportionately high number of secondary school students were the sons of civil servants.

Modern research has modified the picture of a rigidly centralised, standardised system. Schools adapted their curriculum to the needs of the region and their market. Secondary school education was directed to the baccalaureate, but the *collèges* often provided only the early stages of the programme. From the 1830s some offered a curriculum without Latin, including practical subjects often more appealing to their less well-off clients. Some set up workshops. The *collège* at St Amour, Jura, offered a course at the *école professionnelle* to prepare students for the Ecole des Arts et Métiers. The syllabus was often geared to the perceived opportunities of the region. In some more backward areas literacy was prized because job possibilities were so few in the locality. Thus classical studies were well received in rural Brittany. The small *collège* at St Meen, Brittany, was turned into a *petit séminaire* in 1823 because the priesthood seemed the only route to advancement for the local peasantry. In some industrial areas job availability encouraged parents to withdraw their children from school. The children in the textile and mining areas of the Nord had low rates of literacy because of this temptation. Lack of interest in the classics in Armentières, north of Lille, led to a cut in the salaries of the classics teachers. Parents did not always make obvious choices of schools. Lille founded an *école primaire supérieure* in 1837 in accordance with the Guizot law, but local artisans preferred the *collège municipal*. The prosperous middle class of Lille, however, did not want their children taught industrial subjects but how to behave as members of the élite to which they aspired; in consequence they sent their children to the Assumptionist *collège*. If the local *collège* did not offer a practical course instead of the classical, a few larger industrial towns like Mulhouse might sport an industrial or commercial school. Some Catholic schools were also geared to the needs of the industrial middle class, like the *pensionnats* of the Christian Brothers. Thus, although the baccalaureate was important, education was adapted to local needs.[10]

If current research suggests that a wide range of parents were prepared to pay for secondary education, does this mean that education was, despite common assumptions, a vehicle of social mobility? A survey was made in 1865 of secondary school graduates, comparing the careers they sought and the jobs they actually obtained. The determining factor in a boy's decision was not the type of school he attended and the course taken, but his father's job. While 50 per cent planned to apply to a *grande école*, 20 per cent expected to farm or be small businessmen. Among the professions, the law, the civil service or St Cyr was preferred. Medicine and teaching, especially at the elementary levels, were unattractive. Pharmacy and veterinary science, also of low status, trawled the peasantry for applicants. Only 10 per cent of those who entered elementary school teaching were secondary school graduates; most had only an elementary background. The Ecoles des Arts et Métiers offered both a training in engineering or a craft and a chance of social advancement for the sons of artisans, peasants and clerks. But not all families of modest means who had scraped to educate their sons at secondary level dreamed of future teachers, vets or civil servants. In the 1860s 40 per cent of shopkeepers' sons at secondary school planned to enter the family business. Unique among middle-class parents of secondary schoolboys, members of the industrial bourgeoisie did not plan for their sons to follow their example. They hoped to transform their offspring into civil servants. Only one in eight of the sons of the industrial middle class expected to imitate their father and only one in three planned a business career of any kind. Commerce was ranked higher than industry. Forty per cent of the sons of the commercial middle class expected to be like father.[11] Others in the industrial and commercial groups looked to the Ecole Polytechnique, the law or the army for future generations and thus provided their sons with a classical education, though most undertook relevant vocational training. No boys from other social categories planned to be entrepreneurs.

It is apparent from these contemporary surveys that schools were not vehicles of social change. A boy usually followed his father's career and the father would select a school accordingly. There was some lateral movement within the middle class which allowed boys from more modest backgrounds to progress. Parents with a family business were disinclined to opt for a secondary school. Business families who spent money on secondary schooling often did so to direct their sons into a different career from their own. Education was unquestionably appreciated for its social advantages.

The lower middle class who did not opt for secondary schooling, but were prepared to educate their children beyond the primary level, had the choice of diocesan colleges, *petits séminaires* or the higher primary schools, which in the 1880s developed a 'modern' curriculum. By 1902 there were 302 of them. In a survey of their pupils during the 1890s, it was found that 30 per cent of fathers were in industry, mainly as workers, 23 per cent in business, chiefly as clerks, and 17 per cent in agriculture. Government employees and teachers provided another 23 per cent. Pupils seem to have followed their fathers' jobs. Those from small family firms and farms went back to them, 37 per cent went into industry, mainly as workers, 22 per cent into business, 11 per cent into agriculture, 17 per cent became clerks and 5 per cent entered government service or became teachers.[12] Clearly the higher primary schools, responsible for educating most of the middle class, were equally preservers of the status quo. By 1881–2, when the Ferry laws decreed the introduction of a universal primary system, most boys and girls already received a basic elementary education, while a minority of the less well-off went on to the higher primary schools. But Ferry's additional expectation, that the French system would be lay, was never realised. By 1914, 25 per cent of girls and 12 per cent of boys were still in Catholic primary schools and 40 per cent of secondary pupils attended Catholic institutions.

Thus in nineteenth-century France there was expansion, standardisation of organisation and some limited diversification in curriculum, but no wavering from systems designed to preserve, perpetuate and accentuate class differences and divisions. The emergence of a democratic political framework after 1871 did nothing to alter this situation, indeed some of France's most élitist institutions like Sciences Po developed during the Republic. There were perhaps more opportunities for sideways and upwards movements for sons of the lower middle class when the 'modern' baccalaureate was recognised for entry to the Ecole Polytechnique, and there was also a noticeable increase in the numbers of sons of the industrial and commercial middle classes in both 'modern' and classical streams.

There were many similarities between the attempts to develop an education system in nineteenth-century Italy and those in France. As in France, the Church was the main educator in the eighteenth century, providing exclusive secondary establishments and embryonic primary arrangements for the less well-off, mainly concerned with instilling adequate literacy for religious practice and encouraging some boys to join the priesthood. Interest was concentrated at the secondary and tertiary levels, with elementary education left in a parlous state in the second half of the century, the Church having been discouraged and the local authorities having been left both to provide and pay for the schools. Before the years of Napoleonic control, there had been plans for changes in Italian secondary education, particularly after the expulsion of the Jesuits from Naples in 1767, but they had not come to fruition. French conquest brought the French system. In 1806 Joseph Bonaparte started to found royal colleges for boys and some for girls. They were similar to *lycées* and he planned a centralised system of colleges and sixteen higher secondary schools, or *lyceums*. Other parts of Italy produced schemes along the same lines, with Piedmont, Tuscany and Parma in the lead. The Restoration rulers inherited these plans, but did little to develop them, finance being a not inconsiderable factor. In the 1830s and 1840s opposition liberals began to put forward plans for primary education in a spirit of enlightened self-interest, aware that Restoration regimes were becoming more sensitive to the problems of the poor, but were not anxious to educate them. Apart from Lombardy, where the ratio of primary school pupils to the population was 1:13 compared with 1:30 in France, there were very few primary schools. The concern of the liberals with primary schooling centred around visible aspects of social decay, a perceived rise in criminality and an increase in the number of abandoned babies. Women working in the industrial workshops of Milan left their children in order to survive themselves. Liberals agonised that industrialisation was undermining the whole basis of the family and led to immorality and social collapse.

Once in power in Piedmont after 1848 they laid plans for a centralised state educational system in the Casati law (1859), which was subsequently applied to the whole of Italy.[13] It provided for the setting up of a two-year programme of primary education, but few municipalities had the cash to build a school, never mind pay a teacher. Illiteracy remained around 78 per cent. The dissolution of the religious orders and the sale of Church lands in 1866, following the Papal condemnation of liberalism and refusal to recognise the new government, eliminated orders which had provided some rudimentary facilities in the south. The Church constantly opposed the spread of lay schools, and communes deplored the expense. However by 1876 only 96 communes out of 8000 had no school and nominally there were nearly 2 million pupils between six and nine according to the Coppino law of 1877. But annually at least one-third left before the end of the year. By 1876 there were 112 normal schools to train elementary teachers, mostly in northern and central Italy. Teachers were unwilling to teach in the south because of language and cultural problems. Many parts of the south would not accept a woman teacher. Pay was very low, 600 lire, the equivalent of about £24. In the 1860s 27 per cent of teachers were still priests, nuns and monks. In 1900 50 per cent of children were illiterate; 70 per cent in the south, 32 per cent in the north. By 1904 25 per cent of children still did not attend school.[14] Rural schools provided only two years of schooling, with most children still leaving at nine. Educational opportunities for those from poor backgrounds, particularly from rural areas, were very circumscribed indeed. However, unlike the other countries we have discussed, Italian primary schools were not necessarily a dead-end. The Casati law provided for transfer from primary to secondary school, making an 'open' system and thus offering some chance of social mobility.

After unification secondary education was also standardised and low fees made these schools far more accessible to the lower middle class than comparable establishments elsewhere. There were two stages: a five-year course at a *gymnasium* was followed by three years at a *lyceum*. The *gymnasium* concentrated on Italian, Latin and Greek. Physics and chemistry were started at the *lyceum*. Teachers were meant to be university graduates. Each province was supposed to have a secondary school, but the distribution of *gymnasia* was better than that of *lyceums*. Some secondary schools were state-run, some by religious orders, while some where seminaries. By 1876 there were 104 *gymnasia* and 80 *lyceums*, with over 40 000 pupils. Of these over 10 000 were in seminaries and 5743 in privately run schools. The schools run by the religious orders were the most effective. Only 36 schools offered the full three-year *lyceum* course. Many of the wealthy were still taught by private tutors. There were some state boarding schools for the rich, the *convitti nazionali*. These were expensive and very aristocratic, although there were government grants for pupils. In all about 65 000 students received a secondary education,[15] a higher proportion than in the other states we have examined. In the early twentieth century, when commentators became alarmed at the existence of a large educated 'proletariat', secondary school fees were raised to discourage the poor.[16] Educational development in united Italy was very sparse and overtly responsive to political and social pressures. Her educational resources were unequally applied, a disproportionate amount being devoted to secondary and higher education, not in itself unusual but in Italy leading uniquely to the production of a virtually unemployable educated lower middle class. This phenomenon underscores the fact that nineteenth-century education was used as a blunt instrument by politicians. Instead of trying to encourage the economic development of the south, which would have been a long-term policy, successive governments responded to the immediate demands of local politicians by supplying cheap education for their voters. The provision of education was entirely subject to the pressures of the clientage and patronage network. Other political problems did not help. In the years before 1914 there were 35 Ministers of Education, which both indicates the undesirability and low-ranking of the appointment and offers a salient explanation for the absence of long-term planning and serious development.

In Germany too social and political pressures were increasingly apparent, but for opposite reasons. The rapid industrialisation which accompanied equally fast population growth in the later stages of the nineteenth century made restructuring to preserve traditional values essential. Governments had assumed a dominant role in German education over a long period and at all levels. Even more than in France, secondary and higher education were designed specifically to create and sustain a recognised ruling élite. The significance of the classics, of long, strenuous courses and successive

examinations, state-run, committed the embryonic professional or
civil servant to a rigid and centralised state system. The Prussian
government made the first moves in the direction of compulsory
primary education in 1711, with limited success at first. However
by 1835 75 per cent of children were receiving education in Prussia
itself, 61 per cent in Posen. By the end of the century literacy rates
ran at 99.5 per cent. German educational systems were fairly
homogeneous even before unification. University students would
habitually attend successive universities in different states. By
the mid-nineteenth century primary education was more or less
universal. *Volksschulen* were provided for children between six and
thirteen, offering basic literacy skills and religious teaching. Pupils
could go on to higher primary or vocational schools, both of which
charged low fees. Higher primary schools, or middle schools, had
more pupils than all the secondary schools in the 1860s, and between
1885 and 1905 there were 50 per cent more children at middle
schools than at secondary schools. The figure included a substantial
number of girls: two-thirds of middle school pupils were girls in
1886. This was because until 1911 all girls' schools were listed as
middle schools. In principle a boy could move from a primary school
to a secondary school at about ten, but it was so rare that the system
can be considered quite separate. The curricula were different and
secondary school fees were high, 110–50 marks in 1900. The relative
cost can be gauged from the fact that a primary school teacher was
paid 1500 marks and a teacher in a secondary school 3000–7000
marks. Parents intending to send their children to secondary school
began with a private tutor or a pre-secondary school as in France.

The Prussian government was principally interested in education
to train and test bureaucrats and members of the professions,
including the clergy. In the *gymnasium* 46 per cent of the time was
spent on Latin and Greek, 4 per cent was devoted to French, 17.5
per cent to maths, physics and philosophy, etc. The nine-year course
was punctuated by annual examinations, which had to be repeated
if failed, and crowned by a final examination, the *abitur*. In 1812
this test was made more specific and standardised. The *abitur* was a
qualification for university, and until later in the century the
gymnasium remained the only institution teaching the *abitur*. Other
secondary schools, the high *burgher* and *realschulen* followed a separate
modern curriculum, reflecting social divisions in the same ways that
we have seen in France. Founded in the eighteenth century, *realschulen*

tried to offer the sort of practical education suitable for the sons of businessmen and farmers. It was intended that some would go on to intermediate provincial trade schools or vocational and technical academies. However, as in France, the industrial and commercial middle classes often felt that such an education was second-best, and in 1859 the schools were reorganised into *realgymnasien*, running a nine-year course with Latin, no Greek, but introducing modern languages. More natural science was taught. But the course did not offer the educational and professional privileges of the classical *abitur*. Some schools remained as traditional *gymnasien*. In 1882 a technical secondary school was created, the *oberrealschule*.

Social as much as pedagogical criteria were used to judge the schools. The classical *gymnasium* was the ideal and its standing rose in comparison with other schools. *Gymnasien* were revered as the defenders of social order and privilege. In the 1840s the Minister of Culture criticised the *realschulen* as centres of materialism and possible revolution. The 'modern' *abitur* was fiercely attacked because it might undermine established social and political values. The classical ideal became tangled with political conservatism and social snobbery, particularly after the failure of the 1848 revolutions. The universities and the professions resisted change, condemning the modern, technical *abitur* as inferior. Students with these *abitur* could only go to the technical institutes. From 1870 graduates of *realgymnasien* could enrol in faculties of philosophy, but by 1879 the number of 'modern' *abitur* students in these faculties had grown so large that experts were urging either withdrawal of the right or its extension. Finally in 1901 all *abitur* were recognised by universities. Priests still had to be *gymnasium* graduates, law students also had to know Latin, and Greek was still demanded of medical students.

Just as in France the various types of schools attracted pupils from quite different social backgrounds. The *gymnasium* was dominated by the bureaucracy. In the last years of the eighteenth century 40 per cent of fathers were officials, officers or professional men, 33 per cent were clergymen or secondary school teachers, 14 per cent were non-commissioned officers, soldiers, primary school teachers, artisans and workers, 6 per cent were merchants and manufacturers, 5 per cent were peasants and day labourers, and 2 per cent were landowners. The *gymnasium* was far more of a middle-class school than comparable ones in Britain or France. Even in the nineteenth century they taught few sons of nobles. During the century they were increasingly attractive to the growing industrial and commercial middle class, who took up a third of the places in the later years. As in France the lower ranks of the civil service and teachers' families were disproportionately represented. The liberal professions, clergy and higher civil servants continued to dominate and set the tone. Secondary schools did not encourage upward social mobility for the poorer groups. The few who broke through entered the Church, as in France, or the civil service. By 1900 two-thirds of those in the *oberrealschulen* came from families where the father was in industry or commerce or the technical professions, compared to one-half of the *gymnasium* boys. Middle-ranking civil servants sent their children to all types of school. At the *gymnasien* 22 per cent of fathers had attended a university, compared to 7 per cent at the *realgymnasien* and 4 per cent at the *oberrealschulen*. One fifth of fathers had themselves passed the *abitur*.[17] Thus the school system deliberately echoed and reinforced the established social groupings in the country.

The pedagogical and social opportunities of secondary education were specifically and increasingly restricted to the rich. In 1820 1000 boys passed the *abitur*. By 1830 this number had doubled, but was to fall subsequently, reaching 2000 again in 1860. As the population was rising sharply this reflects a real drop in the number of boys in secondary education and seems to have corresponded to a period when there was serious concern that the system was producing too many educated men.[18] In these years the *realschulen* had about half as many pupils as the *gymnasien*. From the 1860s the numbers studying the non-classical curriculum grew more rapidly than did those of the *gymnasien*. In 1860 the *gymnasien's* share of secondary school pupils was 69 per cent, but by 1911 it was under 50 per cent. However their pupils continued to gain a higher proportion of *abitur* – 66 per cent in 1911 – and *gymnasien* continued to dominate secondary education, in tone, numbers of schools and intake.[19] Actual growth in secondary education before 1914 remained fairly modest. Non-classical education expanded in times of industrial optimism: most of the 50 per cent increase in secondary numbers between 1870 and 1914 occurred after 1890 in non-classical schools. Girls were not allowed to take the *abitur* and it was not until shortly before the First World War that a girls' leaving examination was introduced. Baden was the first university to accept women, Prussian universities the last. They gave way in 1914.

Up to 75 per cent of those who attended secondary school did not complete the *abitur* and the age at which many completed had become so advanced that educational experts became concerned about rather geriatric *gymnasien* generations. In the 1880s a substantial proportion did not finish until twenty and 25 per cent were actually over twenty.[20] The proportion going on to university fell from 98 per cent in 1832 to 73 per cent at the end of the century. In the 1860s *realgymnasien* began to award *abitur*, but only 30 per cent of their students entered university and only 20 per cent of *oberrealschule* graduates. The opportunity to take the *abitur* remained a privilege of a very narrow, mostly wealthy group. In 1870 0.8 per cent of 19-year-olds had the *abitur*; in 1911, 1.2 per cent. What did they do with it?

In the last quarter of the nineteenth century a survey was done of the 85 000 who passed the *abitur* in all secondary schools to determine their choice of careers. Unlike the somewhat similar survey of 1865 in France, it did not compare career choices with the father's job. Nor did the survey measure the dream against the reality; we do not know how far the graduates achieved their ambitions. The survey did not cover the 75 per cent of secondary school pupils who left before graduation, or otherwise failed to graduate. It is assumed that most went into industrial or commercial jobs. Of the graduates, 71 000 were from *gymnasien*, 13 000 from *realgymnasien* and 1000 from *oberrealschulen*. About 13 000 planned business or technical careers and 62 000 hoped to be judges, lawyers, officials, theologians, doctors, officers and teachers in secondary schools or universities. The *gymnasium* graduate expected the best job. Nearly 25 per cent hoped for senior posts in the law or government service, 42 per cent planned to be doctors or enter the Church and 10 per cent expected to be secondary school or university teachers. Thus 75 per cent expected to work in senior public service jobs or the liberal professions. Most of the rest opted for the army or less senior bureaucratic posts. Only 7 per cent chose a technical career and a mere 4 per cent commerce or banking. The *oberrealschule* graduates displayed very different preferences. Well over 50 per cent looked forward to careers in engineering, mining, architecture and the like, 11 per cent planned to take jobs in industry or commerce, while 25 per cent thought of teaching or applying to the middling ranks of the civil service. The *realgymnasium* pupils fell between the two, though nearer the latter, in their choices. Technical careers drew 30 per cent, commerce 10 per cent, and only 8 per cent planned to enter the liberal professions or senior levels of the civil service.[21]

In estimating the significance of such a survey which seems to confirm that German secondary schools, like the French, promoted or at least were a reflection of social stability, one should note that official posts carried such status that the growing entrepreneurial middle class, unsure of its position and ranking in society, were inclined to make private and commercial occupations sound as official as possible. Thus the statistics for those who planned to go into industry and commerce would be greater than they appear and the number who actually undertook such work considerably higher. Lower-middle-class craftsmen were increasingly anxious that their sons diversified, and they sent them to non-classical secondary schools, occasionally to *gymnasien*. But few went on to university: between 1840 and 1860 only one master artisan's son and one shopkeeper's son were among the 110 students from Cologne who entered Heidelberg University. Only in the years immediately before 1914 was there a marked change. As the civil service grew, craftsmen and shopkeepers, perhaps disenchanted with the prospects in their own calling, saw the prospects of 'clean' and reliable jobs for their sons, while the growth of clerical work offered similar, superficially non-servile work for their daughters.[22] It has to be recalled that the cost of fees made universities a daunting prospect for the lower middle class. Tuition, excluding examinations and registration, would cost 120–40 marks in theology, philosophy, maths and law and 230–40 in chemistry and medicine. It cost between 1000 and 2000 marks to study at university for one year.

The status of the *gymnasium* had a profound influence over the whole of secondary education, which was always seen as a pyramid with the *gymnasien* at the peak. They were almost entirely geared to training boys for the professions and the bureaucracy, and in doing so diverted the brighter from 'inferior' pursuits in trade and industry. Within their own terms they offered some upward mobility, for sons of minor officials to rise probably in the bureaucracy itself, and for sons of industrialists to enter the professions. There can be no doubt of the social dominance of the *gymnasien*, unchallenged by rivals such as the *lycées* faced in the Jesuit and Assumptionist schools. In 1905 among the army general staff officers, 101 had a *gymnasium* education, four had been to a *realgymnasium* and only four to an *oberrealschule*. A classical education was now part of the weaponry of the middle class in the struggle against working-class socialism.

The education system was used deliberately by the German government to maintain a privileged and hierarchical society. For more than in any other of these states, except Russia with its Table of Ranks, the privileges gained through education were specifically in the gift of the government. Six years of secondary education conveyed the desirable privilege of doing only one year of military service, and that as a volunteer not a conscript. The *abitur* was an automatic qualification for university and certain bureaucratic posts, and was a step on the ladder to further state examinations. Registration at university for three to five years gave a man the right to take other state examinations, regardless of whether he had taken or passed any exams set by the university. Universities and the professions combined to reinforce the system of privilege. Although after 1870 *abitur* graduates who had not attended a *gymnasium* could enrol at a university, none of the professions would accept them.

Education conferred social standing and perpetuated social divisions:

> Differences of education are one of the strongest . . . social barriers, especially in Germany, where almost all privileged positions, inside and outside the civil service, are tied to qualifications involving not only special knowledge but also 'general cultivation' and where the whole school and university system has been put into the service of this [ideal of] general cultivation.[23]

The educated élite scorned the newly rich industrialist, whatever his wealth. Education was as desirable to a middle-class German as was land to a Frenchman. Indeed the educated élite was the functional ruling class. It was also a fairly closed group. In 1885 out of a population of 47 million, 7.5 million were at primary school and 238 000 at secondary school, of whom 128 000 were at *gymnasien*. There were 27 000 university students, 2500 at technical institutes, and 1900 at academies of forestry, mining, veterinary science and agriculture. In Prussia over 85 per cent of *abitur* certificates went to students in *gymnasien* and 83 per cent of *gymnasien* students went on to university. There was almost no opportunity to rise socially through education. Education created a gulf in the German middle class similar to splits in Russia, dividing the industrial and commercial groups from the professional and bureaucratic. The latter recruited and replaced itself largely from within. Where there was some mobility, it was restricted to the upward movement of a very small number from the old traditional lower-middle-class groups.

As in France the existence of the *abitur*, expensive fees and rigid social norms concerning education made university the preserve of the rich. Only 1 per cent of the adult workforce went to university and over half of these followed their fathers in choice of subject and career.[24] Three contemporary surveys of the origins of students enable some comparisons to be made. A survey of the students at the University of Halle from 1770 to 1870, the university attended by most future civil servants, shows that few were from aristocratic families. In 1770 fewer than 25 per cent were sons of landowners or officers. Over half were from the professions, including the clergy (28 per cent), high officials and lawyers (19 per cent). By 1870 the proportion had dropped from 55 per cent to 33 per cent, and sons of minor officials and school teachers had replaced them, together providing 23 per cent of students. Just as in the *gymnasien*, education was offering lateral social mobility within the middle class. Few landowners, industrialists, businessmen or artisans sent their sons to university, accounting for 20 per cent in 1850 and rising to 25 per cent in 1870. Only 2–3 per cent of students were sons of industrialists. The few sons of the old 'burgher' group of artisans, merchants and shopkeepers who did go to university, a total of 9 per cent, were sent to 'improve' their job possibilities by qualifying for the professions or the higher civil service. Law students had the most highly educated fathers, followed by theologians: 40 per cent of the students in the Protestant faculties of theology in Prussian universities in 1900 had fathers who had attended university. This was in sharp contrast to the Catholics, only 4 per cent of whose fathers were university educated.

A survey of the students at Leipzig University who came from Württemberg, a larger and more commercial town than Halle, revealed a much larger proportion of students from commercial, industrial or artisan families, 30 per cent of the total. The faculties of law and philosophy, both arts and science, were large. But here too the proportion of students from professional or higher official families fell from 50 per cent at the beginning of the century to 30 per cent by 1880. The gap was filled, as in Halle, by sons of minor officials and teachers, with a larger share here being taken by sons of artisans and merchants and, to a lesser extent, as in Halle, by sons of industrialists. In all three surveys the proportion of lower-middle- and middle-class students rose in the nineteenth century. However after 1880 landowning families began to show a greater interest in education. A 1910 survey of Berlin students calculated that the proportion from propertied and commercial families had risen from 25 per cent in 1810 to 40 per cent. A 1925 survey of all Prussian universities showed that the numbers specifically from industrial and commercial backgrounds had risen from 25 per cent in 1870 to 40 per cent by 1900, and that the proportion whose fathers were university educated had dropped from 37 per cent in 1870 to 20 per cent by 1910. Thus universities were beginning to make an appeal to the new industrial and commercial middle classes, but not in proportion to the increasing wealth and numbers of these groups themselves. The sons of their employees did not even consider university entrance.[25]

The choice of subject and faculty tended to be determined by the social class of the father. The faculties of philosophy and theology drew from lower groups, especially minor officials, elementary school teachers, shopkeepers and artisans. Sons of clergy and officials had the added inducement that the already modest fees were organised as a loan for them, to be paid within their first six years' work. Few peasants or artisans reached university; the prerequisite of the *abitur* may have been even more daunting than the entrance tests previously set by universities. About 1 per cent of students came from such backgrounds and this proportion remained constant from the 1780s for at least a hundred years. They entered the faculties of philosophy or theology, the first to admit students with the modern *abitur*. They chose careers regarded as accessible by them and their families: theology and teaching. Salaries in the Church were so low, especially after 1875 when the functions of registrar and pastor were separated, that they held no attractions for the middle class and were a declining prospect for the poor. The courses in the faculties of philosophy and theology were the shortest, there was the chance of private teaching while they were studying and they would expect to enter paid employment on graduation, all factors of pressing concern when the family was not well-off. Clergymen could expect to earn about £90 at first, rising to £120 after five years. A teacher in a *gymnasium* would start at about the same level, but prospects for some were better. A head teacher would earn between £240 and £330. The faculties of philosophy, which at this time included science, were unusual in that their numbers grew constantly in the nineteenth century: from 2395 in 1831–6 to 6031 in 1871–6 and then, in common with other faculties, experiencing a rapid rise in the early 1880s to reach 9433 in 1881–4. But the greatest growth area was in science. In this 40-year period the number of science students multiplied by ten, whereas the number studying philology and history doubled. A substantial proportion of the science students planned to teach; scientists going into the business world would enrol in one of the specialised technical institutes.

Contemporary surveys[26] showed the tendency for a disproportionate growth in the numbers of students from the old traditional lower middle classes, minor officials, elementary school teachers and artisans, but a relatively small and slow increase in those from the new wealthy industrial and commercial middle class, with almost no representation at all from the new industrial working class. In Prussia between 1871 and 1900 only one student in a thousand was the son of a worker. But by 1902, over 38 per cent of students came from some sort of artisan or industrial and commercial background, compared to 35 per cent who were sons of officials of one kind or another, as Table 1 shows. Thus although the German educational system responded slowly to economic change, by the beginning of the twentieth century, although the classical *gymnasium* was still dominant, the need for men trained in the sciences had produced positive growth and the industrial and commercial middle classes were more involved in education.

There were many similarities between the French and German educational systems, and the development of each was carefully studied by the other, particularly when one thought the other had the military edge. Duruy consciously tried to imitate the German modern *abitur* in the mid-1860s, and after military defeat in 1870 the French became rather paranoic in trying to assess the contribution of Germany's supposed superiority in education to her military victory. More passed the baccalaureate per age group than passed the whole *abitur*, but more started the *abitur* and completed part of it, especially in the *realschulen*. The classical stream grew in neither state after mid-century, but fewer dropped out and more began to complete the whole programme. In both, non-classical examination courses were introduced, more consistently and rapidly in Germany, which

TABLE I   Social Origins of Prussian University Students, 1902–3[27]

	%
Lesser merchants and artisans	26.3
Middle and junior officials and elementary school teachers	22.6
Entrepreneurs and senior business employees	9.7
Farmers	6.3
Senior officials, judges, lawyers	6.1
Clergy	5.8
Large landowners and tenants	5.2
Doctors and vets	5.0
University-trained teachers	4.5
Supervisors and clerks in industry	2.3
Army officers	1.9
Workers	1.0
Rentiers	0.6
Unspecified	2·6

after 1870 the French held to be a factor in German victory. The modern courses of the *realschulen* were a model for French experiments. If one compares the *gymnasium* and the *lycée*, the former appears somewhat more 'democratic' in its intake: 50 per cent of students were upper middle class in Germany compared with 60–80 per cent in France. There were many more children of landowners and *rentiers* at French *lycées* than at *gymnasien*. Another striking difference was the high and growing proportion of sons of minor officials, elementary teachers and clergymen at the *gymnasium*, that is the traditional, non-entrepreneurial lower middle class, whereas in France the *lycées* were predominantly, though admittedly far from exclusively, the schools of the notables. In both countries the children of the entrepreneurial middle class went to *realschulen* and municipal *collèges*. One not inconsiderable element in the *gymnasium* and university was entirely lacking in France, the clergyman's son. In France the celibacy of the Catholic clergy constituted a species of brain drain, as the more energetic and intelligent peasants' sons were educated, promoted socially into the clergy, but were denied the right to produce a family whose social ascent would, to a modest degree, continue. University enrolment seems substantially higher in Germany, but theology, a popular subject in Germany, accounting for a third of students in mid-century, was not taught in French universities. University courses tended to be shorter in France, and until the shock of 1870 it was assumed that a boy's general education ended with the baccalaureate. In both the numbers in the technical institutes and the *grandes écoles* need to be taken into account to arrive at a realistic total of undergraduates.

Russian educational policy was more liberal in the early years of Alexander I's reign than at any other time before 1914. Subsequently successive ministers tried to use education as a tool of social engineering, to limit educational opportunities to a narrower and narrower group within the wealthy élite. In some ways one can compare this with attempts in Germany to restrict the size of the undergraduate population for fear of social and political upheaval. Certainly education, or rather its withdrawal from all but a wealthy élite, was seen as a prime means of social control. In France the significance of the Church in education became an increasingly contentious issue in Church–State relations. In Germany the Church was permitted a role in elementary education, to the displeasure of the teachers, but in other respects German education was indisputably a department of state. In Russia the relationship between Church and State was so close in educational matters that in 1817 the two ministries of education and religious affairs were merged. Nineteenth-century education policy swung between successive ministers, some of whom tried to promote a modest growth in scientific education and speculative thought and others for whom science and speculation were anathema and the main aim of education was the nurturing of religion. Thus Russia's educational development in the nineteenth century can only be understood by first grasping the scale and timing of policy changes.

The educational reform programme of Alexander I was similar in direction to those of Prussia and of France at the same time, and like them was designed to promote a privileged classical education for the élite and modest provision of basic skills for the less well-off under the aegis of the Church. The statute of 1804 divided Russia, under the supreme control of the Minister of Public Instruction, into six educational districts, each under the direction of a curator and each to have a university and a teachers' training institute. There were to be 3 *lyceums*, 57 *gymnasia* and 511 district schools.

Parochial schools were left as before to the municipalities, Church or local landowner, depending on who was willing to accept responsibility. By the time of the death of Alexander I in 1825 the number of universities had been doubled to six, with a total of 1700 students. There were 5000 pupils in the full complement of *gymnasia* and 30 000 in 370 district schools, and for the less well-off there was a very patchy provision of elementary education under the direction of a variety of agencies, including 100 000 in schools run by the army for the children of its own men.

Much was promised at the outset. The status of teachers, poor in Russia as elsewhere, was to be improved both by better training and pay and by including teachers in the Table of Ranks. A man who completed a doctorate of philosophy entered at the eighth rank and thus qualified immediately for hereditary nobility. University students were encouraged to study abroad. Education was to be available to all, regardless of sex and social status, a very daring prospect for any country in 1804. Scholarships were to make it easier for the less well-off to pursue a course of education and serf-owners were not to stand in the way of sons of serfs who wanted to study.

Elementary and secondary education were deliberately kept separate in Russia, as in other countries, and as the century progressed secondary schooling became the preserve of a smaller and smaller social élite, while the provision of primary schooling grew very slowly. Alexander I tried to open secondary education to all those with sufficient intellectual merit, regardless of social class. In line with the plans of Peter the Great and with the original Napoleonic schemes for the *lycées*, students were to take practical and technological subjects and to visit local factories. Neither technology nor education itself appear to have been taken very seriously by the Russian landed aristocratic élite at this time. An attempt by the minister Speransky to erect an educational hurdle in law and various scientific and commercial subjects at the eighth grade in the Table of Ranks led to his dismissal.

Imperial enthusiasm for liberal ideas did not outlast the French invasion and had started to wane earlier, in the face of noble resistance. The St Petersburg *gymnasium* adopted a classical bias in 1811 and it was decreed that children of serfs could only attend a *gymnasium* with special permission. Fees of 5–15 roubles were charged from 1818. The new minister, Prince Golitsyn, withdrew morals and civics from the syllabus of the *gymnasium* in favour of a new subject, bible-reading. As part of the wave of religious revival of these years, scientific and spiritual knowledge began to be seen as antithetical. Science was thought to be a danger to social stability and courses in technology and commerce in the *gymnasia* were eliminated.

There was a generally reactionary atmosphere in Europe in these years. In Russia the personality of the new ruler had an additional impact. Nicholas I was not intended for the throne and had trained as a soldier. He recognised the need for a number of educated men to staff the bureaucracy, but could see no justification for a broad, general education. Education was 'a pernicious luxury'. His policy widened the gulf between the intelligentsia, the upper classes and the rest of the country as schools and universities became exclusive and privileged bodies. Nicholas was convinced by his advisers that serfdom could only survive in an élitist educational system. Serfs were denied the right to attend *gymnasia*. The tsar blamed the Decembrist conspiracy on education. If serfdom were to survive, social groups had to be rigidly separated at school. Sons of peasants and craftsmen only were to attend parochial schools, sons of merchants and townsfolk district schools, and the sons of gentry and officials the *gymnasia*. In 1828 special scholarships were given to sons of gentry and government officials at the *gymnasia* in order to make their intake more socially exclusive. Certain *gymnasia* were designated for the sole use of the gentry, including Moscow, St Petersburg, Vilna and Kiev, where sons of nobles could complete the course in six instead of seven years. In 1845 fees were deliberately raised to 30 roubles to try to exclude sons of merchants, other members of the middle classes and the 'lower' orders. The provision of scholarships was extended and a proportion reserved for the sons of nobles, many of whom were far from wealthy. Sixty state scholarships of 600 roubles a year were provided in the St Petersburg *gymnasium*. Most went to nobles. The impact on the social composition of the *gymnasia* was marked. In 1826 there were 3608 sons of gentry, 885 of government officials, 257 of junior officials, 425 of merchants, 372 of citizens of modest means, 203 of clergy, 136 of craftsmen, 131 of private soldiers, 124 of peasants and 392 of free men in *gymnasia*. In other words there was still a fair proportion of unprivileged pupils. In 1826 69 per cent of pupils were sons of nobles, but by 1853 this had risen to 80 per cent. In 1826 27.8 per cent were sons of middling and poorer groups, in 1853 17.8 per cent. But only poorer gentry and noble families took these opportunities, which must have somewhat negated the official plan.

The syllabus of the *gymnasia* was narrowed in stages in the belief that a solid diet of the classics and religion was the best protection against radical thinking. *Gymnasia* offered two syllabuses, one totally classical, the other more scientific. But the scientific elements in the alternative syllabus were reduced in 1828. Greek was introduced into the alternative seven-year course to replace natural science, psychology, law, political economy, commerce and technology. French and maths were permitted, and a course with a commercial bias was tried in six *gymnasia*. By 1849, in response to consumer demand, only 9 out of 79 retained the entirely classical curriculum. In the 1860s the German system was followed even more closely. After much public debate on the value of a classical education and prolonged first-hand investigations of foreign systems by the Minister, Tolstoy, *gymnasia* were organised into two categories, *gymnasia* proper, which taught a uniform classical programme including Latin, and *realgymnasia*, which taught only a modern syllabus, but with a restricted diet in science for younger pupils. Only the *gymnasium* course offered a university entrance qualification, the *realgymnasia* prepared students for technical institutes. But only 5 out of the 80 *gymnasia* opted to be *realgymnasia* and 50 new *realgymnasia* were founded. Tolstoy tried to establish links with the district schools, encouraging them to prepare their pupils for the senior classes in the *realgymnasium*. Four-year *pro-gymnasia* were set up to prepare pupils for the *gymnasium*.

Alexander II met with a great deal of criticism of his education changes at all levels. The *pro-gymnasia* attracted peasant and worker families, who quickly took up a third of the places. Alexander III, convinced that education should prepare boys for their station in life, that is the one to which they were born, opposed this fluidity. In 1887 the preparatory classes were closed down. Many in the government would have liked a new onslaught on the propensity of the less well-off for education. Instead, certain social categories were banned from the *gymnasia*, including sons of prostitutes, cabmen, cooks, waiters, washerwomen and shopkeepers. The proportion of gentry rose from 47 to 56 per cent. Even so 25 per cent of nobles were still illiterate at the end of the century. Merchants became keen on *gymnasium* education because the leaving certificate entitled their sons to enter a university and enabled their daughters to mix in suitably exalted circles in preparation for marriage. The Ministry of Public Instruction came to regret the increasing popularity of the *realgymnasia*, but failed in its attempts to downgrade the course by reducing it to five years. Instead the State Council encouraged the passing of legislation which changed the practical syllabus into a more academic 'general' course, but made transfer from elementary schools impossible. In both France and Germany a similar transformation of these courses took place. A parallel reduction in the hours devoted to the classics in the *gymnasia* narrowed the gap between the two types of school. By 1914 there were 453 *gymnasia* for boys with 152 110 pupils, 291 *realgymnasia* with 80 000 boys. In total contrast to the other countries studied, here schools became increasingly politicised, in protest against rigid centralised control and the impossibility of transferring from one type of school to another. There were active protest movements in schools. All secondary school teachers and pupils in Odessa were on strike from October 1905 to the beginning of 1906. The absence of a national elected assembly may have been a factor in the behaviour of schools.

The Russians always seem to have been more willing to educate girls than other European societies. In 1808 there were girls in the *gymnasia* and in the district schools. The Smolny Institute had been opened by Catherine II as a secondary boarding school for girls and others were started, all for nobles and officials of course. Nicholas I was suspicious of women's education and it was left to Alexander II to regenerate Russian interest. The government began to give grants to district schools and *gymnasia* and day schools for girls were also established. Girls' boarding schools were divided into three types, those for the nobility alone, those for nobles, officials and merchants, and those which catered for all comers. During Alexander II's reign the first two were merged. By 1914 there were 323 577 girls in *gymnasia* and *pro-gymnasia* and two years later Duma legislation recognised that the girls' courses were on a par with those taken by boys. Long before this universities had begun to allow women to enrol. In 1868 the first courses for women were held at St Petersburg University, attended by 767 women. Four years later women were admitted to the Military Medical Academy in St Petersburg and women were employed by the bureaucracy, particularly in medical and teaching jobs. By 1881 there were 990 courses for women at St Petersburg University. In 1897 a Medical Institute for Women was founded in St Petersburg. By 1904 there were 5000 women in higher education and by 1908 all universities were running courses for women, still as external students however. Typical of Russia, there were bureaucratic setbacks; in 1908 it was made illegal for a university to enrol a woman and all were expelled, including those who had almost completed their courses. Nonetheless, by 1910 there were 20 higher institutes solely for women, with 20 000 students. At that time there were 40 000 men in higher education and a total of 90 000 women and men in all branches of higher education.

At the start of Alexander I's reign university tuition was free and anyone could enrol who passed either the university entrance exam or the *gymnasium*-leaving exam. Well over 1000 of the 3000 students in higher education received state scholarships which covered all their living costs. The majority of these were from the clergy and the lower classes. Most of those who paid their own way were also from the lower classes and some were serfs. Serf-owners had to agree to support them and not call upon them for labour while they were studying. Serf doctors had to serve their lord as doctors for six years, after which they were free.[28] Thus the social composition of Russian universities was unique in the early 1800s and indeed they were apparently more democratic in intake than the universities of any modern state. In the later years of Alexander I's reign the picture began to change and his successor was convinced of the total incompatibility of the education of serfs and the lower orders with the maintenance of serfdom and an autocratic system of government. The introduction of fees and a policy of restricting enrolment to the nobility were the means employed to revolutionise the student body. In 1828 at St Petersburg University there were 84 students, 28 on state scholarships, nearly all of them clergy. Of the rest, 26 were nobles or officials, 13 were middle class, 10 were Roman Catholic monks or priests, 4 were orthodox clergy and 3 were lower class. By 1838 the proportion of upper-class students had risen, corresponding to the determination of the government. Out of 241 students in St Petersburg, 193 were upper class (157 nobles, 36 officials) and there were a smaller proportion of middle- and lower-class students, 39 and 9. The number of state scholarships, providing everything for the students, increased, but the nobles were now the beneficiaries. The government was the most generous in Europe in scholarship provision. The Mining Institute had 60 scholarships. Holders had to work for the state for six years after graduation.

Nicholas I was determined to eliminate unprivileged undergraduates. Universities were restricted to taking students only from the nobility and the bureaucracy. Fees were introduced in 1839 and increased in 1845 to 40 roubles and again in 1848 to 50 roubles. In 1840 curators were instructed to interview prospective candidates 'in order to keep away from the universities young men who have received no education in the homes of poor parents of lower origin'.[29] In 1845 university entry was restricted to the privileged, which included first-grade merchants, unless a man had a certificate discharging him from his class. The events of 1848 in western Europe appalled Nicholas and convinced him that too many young men were being educated. Universities were limited to an enrolment of 300 and were ordered to fill their places, where possible, with sons of nobles, 'persons of lower origins . . . generally become restless citizens'.[30] By the end of Nicholas I's reign this aim had been accomplished. Other restrictions were also introduced. Only members of the Orthodox Church could enter a *gymnasium* or a university. In 1852 there was a further increase in fees. Municipalities were obliged to support nobles in university hostels, which tended to use up the municipalities' entire budget. The government provided scholarships for 140 nobles in each of the medical faculties. Despite the efforts of successive governments, the proportion of nobles at university fell. In 1880 over 46 per cent of university students were hereditary nobles; by 1914 this had fallen to 36 per cent. But they were still the largest single group[31] and the hostility displayed by universities to all governments demonstrated beyond doubt the failure of the regime to ensure its own security by protecting and enhancing the privileges of the nobility.

Successive tsars were in no doubt that a formal education system should succour the autocracy and its main prop, the nobility. Overzealous to learn from the mistakes of western Europe, Alexander I's liberal policies were reversed in his own lifetime and education became increasingly narrow in all respects. Fees and social and scholarship restrictions were designed to carry favour with the nobility and failed. The tsars cut themselves off from the potential support which liberal policies might have won. Educational policies prevented the emergence of an educated, politically co-operative middle class, such as was the cornerstone of the ruling élite in the other states under examination here. Education became more and more of a political and actual battlefield in Russia, with strikes in schools and universities and confrontation with police trying to assert the dominance of the government. In this respect Russia was not unique. In France repeated conflict occurred between universities and individual governments and in the early years of the twentieth century there was prolonged dissension and unrest in medical faculties over the scope of medical education.[32] Given the expectations and assumptions of the ruling élites, education could never be politically neutral, and given the repeated Church–State wranglings in France it was likely to remain a witch's brew. As a prime instrument of social control and engineering, education increasingly left children of the poor, especially of the industrial working class, alienated and excluded from all but elementary education and limited vocational training. For such groups the priesthood, the traditional bolt hole of the intelligent son of a poor family, was inappropriate. To some degree educational facilities within other institutions, particularly the socialist parties like the SPD in Germany and associated bodies such as the WEA in Britain, provided an answer and averted the exacerbation of social tensions. The persistent assertion of the pre-eminent merits of a classical education for the better-off, and the dilution of the scientific content of the modern syllabus, left many of the industrial and commercial middle class uninterested in anything more than a fairly rudimentary education for their sons, unless they wanted to divert them into a different career. By 1914 such groups were beginning to be more active consumers of education and assumptions about the nature of education itself showed signs of change. Of one thing we can be sure. Education was no civilising universal panacea, as some eighteenth-century philosophers had hoped. It divided society, and especially the middle class itself, and it was the positive intention of most nineteenth-century politicians that such divisions should be permanent.

8. The Bourgeois Revolution 1789–1815

In explaining the nature of class Marx stressed economic and political constituents: a group only became a class when they were aware of their common interests and co-operated to protect them. The two elements appear somewhat contradictory since Marx also believed that the economic drive behind bourgeois capitalism was cut-throat competition. So far in this account each aspect investigated has revealed, if not rivalry, differences and divisions: within the industrial and commercial element, the identification of middle-class landed interests with those of the aristocracy; within the professions, the most typical bourgeois groups, in splitting the bourgeois who served the state, either in a civil or a military capacity, from other sections; and finally, although the four countries have demonstrated similar philosophies of education, schools themselves reinforced the fragmentation and hierarchical tendencies within the bourgeoisie. The political dimension remains. Did political concerns draw the middle classes together? There are indications of a single thread. Historians have emphasised the importance of bourgeois revolution in 1789, 1830 and 1848, the subsequent decline of liberal ideas and the emergence of anti-socialist and conservative nationalist movements later in the century.

'The French Revolution marks the rise of bourgeois, capitalist society in France,' insisted one of France's leading Marxist historians.[1] Marx and his followers asserted that the 1789 revolution in France was a bourgeois revolt which facilitated a middle-class takeover of the state and the development of a capitalist, entrepreneurial economy. It has also been suggested that French victories in the wars 1792–1814 permitted the rise of new middle-class élites in conquered territories. In recent years a revisionist school of historians, part anti-Marxist, part empirical, has attacked this thesis. Currently the revisionists themselves are being revised. While this debate is in some respects a French hothouse, the revisionist 'industry' has had repercussions on detailed studies of the Italian and German states under French occupation and on broader issues of political and social change in these areas. In this chapter we shall consider the French, German and Italian experience between 1789 and 1815. In Russia in these years the autocracy was totally unchallenged by the bourgeois groups, whose political concerns were municipal. Therefore no mention will be made of Russia. We may reasonably assess the significance of 1789 and its aftermath for the bourgeoisie by considering to what extent the revolution was bourgeois first in origin, second in its processes and institutional achievements, and finally in its long-term consequences.

The Marxist thesis is weakest in its presentation of the origins of the revolution as a bourgeois capitalist onslaught on aristocratic feudal structures. Although France was the most industrialised power in continental Europe in 1789, well over 75 per cent of her population lived by agricultural pursuits and most of her industry was artisanal and rural-based. There were entrepreneurial capitalists, but a not insubstantial number were nobles, just as there were many bourgeois landowners, as we have already observed. Alfred Cobban, who pioneered the empirical questioning of previously very vague, but very influential, Marxist generalisations, chose as the title for his inaugural lecture at University College, London in 1955, 'The myth of the French Revolution'. He questioned the republican, Marxist views of Lefebvre and Labrousse, then wholly accepted by the academic establishment in France. His argument, that it was a nonsense to say that 1789 witnessed 'the substitution of a capitalist, bourgeois order for feudalism' is now very well known and was based on, and has been supported by, a vast accumulation of evidence especially of British and North American historians. Cobban emphasised the gradualness of social change; that feudalism as a system run solely by noble landowners alone no longer existed, but that feudal dues were in 1789 additional rents, sometimes payable to bourgeois 'feudal' lords, who exploited them ruthlessly. On the other hand there was no distinct new capitalist bourgeoisie ready to take over in France. Historians were thus urged to re-examine old assumptions and ideologically based constructs both about the significance of 1789 and the definition of 'bourgeois'. Cobban also attacked the woolly language then used by some social historians. He challenged the continued use by Marxists, anti-Marxists and non-Marxists of unqualified terms like 'feudalism', 'capitalism', 'bourgeois' and 'noble'.[2] Cobban's challenge was timely. The unpalatable form of the development of socialism in the USSR and the setbacks experienced by the French republic in the twentieth century contributed to a willingness to reconsider the orthodox French republican view that 1789 had launched the country along the road of progress towards socialism, marked by 1830, 1848, 1871 and, for Europe, by 1917 in Russia. Social history itself was becoming a more precise discipline at this time and technical developments permitted the quantification of the previously unquantifiable.

The Marxist analysis of the origins of 1789 depended on the belief that at the end of the eighteenth century there was an inevitable conflict between declining aristocratic landowners and ascending bourgeois capitalists.[3] 'In the second half of the eighteenth century the growth of a capitalist economy, the essence of bourgeois power, was held back by feudal structures.'[4] The detailed nature and composition of the pre-revolutionary élite began to come under scrutiny. Historians were beginning to question not only whether the revolution had been made by, and/or in the interests of, a frustrated new commercial bourgeoisie at odds with the traditional landed nobility, but also whether some bourgeois and noble interests were so very different before 1789. Forster's work on the nobility of Toulouse showed that the Saulx-Tavannes were very involved in the commercial management of their noble estates.[5] George V. Taylor demonstrated that the bourgeoisie did not dominate eighteenth-century capitalism and that indeed capitalist wealth was a minor element in the French economy of 1789. The acquisition of land and government stocks was as absorbing for bourgeois as for noble families.[6] In 1973 Colin Lucas concluded, 'The middle class of the late Ancien Regime displayed no significant difference in accepted values and above all no consciousness of belonging to a class whose economic and social characteristics were antithetical to the nobility.'[7] In France a new generation of historians also became revisionists, with Furet and Richet in the van.[8] A recent general survey of the revolution concludes that the nobility and bourgeoisie shared so many economic interests that they constituted a single class.[9]

The publications in the 1970s of historians such as Bergeron, Chaussinand-Nogaret and Tulard on the élites of the eighteenth century, the revolutionary and the imperial years continued this French reassessment. Basing their work, like Forster, on detailed and where possible statistical evidence, they stressed the evolutionary aspect of the social transformation of the period. They refuted totally the idea that the origins of 1789 are to be found in an ineluctable conflict between nobility and bourgeoisie. Chaussinand-Nogaret stressed the merging of nobles and rich bourgeois into a consolidated élite during the *ancien régime*, in which landed wealth was the key to status, marriage alliances a convenient social cement, and a noble title the crowning glory, readily available through the purchase of office. The contemporary term 'notable', employed by Napoleon's bureaucrats, has been used to describe this group by revisionists keen, as perhaps Napoleon's officials were also, to avoid 'class' terms. Wealthy nobles and bourgeois tended to have similar interests and ambitions. Both royals and nobles were deeply involved in industrial investment, the duc d'Orleans was in glass, the comte d'Artois chemicals and the nobility were enthusiastically financing the exploitation of the resources under their lands and the forests on them to develop substantial mining and metallurgical concerns. Choiseul and de Broglie were prominent in the iron-smelting industry. Wealthy bourgeois, whatever the original source of their wealth, preferred to renounce industry in favour of land, office and titles.[10] The revisionist conclusion was that society was evolving gradually towards capitalism, but that the bourgeoisie did not dominate the transition and, far from being in conflict with the nobility, were barely distinguishable from them. Unlike Marxists, revisionists denied that the revolution had a social imperative. The Marxists seem to have no case and to have retreated into condemning revisionists as unpatriotic belittlers of 1789.[11]

The initial challenge to the Crown came from the privileged orders. In the second half of the eighteenth century, the writings of the *philosophes*, the political conflict of the French monarchy with established corporate groups like the *parlements* and the financial insolvency of the Crown led to profound and prolonged debate on the nature of French government and the desirability of political change.[12] The serious financial embarrassment of Louis XVI seemed at first a chance for nobles and wealthy notables like the *parlementaires* to defeat modest attempts by government ministers to control the political and financial privileges of the wealthy and extend the power of the Crown. A proportion of the privileged favoured innovation, but in the hope of reducing royal prerogative in their own favour. In their quarrels with the Crown the *parlements* raised the question of representation, but anticipated that they would be considered the most appropriate representatives of the nation. The calling of an Assembly of Notables in 1787 and the introduction of provincial assemblies aroused expectations of change among diverse groups, which caused some members of privileged groups to hesitate. There was widespread peasant insurrection long before the calling of the previously moribund Estates General in May 1789. The attempt of the *parlementaires* to insist that the three estates met separately as in the last assembly of 1614 began to expose the many divisions among privileged groups, but they had set in motion a process which for a time at least was beyond their control.

The initiative passed, with the calling of the Estates General, to the bourgeoisie, but not the entrepreneurs. The Third Estate assembly was dominated by traditional groups: 43 per cent were office-holders, 25 per cent lawyers and only 13 per cent, 85 members, were in trade, industry and banking.[13] Motives were varied. The quarrel between the king and the privileged bodies, the writings of the *philosophes*, career frustrations experienced by office-holding groups all contributed to the expectation that the meeting of the Estates General would produce political change. To conclude on the origins of the revolution: there appears to be no case for the Marxist argument, which indeed was elaborated by later socialists beyond Marx's original idea, that 1789 merely began a process of change.[14] On the other hand, the revisionist contention that France had a totally consolidated élite in 1789 seems to move too far in the opposite direction and would seem to ignore the political and social conflicts of the 1790s as much perhaps as Marxists have overemphasised them. An industrial bourgeoisie did not initiate the revolution, but in the 1790s traditional bourgeois groups assiduously tried to dismember much of the apparatus of privilege of the *ancien régime*. Thus 1789 was no capitalist bourgeois revolution in inception, but in its processes and new institutions the traditional bourgeoisie attempted to consolidate its position and assume control.

We may therefore turn to consider the revolution itself, the events of which have been somewhat neglected by revisionists, but interest in which is now reviving.[15] The revolution may not have begun with aristocratic and bourgeois rivalry, but to believe that such conflicts were insignificant involves ignoring the events of the 1790s. In the summer of 1789, many nobles, alarmed at the growth of urban unrest and by the mounting attack on the Church, made common cause with the king, an alliance which nineteenth-century ultras conveniently forgot was far from predictable in the country of the Frondes. This alignment of king, clergy and nobility against the revolution was somewhat unexpected and far from total, for some poorer nobles and clergy joined the Third Estate in the self-styled National Assembly. But it was sufficiently comprehensive to isolate the nobility, altering an argument that began over finance and political representation into one which significantly divided society. The scale of popular disturbance and foreign war, in which *emigrés*, many of them noble, fought against France, turned nobles into enemies of the state and thence into enemies of society. An 'aristo's' crime lay far more in his political and religious attitudes than his birth, which was often not noble. Only 8 per cent of the heads of noble families became *emigrés*. But *emigré* land was confiscated, those accused as traitors were guillotined. The whole concept of nobility came under attack, the term 'aristo' became one of vituperative abuse and nobles were deprived of a vote and the right to sit in revolutionary assemblies. In some respects, once the Crown had been challenged, the nobility with their distinctive privileges, were obvious targets. But the nobility were not the only privileged group: wealthy members of the bourgeoisie also owned feudal rights and were not keen to lose them. However the cascading violence and uncertainty of revolution were self-sustaining and exacerbated by foreign war and serious food shortages. Wealthy nobles, rich clerics and the royal family were convenient scapegoats. Traditional social rivalries and jealousies were transformed into an ineluctable conflict, violently interrupting gradual changes in norms and in society itself, provoking an unnatural and, as it emerged, sometimes temporary divorce between noble and bourgeois élites, within the bourgeoisie itself, and between them and sans-culottes, and exacerbated long-standing and profound rivalries between country and town, and between Church and State.

In sympathy with the ideas of some of the *philosophes*, the bourgeois leaders of the revolutionary assemblies hoped to replace the privileged society of the *ancien régime* with codified legal equality and political and constitutional rights permanently conferred on French citizens in a written constitution. All adults were deemed citizens and equal before the law, but few politicians in the 1790s believed that all should be politically equal. The sovereignty of the people was translated into regimes of electors and legislators, and the various constitutions of the 1790s provided for a restricted direct suffrage, or for indirect elections. The first constitution of 1791, which created a constitutional monarchy, distinguished between passive citizens, equal before the law but with no political voice, and active citizens, who had to be male, twenty-five or over and pay a substantial sum in direct tax. Hence 4 300 000 active citizens chose an élite of 50 000 electors. Popular violence convinced the comfortably-off members of the assembly that a tax qualification for political participation was vital for their own security and that of their property. The attitude of the king, the vicissitudes of war and the intervention of the Parisian crowd against the monarchy in August 1792 was to signal the collapse of this constitutional experiment, the declaration of a republic and the execution of the king.

Whereas the traditional professional and office-holding bourgeoisie dominated the assembly of the limited monarchy, the Convention was elected directly by all adult males. In the confusion of war, invasion and civil war, power appeared to pass to the Parisian sans-culottes, a term more political than social but including mainly artisans. Ambitious politicians of the Jacobin faction used the threat of 'popular' intervention to defeat their political rivals and concentrate executive power into a twelve-man Committee of Public Safety, for which Robespierre became the spokesman. The arbitrary use of power, and particularly the bloody events of the Terror, subsequently discredited democratic republican institutions. For over half a century élitist regimes, both oligarchical and dictatorial, were justified by the well-off by reference to the so-called extreme and violent proclivities of the poor. An oligarchical republican Directory was succeeded, amidst rumours of a royalist takeover, by a three-man Consulate, in which France's best-known general, Bonaparte, was the dominant figure. In 1804 he made himself Emperor and the republic was formally abolished. The Directory had reintroduced indirect elections, Napoleon made consultation of the popular will through elections totally meaningless. Despite the existence of consultative assemblies, Napoleon conserved real authority for himself and his Council of State, appointed by him to prepare legislation; this prompted de Tocqueville to conclude that ultimately the revolution merely consolidated the centralisation of the Bourbons. Napoleon introduced a new device, the plebiscite, ostensibly to permit consultation but in fact doing no more than orchestrate uncritical applause. The military, bureaucratic dictatorship seems to have been acceptable enough in France, at least while the armies were victorious, and the extent of French conquests appears to have been sufficient compensation to the revolutionary politicians for the loss of the ephemeral political rights they had claimed with such vigour in the 1790s.

The key to the willingness of those who had previously demanded a share in government to live, frequently enthusiastically, in a dictatorship more complete than that of the Bourbons lies partly in the fear of those with property of repeated social upheaval and the need to protect French territory. There was also the belief that Napoleon epitomised their aspirations in his efficient completion of much revolutionary legislation including the codes of law. Perhaps there was also an expectation that, once war was over, somewhat more effective parliamentary institutions would be established, although this last, asserted in the *Acte Additionel* of the Hundred Days, has the ring of cynical imitation of the Bourbon constitution of 1814. Perhaps the administrative, judicial, military and other appointments which the Empire offered were sufficient compensation for the withdrawal of political responsibility.

The political inheritance of the revolutionary years was thus varied and ambiguous, but resonant with models for both nineteenth-century France and the rest of Europe. Despite the presence of occasional members of the nobility and clergy such as Mirabeau and Sieyès, the prosperous middle class of professional men, land-owners, etc. was undoubtedly responsible for the experimentation of the 1790s and the acceptance of a military dictatorship. It would be impossible to claim, in the light of France's economic development in 1789, that this was a capitalist bourgeois affair, but it did represent an attempt by the middle class to achieve political power for property-owners like themselves and to control unseemly popular movements.

Our two remaining questions concern the long-term social implications of the revolution. To what extent did the revolution transform agrarian feudalism into industrial capitalism? Did a new élite emerge? Some policies in the 1790s intensified social conflicts, although often more for political than social reasons. The abolition of feudal dues on the night of 4 August, the confiscation and sale of *emigré* and Church lands in the 1790s and revolutionary legislation which continued the dismemberment of the communal and artisanal systems seem substantive evidence for Marxist claims that the social legislation of the revolution contributed to the development of capitalism.

However, as we have already observed, research on the sales of *biens nationaux* and corroborative evidence from lists of Napoleonic notables and electors of the subsequent period suggest that the old élite survived rather than that a new one emerged. As we have already noted, some nobles used the opportunity of the *biens nationaux* to buy additional land, or to repurchase their own land through their agents. In the Sarthe 50 of the purchasers were noble. Maupeou, grandson of the *ancien régime* minister, was a purchaser. War, civil war and Napoleonic policy called for a compromise and during the Consulate *emigrés* were given the opportunity to return and re-establish themselves. Legislation halted further sales and facilitated the return of unsold land, particularly in the west, centre and Midi. About 25 per cent of confiscated land was repurchased. In areas where the nobility were the dominant landowners before the revolution, their position remained secure. Investigations during the Consulate to find the twelve wealthiest taxpayers in each department produced lists headed by, and filled with, the names of *ancien régime* nobles. Only in a few industrial departments were non-nobles in prime place, for instance in Ardennes, Bas-Rhin, Haute-Marne and Nord. The richest man in the Nord was not an industrialist but a grain merchant who added to his already extensive estates by buying *biens nationaux*. Sometimes those rare lists dominated by industrialists could be ambiguous. Ironmasters led the lists in the Haute-Marne but, like Vandeul, were essentially landowners. In the July Monarchy Vandeul sometimes listed himself as a landowner first, sometimes as ironmaster, a warning to those who try to make too hard and fast a distinction between landed and business interests. Despite his major business concerns, Vandeul paid a much higher *foncière* (land tax) than *patente* (industrial tax), the latter of which was assessed on property, not profits.[16]

Members of the bourgeoisie took full opportunity to buy *biens nationaux*. The position of the urban bourgeoisie was considerably strengthened in the rural areas. The Périers bought a major share in the Anzin mines, and well-established forge-owners like Dietrich and Rambourg added to their property. Some of the new cotton firms in Alsace were set up in former monastic buildings. The enthusiasm of businessmen for land was unabated. In both the Ardennes and the Nord five manufacturers or forge-owners were among the twelve biggest landowners during the Consulate. But the most successful and largest group of purchasers were members of the traditional professional and office-holding bourgeoisie, many of whom were already well-established landowners. Ironically the biggest single group of purchasers were former owners of venal office, who spent the compensation paid to them by revolutionary governments on land.

During the Napoleonic era prefects were asked to compile lists of those who paid most tax, or 'propriétaires les plus distingués' or 'personnes les plus marquantes', a fair number of which survive and enable us to have detailed knowledge of the composition of the élite. Such quantification was useful partly because, after the turmoil and with new administrative and electoral systems, a prefect needed a set of criteria in recommending individuals for various posts. Prefects were required to assess political behaviour as well as income and to compare a man's role before and after 1789. In recent years historians have made extensive use of such lists. They reveal a high level of social continuity and in most cases document the survival of the landed élite. But because prefects or notables themselves sometimes left off their names for political reasons, the lists have to be used with care.[17] Presumably because of these pitfalls, a national survey of the imperial élite on a departmental basis comprises a brief statistical analysis, but mainly confines itself to biographical details.[18] In the Bas-Rhin 20 per cent (13 out of 69) of the Napoleonic élite were pre-1789 nobles, 20 per cent (14) had imperial titles, and in all nearly 50 per cent were old or new nobles, or members of the long-established rich bourgeois patriciate of Strasbourg.[19]

Far from encouraging the emergence of a commercial and industrial bourgeoisie, the revolution, by putting more than 10 per cent of the land of France on the open market, encouraged those with wealth to buy land. The vicissitudes of war and civil war accentuated this trend in the pursuit of the most secure return on an investment. Legislation of the revolutionary years may have cleared the ground for the development of capitalism, but the impact of war left it barren in many cases. Some with commercial and industrial interests may have benefited at times; wine-producers, ironmasters and cotton manufacturers during the crisis of 1827–32 certainly looked back on the Continental System as a golden age of growth.[20] But the overall political uncertainty and the financial drain of continental, colonial, maritime and civil wars, in which Napoleon came near to becoming a second Charlemagne, left France relatively backward in 1815 comared with 1789, although she was still the leading industrial power in continental Europe. Indicative of the trend were the demographic fluctuations of Paris in these years. The fastest-growing and largest industrial centre in France, Paris, lost nearly one-fifth of her population during the wars, falling to 550 000. It could be said that these were short-term, accidental setbacks. The deficit was made up by 1817 and the process of greater centralisation of finance and industry in Paris had been intensified during the Empire.[21] The first decade of the Restoration produced a fairly rapid development in the newer textile trades and metallurgy, so perhaps one should not overstress the degree to which land sales absorbed surplus wealth. But no case can be made for the Marxist claim that the revolution made a distinctive contribution to the transformation of the economy. Not only in France but throughout continental Europe, the effects of prolonged war, the Blockade and the Continental System were disturbing interruptions to a process of gradual change.

During the vicissitudes of the 1790s the traditional property-owning middle class created new institutions which gave them a political role and added to their estates. This may not have constituted a classic Marxist bourgeois revolution, but it was a revolution and those who gained were middle class. The revolution dispossessed former office-holders and turned many of the old élite into public enemies. Did a new bourgeois élite emerge, as commentators of all political persuasions have suggested?

The revolutionary and Napoleonic years produced spectacular changes in the organisation of the official world, with a complete restructuring of the civil, judicial, fiscal, educational, clerical and military establishments. The Council of State, the prefectoral system, the new courts, the Bank of France, the University and specialised colleges, even the high death rate among military personnel, permitted a major transformation of the official élite. A strong family and dynastic tradition quickly emerged and became permanently entrenched. Under Napoleon the new institutions were imbued with increasing professionalism. But the dynasties which emerged were not uniformly new, especially in the administrative and judicial spheres. The élite may have looked more professional and more opportunities were provided for training within the Council of State, but training was not open to all and men with experience were valued. A recent quantitative study showed that there was considerable continuity in central government (27 per cent), local administration (34 per cent), the judiciary (32 per cent) and financial administration (20 per cent) between the pre-revolutionary and Napoleonic periods. In general those who had held honorific posts did not survive, those whose job was functional did. The main exception was in the upper ranks of the judiciary, where few of the really senior *ancien régime* men were in similar posts in 1810. Age may have been a factor. In total, just over 30 per cent of imperial officials had started their careers before 1789; indeed the central administration was staffed almost entirely by *ancien régime* men.[22]

The Empire was thus a time for some of the pre-revolutionary élite to rebuild their careers. Bourgeois lawyers, administrators and professionals found even more outlet for their ambitions than previously. The epithet 'citizen' gave way to a panoply of Bonapartist appendages. Napoleon was no enemy of privilege and was keen to reward those who would serve him. Men with *ancien régime* titles did not despise the new Legion of Honour. They comprised nearly a quarter (22.5 per cent) of those who accepted imperial honours and members of the pre-revolutionary wealthy bourgeoisie were equally complacent. Continuity and the revival of the *ancien régime* bureaucracy are the most striking features of the imperial élite. Less strident revolutionary personnel were retained and some individuals gained accelerated promotion, especially in the army. But those who ultimately prospered from the years of revolution were men already established in the professions, the administration or the judiciary. Most were indeed middle class, but the revolution had no permanent impact on their careers. Although the revolutionary years brought great upheaval, ultimately the best recipe for survival was established landed wealth, which both nobles and members of the old official and professional classes possessed. Thus much of the fairly homogeneous 'upper' class which existed in France on the eve of 1789 survived and their landed interests remained predominant. However, although it can be demonstrated that the pre-revolutionary and post-revolutionary élites were notables, and that the constituent elements shared many common interests, the term 'notable' is so transparent and neutral that vital social and political conflicts are obscured and fudged. It would be naive to suppose that the revolutionary years had no effect upon the attitudes of families who may have survived but who certainly came under attack. The hostility shown in the 1790s to the Church, to the nobility and so on, accentuated divisions within the notables. The revolution may not have had much impact on the composition of society, but it left a permanent impression on political attitudes. In emphasising the gradualness of social change, revisionist historiography risks losing sight of the political significance of the 1789 revolution. The term 'notables' is best used as a shorthand form of 'the wealthy, mainly landowners, some of whom were noble, some not'.

Social and accompanying political change took far longer than nineteenth-century socialists hoped and was far from continuous, and the old élites retained much of their power through the years of industrialisation. The growth of the centralised bureaucratic state often helped to underline their influence and encourage the consolidation of the wealthiest segment of the upper middle class with nobles, the antiquity of whose titles mattered much less than previously, to form a more segregated and more politically divided 'upper' class. The political achievements associated with the French Revolution had their antecedents in the earlier period, notably the refinement of the centralised bureaucratic state. However, much was novel in continental Europe, such as the codification of the law under the principle of legal equality, excluding only women and those unable to pay legal fees (effectively the vast majority). The political experiments and experiences of the revolution were unique in Europe at that time, challenging traditional notions of privilege. But their success was very limited. The new egalitarian-sounding language of politics was translated by the élite into a justification for an oligarchy of wealth, more secure because elections of sorts existed along with an aura of social mobility. The bulk of the middle class, along with working men of all kinds and all women of whatever class, were excluded from political life until 1848 in France, and even then the notables were able to utilise for their own advantage the democratic franchise which continued to exclude women until 1945.

What of the other states with which we are concerned? Nineteenth-century liberals, and indeed fearful conservatives, believed that French revolutionary concepts infected middle-class groups in other states. After the Second World War, perhaps themselves influenced by ideas of European co-operation, historians like R. R. Palmer conceived of an 'Atlantic' revolution, in which precepts of liberty and equality arose as native plants on both sides of the Atlantic. The French historian Jacques Godechot warmed to the notion of 'une révolution occidentale'.[23] They argued that social groups anxious for influence, but excluded by the traditional order, had nurtured radical concepts during the eighteenth century and seized on the opportunities which the French armies afforded them. Some writers, notably Denis Mack Smith writing on nineteenth-century Italy, labelled them 'bourgeois',[24] although Palmer himself was careful to pinpoint the presence of both noble and commoner among the new aspirants. Palmer described the whole process as a 'democratic revolution', in favour of equality and against privilege. The democratic revolution he described was one of an educated minority, anxious to participate in making political decisions monopolised by traditional rulers. It was a revolution which enlightened rulers themselves could have undertaken and physical revolution would then have been superfluous. The broad canvas of this decidedly élitist view of a movement for political representation found favour in the 1960s, but perhaps the problems of contemporary Europe and the less attractive side of international radicalism displayed in the 'Atlantic' neo-Marxist student revolts of 1968 caused the varnish to crack. Detailed empirical regional investigations were undertaken. Historians began to ask whether there was a revolutionary initiative independent of France. They traced the actual impact of French domination, considered the extent of local support for the invading armies and, to a certain extent, asked whether French 'liberation' launched new élites.

Outside France the writings of the enlightenment found a receptive educated public and the autocratic rulers of some Italian states and of Prussia attempted the reform of structures of government. The Revolutionary Wars had a dramatic impact on European frontiers. All of the major continental powers were defeated. French armies redrew the map of Italy, absorbing northern, western and much of central Italy directly into France, which made Piedmont, Parma, Genoa and Tuscany French. The French frontier reached to the Rhine, including hundreds of tiny former principalities, present-day Belgium and Holland and the whole of the North Sea coast beyond the Elbe. All were divided into departments like the rest of France. Even Illyria was split into departments under the direct control of Paris. Prussia lost her western Polish lands to a new Grand Duchy of Warsaw, Austria ceded Italian territory in addition to suffering the dismemberment of the Holy Roman Empire which she had led. Superficially the result was simply the extension of French power, and neat, new kingdoms for well-behaved generals and not-so-obedient relatives. Napoleon's stepson, Eugene Beauharnais, became viceroy of the Kingdom of Italy, which consisted of former Lombard and Venetian land. The Kingdom of Naples was ruled first by Joseph Bonaparte and then by Marshal Murat, husband of Caroline Bonaparte. The German states were revolutionised. The Confederation of the Rhine was formed, absorbing Bavaria, Württemburg, Baden and other smaller states. Westphalia was handed over to Napoleon's brother, Jerome, and Brunswick, Hesse-Cassel and part of Hanover merged with it. Add to this the Helvetic republic, the alliance of Denmark and Norway and the abortive invasions of Spain and Russia, and it is easy to appreciate that the impact of the French armies was, if only temporary, colossal in scale. How much native revolutionary impetus was there, and to what extent were the changes conditional upon the emergence of a new élite?

On the eve of the French Revolution the German lands of the Holy Roman Empire consisted of 300 states, 50 free cities and 1000 or so territories of imperial knights. The Austrian monarchy exercised a nominal overlordship and the imperial writ continued to run in terms of the administration of justice. But Prussia was an effective challenge to Austrian authority, given the extent of her land, the success of her armies and the forcefulness of her rulers. The landed nobility were dominant in Prussia. The leading elements within the middle class consisted of bureaucrats and professionals; the industrial bourgeoisie was tiny and towns were run by very static bureaucracies. Particularism was entrenched. The French Revolution had a major impact, not in the realm of ideas but because territorial divisions were reduced to about twenty. This was achieved by French troops, but also by the princes and their bureaucrats keen to take advantage when the French upset the balance of power between Austria, Prussia and a handful of mutually jealous medium-sized states. The French deliberately encouraged Austro-Prussian antagonism and the conflicting ambitions of the other princes. Thus the 'revolution' in the German states could be left to the princes liberated by the successive defeat by France of Austria and Prussia. Their collaborators, it is true, were largely bourgeois, bureaucrats, writers, professors and, in Protestant areas, pastors. The entrepreneurial middle class, largely rather old-fashioned in their outlook, had little active interest in politics. The bureaucrats thought in terms of state-led change, finding adequate expression for their own political ambitions in rendering the centralised state more efficient. Their reward lay in the high status accorded them, especially in Prussia. For ambitious rulers of medium-sized territories the pickings were lush. The knights were dispossessed but, more important, the secularisation of Church lands by the French afforded princes adequate compensation for other losses and completed the process of the elimination of ecclesiastical states begun by enlightened despots. The social consequences were considerable, including the withdrawal of the aristocracy from senior ecclesiastical posts, made much less attractive by secularisation. The old-fashioned, conservative bourgeoisie of professors, doctors, etc. who had dominated the old cathedral towns was also discountenanced by the changes, which by the withdrawal of Church funding caused religious and charitable foundations to collapse.

Internal centralisation and reform were not wholly contingent upon French imperatives. The Prussian government undertook extensive spring-cleaning, not because the French demanded imitation but because the Prussians resented defeat and sought earnestly to avoid its repetition. Elsewhere the initiative was Parisian. When the Confederation of the Rhine was set up in 1806 all old imperial laws were nullified. Napoleon hoped that the clean slate could be written in French, while the princes vied to consolidate their own patches of territory. Civil servants were urged to centralise and codify. In some areas even French terminology was employed. Burgermeisters were replaced by mayors in the north-west perimeter lands and prefects were appointed. Local magistrates were forced to hand over to state courts. Thus the administrative, judicial and also the economic powers of the individual towns were eroded. State citizenship was given precedence over membership of the smaller corporation.

Initially local notables were appointed as state bureaucrats and lawyers and merchants were put on to town councils, but when the results were unsatisfactory, newcomers, usually trained lawyers from the central government bureaucracy, replaced them. The diversity and long tradition of local communities made them a gruelling challenge for centralising bureaucrats, who were regarded as enemies by the local notables. The new Imperial Codes were far from comprehensive, indeed they were sometimes totally ignored. In order to hold on to the territory, the French compromised, not with the towns but with the princes, rendering unequal the traditional struggle between centralising princes and towns eager to preserve their autonomy. The French often left the prince and his officials in control, with no buffer between the community and the state, except for the detested bureaucrats. In addition the old guild restrictions were abolished totally in Westphalia and the Rhineland, despite the opposition of local communities. Thus, far from liberating a new ruling élite, it seems that the French cemented the princes more firmly in place.

Only in a few areas was there any hint of an autonomous radical impetus. Palmer and others have suggested that the Rhineland was receptive to French ideas and that French success rested on an alliance with a thrusting and aspiring middle class. But detailed investigation of the French occupation gives a different picture of politics and society.[25] The local bourgeoisie did not rush to fill official posts, which were poorly and irregularly paid and whose incumbents were unpopular with both the occupying French troops and the local population. It has also been suggested that French institutions found favour with the local bourgeoisie, charmed by their rational and enlightened nature. In 1798 the French abolished the existing universities and grammar schools in the area, which had been starved of funds since the occupation because most of their income came from Church property, which the French sequestrated. New French-style schools were founded, but lacked money, teachers and pupils. The occupation was seen for what it was, military exploitation. The bourgeoisie already dominated. What has some-times been interpreted as native political radicalism was more akin to local patriotism and religious zeal. Protestant and Catholic communities were both very active. French policy was considered to be outrageously anti-clerical, even when French administrators merely continued a well-established onslaught against popular superstition.

The French did change the ruling élite. The former clerical rulers were dispossessed and the ban on Protestant participation in government was lifted. Aristocratic bishops and bourgeois bureau-crats, professionals and academics, who had dominated the local urban community, were joined by businessmen, who took an active role for the first time. In 1794 the French set up a twelve-man administration involving local wealthy business leaders, previously excluded. From 1797 the area was integrated into France. The prefectoral system was introduced, and in traditional French fashion the new prefects were all outsiders, with local notables as sub-prefects. Forty-three per cent of the new *conseil général* were business leaders, as were 25 per cent of the electoral college. Rhinelanders were elected to the national assemblies in Paris. A French-style judicial system was set up. But a new élite? Cologne's new mayor was in fact the pre-revolutionary incumbent. The French tried to win over the notables – a number received Napoleonic titles and freemasonry was encouraged – but they never forgot that they lived under a military occupation. They began to talk the language of popular sovereignty only as a way of undermining the French. Religious and patriotic sentiments were closely intertwined. Some aspects of French rule were palatable, excluding always financial exactions and the new system of taxation. The Imperial Codes remained in force until unification in 1871. Elsewhere princes and local communities were glad to be rid of all things French. After the battle of Leipzig in 1813 the title of burgermeister was restored in Westphalia, together with the old town council. In 1814 the whole Napoleonic edifice collapsed, but there was no thought of reconstructing all the old states. The rulers of the larger states held on to their prizes. Thus the revolution had strengthened the traditional rulers and their bourgeois bureaucrats, but the disruption of war and the Continental System did nothing for the entrepreneur.[26] A subsequent myth talked of the final campaigns against Napoleon as a 'war of liberation', a 'volkskrieg' or 'people's war' but, just as there was no spontaneous support for the French armies, nor was there for their removal. The princes, who retained control throughout, were careful to prevent the growth of democratic notions, although they were obliged to mobilise militias under the command of regular troops in the final battles.[27]

French success in the German states rested not on the ambitions of a frustrated bourgeoisie, but on the exploitation of the rivalries of princes. In the Italian peninsula, French victories were also due to the collapse of Austrian power and the diversity and divisions of their potential adversaries. But in addition there were elements of local revolutionary initiative, absent in Germany, which have been explored by Italian historians since the Second World War. It should be emphasised, however, that Italian revolutionary activity

was confined to an educated urban élite, who were regarded with
suspicion and cynicism by peasants who knew them as ruthless
landlords. Revolutionary inspiration was varied and very local,
ranging from the Buonarotti's radical ambitions to do away with
monarchies and feudal institutions to the noble landowners of
Lombardy, who wanted modern administration free from Austrian
control. In different regions the politically dissatisfied might include
journalists, lawyers, doctors, other professionals, students, some
merchants, modernising landlords and some nobles and priests.
Radicalism was by no means confined to the bourgeoisie, nor were
the nobility much of a target, for in the peninsula nobles rarely
exercised the influence they did in Prussia and parts of France. In
Italy nobles were far less likely to consider themselves innately
superior. There was no central royal court to dominate society and
no noble military tradition. Indeed, both in the eighteenth century
and later, nobles were likely to be radical and lead discontent.
Italian cities were usually governed by long-established, closed
oligarchies impenetrable even to wealthy outsiders. Hence most
cities encompassed groups of often long-settled 'newcomers', who,
however wealthy, were excluded from government. The French
merely had to find the right form of compromise with such groups.
The social cleavages in late-eighteenth-century Italy were by no
means simple noble–bourgeois rivalries. The divisions which occurred predated the French Revolution. There was already a strong
reforming Enlightenment tradition of varying regional intensity, but
no radicalism before the intervention of the French. The Italian
'Jacobins' of the 1790s were a new generation, some of whom, like
Buonarotti, had lived in Paris, supported Robespierre, taken French
citizenship and were keen to import French egalitarian republican
ideas into the peninsula. But they were also élitist and paternalist
in their approach, debating the best ways to educate the masses to
republican awareness, the need for schools, etc. Some were conscious
of the need for peasant support, but the French occupation aroused
peasant hostility and the Jacobins' own definition of 'the people'
tended to exclude the poor.[28]

The republican experience in the peninsula was brief, crushed
between the indifference of French governments, the privateering of
her generals and ubiquitous traditional popular brigandage and
rebellion. Their constitutions were resonant with Directorial over-
tones. Ten constitutions were prepared for different republics

between 1796 and 1799, all very like that of the year III. All men were citizens, but not all were enfranchised. Elections were indirect and candidates qualified on a high tax payment. Deputies were paid, on a scale related to the price of wheat. Each had a two-house legislature and five directors. All promised religious toleration. Each republic was split into departments administered by a centrally appointed nominee, prefects in Rome, commissioners elsewhere. Central government changes were everywhere transient, but the reorganisation of local administration was often more enduring.[29]

After a very brief initial period when there was some hint of local radical Jacobin inspiration, the French gradually assumed a monopoly of power in the peninsula and Italian territory was either distributed at the behest of the French to Napoleon's relatives or absorbed directly into France itself. French military superiority was unanswerable. In 1799 five revolutionary republics were set up by the French, the Cisalpine, Luccan, Roman, Neapolitan and Ligurian. None lasted more than a year and each had a written constitution, in Rome composed entirely by the four French consuls in the city, closely modelled on that of the Directory. In effect the Directory had no concerted strategy towards the peninsula. French conquest was mainly a matter of freebooting generals taking advantage of the collapse of Austrian power to enrich themselves, in the process of which it was usually expedient to negotiate with local notables. There was little pretence at this stage that the Directory was in control of its generals. The occupation of Milan was typical of the confusion. Local moderates, most of whom were owners of rural estates, supported the French civilian administrators. More radical urbanites, resenting the imposition of French civilian control, urged the setting up of an independent republic and the unification of Italy. Although many of the radicals also owned land, usually of more recent provenance, they had little care for the rural poor, who returned the compliment. Some French generals sided with the radicals, and they won the day as the moderates had no military resources to support them, but the alliance with French troops was one-sided and ephemeral, in Milan as elsewhere. The most powerful French generals ultimately dictated the future. At the end of the 1797 campaign Napoleon, who had shown more sympathy with Italian patriots than had the Directory,[30] made peace with the Austrians without consulting the Directory, seizing Lombardy and setting up a French-style regime with little concern for the ambitions of local notables. Venice, on the other hand, was presented to the Austrians at Campo Formio, to the dismay of the Venetian radicals, eager to be free of Austrian domination.

The traditional élites were sometimes willing to back plans for reform which they had resisted when proposed by their previous rulers. In some respects the succour for the revolution provided by a number of senior clerics appears contradictory, given anti-clerical policies such as the sale of Church lands. The nobly born bishop of Imola referred to himself as 'citizen cardinal' and was termed a 'Jacobin' by his opponents. A surprising number of Roman clerics accepted the republic set up in 1798 by the French after they had chased the pope from the city. Just over half of the complement of cardinals took part in a *te deum* to give thanks for 'liberty regained'. The explanation lies in a genuine desire among churchmen for the reform of both the clerical and civil government of the area. Sometimes the French gave previously unheard of opportunities for political office to professional men, but they usually kept the best jobs for those senior members of the landowning aristocracy who would work for them. The 'Jacobins' of Rome included some nobles and lawyers, and others who had formed part of the papal administration but had been balked in their promotion prospects because they were not clerics. Many within the Church did not oppose the sale of Church lands and the constitution was careful to recognise the spiritual power of the pope. But the need to defend the new republic from attacks by Ferdinand of Naples led to a radicalisation of policy and Catholic support quickly waned. A not dissimilar structure of support for a republic occurred in Naples itself, when the French defence of Rome was followed by the invasion of Naples and defeat of the monarchy. There was little support for, and much criticism of, the Spanish Bourbon house, a fairly recent acquisition for Naples, among the old landed nobles and newer rich landowners, many from legal or medical backgrounds. Like the notables of Rome, some were genuinely convinced that social and political reform was needed. The Neapolitan 'Jacobins' were nearly all from the upper classes and a number were senior churchmen. Among the hundred-odd republicans executed after the brief six-month life of the republic, there were two princes, four marquises, a count and a bishop. Their republicanism was exceptionally élitist and self-seeking, with little care for the poor and much affectionate longing for the old Italian city states. There was no attempt to secure mass backing, indeed the republicans' defeat was exacerbated by a jacquerie directed against them. The rural poor were only too well aware that the new republicans were the urban absentee landlords who had been exploiting them for years. The poor of Naples and local peasants aptly described a Jacobin as 'a man with a coach'.[31]

After the collapse of the short-lived republics, the French presence became increasingly exacting and dictatorial. Napoleon wanted Italy to supply men and money for his armies. He redrew the borders of Italian states to suit himself, in far more cavalier fashion than in the German states. Most of central and north-east Italy became departments within the French Empire. A second group of provinces including Lombardy and Venetia was called the Kingdom of Italy, but was so subject to France that her leading administrators had to pursue Napoleon throughout Europe to obtain even minor decisions. Naples proved far less reconcilable than other parts of Italy. Popular risings were endemic. The attempts to win over local élites, actively pursued elsewhere in the peninsula, was hampered by the memory of the violence of 1799. Poverty and corruption made reform imperative but almost impossible. As we have already noted, the French attack on feudalism brought a catch-22 solution. Noble landowners gained more land, communal rights grew weaker. However, the *galantuomini*, the rural middle class, also did well out of land redistribution. In 1810 in Calabria peasants were often unable to pay even modest rents or supply their own seeds. The *galantuomini* moved in, creating a new layer of oppression to crush the peasant, but leaving the old barons in ultimate control. The *galantuomini*, who owed their advancement to the French, began to emerge as local administrators under the French.[32]

Although the Italian and German states were no strangers to enlightened reform before 1789, the established élites had resisted attempts to eliminate feudal institutions and only modest progress had been made. The French revolutionaries found few independent revolutionaries abroad. There is little evidence of revolutionary initiative in the German states; somewhat more in Italy, but the Italian 'Jacobins' did not represent a new thrusting, bourgeois group on the whole. They came from varied social backgrounds, including the Church and nobility. Most were established landowners and had a very limited and élitist view of revolution. They were completely at odds with the urban poor and with peasants, who were struggling to combat the attack of the élite, including the 'Jacobins', on communal property.

Co-operation and collaboration were as important as conquest in redrawing the map of Europe, which was changed more extensively than at any time since the Roman Empire. In the Italian peninsula and in the Rhineland the French sought the support of established élites and if necessary encouraged the emergence of alternatives, who thus had a vested interest in the survival of many aspects of government introduced under the aegis of the French, notably the administrative, legal and judicial structures. In Lombardy and Tuscany, families who had worked for enlightened reform before 1789 regarded the French as fairly natural allies and readily accepted jobs in the new French-style institutions.[33] The French also sugared the pill of collaboration by giving both old nobles and, in southern Italy, newer rural middle-class families the opportunity to buy Church lands and acquire communal rights. The demolition of feudal structures in Naples had to be modified to keep the barons acquiescent, for there were no other suitable candidates for the top jobs. Napoleon was as keen to conciliate the nobility abroad as in France, and senior government posts were efficacious in wooing the old élites in both Piedmont and Naples.[34] Providing jobs for bourgeois families who had not previously worked for the state did not necessarily mean that the French created competition for office. In southern Italy the *galantuomini*, who profited from French rule and served Napoleon, constituted another layer in the rural hierarchy, below the barons. Thus, the idea that the French stimulated the development of an alternative bourgeois élite in conquered territories, which subsequently turned to radicalism when jobs were lost after Napoleon's fall, needs some modification in the light of recent detailed studies. Once Napoleon was established in power, his policy of conciliating the old élites, noble and bourgeois, was pursued both at home and abroad. The opportunities of war, de-feudalisation and governmental reform permitted, as in France, the enrichment of some newer families, such as the Cavours, and a number of the established élite refused to collaborate. It should also be remembered that those natives who served Napoleon abroad were opportunists and never enthusiasts. No one ever forgot that French rule was military dictatorship, not revolutionary liberation. Even for those who made their fortunes out of the foreigners, French rule was at the least distasteful. The French provided Piedmont with reform which brought long-term benefits to her administrative, judicial and educational systems. But the state was absorbed into France, her representatives were sent to Parisian assemblies. The dissolution of religious houses brought protests, as well as profit to the local élite purchasers. French taxes, especially on salt and tobacco, were universally detested.[35] As in France the poor, artisan and peasant, suffered most from de-feudalisation, the decline of artisan structures and the effects of prolonged war and civil unrest. Despite the new codified legal equality, the notables prospered, gaining from the sale of Church and communal land and the increased opportunities to serve a vastly expanded state machinery. Bourgeois families, including professionals, especially lawyers, some of whom had not previously been considered for the bureaucracy, obtained employment and a rapidly growing army of lower-middle-class civil servants were taken on. Thus there was some modest change, but far less revolutionary in society and the personnel of government than in the new institutions which the French constructed.

Herein lies the real revolutionary impulse of the bourgeoisie in 1789 and subsequent years: they sought institutional, never violent change. At the beginning of 1789 none of these states possessed elected representative assemblies. There was some consultation of meetings of the estates, but intermittent, regional and unrepresentative since members of the nobility invariably had a preponderant influence. By 1914 all four countries had elected national assemblies and with the exception of Russia, where the franchise for the recently created *duma* was strongly biased in favour of landed nobles, elections were either held with a democratic male franchise (Germany and France) or moving rapidly towards democracy (Italy). Apparently France set the trend in continental Europe with her revolutionary political experimentation of the 1790s, the results of which she exported with her armies into the Italian and German states and elsewhere in the following decade. An essential component was the replacement of traditional privilege by electoral rights based on the amount of tax a man paid in different forms of middle-class enfranchisement. A variety of constitutional regimes were accompanied by the remaking of basic state institutions, involving local assemblies and the judicial and administrative framework, and here too the intention was to extend participation beyond traditional venal and privileged office-holders. Although the revolutionaries of the 1790s had to respond to a conflicting range of imperatives, food shortages, civil and foreign war and the escalating cost of both, on the whole they represented primarily the interests of a bourgeois property-owning, tax-paying, educated minority. Popular unrest left them nervous of the poor and increasingly more concerned with stability than constitutionalism. The reform and elaboration of the institutions of the state was the real triumph of the bourgeoisie in all these states, for the process, stimulated by the Enlightenment and the policies of the French revolutionary leaders, provided employment at all levels for the middle classes. But the new gravy train was still driven by the old élites. Political change did not promote or substantially accelerate social change, almost the reverse. The elimination of venal office and some elements of traditional privilege, the sale of Church lands and the remaking of the institutions of the state in fact enabled the old élites, noble and bourgeois, to consolidate their position.

The political consequences of the revolution were irreversible. The Bourbons were restored in 1814 with a written constitution and the institutional framework of the revolution survived both in France and in some areas of Italy and Germany. The political and institutional revolutions were bourgeois; the attempt to challenge privilege by sequestrating Church property and creating egalitarian codes of law and a rational judiciary was the work of an educated, professional middle class. But the revolution had very little impact on the emergence of an entrepreneurial bourgeoisie. De-feudalisation sounds impressive, but former feudal lords found ways to retain the lion's share. The revolution may have accelerated the decline of artisan organisations, especially in the disruptive twenty years of war. But major social change ensued apparently only in Russia, where the impact of the wars permitted the rise of enterprising peasants to become a new entrepreneurial élite.

The self-image of the revolution was quintessentially educated and bourgeois. Individual moral worth replaced traditional privilege. In 1798, to celebrate 9 Thermidor, a big procession was organised in Paris. It included professors and students from the Museum of Natural History, followed by their exhibits such as bears and lions. Behind them came printers and librarians from public libraries and professors from the new Polytechnique and the old Collège de France. Copies of manuscripts and rare books were carried. Works of art brought from abroad were also displayed. Later, on the *Champ de Mars*, there was an industrial exhibition, the first of its kind. A prize was awarded to the inventor of the lead pencil and to a man who had devised a new typeface. In the brave new world education

9. The Bourgeoisie and Liberalism

IT has been argued, quite persuasively if somewhat perversely, that despite the economic, demographic, political and other changes of the nineteenth century, the old élites retained their dominance in society and in the state.[1] Our investigations into land ownership and the civil and military bureaucracies would seem to support this claim. The French Revolution, while reshaping political structures, appears to have had only a very limited impact on the élites who were in control. In these final chapters we shall select four themes in the nineteenth century which illuminate the role of the bourgeoisie in politics. The French revolution of 1830 is an irresistible choice, combining both liberal and 'bourgeois' aspects:[2] nineteenth-century liberalism was apparently quintessentially bourgeois. We shall also review the role of the liberals in Prussia, Italy and Russia, taking as our focus the apparent predominance of liberal parliamentarianism in Prussia after 1848 and its rapid evaporation in the 1860s, the significance of regional divisions in Italian politics and finally the absence of the middle class as a political force in Russia. Obviously other aspects could have been chosen and it might have been desirable to trace the evolution of the influence of different sections of the bourgeoisie over the whole century. Realistically, however, such a project would entail a separate book and it is hoped that the four topics chosen will acquaint the reader with aspects of current debates among historians.

Nineteenth-century liberals were members of the political and social élite in their respective countries. Some were noble, most were bourgeois. Many were landowners and the bulk formed part of the traditional middle class of professionals, bureaucrats, etc. In France those with commercial and industrial interests were involved in liberal politics from the 1820s, elsewhere considerably later. The writer of this book could be considered a masochist for, if 'middle class' is often used loosely, 'liberal' seems to be stuck on quite vaguely to a curious assortment of politicians and political movements. It is as easy to assume twentieth-century concepts when discussing nineteenth-century liberals as it is when delineating the nineteenth-century bourgeoisie. In the twentieth century a liberal is a political democrat, believes in the liberty of the individual, free speech, freedom of association and religious toleration, and is most likely also to oppose restrictive commercial practices and favour free trade. The most recent generation of liberals this century are also inclined to want to limit the power of the centralised state. While there was no single liberal dogma in the nineteenth century, the term meant almost the opposite of its twentieth-century meaning, especially in the first half of the century. Liberal ideas had their origins, which they shared with other philosophies, in eighteenth-century enlightened concepts which anticipated a more rational state and the elimination of irrelevant and damaging traditional privilege. The French Revolution of 1789 was central to the thinking of French liberals, though they, and liberals elsewhere in Europe who also respected the dynamic influence of 1789, would have been unable, in 1830, to agree on the exact contribution the revolution made to the way in which they looked at the world. Strong government was vital to the health of society and the welfare of the individual, and liberals hoped to combine a monarchical and effective executive with elected representative institutions. French liberals quickly replaced Charles X with his cousin Louis-Philippe in 1830; Prussian liberals never envisaged the removal of Frederick William IV, nor the Piedmontese the House of Savoy. They expected that monarchy would be based on rational and utilitarian principles; the French liberals presented Louis-Philippe with a constitutional preamble in which a contractual arrangement was offered him, in contrast to the 'royal grace and favour' tone of the constitution of 1814.

The interests of the individual woud be protected by the existence of elected representative assemblies, in which both voters and candidates were obliged to qualify by paying a substantial amount in direct tax, primarily on land. In 1830 the French liberals were happy with a 300-franc franchise, which provided an electorate of about 90 000 out of a population of 31 million. Only after considerable debate was the tax qualification reduced to 200 frs. following the revolution. The Prussian *landtag* of the 1850s was elected by a three-class franchise in which a tiny minority of first- and second-class voters elected two-thirds of the MPs. United Italy adopted a 40-lire tax qualification, which enfranchised about the same proportion of wealthy Italian males as did the Orleanist system in France, 2.2 per cent of the population. In Russia, when a national assembly, or *duma*, was finally established after the revolution of 1905, liberal opinion did not oppose a voting system more hierarchical than that of Prussia, which the tsar twice narrowed still further before 1914. Liberals were political élitists. In France in the 1840s the Banquet campaign's plan to lower the tax qualification for voters was anathema to Guizot, virtually chief minister for the last eight years of Louis-Philippe's reign; Prussian liberals were horrified when Bismarck insisted that the *reichstag*, the representative assembly for the new North German Confederation in 1867 and the German Empire in 1871, should be elected by universal manhood suffrage; in Italy the tax qualification was reduced in 1882 only in the expectation that the new voters would show their gratitude by supporting the status quo. Liberals assumed that the rule of the rich would be government by independent and morally upright citizens like themselves, an illusion somewhat shaken by the scandals of the 1840s in France. It was also argued that a taxpayers' franchise was egalitarian, since, by hard work, anyone could qualify. Democracy became the instrument of those with autocratic tendencies such as Napoleon III and Bismarck. Liberals found adaptation to a broader franchise and especially to democracy very painful. Where local landed élites remained entrenched the transition was easier, as in France in 1848 and 1871. A combination of suspicion, ignorance, fear and lack of understanding of a mass electorate denied them the new votes they needed if they were to retain their influence. Political groupings of liberal persuasion were, by 1914, facing replacement by organised parties. The SPD, SFIO and PSI, the socialist parties of Germany, France and Italy, were the largest parliamentary parties in these countries and in Italy the next-fastest-growing party was the Popular Catholic Party or *Popolari*. Only in the most backward and remote regions were the notables able to retain their control over the democratic vote.

Liberals saw no essential conflict between a strong executive and an elected assembly. Both Guizot and Cavour were convinced of the power of parliament, even though in the 1830s Louis-Philippe began to interfere more than had done his predecessor; Bismarck defied the elected *landtag* with its liberal majority from October 1862 until after the defeat of Austria in 1866; and Cavour, the Piedmontese Prime Minister, was ignored by the king in peace negotiations after the war with Austria. Liberals appear to have seen no sinister contradiction between the growth of the power of the state and elected assemblies stuffed with men holding official appointments. The demise of intermediary bodies in the state, which liberals supported in the name of efficiency and rationality, served to increase the role of the state, in administering justice, running local affairs, etc. In some respects liberals were enthusiasts for the modern state: many Prussian civil servants in the 1840s who were inclined to liberalism were keen to expand the machinery of the state, not just to feather their own nests but because they believed that an effective state was crucial to a civilised and settled society. Press censorship, the banning of 'unsuitable' political groups, the use of the army in industrial disputes, all of which liberals supported at different times, served to expand the role of the state. Liberals were ambivalent in their approach to the relationship between the individual and the state. *Laissez-faire* meant freedom for the better-off. From the 1830s there was some disagreement between entrepreneurs and the more traditional bureaucratic and professional middle class who became increasingly aware of the poverty and injustice in modern urban society. Conscience and moral judgements were vital in determining the juxtaposition between the individual and the state. Groups were sometimes at odds with their apparent 'natural' interests: many of the nineteenth-century reformers in Russia were nobles, the liberal leaders in Prussia in the 1840s and 1850s were mostly bureaucrats.

Liberals had no firm political platform. In France in the 1830s and 1840s they claimed to represent a *juste milieu*, a middle road. The belief in freedom of association, as originally recorded in the constitution of 1791 and reiterated in the constitutions of 1814 and 1830, was even more dented by the 1830 liberals than by the monarchists, for in 1834 all political associations, whatever their size, were banned. All subsequent liberal formations were so convinced that social democracy was an emanation of the Devil that they subscribed to outlawing the party (Germany) or condoning the use of troops to break up strikes (every state). Freedom of speech was another liberal 'belief' that was recorded in constitutions and rapidly legislated away. The French liberals imposed stricter press censorship than had the Restoration; from 1835 no newspaper or periodical was allowed to use the word 'republic'. Liberals believed in religious toleration, but in practice this amounted to little more than official anti-clericalism, in France in 1830 admittedly chiefly directed at the political manifestations of Roman Catholicism, especially its close links with ultra-royalism, but later translated into an active laicisation of education. In united Italy liberals pursued the Piedmontese anti-clerical line and sold off the remaining lands of the Church, often to the benefit of liberals. Although the National Liberals did not launch the *kulturkampf* against the Roman Catholic Church in the 1870s, they actively supported the ban on the Jesuits, the dissolution of religious orders and so on.

The fundamental intolerance and illiberal stance of nineteenth-century liberals is thrown into even sharper focus when attitudes to social and economic questions are compared. In their lack of sympathy for the urban and rural poor they often exceeded the approach of more overtly conservative groups, for liberals often displayed what is frequently referred to as a 'Protestant' ethic in their reverence for visible physical and mental effort. By this token both the landed aristocrat who lived off the fruits of the labour of others and the poor were culpable. Overt supporters of 'progress', liberals underwrote the erosion of communal rights. The *galantuomini* of southern Italy were as keen to buy communal land as the barons. In Prussia rural communities could expect no backing from liberals; all types of prosperous bourgeois bought up available land. In Russia also 'reform' was seen to mean the destruction of communal rights and the legalisation, by Stolypin in 1907, of the right of the individual peasant to own his own land. Peasants and artisans were merely disruptive and untidy elements. The last major attempts of artisans to preserve traditional rights and organisations in the 1830s and 1840s, met with the consistent opposition of both liberals and conservatives. The full force of the Orleanist state was used against silk weavers in Lyons, struggling to maintain their traditional independence against merchants who were developing into embryonic entrepreneurs. *Laissez-faire* did not prevent employers calling in government forces to control their workers, but denied to workers reciprocal rights to band together to protect their interests. Liberals in the Côte-d'Or and other wine-producing departments thought it quite reasonable to organise petitions against the wine tax in the late 1820s, but were discomforted when wine-producers attacked the offices of the tax collectors and burned their records.

In 1848 only the violent demonstrations of artisans and peasants, in response to both short-term harvest failure and industrial depression and long-term economic 'modernisation', created the circumstances in which liberals could promote their own ideas. Yet liberals manifested complete hostility to both peasant and artisan grievances, apparently unaware that, without popular unrest, their own case would never be heard.

Liberal ideas on the role of governments in the national economy swung with the pendulum of perceived economic wisdom and opportunity and were indistinguishable from the opinions of other comfortably-off citizens. Well into the 1830s they pursued the opportunism of protectionist tariffs, although attitudes varied according to the particular interests of specific industries. However it was accepted that free internal trade was desirable: free trade among the various provinces of Prussia was instituted between 1818 and 1834; Italian liberals began to observe the disadvantages of competing commercial arrangements in the peninsula in the 1840s and the merits of the *zollverein* created by Prussia. The *zollverein* treaties introduced a novel concept, low external tariffs, heralding a more recognisably liberal economic philosophy of free trade, in vogue from the late 1850s to the 1870s, to be replaced by fierce protectionist tariffs with the onset of the World Depression.

This attempt to set out common liberal principles has shortcomings. The ideas mentioned were often far from unique to liberals; above all liberals almost never operated as a concerted group. The label 'liberal' may be attached in a random and indiscriminate way. In the 1820s in France the appellation 'doctrinaire' was more usual; the term 'liberal' was commonly applied in France only in the 1830s and 1840s. In Prussia 'liberal' was replaced by the distinction between 'moderate' and 'progressive' in the 1850s and the label 'national liberal' thereafter. Until the growth of socialist parties, political formations tended to be based on individuals and issues, not formal party structures. Although socialist organisations obliged their rivals to imitate them, in Italy parties remained fundamentally patronage and interest groups. At the beginning of the nineteenth century Madame de Stael described her own political views as a list of proper names, not principles;[3] this categorisation could be applied to liberalism, and was still true of traditional Italian political formations in 1914. In Germany parties became more structured, but it is noteworthy that the supporters of Hugenberg's party, the successors to the national liberals, were transmogrified rapidly into Nazi voters in the economic crisis of 1929–32. Historians chart the existence of a liberal opposition in the *duma* in Russia in the years up to and including 1917, but the description suggests a unity which was never there. Moscow merchants described themselves in 1905 as the 'trade and industry' party, well aware of their own isolation from similar groups elsewhere and from the lower middle class too.

Only in Germany did liberals adapt to become a parliamentary mass party and there the *reichstag* was of marginal importance. In a society of notables liberals could be interest and patronage formations, a 'party of names', closely associated only for specific issues. The fate of liberalism typifies the division of the middle class and explains why the old notables were able to retain the essence of political power for so long. The *juste milieu* will always be a matter for transaction and trimming. The centre ground will always be a quicksand.

The Marxist and revisionist dispute over the bourgeois nature of the 1789 revolution in France has been continued naturally into the 'bourgeois' revolution of 1830, with Marxists arguing that 1830 was positively the triumph of the middle classes and revisionists pointing to the community of interests of wealthy notables, whether noble or bourgeois. Revisionists prefer to stress the presence of many former Bonapartists in the élite after 1830, indicating political, rather than social change. What was 'bourgeois' about 1830? The liberal political opposition? The fighters in the July Days? The consequences of the revolution? The origins of the 1830 revolution may be traced to two crises, one political, one economic, which were only loosely connected. The political crisis turned on the interpretation of the 1814 constitution. Were ministers appointed by the king responsible to the king or to parliament? Napoleon's defeat was followed by the setting up of a constitutional, representative regime in which a tolerable working compromise was reached, combining the imperial framework with the restored Bourbons in place of the emperor harnessed to a two-chamber parliament. The Allies replaced Napoleon with the guillotined king's brother, Louis XVIII, who agreed to govern within the terms of a constitutional charter, worked out by a group including the liberal thinker, Benjamin Constant. France retained all but the political institutions of the revolutionary and imperial era. Louis was made hereditary head of the executive, appointed his own ministers and shared legislative power with a parliament consisting of two assemblies, one hereditary, one elected. The franchise was limited to adult males of thirty and over who paid at least 300 frs. in direct taxes each year. Candidates to the assembly had to pay 1000 frs. in taxes and be at least forty. There was a fair measure of agreement among the wealthy that the effective functioning of the constitution was vital to avoid renewed civil war and political upheaval. Thus the Napoleonic concordat and the revolutionary land settlement were confirmed. The biggest political threat to the compromise were the ultras, many of them *emigrés*, who were more royalist than Louis XVIII and could come to terms neither with the historical reality of 1789 nor the present existence of a limited monarchy. As a consequence of the Hundred Days and the necessity of a Second Restoration of the monarchy, ultras were in control of the first elected parliament, which the king, anxious for a more sedentary life, immediately dissolved. Never again were the ultras to have a numerical advantage, but when their leader, the duc d'Artois, became Charles X in 1824, they had a renewed psychological one.

On the left were a number of parliamentarians and journalists who, while well aware of the practical necessity of a monarch (the memory of the conflicts of the First Republic were too painful to contemplate) were rather more attached to representative institutions than to the person of the king. These *doctrinaires*, or liberals, were committed to the 'doctrine' of the 1814 constitution and apprehensive of ultra intentions. At no point in the Restoration were the liberals revolutionaries, but they were always depicted as such by their opponents. Liberalism was not a political programme, but a tendency or attitude of mind which crystallised in response to government policies. The first real affront to the constitution for the liberals was the law of the double vote, pushed through parliament in 1820 by ultra outrage after the heir to the throne, the duc de Berri, was murdered, it was claimed, by a liberal. The law gave the richest quarter a second vote. Thereafter fewer than 25 000 voters elected 165 deputies in special departmental electoral colleges; they then joined the rest of the electorate to choose the remaining 265 members. It was assumed, fairly correct at first, that wealth equalled conservatism. Liberals were equally antagonised by the *Loi Septennale*, which swopped from a system by which the Chamber of Deputies was renewed annually in fifths to a single general election every seven years. What annoyed the liberals was that this law was passed shortly after the election of 1824 when their own representation reached its nadir. Another law of 1824, permitting the setting up of a state loan to indemnify those who had lost land during the revolution, also worried liberals, many of whom had bought *biens nationaux*, that the revolutionary land settlement was in jeopardy, or at the very least that families who had emigrated were being rewarded for their opposition to the revolution. As self-appointed heirs of the revolution, liberals were inevitably suspicious of the increasingly close association between State and Church; a number of senior clerics were ultras and a missionary campaign in the 1820s was conducted by ultra-inspired priests. A high point of the missionaries' visit to a commune was a service to bemoan the evil consequence of the revolution for the Church. In 1825 a law of sacrilege passed by parliament made profanation of the host punishable by death, a law never implemented but a clear indication of the growing confidence of the Church. Charles was crowned with unprecedented and devout medieval-style splendour in Reims cathedral. He was often depicted by contemporary cartoonists in clerical dress. Most damaging of all, in the election campaigns of 1827 and 1830 senior clerics were enjoined to order priests to preach in favour of ultra candidates. As a result of these actions anti-clericalism was refined as a more precise ingredient of liberalism. Liberals were also antagonised by successive laws strengthening press censorship; liberal newspapers were the most successful. Such were the preconditions of a lively, but controllable, political debate.

Government strategy pushed debate into crisis. Convinced, wholly erroneously, that liberals were a revolutionary threat, Charles was prepared to use any tactic to defeat them. In successive elections the government falsified electoral lists in order to preserve a royalist majority, with remarkable success in 1824 when only 40 liberal critics were elected. Overt falsification of electoral lists and elections provoked the casual and temporary association of liberal opinion critical of the government to coalesce into a more formal arrangement. The 1824 election had been accompanied by blatant falsification of electoral lists, omitting known liberals and including royalists who had died and those who did not qualify as electors. The electorate shrank from 110000 in 1817 to 79000 by 1827 as a consequence. Electoral malpractice was all the more misjudged since many liberals were trained lawyers. In 1827 Parisian liberals set up a committee, *Aide-toi, le ciel t'aidera*. They published a series of short pamphlets informing prospective voters how to ensure that they appeared on the electoral list if qualified and encouraged the setting up of electoral committees in the departments.[4] A regular procedure for annual revision of lists was introduced in 1827 to replace the previously rather haphazard arrangement. Charles, advised that Villèle, his chief minister, was losing support, gambled on an early election, hoping to revive the fortunes of his government. Instead the new parliament contained 180 liberals, the same number of royalists and 60–80 ultras.[5] The king conformed to traditional practice and accepted Villèle's resignation. A moderate royalist, Martignac, became spokesman for a new royalist government in parliament, and as a concession to the liberals Royer-Collard was made president of the Chamber of Deputies, which was a great sacrifice for Charles.

Thus after the election of 1827 the king deferred to parliament. Yet, within less than three years, an intractable political crisis developed and Charles found himself in exile. The explanation for the worsening political situation lies mainly in the history of this last Restoration parliament, but one has to turn away from the arguments of the enfranchised political nation to comprehend the outbreak of revolution. The Martignac government was quite ineffectual, opposed by both ultras and liberals, the latter of whom strengthened their hand in nearly all the hundred or so by-elections which followed liberal appeals against malpractice in 1827. No modification of the composition of the government was made to take into account the voting power of the liberals. Martignac hoped to please both liberals and ultras by proposing that local councils be made elective, not appointed by the central government; the ultras because they favoured regional power, the liberals because they put their faith in elections. However only the double vote electors were to be enfranchised, so the liberals were implacably opposed and the proposal was withdrawn. It became virtually impossible to legislate.

Between 1827 and 1832 France experienced a dual economic crisis. There was a serious shortfall in the grain crops and the potato and wine harvests were poor. Bread prices rose by up to 75 per cent. In addition French banks were affected by a credit crisis which began in London in 1826; commerce and industry were hit, with reduced wages and hours. Thus major cities, especially Paris and Lyons, experienced constant and disruptive artisan demonstrations. The wealthy who voted and sat in parliament reacted by providing charity handouts and demanding that troops were on hand to maintain their idea of order. Increased bankruptcies and problems in major industries like iron, silk and wine-producing brought demands for government investigations and action. Industry was becoming increasingly concentrated in Paris and northern and eastern France. The liberal vote was strongest in these regions and Martignac responded by agreeing to hold a parliamentary enquiry into both the iron and wine industries. Liberal deputies organised petitions from wine and iron producers, large and small. Producers were asked to give evidence to the Chamber of Deputies. The crisis was taken seriously, and by implication it was accepted that the proposition of solutions fell within the remit of the assembly. Unfortunately, it soon transpired that producers were only in accord in blaming either the government's taxation or its commercial policy, or both. While silk and wine producers wanted France to reduce her high tariffs on imported goods like iron and coal in order to encourage other nations to reduce their customs duties on French silk and wine, iron manufacturers wanted even higher duties on foreign imports. It is clear that official opinion found the ironmasters at fault, shielding behind tariff barriers, failing to innovate and forcing French iron prices to remain unreasonably high. But it was recognised that to try to alter the situation by a change in government policy would have aroused the iron lobby, composed of very rich landowning ironmasters, to even greater opposition. The only measure taken relevant to the crisis was a minor relaxation of the sliding scale on wheat imports. Because no steps which would have divided the liberals were pursued, the economic crisis served further to bind liberal opposition together against Martignac.[6]

In this period of deepening economic depression, France was virtually without a government, for liberal–ultra disagreements left Martignac so helpless that he resigned in the summer of 1829. Rumours abounded of an ultra *coup d'état* and in effect an ultra administration was appointed in August 1829, an unprecedented constitutional decision, for the liberals had a clear majority in the chamber and an ultra government could only render France even more ungovernable. The ultra of ultras, the prince de Polignac entered the government and in November 1829 was made chief minister. The parliamentary session was postponed until March 1830, by which time liberal electoral committees and newspapers were in full cry. Petitions of citizens refusing to pay taxes unless sanctioned by parliament were circulated. When parliament finally reassembled on 16 March the response to the speech from the throne was an unprecedented and outspoken motion of no-confidence in the government, supported by a majority of 221 of the deputies present. The king peremptorily closed the session and, after some delay, dissolved the assembly. The result was even more unsatisfactory for the king, even though he had used the full resources of paid officials in State and Church to press the case for royalist, preferably ultra, candidates. Of the 221 who had voted the motion of no-confidence, 202 were re-elected and in all 274 opponents were returned. Only 143 deputies were prepared to vote for Polignac. Because the king would not countenance a liberal government, a political argument had turned into confrontation. Unfortunately, on this point the constitutional charter of 1814 had been, probably deliberately, vague. The king appointed his own ministers who, according to the charter, were 'responsible', but it did not say to whom. In effect until 1828 ministers matched the parliamentary majority. When they ceased to do so, the liberal majority demanded that the king conform not only to previous practice but also to the charter, claiming that the king was defying both political reality and the written constitution. There was apparently no way out of this double impasse.

In 1830 Charles X faced an unprecedented liberal majority in parliament. Did the political conflict have social dimensions? Did the liberals represent the bourgeoisie? In the late 1820s official reports on political attitudes were frequently couched in class terms. Prefects often commented that the industrial and commercial middle classes were wholly hostile to the regime. One of the four ordinances which triggered the revolution planned to reduce the electorate by 75 per cent, eliminating such unreliable voters and enfranchising only the very rich landowners. The ultras were incorrect in believing that rich landowners were loyal monarchists and that opposition was limited to a less well-off bourgeoisie, as Table 2 indicates. Regional differences were more significant than class or wealth in determining electoral patterns. Paris and eastern France were predominantly liberal, the west more inclined to ultra-royalism. The generalised view that the bourgeoisie was hostile to the monarchy was an ultra myth, nurtured by their implacable hatred of the French Revolution and an *emigré* ignorance of political reality. The ultras were political romantics, who would have liked to destroy all memory of the revolution. Ultras dreamed of a France ruled by king, Church and aristocracy, even though not all ultras were aristocrats and the majority of royalists were not ultras. The ultras defined political conflict in simplified class terms, forgetting that a number of nobles had rallied to the Empire and many Restoration officials began their careers under Napoleon. The longest-serving Restoration chief minister, Villèle, was bourgeois, ennobled by Martignac after his resignation in 1827. In the hierarchical view of the ultras the bourgeoisie were natural enemies of the traditional order.

TABLE 2   Chamber of Deputies, 1827[7]

Tax Paid (frs.)	Political Views			
	Left	Centre Left	Centre Right	Right
Up to 1000 (the minimum)	0	4	5	1
1000–500	42	42	59	39
1501–2000	17	17	26	33
2001–3000	18	24	26	22
3001–7000	18	18	10	7
7001–14143	1	1	0	2
Total	96	106	126	104

But why should official reports have reiterated such a naive interpretation? The explanation lies partly in the inexperience of a section of the prefectoral corps in the late 1820s, when frequent reshuffles occurred to try to obtain more royalist election results. Charles was even more intent than his predecessor on appointing nobles to official posts. Indeed some young men with an ancient pedigree but a minimum of administrative experience were appointed who contributed to the king's loss of the elections of 1827 and 1830. The attempt to construct a noble administrative, clerical and military élite antagonised bourgeois officials, whose promotion was blocked or who were kept out of office when they made the wrong choice during the Hundred Days. They were often the fulcrum of liberal opposition in their region. The worsening economic crisis added another dimension to liberalism. Many industrialists blamed the government's commercial strategy and the majority of industrialists were both bourgeois and liberal. However a fair number of the richest were noble. More important, the industrial and commercial middle class may have been united in blaming the government for the crisis, but they were very divided over whether the best solution was to reduce or increase tariffs on imported goods. The liberals constituted far more of a political than a social opposition to Charles X. Some of them were titled, just as some ultras were bourgeois. Most were not the entrepreneurs of the prefect's fancy, but landowners, professionals and bureaucrats. However the aristocratic–bourgeois duel was not simply the product of the ultra publicity machine. Liberal leaders were equally convinced that 1789 had permitted the political maturation of the bourgeoisie: Guizot, Tocqueville, Remusat refer to the close connection between the middle classes and the revolution. Even liberals who were nobles enjoyed the 'bourgeois' label. Those who considered themselves the political heirs of 1789 took pleasure in believing that the revolution inaugurated a period of social progress. However the liberals did not believe that the security of these triumphs was at stake in the political crisis of the late 1820s. Thus in evaluating the preconditions for revolution within the scope of the political conflict the psychological factor was uppermost. The ultras detested the memory of 1789, failed to appreciate that the liberals were fervent patrons of the status quo and constantly anticipated a revival of the upheaval of the 1790s. But surely they did not see Guizot as Robespierre? Neither were the liberals innocent of blame. They tended to have an equally carica-tured impression of their opponents. Most royalists accepted the charter and were willing to work within it. Charles X tried to govern constitutionally by appointing Martignac, but the liberals refused to co-operate.

The political conflict was converted into confrontation by the king. The charter allowed him to issue laws by decree in an emergency when the state was in danger. Charles claimed that the liberal electoral victory in 1830 posed such a threat. Thus he issued four decrees or ordinances from his palace at St Cloud, near to Paris, on 25 July 1830. No newspaper or pamphlet of less than 25 pages could be published without authorisation, which could be revoked at any time. Parliament was dissolved without meeting and a new election was called for August. The electorate for this and future elections was to consist only of the 25 per cent most wealthy who had qualified previously for a double vote. Liberal journalists immediately denounced these ordinances as a breach of the constitution, but liberal deputies were divided, hesitant and uncertain how to proceed. The liberal newspapers, the *Globe* and *National*, defied the authorities and published editions condemning the ordinances on 27 July. The king's decision was thus challenged, but the liberals had put up with many rebuffs in the 1820s, and in the July crisis, although they were in a majority in parliament, there was no indication that they would defy the king.

The Three Glorious Days was an artisan, not a liberal notable revolt. Since 1827, when food prices had risen, supplies of bread had been threatened from time to time and wages and hours had been reduced, there had been frequent demonstrations and marches by groups of artisans urging government intervention and help. Paris was a volatile city. She was the largest and fastest-growing industrial centre in France with an artisan population crowded into the central districts, close to the seat of government. These narrow streets were notoriously difficult to control, particularly as no troops were garrisoned in the capital. In late July 1830 demonstration tipped over into revolution as printing workers joined other artisans on the streets. The king had failed to ensure that there were enough troops to contain rioters and those available rapidly deserted to the rebels. The king took no further steps to justify his position or rally supporters. On 30 July, with rebel control of the streets stiffened by the hastily reassembled national guard which Charles had dissolved in 1827, liberal journalists put up placards demanding Charles' replacement by his cousin, the duke of Orleans as *lieutenant-général*. A provisional municipal administration containing several republican sympathisers, including Lafayette, took over the *hôtel de ville* in Paris, and also demanded the resignation of Charles. Liberal deputies hastened to gain control of a situation in which they had played little part except as individuals. Thus the actual revolution and the catalyst for the solution of the political crisis was the work of Parisian artisans, although presumably the journalists would have argued that without their intervention no change of regime would have occurred.[8]

The label 'bourgeois revolution' was initially pinned to the July Days not by a jubilant liberal notable or by Marx, but by contemporary republicans and socialists to express their disgust that what was in their view an artisan revolt was quickly filched from the fighters, leaving the old élite still in control. For them 1830 was 'une révolution escamotée',[9] a revolution smuggled away from the real victors; 'bourgeois' because the bourgeoisie remained in charge, making none of the social reforms desired by the socialists. The socialists were correct in their claim that little was altered. The liberals had been happy enough with the 1814 settlement. At the beginning of August 1830 the liberal deputies present in the capital rapidly convened parliament, which on 7 August offered a vacant throne to the duke of Orleans. The constitutional charter was quickly revised on 14 August, with almost no discussion. The king's right to make laws without parliament was rescinded, otherwise his powers were identical to those of his predecessor. But he was 'king of the French people' not 'king of France' and it was stated that his throne was the gift of his people. In 1814 the constitutional charter had claimed that the constitution itself was the gift of the king to his people. Furthermore it is worth remembering that Louis-Philippe was Charles X's cousin and might well have been regent had Charles died, for his successor was Henri, nine-year-old son of the heir murdered in 1820. The electorate was doubled to 160 000 by halving the tax qualification, which was also halved for candidates. The principle of election was extended to local councils and a democratic franchise was established for the election of national guard officers. But the idea that voters had to be substantial property-owners remained entrenched, with arguments that wealth guaranteed independence and that the poor would not bother to vote. In its electoral arrangements this was indeed a bourgeois regime, as was also that of the Restoration.

The narrowness of the Orleanist electorate and especially the presence of two bankers, Jacques Laffitte and Casimir Périer in government, contributed to Marx's contradiction of earlier socialists. He argued that 1830 was indeed a bourgeois revolution which had changed the ruling élite, bringing to prominence a wealthy business class: 'It was not the French bourgeoisie that ruled under Louis-Philippe, but one faction of it: bankers, stock-exchange kings, railway kings, owners of coal and iron mines and forests, a part of the landed proprietors associated with them – the so-called finance aristocracy.' The industrial bourgeoisie, on the other hand, were in opposition to Guizot.[10] Marx was thus quite specific in his delineation of the Orleanist ruling élite, in which he included landowners. Subsequent followers of Marx tended to adopt a more general 'industrial and commercial' definition of the bourgeois élite and 1830 then entered into the Marxist 'rise of the bourgeoisie' hall of fame. Thus 1830 became the revolution which completed the process, begun in 1789, in which the entrepreneurial bourgeoisie replaced the landed aristocracy in power. Just as recent historians have questioned the viability of the Marxist thesis in relation to 1789, so have they for 1830, although the standard Marxist concept of rising and falling classes is quoted without comment in a revisionist survey of élites.[11]

Was 1830 a social revolution in its consequences? First, was it anti-aristocratic? At one level, this question can be answered in the affirmative. Of the 365 members of the Chamber of Peers, 175 refused to take the oath of allegiance to Louis-Philippe and were excluded, along with peers nominated by Charles X. As promised in the immediate aftermath of the revolution, in December 1831 the automatic right of nobles to belong to the Chamber of Peers was abolished. Members were to be appointed by the king from a list of specific categories. The upper house became bourgeois. Louis-Philippe used the right to nominate to the Peers to reward well-behaved bourgeois bureaucrats, including 235 generals.[12] The attempt of the Bourbons to construct an aristocratic ruling élite was abandoned in a dramatic 'émigration à l'intérieur'. However, shrewd conservative Orleanists soon set out to woo legitimist notables, rather than risk the formation of a legitimist–republican opposition alliance. By 1840 the legitimist élite was firmly back in harness in local government, particularly in western France.[13] Nobility itself had become a political issue, especially in Charles X's reign, and many of those who secured official posts after the 1830 revolution were men whose career had been blocked at the Second Restoration or subsequently. Thus there was mutual antipathy. It is true that a substantial proportion of those involved in politics held noble titles throughout the period of constitutional monarchy and the 1830 revolution had no marked impact on numbers. In 1821 58 per cent of the Chamber of Deputies were titled, in 1827 40 per cent and in 1840 just over 30 per cent. A title was seen as sufficiently desirable for many to be invented: in 1840 45 of the titles in the chamber were spurious. But contemporaries were very conscious of the distinction between different types of title and when they were awarded. Louis-Philippe's nobles were of Bonapartist stock. The nobility continued to make a substantial contribution to entrepreneurial activity of all kinds, but this did not mean that they were indistinguishable from the wealthy bourgeoisie. The 1830 revolution made a substantive difference to the role of the traditional nobility in halting Restoration attempts to make the ruling élite and the nobility synonymous. Just as Charles X fell because he refused to separate his fate from that of his government, so loyalty to the Bourbons and to the Catholic Church split the notables and excluded one section from national power politics. That does not mean that 1830 was a stage in the decline of the landed nobility. We have already noted that in economic terms this was far from the case: in the 1840s 235 of the 512 richest notables were landed aristocrats. But in political terms the ultra hope of equating the ruling class with the nobility was never more than a dream, although it may have been a nightmare to the liberals.

Politically 1830 split the élite. Were there other social differences? Recent research on electoral lists shows that voters and deputies were primarily landowners both before and after 1830. Marxist claims that 1830 gave power to big businessmen are not born out by analysis. In 1829 14 per cent of the deputies were businessmen, in 1831 17 per cent, in 1840 13 per cent. France was primarily a prosperous agrarian country and much entrepreneurial activity developed directly by large landowners from the produce of their estates. Men qualified as electors through their tax contributions. The most onerous direct tax was that on land, so it is not surprising on both counts that the bulk of voters were landowners, before and after 1830s. In 1827 60 per cent of voters and 73 per cent of candidates were landowners. In 1829 31 per cent of deputies were landowners, in 1831 23 per cent. But the most frequently cited occupation, before and after the revolution, was civil servant: 40 per cent in 1829, 38 per cent in 1831. Statistics show that few deputies were professional men: 5 per cent in 1827, nearly 9 per cent in 1840.[14] Such figures are misleading. Most candidates would list more than one 'occupation', yet only a sophisticated computer analysis can take adequate cognisance of the fact that a man would be quite likely to be a landowner, a forge-owner, a mayor, etc.[15] There is no evidence to suggest that the élite of the July Monarchy differed markedly from that of the Restoration in occupation. Economic change was proceeding far too gradually for that to be the case. The most striking feature of the Chamber of Deputies in both periods is not the proportion of entrepreneurial or professional MPs, but the dominance of paid state servants.

It has been suggested that the real difference lay in the attitudes of the two regimes to economic and social questions, that the July Monarchy was more supportive of the industrial and commercial middle class. Both regimes followed highly protectionist commercial policies at the behest of producers and both favoured the employer in his relations with the employee. Both had great respect for accumulated wealth. The economic crisis of 1827–32 aroused criticism of Bourbon commercial policies among producers, but, as we have seen, there was no 'bourgeois', capitalist or other, consensus of condemnation of the economic policies of the Restoration. The priorities of different entrepreneurs were diverse, and continued to be so in the July Monarchy, when protectionist policies were pursued and strategies developed, as in the previous regime, in response to pressure from the most powerful economic interest groups. Just as the early 1820s had been a time of economic prosperity, so were the 1840s. It has been suggested that the Soult–Guizot administration was more constructive in its attitude to capitalism, but this may correspond more with evolutionary economic change than contrasting government preoccupations.[16] The only real difference between the élites of the Restoration and the July Monarchy lay in their attitude to, and in the respect they accorded, the Church and the house of Bourbon. The label 'bourgeois' was a red herring. The development of society had, long before even the 1789 revolution, allowed wealthy non-nobles to exercise some political influence. On the other hand, despite the abolition of the hereditary peerage in France in 1831, the social and economic power of the nobility remained very considerable and titles and many aspects of privilege remained embedded in social norms. These were untouched by revolution. Liberal sentiments cut across class lines, although they were the preserve of an educated minority, sometimes titled, sometimes bourgeois. The political issues of the period were not exclusively class interests. The diverse elements of the middle class, landed, bureaucratic, professional, commercial and industrial, were far from united in their goals, or even conscious of any commonality of purpose.

Finally, as a postscript to the more nonsensical claims that the July Revolution heralded a new bourgeois era, the king himself was often referred to as a citizen or bourgeois king. His father had, of course, temporarily abandoned his title, but not his wealth, when he called himself 'Philippe Egalité' in the 1790s. Louis-Philippe gained his appellation not because he was a regicide like his father – Charles X was allowed to flee into exile unchecked – but because of his lifestyle, his famous umbrellas, the shops, whores and accessibility of the Palais Royale, because his sons went to school with the rest of the élite and because of the cosy domesticity of his private life. But one has to recall that he was the king's cousin, and that he and his sister were the chief beneficiaries of the indemnification of the *emigrés* to the tune of 12 million francs. The July Monarchy was only slightly more bourgeois than the Restoration in the composition of the political nation and the ruling élite. During the Restoration the ultras, beleaguered dinosaurs in the modern world, tried to construct a golden age, to 'recreate' what was not there even in 1789, an aristocratic ruling class. The illusion was sustained by *emigré* ignorance of modern France and by the romantic novels of Scott and others exploiting the need for anachronistic security in a medieval past. But mythology became confused with reality, as the cascade of ultra-inspired legislation of the 1820s revealed. Temporarily the 'aristocratic' image of the Restoration seemed more than an aura, transcending the fact that the regime was a continuation of the political and social compromise of the Empire. But the liberal notables were sufficiently secure in their land, official appointments, careers and businesses. This was a political, not a social revolution. The Orleanist liberal élite enjoyed thinking of itself as 'bourgeois', which they equated with 'modern, educated and industrious'. They claimed to represent opportunity for all, an end to traditional privilege and the liberty of the individual. Perhaps they lived in as much of a dream world as the ultras; within five years press censorship was more rigorous than before, even the word 'republican' was banned, all political associations, however small, were forbidden, and the response of governments to the problems of the silk weavers of Lyons in the early 1830s was just as repressive as Bourbon attitudes towards artisan grievances.

The liberal notables when in power in France proved to be extremely conservative, fearful of popular unrest and promotors of an élitist educational system. Although they had clashed with Charles X over ministerial responsibility, they did not attempt to make France markedly more of a parliamentary state, indeed Louis-Philippe interfered in politics more than his predecessors. The liberals proved to be determined opponents of franchise reform. The distinction between state power and parliament was increasingly blurred: although liberals introduced legislation obliging those deputies with official jobs to seek re-election to the chamber, the result of the poll could always be taken for granted. However, despite their misgivings, the élite, Orleanist and legitimist, survived revolution in February 1848, the introduction of universal suffrage and the establishment of the Third Republic in 1871. Liberal philosophies were overtaken by others, but the issues of monarchy and Church continued to distinguish legitimist notables from others. Only to-wards the end of the century, as their local power base began to beeroded in some areas by economic change, was this position to alter.

Prussian liberals started from the same premise as those in France, enthusiasm for a constitutional regime, but unlike the French they lost the power struggle with the ruler and parliamentary institutions failed to develop. How can one explain this contrast? One obvious difference between liberalism in France and Prussia was nationalism. The French liberals were, as self-conscious heirs of selected aspects of the 1789 revolution, patriots and nationalists. This was one factor in the appeal of liberal ideas in eastern France, which suffered from invasion and occupation at the end of the wars. Subsequently, however, claiming to be a patriot merely had very tenuous radical associations and was relatively harmless and undivisive. There was no contradiction in France between patriotism and liberalism; France had been a united country over a long period. In Prussia, where nineteenth-century liberals also considered themselves nationalists, circumstances were very different. They thought of themselves not as Prussian nationalists but as German, and Germany was no more than a confederation of 39 independent states, under the moral leadership of the Austrian ruler, with no common institutions other than occasional meetings of ambassadors of each state in Frankfurt. Austria's authority was weakened by the cares of her multinational empire, while the second largest state, Prussia, acquired influence and power through her economic growth and her leadership of the *zollverein*, a customs union which between 1834 and 1854 attracted the participation of all the German states except Austria and two free cities. The question of Germany was likely to involve a power struggle between Austria and Prussia. The issue was particularly vexed because ethnic groups were so untidily arranged in central Europe. A majority of Austria's population was non-German, as was a large section of Prussia's eastern provinces. Another contrast with France, which proved to be a serious weakness, was that the leaders of the attempt to turn Prussia into a parliamentary state were members of the king's own bureaucracy, especially members of the judiciary, and as we have seen they were motivated partly by professional frustration. Bureaucrats were held in such high regard that their leadership was unquestioned. But only a small proportion of the middle classes were interested in liberal ideas; outside the bureaucracy they were mainly drawn from professional and intellectual groups. In France the liberals were notables, constituting a powerful and wealthy section of landowners and including also professionals, bureaucrats and those with financial, commercial and industrial interests. In Prussia the landed nobles remained the ruling élite, particularly in the heartland of the state, and liberal and nationalist notions were wholly repugnant to them. Only in the newly acquired Rhenish provinces was the élite partly entrepreneurial – and liberal.

A further contrast with France was that in Prussia liberalism was intertwined with particularism, the defence of the small community, of a single province or group of provinces, against a larger authority, which was regarded as foreign and hostile, whether that power was Prussia or Austria. Particularism was a potent force in the confederation exacerbated by the increased power of the larger states during the Napoleonic period and after. It is not surprising that early-nineteenth-century German nationalists stressed the mental and spiritual unity of all Germans.[17] In France, of course, it was easy to be a patriot and a liberal, and the issue of the local community versus the state did not arise in an extreme form, but it is interesting to note that the Restoration monarchists, later the legitimists, were the champions of provincial rights against the power of the centralised state. In the Rhineland the local notables, many of them non-noble businessmen and industrialists, rightly accused the Prussian central government of imposing an undue tax burden upon them. They fought against the *zollverein*, which in its infancy worked to their disadvantage, but above all detested the incursions of the Prussian bureaucracy into their province. These Rhenish liberals, many of them Protestants, favoured a constitutional monarchy for Prussia in the hope of thereby reducing the interference of the Prussian state machine in the affairs of their area.

The Prussian liberals lacked the bedrock of alignment behind a phenomenon akin to the 1789 revolution, which was a uniting factor for French liberals even though the revolutionary heritage was confused. In Prussia the reforming and modernising agent was the state, hence perhaps it is not surprising that bureaucrats subsequently became prominent liberals. In Prussia a major programme of reform was undertaken at the beginning of the century, partly as a reaction to the success of the French armies. In 1806 Stein, the leading reformer, hoped that eventually a national representative assembly would be formed. His successor, Hardenberg, while arguing the case on the grounds of rationality and efficiency, was less optimistic, although he called an interim assembly of notables from Prussia's eastern provinces in 1811. In May 1815 Frederick William committed himself to provide a written constitution and assemblies for each of the provinces. The strongest pressure came from the western lands. Three thousand Rhinelanders, led by the publicist Gorres, signed the Coblentz address, urging Frederick William III to keep his promise. The new Minister of the Interior, von Humboldt, also pressed for direct elections. But the king procrastinated. The murder, by a member of a students' association, of Kotzebue, a right-wing Russian playwright, gave opponents of change, like the influential Austrian minister Metternich, the opportunity to urge repression in the Carlsbad Decrees. Student societies, the *burschenschaften*, were banned, censorship was tightened and, with the resignation of von Humboldt, hopes of an elected national assembly withered away. Conservatives, especially the east Elban nobility, pressed for the revival of the old estates in each province and their view prevailed. In 1823 it was decided that a diet should be elected by the estates in each province. There was to be a three-class franchise of nobles, burghers and peasants, with property ownership the basic qualification for voting. Entrepreneurs and others, however rich, only qualified if they were also landowners. Hence the diets for the Prussian provinces contained 1329 deputies for the towns, 2207 propertied peasants and 12654 estate-owners. In addition to the property-owning franchise, 69 per cent of seats were allocated to nobles, owners of entailed estates and rural areas. Thus the cities of Cologne and Aachen, with populations of over 100 000, elected only three members to the diet of the Rhineland, whereas 7000 nobles elected 25 representatives. In some states, such as Hanover, bourgeois landowners were totally disenfranchised. Despite the electoral system, businessmen were often the outstanding leaders in the diets, although liberal bureaucrats exerted an increasing influence.[18]

Nationalist ideas were gradually becoming more popular and were beginning to appeal to other groups within the middle class and beyond. At the time of the battle of Leipzig (1813), German nationalism was primarily an anti-French sentiment, laced with the enthusiasm of some intellectuals for a common historic, linguistic and cultural heritage. But writers interested in nationalism, like Heine and Arndt, did not associate patriotic feeling with a political entity, and often roundly condemned any concept of a single German state as likely to be destructive of German patriotism, which would be swamped in the vitality of particularist state traditions and power structures. The *burschenschaften*, associations of university students, gloried in a romantic historic nationalism, but respected existing boundaries and institutions. Occasional war scares, like that of 1840, and the first round of the struggle for succession in Schleswig-Holstein a few years later, encouraged fairly popular patriotic sentiments. What began to make association between the sovereign states of the confederation more meaningful was not poetry, or the intangible sense of being one *volk*, but a growing awareness of common economic interests. In the years after 1815 all of the states adopted protectionist tariffs, and often tariff boundaries persisted within individual states such as Prussia. As the slow development beyond very limited local markets began to gain momentum, these tariffs were seen more as obstacles than a protection. The Prussians eliminated internal tariffs and they and other states competed to form larger commercial units. Not surprisingly, in view of her size and economic potential, Prussia became the dominant power, and in 1834 formed a *zollverein*. Membership offered free internal trade, thus a greatly enlarged market and some protection from foreign goods with a low external tariff of 10 per cent. Prussia gained most, but the other states profited and looked to Berlin to provide large-scale capital. Railway construction flourished in the 1840s, Berlin banks provided much of the finance and most lines started in Berlin. Railways created the backbone and skeleton of a new, larger state and the impetus for unprecedented growth in Prussian metallurgical industries.

These economic developments had two important consequences. The power balance in the German states was altered irreversibly in Prussia's favour, and the industrial and commercial middle classes became interested in some aspects of nationalism. Larger markets were obviously beneficial, the *zollverein* provided a good first base.

But it was only a renewable customs union and political boundaries remained. For some men political unity began to appear a more secure alternative, but only when nationalism had been divorced from its revolutionary content, which was more upsetting to trade then the need to renegotiate the *zollverein*. Liberal nationalism had revolutionary implications, at least in the rest of Europe, whereas the development of economic links was best done through the agency of the existing authoritarian states. Rhenish industrialists cooled on the subject of parliaments when Silesian weavers added their contribution to liberal demands, a protest about working conditions.

The constitutional issue was, however, still foremost in the minds of middle-class critics like Schön, a leading figure in the East Prussian bureaucracy, and Hansemann and Camphausen, speaking for the wealthy bourgeoisie of the western provinces. The accession of Frederick William IV (1840–60) to the throne of Prussia encouraged liberals because he appeared sympathetic both to constitutional notions and nationalist hopes. Meetings of the estates became more regular and the king encouraged them to set up committees to discuss local affairs with him. In 1842 he assembled a gathering of representatives from all these committees, consisting of 4 nobles, 32 burghers and 20 landowning peasants. Ambitious railway projects in the next few years seemed to indicate the urgent need for some sort of state assembly which could sanction taxes and a new state loan to float railway plans. In February 1847 the eight provincial estates of Prussia met together as a united estates with over 200 nobles and 300 burghers and peasants. For the king this was a unique occasion, for the participants it was regarded as the first of many such gatherings and a prelude to the compilation of a written constitution. When the king refused the latter, the majority withdrew their support for the railway loan and the king dissolved the assembly in June 1847.

As in France in 1830, it was not the liberals who made the revolution in the following year. Between 1845 and 1848 a further coincidence of harvest failures with financial, commercial and industrial recession aggravated the already difficult circumstances of peasants coping with a desperate land shortage and attacks on traditional rights made intolerable by population increases and artisans resisting the impact of the technical changes of industrialisation. The liberal leaders in the estates, many of whom were senior civil servants, had no sympathy with the objectives and methods of peasants and artisans. They did not see themselves as revolutionaries and, without the escalation of artisan violence and the news of the events in Paris and of radical demands in Baden and elsewhere in southern Germany in February, it is unlikely that they would have countenanced any further action. In March the German Federal Diet, the traditional gathering of representatives from all of the states, published a patriotic appeal hoping to stall radical change by promising to reform the constitution of the confederation. Four days later a meeting of impatient liberals from south-western German states declared the need for a national parliament and set up a steering committee to organise elections. In Prussia discontented out-of-work artisans tried to profit from the patriotic and liberal ferment and uncertainty, itself aggravated by the economic crisis, to draw attention to their own problems by holding mass meetings. Berlin was chiefly a city of small merchants and artisans, and 40 per cent of its budget was being consumed in poor relief for the unemployed. The king tried to counter the agitation of the radical workers and liberal middle class by promising to recall the United Diet in April and support the reform of the confederation. On 18 March he announced that Prussia would help to reorganise Germany into a genuine confederation with a constitution. The disturbances which then occurred and which constitute the Prussian revolution seem to have been almost accidental and to a fair degree the product of royal indecision and idiosyncrasy. While soldiers were clearing the crowds who had gathered before the royal palace to hear about the changes, shots were fired. Artisans and other workers, who had expected that a troop withdrawal would follow the original announcement, concluded that the king was reneging on his promises, threw up barricades and fought with the soldiers. The troops were entirely loyal to the king and could have quelled the riots, but Frederick William, apparently shocked by the bloodshed of civil disorder, and for the moment charmed by the thought of himself as one of the leaders possibly of a revived Holy Roman Empire, withdrew his troops. More indecision and misunderstanding led to the total military evacuation of Berlin, but the army did not desert the king. The liberal middle classes had taken little part: 74 artisans, 13 merchants and 2 students were among the dead.

For those who did fight, the riots were part of their struggle for survival. Along with other artisans, they wanted to limit the embryonic factory system by restricting its output through a revival of guild regulation. Violent Luddite demonstrations grew more frequent. Peasants who joined in unrest were anxious to end feudal dues. But neither group influenced actual decisions. Two liberal leaders, Camphausen and Hansemann, were appointed Minister President and Finance Minister and they were determined to support the king and check the demands and activities of the artisans. A new constituent assembly was to be elected by universal suffrage, but indirectly, to limit the impact of the radicals. Rural and urban disturbances convinced those with property that their interests lay in the preservation of royal, even military, power. New entrepreneurs were appalled by Luddism. Middle-class purchasers of feudal rights opposed their abolition. Civilian militia groups, organised by property-owners, sprang up everywhere. But promises were made to revive the guilds and eliminate feudal rights, and popular violence died out. The harvest was satisfactory. Liberal bureaucrats continued to lead the middle-class movement, but with increasing caution.

The king promised support for the national as well as liberal cause and paraded the black, red and gold flag of the revolution, but active Prussian support was tepid. The Rhineland supplied 100 of the 141 Prussian delegates to the pre-parliament which met in Frankfurt on 31 March. Elsewhere, particularly among the aristocratic eastern landowners, there was total opposition to both liberal and national ideas. All adult males were qualified to vote in the elections to the National Assembly in Prussia, but an indirect electoral system, an open ballot and lack of pay for delegates helped to ensure that only one peasant and four artisans were among the 585 members. Ninety nobles, nearly all professional men, were chosen. The vast majority was bourgeois. The biggest group, 157, were lawyers, including judges. There were 138 higher civil servants and 100 university and high school teachers. Thus the total of men who received a salary directly from one of the states was 395. There were only 40 entrepreneurs. Senior bureaucrats of all kinds, because of the respect in which they were held and the experience of government they enjoyed, were thought of as natural delegates to a federal assembly. But the Frankfurt parliament held only the shadow of authority and by its own decisions exposed the nakedness of its position. It had no income and no army, and was surprised when the armies of the princes of Germany refused to swear an oath of allegiance to it. The definition of German nationality and German territory proved disastrous. The assembly refused the request of the

Polish citizens of Prussian Posen to join an autonomous Polish state. They invited Palacky, the Slav leader, to attend their debates, and he refused. It was completely outside their competence to determine how much of the embattled Austrian Empire should be a German state, and as Austria regained control over her constituent parts she ignored their debates. The question of the nationality of Schleswig-Holstein, ruled by Denmark but part of the confederation, was taken out of their hands by the Prussian army, and Frederick William listened to the protests of the great powers, not the assembly's protests at Prussian military occupation of the duchies.

Thus the authority of the bourgeois assembly was denied by the princes and disregarded by the great powers. It was also attacked by radical artisan groups, impatient for economic reform. On 18 September 1848 delegates were obliged to ask Austria and Prussia for military protection when artisans demonstrated against the withdrawal of troops from the duchies. Two delegates were killed. From this point, and the abortive radical revolt of Struve in Baden which followed, most middle-class Germans were more anxious for the protection of individuals and property, and for the re-establishment of the full authority of the princes to achieve this, than they were for the creation of a liberal federal constitution for Germany. Disillusion was evident in the election results for the Prussian constituent assembly. Few members of the middle class stood. There were 68 peasants and 120 radicals. In June 1848 the Berlin arsenal was stormed and in August the assembly abolished feudal rights. But divorced from the better-off, and with only limited popular support, the power of this elected parliament was a mere chimera. A league for the protection of landed property was formed in Prussia.

The Prussian king, encouraged by the reassertion of monarchical power in Vienna, appointed a conservative government in November, and the radical assembly was dispersed by the royal army. Frederick William refused the federal imperial crown offered by the Frankfurt assembly in April 1849 and a month later, along with the other larger states, Prussia withdrew her delegation from Frankfurt. In June the assembly was brought to an end by the military intervention of the large states. Outbursts of artisan agitation continued in the summer, notably in the Rhineland, Saxony, Bavaria and Baden; and there were even military mutinies in Baden. But the revolutionary initiative was dead and property-owners now put their faith in the princes and their armies. The liberal middle classes, who participated in attempts to create a constitutional regime in Berlin for Prussia and in Frankfurt for a federal Germany, were disillusioned by the experience. They found themselves out of sympathy both with the aims and methods of artisans and peasants. They were obliged to conclude that the king and his army offered more reassurance than a riotous crowd. Although they wanted an elected parliament, they were not democrats and expected that voting rights would stop with property owners. In 1848 these liberals came from traditional elements within the better-off middling ranks of society. The leaders were mainly university-educated senior and fairly senior civil servants, many from the judiciary. They were opposed to what they saw as the increasing conservatism of their fellow bureaucrats and were worried that the bureaucracy was being taken over by the nobility in Prussia. The administrators saw themselves as impartial arbiters in the constitutional argument and were appalled by violent defiance of royal authority. Members of the judiciary were more inclined to radicalism, but not to actual democracy. In 1848 these bourgeois elements had few interests in common with the growing commercial and industrial middle class, who looked directly to the king and his army to solve the problem of Luddism and artisan unrest. Even the liberals were associated with revolution by the accidental concurrence of their political ambitions with the timing of an economic crisis. Until the crisis of the mid-1840s intensified the reaction of urban artisans, the bureaucratic critics of king and bureaucratic system found common cause with urban artisan groups, who were struggling to retain the autonomy of their small towns against the centralising authority of the princes. The events of 1848 revealed that reforming civil servants and defensive home town politicians had nothing in common. The powerlessness of the artisans was thrown into contrast by the loyalty of the troops to the princes. The radical bureaucrats were compelled to accept a more subservient role if they were to salvage their jobs.

Although liberals were hostile to democracy and the demands of peasants and artisans, they did not represent the interests of the middle class as such. Bourgeois industrialists had no sympathy with the attempts of Prussian reforming bureaucrats to oblige Frederick William to set up a parliamentary system. The entrepreneurs of the Rhineland who began to espouse the notion of constitutional monarchy at this time were in total conflict with those bureaucrats and for them an elected assembly would be a means to limit both Prussian bureaucratic and Prussian monarchical intervention in their province. They were motivated by local, rather than class imperatives, indeed they genuinely believed themselves representative of a broad spectrum of Rhenish society. Ironically the events of 1848 made different social groups far more aware of their lack of common interests. Middle-class industrialists became more appreciative of the benefits of a centralised monarchy with a strong army; reforming bureaucrats were made aware of their social isolation and need to cleave to the monarch for their own professional security. The popular violence of 1848, the Luddism of artisans, the archaic fury of peasants in the face of the demise of traditional customs on which their livelihood had depended, caused the educated, well-heeled critics of established authority to realise that revolution was not a romantic game of élitist secret societies, but an anarchic, uncontrollable panorama, in which property-owners were as likely to be victims as victors. Revolution was not class war before 1848, but episodes like the June Days of 1848, when the French army butchered unemployed artisans to maintain the authority of an assembly of notables, albeit elected on a democratic franchise, ensured that in future confrontations issues would be expressed in terms of class conflict.

In Prussia there was strong middle-class pressure, particularly from leading members of the judiciary, for constitutional change in 1848; indeed, superficially, although he was not unseated in the March revolution, Frederick William's authority seemed to be under almost as much threat as that of Louis-Philippe. Yet, as elsewhere in Germany, middle-class liberalism finally deferred to royal authority. The unity of conservative aristocratic and military opinion behind the rulers was in marked contrast to the divisions and disagreements of those who wanted to limit monarchical and aristocratic authority. The constitutional and national achievements of the revolutionaries were nullified by the armies of the princes, and this was confined by the re-establishment of the old diet. The Prussian king replaced his revolutionary constitutional assembly with a new body, created through a constitution decreed by the king alone in December 1848, similar to that of Belgium which dated back to 1831. Initially all adult males voted in elections to the lower house, but this system was replaced by a graded franchise. First-class voters, the richest 4.5 per cent of the adult male taxpayers, elected one-third of the lower house. Second-class voters were those who paid the next third of the direct taxes. They consisted of 12.8 per cent of taxpayers and again elected one-third of the deputies. Those who paid the final third of Prussia's taxes and constituted 82.7 per cent of taxpayers also elected one-third of the deputies. The upper house, at first elected, was later nominated by the king. Only the pressing need for revenue left the purse strings in the hands of the assembly. These constitutional arrangements, although determined entirely by the king and his advisers, were apparently satisfactory to the middle-class liberals, who soon assumed control over the lower house. It appeared that the liberals had taken over the king's constitution.

But the character of and support for liberalism was changing, not just through the fear engendered in liberals by the popular unrest manifest in 1848 and the realisation that, despite their own claims to be a species of 'proletariat', they had nothing in common with the grievances of the poor. The rapid growth in the Prussian economy in the 1850s was a major factor in the change in support for liberalism. The king took some steps to appease the grievances of some of the revolutionary fighters of 1848 during the Manteuffel government in the 1850s. Feudal laws were abolished but, although 600 000 peasants took advantage of low interest rates to buy their freeholds, this did nothing to alleviate the land hunger of peasant communities. Guilds were restored, but industrial developments of the 1850s made them anachronistic. However there was no renewal of artisan and peasant unrest. Poor peasants either migrated within the German states or went overseas. One million left in the 1850s alone, mostly bound for North America. Artisans shunned the nascent social democratic movements of the 1860s and attempts to exert pressure on governments were ineffective. Those members of the professional middle class who had appeared to encourage artisan protest in 1848 proved to be champions of the liberalisation of industry, thus diametrically opposed to their old allies.[19] The coincidence of popular unrest with conflict between the king and diet in 1847 was unlikely to be repeated: antipathies were now more distinct, the bourgeois fear of revolt more pronounced and optimism that a German constitutional nation could be formed by liberal means now almost extinguished.

However the *landtag* remained and was soon under liberal control. By 1858 there were 210 liberals and only 57 conservatives and 58 Catholics. Frederick William IV's brother, William, who became regent in 1858 when the king suffered a series of strokes and then king in 1860, appeared briefly to tolerate the liberals, but soon settled into rigid, but impotent, conservatism. Military leaders, discountenanced by the fiasco of 1848, in which they had been offered little opportunity to show their paces against the radicals, who had retained to some degree a psychological advantage, were anxious for military reform. In 1859, von Roon, Minister of War, put a proposal to the assembly which would have increased the period of military service from two to three years, swelled the annual draft from 40 000, where it had stood since the beginning of the century, to 60 000 and absorbed the *landwehr* into the command structure of the regular army. Liberals were vehemently opposed to the last of these proposals, for to them the independence of the *landwehr* was a precious safeguard of middle-class rights. A political stalemate was soon reached; the liberal majority rejected the army bill, but it was not so easy for the king to discard the assembly. In March 1862, when the king dissolved the *landtag*, liberal representation actually increased to 285, and only 67 deputies were willing to vote for the government of Prince Karl Anton and his programme of army reform.[20] In theory William was in as precarious a position as Charles X had been in France in 1830, but William had greater confidence, based on the total reliability of the army and the precedent of an ignominiously defeated revolution fourteen years earlier. The Prussian liberals were split between Progressives and Moderates, which groups were more suspicious of each other than of the conservatives. The experience of 1848 had left the Moderates with no stomach for a fight with the Crown. Indeed, when William broke the Gordian knot and appointed a radical, unpredictably maverick conservative, Bismarck, the Moderates were convinced that the alternative would be a Progressive government, which they would find even less palatable.

The timidity and internecine conflicts of the liberals, and the willingness of Bismarck to govern without parliamentary consent for his budget, plus the view of some liberals that problems within the German Confederation partially justified such a strategy, contributed to the gradual withering away of the huge liberal majority. They lost only 27 seats in a further election in 1863,[21] but the substantial majority they retained was decisive only on paper. Bismarck continued to rule by decree. Many liberals were won over by military policies which seemed to favour their own nationalist ambitions. In 1866, during the war with Austria, liberal support dropped to 172 and conservatives, in conjunction with Catholic, Polish and other independent groups, could at last outvote them. In the elections for a Constituent Assembly in February 1867, following the formation of the North German Confederation, the majority of liberals, now renamed national liberals, joined conservatives to support Bismarck and indemnify him for the five previous years of unconstitutional rule. How can one account for such a volte-face?

The defeat of the revolution of 1848 left liberals in Prussia, as in other German states, very divided. Some hoped to be able to have a decisive voice in the new assemblies set up by the old rulers. Others belittled these limited constitutional concessions and continued to press for a wholesale revision of the resurrected German federal diet. Parliamentary particularism could be an enemy to German nationalism. The ultimate goal of liberals in the various German states was still the creation of a federal, parliamentary regime, but the political relationships of the liberals with other social groups were changed by the revolutionary experience. Some liberals, disillusioned with their old allies, found the stance of established rulers more reassuring than in the past.[22] Economic growth in the 1850s was supported by the government. The *zollverein* treaties, initiated by the Prussian government, seemed increasingly efficacious. In 1862 agreements to reduce tariffs were concluded between the *zollverein* and France, and in 1865 these were extended to include Great Britain, Belgium and Italy. An economic strategy agreeable to the liberals was gradually adopted in these years in all of the German states apart from Austria. By the mid-1860s most states had abolished guild control over industry and, after Austria's defeat by Prussia in the war of 1866, Prussia, at the head of the new confederation, orchestrated a policy of economic liberalism entirely in tune with that desired by the liberals. There was to be a common banking system, code of law, and railway and transport policy, and weights and measures were to be standardised. Laws decreeing provisions for mobility of labour, freedom of enterprise, freedom of credit and the abolition of state restrictions on joint stock companies, all passed between 1867 and 1870, fulfilled the *laissez-faire* ambitions of employers.

In the realm of politics too, Bismarck's policies ultimately achieved what most Prussian, though not other German liberals wanted, although the process and final form of unification may have worried some. In the 1840s liberals had envisaged nationalism as essentially liberal and individualistic. They expected that united Germany would be a federal, parliamentary construct, in which a national constitution would override the particularism of the traditional conservative élite and the princes. Popular violence and the emergence of a new working class made liberals acutely aware that they had no vested interest in radical change, but could gain more by reaching a power-sharing agreement with the princes. Such naive hopes were shattered by the swift military conclusion reached by the Prussian army to the decades of rivalry between Austria and Prussia in the confederation. The war effectively left the Prussian traditional élite in control of the new empire, somewhat bemused and only slowly appreciating the advantages in the reach of radical or 'free' conservatism. The liberal middle classes were outmanoeuvred by Bismarck's manipulation of the opportunities offered to himself and Prussia in the political and military crises of the 1860s. Bismarck managed to turn Prussia's virtual military conquest of the other German states into something approaching a national victory, which the liberals in Prussia could not but applaud.[23]

The liberals were also outmanoeuvred by Bismarck in the constitutional arrangements made for the confederation and later extended to the empire. Liberals had always been constitutionalists, but only a few had embraced democratic ideals. Most were suspicious of democracy and preferred the Prussian *landtag* franchise. This weighted system had produced liberal majorities so, not surprisingly, liberals could see no gain for themselves in enfranchising the less well-off. A limited suffrage did not favour the Crown; in neighbouring France a democratic electorate was loyal to the emperor. Thus Bismarck took advantage of the revision of the confederation to introduce adult male suffrage. Unlike liberals, and most conservatives, Bismarck did not believe that a mass electorate would be preponderantly radical in the choice of deputies, but, as a safeguard, he insisted that those elected should be unpaid. The constitution affirmed the ascendancy of royal, state power by specifying that government ministers should not be responsible to the assembly, or *reichstag*, that the *reichstag* should have only a limited role in military expenditure and that the new body should only discuss, not initiate, policy. The draft constitution was approved by the assembly by 230 votes to 53, with the national liberals supporting the government. Thus the majority of liberals voted for a constitution which posed serious obstacles to the evolution of a parliamentary state. After the defeat of France in 1870–1, all of the states south of the Main except Austria joined in a federal empire, whose constitution was based on that of 1867. The national liberals, now 119-strong, were members of the government majority and helped to complete the process which made the new empire basically authoritarian and in which the role of the military was enhanced to the point that only a strong or very wily chancellor like Bismarck was able to hold the senior officer corps in check; in other words, an empire in which liberalism had little relevance.

The apparently paradoxical reversal of the national liberals can be explained partly by opportunism. The wars and the imperial constitution of 1871 appeared to achieve the national dream of several generations of liberals. The government's pursuit of a policy of economic liberalism was wholly satisfactory to them. The liberals may have realised that their own political power base was very narrow; unlike contemporaries in Britain they appeared unable even to consider trying to appeal to a broader social spectrum. This last explanation is perhaps flattering. German liberals rarely seemed to regret their failure to exploit the democratic franchise. More relevant to the liberals in the 1860s was the apparent indifference of voters to participation in parliamentary politics. Throughout the 1850s and 1860s voting levels were extraordinarily and indeed in European terms uniquely low. In 1858 only 22.6 per cent of electors voted in the Prussian *landtag* elections. Participation was to rise to just over 34 per cent in April 1861, but to fall to just under 31 per cent in October 1863, during a very significant constitutional crisis which decided the future of parliamentary institutions in the country. The only election of the 1860s which attracted a noticeably higher poll was that for the constituent assembly in 1867, when nearly 64 per cent voted. Thus, on average, fewer than one-third of the enfranchised citizens went to the polls. Why? The better-off, who elected the majority of members, showed somewhat more enthusiasm. In April 1862 61 per cent of the first-class voters turned out, while only 48 per cent of the second class and 30.5 per cent of the third class voted. The low participation of the less well-off presumably indicated in some measure their criticism of a system which permitted over 80 per cent of the voters to select only one-third of the deputies. But voting levels remained low in all three groups, even though it was clear from the outset that Bismarck's government was a threat to the authority of the assembly. The divisions within the liberals themselves were extremely debilitating. The popular violence of 1848 destroyed the confidence of many liberals in elected assemblies. Many Moderates were more inclined to royal than mass power. The bulk of the liberal leaders in 1848 were civil servants and even those who were not disenchanted with their limited control over mass politics in the revolution were subsequently bought off by promotion or by threats of dismissal. The government was determined to exclude civil servants from parliament and its success emasculated Prussian liberalism. In the final analysis the liberals themselves consciously sacrificed parliament for liberal economic legislation and a unified state. They lacked the landed power base of the French notables, on whom democracy had little impact.

Italian liberalism before unification was complicated by the division of the peninsula into separate states, one of which was ruled by a succession of popes who were committed enemies of all change. The two most economically advanced states, Lombardy and Venetia, were part of the Austrian Empire and all the other rulers from time to time utilised Austrian troops to suppress revolts against their autocratic forms of government. Thus in Italy there was little chance that liberalism could promote change by peaceful means. The term 'liberal' is usually applied to constitutional monarchist movements. In some provinces like Venetia republican and/or democratic solutions were propounded, being more in keeping with traditional practice. Liberals were sometimes noble, particularly in Piedmont and Lombardy, sometimes a mixture of bourgeois and nobles; liberalism was not a class phenomenon. Many were landowners, and often, as in France, had added to their estates by buying Church and sometimes common land after the revolutionary takeover by France. Some were members of the traditional bourgeoisie, mostly professional men and bureaucrats, although there was some support from entrepreneurs, noble and bourgeois, in Lombardy and Venetia. It has been suggested that liberals on the whole came from more exalted social ranks than republicans and democrats.

In 1814 old rulers were restored. Did the fact of the Restoration automatically create dissatisfied élites of unemployed Napoleonic officials, which then formed the nuclei of liberal and national opposition? This has been suggested and appears both logical and reasonable. There were bourgeois families who gained land and position under Napoleon greatly advancing the fortunes of their families, such as the Cavour clan in Piedmont and the *galantuomini* in southern Italy. But recent detailed investigations call for a modification of this explanation for the origins of Italian liberalism. After the turbulent Jacobin 1790s, Napoleon preferred to conciliate old élites, noble and bourgeois, by appointing them as senior bureaucrats. Thus, as has already been noted, Napoleon's ruling group were not new, although, as in France, there were some more recently enriched elements. There were a host of new middle-ranking and minor appointments for the lesser bourgeoisie in Napoleon's much enlarged governing systems. At the Restoration the new rulers opted for a variety of solutions. The decision on how many Napoleonic servants to employ was pragmatic and opportunistic. In Lombardy–Venetia Napoleonic local notables were retained but gradually downgraded from senior jobs and their places taken by Germans. In the new Kingdom of the Two Sicilies, disgruntled *emigré* nobles complained that Napoleonic officials were kept on, but many of Napoleon's men had been local barons. Conversely it has been suggested that the leaders of the 1820 rising were frustrated ex-bureaucrats from the imperial era. Officers and men who had served in the Napoleonic armies were the most likely of Bonapartist clients to be unemployed, or to believe that their talents were underused in a peacetime garrison. They were often the centre of complaints about the restoration and the chief orchestrators of the revolutionary, secret masonic-style cells, especially the *Carbonari*. In Lombardy–Venetia lawyers were embittered by the replacement of the French legal system by the Austrian, which denied them the right to represent their clients in court. Manin, the leader of the 1848 revolution in Venice, was a lawyer. In Piedmont the main motive for violent protest was the attempt of the restored monarchy to eliminate all traces of French rule. Thus regional differences had a significant impact on the emergence of opposition. In addition, in Italy the repeated attempts by peasants to combat the destruction of communal rights formed a background of perpetual popular violence. There was no community of interest between the two groups, but peasant insurrection made it easier for the liberals to be heard.

The fragmentation of the Italian states might lead one to expect that nationalism would be a more important component of liberal ideas in Italy than elsewhere. Anti-Austrian sentiment was certainly pronounced in Lombardy and Venetia, provinces absorbed into the Austrian Empire in 1814 and ruled from Vienna. But in these provinces as in others, local patriotism was more in evidence than Italian nationalism, in keeping with strong traditional regional ties. Nationalism was more important to republicans and democrats like Mazzini and Garibaldi. Hostility to Austria also generated demands for constitutional government to replace Viennese centralised autocracy. Local notables in Lombardy and Venetia resented the inefficiency of Austrian rule compared with that of France. The centralising policies of the Habsburgs meant that even less was left to local initiative than before.[24] Central consultative committees were set up in Venice and Milan, with supporting provincial groups. The emperor appointed all members; property qualifications for membership were so high that in Venice in 1846 only 80 people were entitled to be considered for the provincial committee and of these only 32 were rich enough for the central body. Despite their extreme social exclusiveness, the congregations were trusted with little to do and did nothing to improve Austria's image.

Metternich, Austria's chief minister, sought to germanise northern Italy. University staff were appointed from Vienna; the works of Dante and Hugo and Rossini's *William Tell* were banned. The Austrians tried to revive the power of the local nobility who were traditionally francophile, a sentiment heightened by wartime experiences. Senior appointments deemed unworthy of an Austrian went to local nobles, but in Venice their power was only a shadow of pre-revolutionary days. Even so the attempt to rebuild the influence of an aristocracy, in decline before the French invasion, was resented in Venice. Venice was the fourth city of the empire, but the Austrians were determined to develop their German lands and deliberately left Lombardy and Venetia to stagnate. They were not allowed to trade with the rest of the peninsula; Venice was denied a branch of the bank of Vienna. The empire was content to remain land-based and Venice was an irrelevance. The economy of the provinces, damaged by war and loss of trading links, began to develop only after 1830, when Venice became a free port. The local industrial and commercial bourgeoisie resented Austrian policy, and their attempts, through the local chamber of commerce, to revive her economy were inevitably both anti-Austrian and anti-noble. Arguments over railway construction added to this ill-feeling. In

Lombardy noble landowners along with intellectual and professional groups were in the van of opposition. The explanation for the contrast between the social composition of opposite groups in the two provinces lies in Austrian policy. Before the Revolutionary Wars Joseph II had tried to break the Lombard nobility, whereas in Venice nobles had had the monopoly of lucrative jobs. In addition in Lombardy the most active entrepreneurs were nobles, which gave them a potent reason to dislike Austrian rule.[25]

Elsewhere some opponents of the Restoration were men whose careers had been blocked by the end of French occupation, but it no longer seems appropriate to describe this as a bourgeois opposition, for many liberals were nobles. At first opposition was manifest in the sporadic risings of secret societies like the Carbonari, Adelfi or Federati. Their supporters included junior army officers, members of families who had supported the French, dissatisfied with their own fate and that of the peninsula. In Naples in 1820 and Turin in 1821 members of secret societies attempted through limited military revolt to force their rulers to create constitutional regimes. Sicilians rebelled against rule from Naples, imposed in 1814, but the support of the barons for artisan risings soon evaporated because of the scale of popular protest.[26] The movements were sporadic, disconnected and often mutually antagonistic. Neapolitan liberals urged Ferdinand to send troops to repress the Sicilian revolt. The Austrians willingly supplied him with troops to use against liberals in Naples. In Turin also the revolutionary movement was divided. Victor Emmanuel I, restored as king after the wars, tried to reverse Napoleonic innovations. The Napoleonic Code was replaced by Roman law; there was some attempt to restore feudal rights and other privileges of the nobility were restored. Bonapartist officials were dismissed. Religious toleration was abolished. Criticism of the king grew in regional protests in Genoa and Savoy. There were small Carbonari cells in the army which attracted some students and were democratic in tone. A number of discontented nobles formed cells of the Federati and Adelfi which hoped for constitutional, but not democratic change. The news of the uprisings in Naples encouraged the Carbonari and in March 1821 sympathisers in the army took Alessandria and turned to march on Turin. The king's cousin, Charles Albert, encouraged the rebels and was made regent by them. He promised to establish a constitution, like the one recently agreed in Naples. The revolutionaries were, however, a tiny minority and their conflicts allowed the king to use Austrian troops to re-establish an autocratic system of government. Although the rebels had been in discord and few in number, they consisted of members of the ruling élite, most of whom, because of the influence of their families, escaped arrest. Ninety of the 97 death sentences were imposed *in absentia*.[27]

The 1830 revolution in France was some inspiration to the secret societies in Italy, but their activities were small-scale, isolated and intensely regional in scope. Revolt came first to the Austrian-ruled duchy of Modena and spread to the Papal States. The Romagna, formerly part of Napoleon's Kingdom of Italy, had been restored to papal control in 1815. Far from Rome and not very prosperous, the provinces of the Romagna criticised the abolition of Napoleonic institutions and the restoration of Roman and clerical control of much of the land and the best jobs. In 1831 revolutionary activity culminated in the setting up of a provisional government at Bologna, but within three weeks Austrian troops had crushed the revolt at the pope's behest, together with a rising in Modena. The two rebellions were mutually antagonistic. The violence of the repression in Bologna led to the great powers demanding that the area be allowed more municipal autonomy and when the pope disagreed French and Austrian troops occupied some districts until 1838. The dominance of Austria in the peninsula was further reinforced by the accession of Charles Albert to the throne of Piedmont. Aware of his dependence on the Austrian army to control revolutions which he now detested, he established close links with his stronger neighbour. He married a Habsburg and arranged matches with members of the family for his son and sister. Minor revolts continued in the 1830s. Mazzini, the idealist republican revolutionary and writer, led an abortive army revolt in Genoa in 1833. Garibaldi, fighter and patriot, similarly failed to raise the navy. Both Mazzini and Garibaldi, natives of the Kingdom of Piedmont, were condemned to death in their absence for their revolutionary activities. Mazzini tried to convince Italians that they should work not just for the liberation of isolated provinces from Austrian rule and domination, but for the unification of all of the provinces in the peninsula under a single republican constitution. He founded an organisation, Young Italy, to try to co-ordinate patriotic movements into a single volunteer national army to work for national liberation. Young Italy was founded in Tuscany, but its headquarters were in Marseilles where its newspaper was published. Young Italy broke new ground with its emphasis on unity, but its practical impact was nil. It attracted members of the élite, titled and professional, but it was ill-fitted, by its small size and lack of proper military training and equipment, to realise Mazzini's dreams.

The fact that the pope ruled a considerable chunk of central Italy was a permanent block to liberal and national ambitions, but a few Italians tried to convince themselves that a liberal papacy might provide the answer. In 1843 Gioberti, in *On the Moral and Civil Primacy of the Italians*, looked to the leadership of the Church, but a common religion and especially the presence of the head of the Church as a temporal ruler served to divide, not unite, Italians. Some of the poorer clergy, particularly in Naples, welcomed Gioberti's ideas, but the upper echelons judged them dangerous. Revolutionary activity was directed against papal rule and the Austrians were the main military prop for the pope. The Church hierarchy viewed both liberal and national movements as a threat to its religious and temporal authority. Briefly, with the accession of Pius IX in 1846 some liberal Catholics hoped for a pope sympathetic to reform. After an interlude of modest change, including the setting up of lay consultative councils and a civilian militia, the Papacy returned to its dependence upon conservative forces to protect both its territory and its spiritual function.

After 1830 interest in constitutionalism and liberation from Austrian rule began to exceed the scope of revolutionary conspiracy. The success of the *zollverein* brought home to Italians the disadvantage of the customs barriers in Italy. In the 1840s Balbo, the Piedmontese author of *On the Hopes of Italy*, supported the idea of a customs union for the area and cited the benefits reaped elsewhere by free trade. Others, like Cavour, hoped that railway construction would contribute to a desire for greater unity, as it was doing in the German states. The economic benefits of greater unity were particularly appealing in the most economically advanced regions of Lombardy, Venetia and Piedmont and attracted support from entrepreneurs.

An important aspect of nineteenth-century nationalism was the search for a common past, linguistic, cultural and political. But in Italy the rediscovery of past glory tended to reinforce regionalism. Italians even lacked a common language and writers like Manzoni pioneered the revival of a language used only in Tuscany. But the educated Piedmontese preferred French, and Latin was used in Piedmontese universities until 1852. Thus both liberal and national concepts were essentially those of literate, educated minorities, civil servants, academics, professionals and some nobles. In no sense at all were such ideas specifically or solely those of an entrepreneurial middle class, indeed such groups only hesitatingly appreciated the benefits that national unity could bring them. Those who hoped for liberal political change did not see the struggle in class terms. Indeed the democrat nationalist thinker Mazzini argued that class divisions and conflicts would weaken the national cause. Cavour hoped for liberal reform through the combined pressure of aristocratic landowners and the wealthy bourgeoisie. On a dissident note, Cattaneo, the Lombard revolutionary leader in 1848, deplored the role of aristocrats in the movement for change and longed for power to pass to the middle classes, as did Gioberti. Cattaneo believed that the best prospect for Italy lay in economic progress and capitalism.[28]

Economic and social problems in the mid-1840s brought a renewed period of violent upheaval in which peasants and artisans took a lead. In spite of the centrality of Paris in European revolution, the year of revolutions really began on 12 January with a renewed attempt by the Sicilians to regain their independence from Naples in a revolt inspired by economic grievance. This was followed by unrest throughout the peninsula. On 8 February Charles Albert promised a bicameral parliamentary system and a constitution was proclaimed a month later, similar to that of the Orleanist monarchy, which the French were busily demolishing. Similar declarations were forced upon Ferdinand, the pope and the ruler of Tuscany. Hostility to the presence of Austria was a dominant emotion in these movements and the successful revolt in Vienna on 13 March gave an excellent opportunity. But revolutionary leaders were not all liberals. In Venice the rising grew from the demand at the beginning of the year that Venice and Lombardy be accorded autonomous status and that property qualifications for elections to the congregations should be abolished. The economic crisis stimulated unrest, turning Manin into a popular hero, but he feared the poor and merely wanted the resurrection of the old Venetian republic, ruled by a somewhat less selective élite. He included bourgeois businessmen and professionals, not nobles, and those with democratic views were excluded. In Milan, by contrast, the nobility joined the provisional government, in an attempt to restrain disorder. In Lombardy there was less interest in declaring an independent republic and Cattaneo was inclined to look to Piedmont for a lead, an indication of the weakness of the democratic movement he actually represented. After some self-interested hesitation Charles Albert agreed to join Lombardy and Venetia in a war of liberation from Austria. Thus a rising, which began in Milan as an artisan rising backed by middle-class democrats and supported by the large number of Italian troops in the Austrian garrison, was taken over by the moderates, some of whom were bourgeois, but the majority of whom were noble. The democratic–artisan initiative was buried in the scramble of the traditional élites to hold on to power, forming civic guards to keep order which excluded artisans and peasants. They introduced taxes which left the great landowners fairly unscathed and which fell heavily on business and industry. As provincial towns formed provisional governments, they were invariably controlled by the traditional local élite.[29]

But failure in 1848 was not solely the product of social discord. Regional jealousies and rivalries were significant. Piedmont was unprepared for war and was unwilling to give wholehearted backing to the rebellious provinces. The agreement of Naples, the Papal States and the Austrian-ruled provinces to join their armies with that of Piedmont rapidly evaporated, as first the pope and then the king of Naples withdrew. Charles Albert demanded that his allies defer to his monarchical authority, feared the republicanism of Milan and Venice, and detested the aspiration of their peasants for social and land reform. One wonders whether his defeat at Custozza in July 1848 did not come as a relief. His withdrawal to Milan and the subsequent armistice were clearly designed to hold the popular movement in check. In November the pope and Leopold II of Tuscany fled and in February 1849 Mazzini and Garibaldi declared a democratic republic in Rome. That same month, in most unpromising circumstances, Charles Albert resumed the war with Austria, was beaten at Novara and abdicated in favour of his son, Victor Emmanuel II. The Austrian victory heralded the return of Austrian military and political control to the peninsula. The Roman republic fell to French troops in May 1849 and Venice capitulated to the Austrians in August. Ferdinand of Naples resumed power without the Austrians, but in the three duchies and the Romagna there was an Austrian military occupation for most of the 1850s. Lombardy and Venetia were kept in a state of siege up to 1857.

Thus the revolts in the Italian states for liberation and constitutional rule were universally disastrous. With some exceptions, such as Rome, there was no fusion of interest between peasant insurgents intent upon land reform, middle-class democrats working for radical political change, and middle-class or aristocratic leaders pressing for the end of Austrian influence. In Naples, as elsewhere, there were the competing political claims of liberals and democrats plus peasant agitation to try to protect communal rights and artisan Luddite demonstrations. The activities of the peasants and artisans so frightened the middle class of both persuasions that it was easy for Ferdinand to re-establish his position. In Tuscany artisan riots in August 1848, protesting about shortage of work and the nascent factory system, were repressed by the newly organised civic guard. A violent rising of the unemployed in Bologna was also held in check by the middle-class leaders who had gained from the insurrection earlier in the year. Middle-class support for revolution as a means to achieving their own ends collapsed during 1848 when the scale of popular unrest was understood. Only in Piedmont did the liberals gain a foothold. Piedmont alone retained a constitutional government after 1848. She developed a parliamentary system, with two chambers, one hereditary, one elected by the 80 000 richest taxpayers, who each paid at least 40 lire a year in direct taxes. During the 1850s her prosperity and the manner in which foreign investment, especially French, was attracted there made her political system not totally repugnant to others in the peninsula, and made Piedmont a focus for non-revolutionary nationalist ideas. But the liberals, who began to gain ascendency in Piedmont's new parliamentary system, found their attempts to institute educational reform, to nationalise Church lands, etc. checked by the conservative landed élite in the 1850s and were only able to implement their plans during the military emergency of the Italian wars.

Italian unification had little to do with liberal or nationalist plans. There was no tangible sign in the 1850s that these were becoming less mutually antagonistic. Unification was a product of French and Piedmontese territorial ambition. The defeat of Austria was a piece of neo-Bonapartist opportunism on the part of Napoleon III, eager to acquire Nice and Savoy, as promised in the pact of Plombières of 1858, while appearing to 'do something for Italy'. The subsequent crumbling of Austria's influence, and with it the old regimes, came as a shock for Napoleon III and was somewhat unexpected for Piedmont's Prime Minister, Cavour, despite the restrained propaganda of the pro-Piedmont National Society in the duchies and elsewhere. The background to the unrest in the duchies and throughout the south was the economic crisis of the late 1850s. The revolt in Sicily against the Bourbons was strongly underpinned by a peasant jacquerie demanding the restoration of communal lands. Crispi, at the head of the revolutionary administration of Palermo, was obliged to guarantee all combatants a share in communal lands. During the summer of 1860, peasant violence against landlords and against any government grew incessantly. When he landed in Sicily from Piedmont, Garibaldi was hailed by the peasants as their champion, but his goal was patriotic liberation and like Mazzini he opposed class conflict and attacks on private property. As peasant insurrection and disregard for democratic revolutionary leaders increased with the retreat of Bourbon troops, the big landowning barons and the middle-class *galantuomini* threw in their lot with Garibaldi, though not with Crispi, to save their property. Ironically, peasant agitation actually propelled the *galantuomini* to favour incorporation into the new Italian kingdom.[30] The story repeated itself in Naples, where peasants flocked to Garibaldi as to a messiah, rapidly followed by the landowners themselves.

Fear of popular unrest and/or foreign intervention meant that hastily arranged plebiscites acquiesced in the creation of a unitary state. Due to the predominance of Piedmont, Italy thus became liberal Piedmont writ large, adopting her parliamentary system, administration, legal and judicial structures, and her anti-clerical, educational and free-trade policies. The five-year subsequent open rebellion of the south was dismissed as brigandage, but heralded an increasing cleavage, which was intensified by growing poverty and backwardness in the south and the industrialisation of the north. To many southerners, even the *galantuomini* who were quick to profit from the sale of Church lands and the nobles who continued to rule their traditional fiefs, the south was merely a colony of a foreign power.

Italy became a state dominated by a tiny wealthy élite, mainly of northerners. The upper house of nobles had a major voice in decision-making and was an important source of ministerial appointees. The lower house was elected by literate male taxpayers, as in Piedmont before unification. In 1870 about half a million qualified, giving an electorate similar to that of France before 1848, equivalent to about 2.2 per cent of the population. The landed élite and the liberal professions continued to dominate politics, even beyond 1900 when industry was developing rapidly, 'transforming' or absorbing some new elements, particularly the new entrepreneurial élite. But the minute political community was made even narrower by abstensions; no more than 60 per cent of the electors bothered to vote, southerners regarding the new system as a piece of Piedmontese arrogance and neo-colonialism, while Catholics were threatened with excommunication by the pope, who did not recognise the existence of the new state. Extremists of the right and left, whether supporters of one of the old ruling houses or republicans, were excluded. Politics were confined to the élite which, not unnaturally, felt isolated. Little attention was paid to social questions, particularly the problems of the rural poor of the south. The vast majority of Italians remained alienated from the new state, particularly in the south, forming water-tight communities within the new structure, reinforced by traditional southern loyalties and organisations like the mafia.

Regional political fragmentation was accentuated by the process and form of unification and the industrial and commercial development of the north which followed. The political interests of the urban and rural middle classes of the south were, and remained, very different from those of the north. The southern urban bourgeoisie had few associations with industrial investment; they were landowners, but the basis of their prosperity before unification had been intimately linked to the ruling house and their viability was permanently undermined by the removal of the seat of power from Naples. In the north the urban middle class was increasingly involved in industrial enterprise. The rural bourgeoisie in both areas were landowners, acquiring both Church and common land. But in the south the poverty of the soil and poor communications made commercial farming inappropriate and middle-class owners continued to lease land in traditional ways. In the north the rural middle class was more likely to farm its land, or engage tenants who would, like them, farm for the market. Better communications, a larger market and richer soil all contributed to the development of agriculture, especially the mulberry for the silk industry, wool, wheat and high-yielding produce like cheese and wine. Thus the northern rural bourgeoisie invested in their land and shared common interests with the urban entrepreneurial middle class. There was far more diversity within the middle class of the north, with not only jobs in industry, trade and agricultural enterprise, but opportunities in the professions as well as public service. In the south the bourgeoisie was increasingly impoverished, with fewer opportunities because of the condition of the economy and ever greater dependence on the state to provide employment. As a consequence, the southern *galantuomini* did not constitute a separate political force, but were dependent on local barons for their prestige and influence in the local community and for jobs for their sons. Many of the educated and frustrated bourgeoisie turned to politics, also with the help of the local barons. Thus the political practices of the south were committed to perpetuating a system of patronage and clientage. It was assumed that the state should provide jobs to make up for the deficiencies of the southern economy. The contrast with the north added to the sense of bitterness. Thus in politics the bourgeoisie was divided not just by wealth and by attitudes to the House of Savoy and to the Church, but most of all by geography. The northern liberals, who were dominant at unification, never appreciated the dimension of the problem, but believed that the answer lay in transformism, fudging, merging and absorbing opponents, and politics remained a matter of patronage and corruption. The liberals in parliament never understood how to transpose themselves into attractive commodities for an electorate, which through successive legislation was near to adult male suffrage by 1914.

It is often suggested that the extremes experienced in Russian politics in 1917 can be explained by the lack of a middle class. Our investigations so far would suggest that the absence of links between middle-class groups may be more significant. Unique among these states, Russia remained an autocracy until 1905, but the tsar's bureaucrats made many of his decisions. Senior ones were almost exclusively noble. Those with political ambitions joined or allied with the bureaucracy and competed for ministerial office. At the head was the State Soviet, similar in concept to the Council of State in Napoleon's France. Legislation was first debated by the soviet, then referred to the appropriate ministry, and then presented for the tsar's approval. He could issue *ukazy*, decrees made without the approval of the soviet. After the 1905 revolution this soviet became the upper house of the *duma* and elected members from the nobility, towns, guilds, universities and churches were added. There was a supreme court, or senate, which was the court of appeal and also promulgated *ukazy*. Ministers were chosen by the tsar and were wholly responsible to him, even after 1905. Before 1905 they held no joint meetings, although Alexander II had made provision for the setting up of a Council of Ministers. Each ministry had a separate office in each of the 78 *gubernia* or provinces and the 18 regions which were considered too far from the capital to be split into *gubernia*. These offices were independent of the local governor, who continued to be appointed by the tsar and answerable to the Minister of the Interior.

Thus in one sense Russia had no participatory political life until the establishment of local assemblies, or *zemstvos*, in the 1860s and a *duma* after 1905. In both of these the middle classes had but a modest role. The two circumstances appear to bear directly on each other, the smallness and fragmentation of the middle class and its willingness to defer to tsarist and aristocratic authority being a major factor in the survival of an autocratic, non-representative form of government. Whereas elsewhere in nineteenth-century Europe liberals were middle class, in Russia they were normally aristocrats. In 1864 Alexander II's government, following the emancipation of the serfs, set up local assemblies, or *zemstvos*. There were district *zemstvos* with separately elected groups of nobles (40 per cent), peasants (40 per cent) and townsmen and priests (20 per cent). The members of the district *zemstvos* chose representatives for the provincial assemblies. Nobles chaired the meetings and developed an important role in local affairs, including education, health, economic affairs and road construction. In 1870 property-owners in the towns were allowed to elect their own governing councils, which were responsible for most matters except the police.

The absence of a national elected assembly, and the impossibility of peaceful political debate given the censorship, pushed criticism more and more towards revolutionary goals. Small noble-led groups like Land and Liberty, which murdered Alexander II in 1881, developed first into a populist formation and in the twentieth century into a Social Revolutionary movement which tried to orchestrate widespread peasant criticism of the limited impact of the Emancipation Decrees of the 1860s. Social democratic ideas grew up among a minority of the middle class and some isolated groups of workers, but their leaders were forced by censorship and persecution into exile. The movement itself was rent by ideological faction-fighting, finally splitting into a tiny Bolshevik group and (despite their names) a slightly larger Menshevik wing in 1902. Only a few fringe members of the middle class were interested and the total number of industrial workers was too small to have much impact. Hence Lenin developed the notion that his Bolshevik group was a vanguard party of professional revolutionaries. He had few adherents outside the railway workshops of St Petersburg, and most leaders, including himself, were confined to foreign exile and ineffectiveness. The critics of the tsar who had most impact were liberal nobles working in the *zemstvos* for a national elected assembly. In 1905 these formed the Kadets or Constitutional Democrats. It was, however, military defeat by Japan that brought together noble and peasant critics into a temporary alliance against the autocracy. The contribution of middle- and working-class groups to the 1905 revolution was minimal. The tsar conceded a national assembly or *duma*. In the elections the Kadets won 179 seats and the Social Revolutionaries 94, despite a formal ban by the party on participation. Eighteen social democrats, mainly Mensheviks, were elected in Georgia. In addition there were strong national contingents, with fifteen centrists and fifteen rightwingers. The *duma* sat for only two months, clashing over the issue most dear to the peasants, the redistribution of landlords' land. After its dissolution, rural unrest continued unabated. Stolypin, the new chief minister, set up special courts-martial and many peasants were hanged. A second *duma* was elected and swiftly dispatched for intransigence, but a third, elected on a narrower franchise in 1907, survived. Nobles and the wealthy urban upper middle class were given a preponderant say and the number of centrists and rightwingers soared, with only 52 Kadets and a small number of socialists. A tsar's party was positively emerging in this *duma* in the shape of the Kadets, but it was almost entirely noble in composition and backing. The Kadets never produced the fusion of wealthy interests, noble and non-noble, land and industry, which emerged in the conservative groups in France and in the National Liberals in Germany. This was partly a question of numbers, partly a difference in economic role and also a matter of governmental attitude.

In the other countries we have studied noble and wealthy bourgeois interests often coincided. Tsarist governments consciously sought to fragment society to maintain their own power. Nobles and merchants shared some privileges and Moscow entrepreneurs, noble and otherwise, worked together for common economic goals in the second half of the nineteenth century. But tariff and taxation issues, which in Germany united the upper classes in pressure groups, drove a permanent wedge between Russian merchants and landowners. Reforming nobles became convinced that high tariff policies installed in the 1880s benefited industry at the expense of agriculture. The *zemstvos*, where the landowning aristocratic interest prevailed, constantly petitioned for reform of taxation, which they argued gave unreasonable advantages to industry. Although nobles were involved in industry, by the end of the nineteenth century it was mostly in small-scale, rather old-fashioned operations, unlikely to gain from policies promoted by the big industrialists.

Tsarist ministers were in some respect like Bismarck, keen to placate the entrepreneurial class by economic benefits, while limiting their political effectiveness. Profits were high: 40 per cent returns in the iron industry were fairly standard, up to 25 per cent in cotton, and 7–12 per cent was a normal average elsewhere. The government cushioned railway investors by buying most shares and guaranteeing a certain level of profit before finally buying up most lines on terms very advantageous for the private investor. The tax system benefited the industrialist. There was no income tax, direct taxes were low and indirect taxes, from which the government drew most of its revenue, fell most heavily on the less well-off, even after the poll tax was withdrawn. In addition ministers like Witte offered subsidies and other benefits to shield young industries from foreign competition and the absence of a large, wealthy home market. But such protection meant more bureaucracy, which was not appreciated. The repeated anti-Semitism of the tsars brought resentment from the substantial Jewish element in the middle class. It was also apparent that supporting economic policy was only followed subject to the pre-eminent needs of the army and navy. Government support was therefore erratic and tenuous, which turned many members of the entrepreneurial groups into government critics after 1905.

The most notable section of the middle class, the merchants, were notoriously politically passive: the Moscow group anxious to side-step contact with the state bureaucracy; the St Petersburg contingent deeply embroiled with bureaucrats in search of orders; the modern southern group keen to serve on government committees and ingratiate themselves. Merchants ran local government in Moscow and other large towns, and, if space allowed, an exploration of their role in local affairs in the later nineteenth century would reveal

strong liberal tendencies in the realm of the reform of the fabric of
municipal life, from sewers to schools. The absence of a national
assembly, and the perceived needs of growing towns, attracted
bourgeois liberals towards local issues and problems.[31] In the later
years of the nineteenth century, merchants began to form regional
pressure groups to promote specific interests, particularly tariff
policies. New organisations like the Moscow Exchange Society were
formed to speak for merchants, but there were many quarrelling
voices and tongues. The Moscow Society was controlled by a
combination of the 200 most wealthy joint stock banks, insurance
companies and commercial and industrial firms, and by 100 electors,
almost all of whom were Russian, even though Russians only
constituted 60 per cent of the first-grade guild. As a consequence
non-Russian merchants refused to support them both in local
government and in the state *duma* after 1905. Generational differences
exacerbated the problem. The Moscow Exchange, dominated by
traditional merchants, was restrained, but a younger group was
more eager for a political role. G. A. Krestovnikov, Exchange
president in the years before 1914, belonged to the younger generation. He had graduated in physics and maths from Moscow
University, was a founder of the Moscow section of the Russian
Technological Society, was involved in industry and had married
into one of the top merchant families, the Morozovs. He might have
been expected to be a catalyst for change, but his close involvement
with the bureaucracy (he was twice considered for ministerial office),
channelled his political energies in a more traditional direction.

In 1905 the Moscow Exchange hosted conferences with delegates
from other exchanges to discuss political reform, but despite the
revolution there was only discord. The Moscow group persisted
with a conservative, élitist strategy, trying to exclude lower-middle-
class artisans from the new electorate. They set up a Trade and
Industry Party, but deliberately did not seek a mass following. Thus
only two of their candidates were elected to the first *duma* and the
nine or ten merchants elected in all belonged to six different parties.
The seven non-Russian merchants elected in outlying regions were
interested only in regional, not class affairs. Trading peasants who
were elected related not to the merchants, but to their local
community. Shop assistant representatives in the *duma* regarded the
merchants as enemies who had oppressed them. Members of the
intelligentsia were entirely hostile to the merchant deputies and

generally supported workers against employers. Such doctors, lawyers and engineers joined the Kadets, distancing themselves, as they put it, from the narrow class interests of landowners and industrialists. Deputies from the intelligentsia defined themselves as anti-bourgeois. Merchants looked down on lower-middle-class artisans, despised the intelligentsia as mere theoreticians and retained a distant deference to the nobility. None of the groups a western European would consider middle class and likely to work together, especially in a crisis like 1905, saw the situation in this light. Thus middle-class deputies to the assembly were few and hopelessly divided. The first *duma* was 9 per cent composed of merchants. The business community of Moscow took a lead in promoting entrepreneurial representation. Two Old Believer textile magnates, Riabushinskii and Knovalov even formed a Progressive Party and, convinced that the autocracy was on the verge of collapse, considered an alliance with the Bolsheviks. Most were conservatives and aligned themselves with landlord groups; however they were disappointed with developments after the 1905 revolution and turned to criticism of the regime, though in a persistently fragmented and isolated fashion.[32]

Hence the political nullity of the middle-class elements in Russian society. It was not simply a question of numbers and limited economic and political development; at root the obvious 'middle-class' groups remained far more mutually hostile than elsewhere. In the years before 1914 there was no question of bourgeois members of the *duma* co-operating; they did not even pretend to think of themselves as a class. The main proponents of liberal ideas remained nobles. This polarisation and resulting isolation were to some degree the product of geographical and regional differences, the presence of a number of conflicting national groups, different stages of economic development, the dominance of foreigners in the Russian economy and consequent huge variations in social and political norms. Western observers often look for familiar political assumptions in Russia and ascribe their absence to backwardness and devious tsarist/communist strategies. But it was and still is also the case that 'politics' had and has a different meaning in Russia. The number of different languages and cultures renders western European 'national' politics somewhat superfluous and ineffectual. Local assemblies were perhaps more relevant. The dominant role of the bureaucracy, then as now, meant that the politically ambitious sought bureaucratic posts and, conversely, bureaucrats moved easily into industry. Typical were Putilov and Vyshnegradkii, both graduates of St Petersburg University and protégés of Witte in government service, who became senior bankers later in their careers.

Our investigation of liberalism illustrates the strengths and weaknesses of the middle class in politics. In none of these states was liberalism a class-based philosophy when looked at from above. In Russia the majority of those sympathetic to liberal ideas were noble, as were a sizeable proportion of liberals in France and Italy. Yet liberal notions were quintessentially bourgeois and studied from below liberals were often oppressors to the urban and rural poor. The apparent paradox is clear when one appreciates that most liberals were conservatives, and that even those who wanted change preferred to retain major aspects of the old order. During these years all of these countries experienced political change which increased the 'bourgeois' character of the state and of society, particularly in the growth of both parliamentary and bureaucratic institutions. The élites may have been an amalgam of traditional landed aristocrats and rich bourgeois, many of whom were also landowners, indicating that at its apex, especially in more backward regions, society was changing very slowly, but industrialisation and the growth of state institutions were beginning to modify this picture by the end of the nineteenth century.

Liberalism in many respects was a flag of negotiation, compromise and convenience evolved by those with some power and influence to retain their position in changing times. There was no single liberal doctrine or set of policies, for liberalism represented a *juste milieu* between the perceived injustices of 'traditional' societies and the supposed evils of mass power. Liberalism was a compound of the belief that society should be based on moral, rational foundations, respect for wealth and private property, and the horror of uncontrolled popular violence, or other forms of extremism. During the century those of liberal persuasions had to come to terms with the problems of the modernisation (and formation) of the state and the social problems of industrialisation and urban growth. The tensions resulting from both of these interrelated developments meant that a liberal *juste milieu* would be subject to constant modification. But, ironically, a set of ideas supposedly designed to accommodate change repeatedly manifested self-destructive rigidity. Guizot would not budge on electoral reform in the 1840s and the liberals in Prussia put their faith in an electoral system in which only a tiny minority bothered to vote. To try to relate a belief in absolute moral standards to the size of an electorate was unconvincing. There was no absolute or moral justification for a 200-franc, predominantly landed franchise in France before 1848, as was implied by inclusion of 100–franc *capacités*, who paid less tax and qualified because of distinction in a variety of fields. The Prussian three-class franchise was also simply based on the assumption that the richest men were the most conservative, as was the Piedmontese, later the Italian system. Liberals opposed franchise reform and feared democracy. But they could not define their idea of the social parameters of the political community without sounding selfish and a little ridiculous. Ostensibly in the name of order and stability, but really to assert their own influence, liberals argued not only that certain elements of society were fitted by their wealth to govern, but also that absolute standards could be established in other areas of life. Oral and written examinations were instituted to determine entry to university, the civil service, etc. But the standards set restricted entry to the professions and education to a rich, not a proven moral, élite. It was apparent that here too liberals were afraid of social change. While bureaucrats, professional men and intellectuals were establishing criteria for 'active' membership of the state, industrial change was increasing the size of the entrepreneurial middle class. However the composition of elected assemblies continued to resemble a more traditional society.

A democratic electorate did not bring the collapse of the social fabric which Orleanist liberals had feared. In the first election after the 1848 revolution the old Orleanist notables were re-elected in large numbers and there were not the mass abstentions which those previously opposed to reform feared: 84 per cent voted; 165 of the old Orleanist chamber were returned. Of the 900 deputies 200–300 were Orleanists, 100–150 were legitimists and 500 were moderates, many converted from monarchism since February.[33] Almost all were local notables; only 25 small farmers or workers were elected. Most would have fulfilled the stringent conditions for candidates in the previous regime: 80 per cent were over 40 and 700 of the 900 paid over 500 frs. in direct tax a year. The elections in May 1849 confirmed the ascendancy of the notables. The so-called 'party of order' secured 500 of the 750 seats. In over two-thirds of the departments the political preponderance of the notables was total, particularly in the north and east but also in the north-west, west and south-west. But the notables were still alarmed at the incidence of radicalism. The Massif Central emerged as an area of peasant radicalism, relatively free from the dominance of big landowners. Paris continued to elect leftwingers. In May 1850 the assembly decided to restrict the right to vote, after eleven leftwingers were elected in the 21 by-elections held in March 1850. The vote was limited to taxpayers who could fulfil a three-year residence qualification. The law disenfranchised three million voters and allowed the elected president, Louis-Napoleon, great-nephew of Napoleon I, to appear as the champion of democracy.

Universal suffrage was a new and little-understood instrument for the notables, accustomed to considering the views of only a small and like-minded electorate. It is curious that, although the only elections they had known under universal suffrage had been triumphs not just for the middle classes but for the notables, the members of the legislative assembly were still convinced that universal suffrage was a radical phenomenon, to be curbed at all costs. It was only in the large towns that leftwingers were chosen, and, given the fact that there were only four towns with more than 100 000 inhabitants in France at this time, no really subversive threat was on the horizon. The notables fled from the ghosts of the First Republic during the brief life of the Second, unable to comprehend that they could dominate a conservative republic. Hence it was with some relief that they watched Louis-Napoleon dismantle the republic during 1852 and establish a plebiscitary dictatorship, in which the tolerance of the notables was of more significance than the frequent appeals for popular acclaim in plebiscites. Safely circumscribed within an almost powerless legislative body, universal suffrage was restored. In many ways the Second Empire was even more conclusively the regime of the notables than the July Monarchy had been. Only the capture of the emperor after Sedan necessitated further change.

In contrast to the June Days, the experience of the Commune of 1871 probably made it easier for the well-off middle class to devise, over a period of years, a conservative republic.[34] The Chamber of Deputies was elected by universal male suffrage, but constituencies were deliberately organised to accentuate the power of the notables. In 1875 19 million northern voters elected 220 representatives, whereas in the south, which was far more rural and where the notables were strongest, 16 million voters elected 280 deputies. The reluctance to pay deputies, the salary was only increased to 15 000 frs. in 1906, meant that only the wealthy could consider a parliamentary career. Many seats were effectively family fiefs. In 1871 one-third of deputies were nobles; this had fallen to 9 per cent by 1914. There was a preponderance of lawyers: in 1906 37 per cent of all deputies and 60 per cent of all ministers were lawyers. There were only a very small number of entrepreneurs, although they were far more prominent in local politics.[35] The chamber shared power with a president, elected not by universal suffrage, but by the Chamber of Deputies and upper house, the Senate, meeting together. The method of electing the president and the creation of a Senate were meant to preserve the conservative character of the republic. The Senate was partly chosen by the chamber, partly elected. The electoral colleges consisted of the deputies, general councillors and *arrondissement* councillors from each department plus one representative from each municipal council, whatever its size. Rural areas were overrepresented. The Third Republic was primarily a conservative regime, but in the later years of the century it was somewhat less dominated by the landed upper-middle-class notables. The emergence of a substantial Radical/Radical Socialist grouping gave opportunities to some from more modest backgrounds, as did the socialist groups which came together in a united Socialist Party in 1905. But it is noteworthy that the main socialist leaders, like the future Prime Minister, Blum, were from wealthy professional families. It was this element in the middle class which came to dominate politics.

In Italy the political community was extremely narrow, circumscribed both by the initial enfranchisement of only 2.2 per cent of the population and by the papal ban on a Catholic vote. In 1882 the electorate was increased to two million, the voting age being reduced to 21 and the qualifying tax payment to just over 20 lire. Men who had completed two years' schooling were exempt from this tax qualification. In two further stages, in 1912 and 1919, Italy adopted full male suffrage. Initially most MPs were northern landlords, but gradually professional politicians, mostly lawyers, took over. In 1900 114, or just over 25 per cent, were landowners, but this had fallen to 73 by 1914. By 1913 just under half of the members of the lower house were lawyers. There were only a handful of industrialists and men involved in agriculture. Teachers and journalists abounded. Most socialist MPs were lawyers or teachers. Deputies were thus a middle-class urban phenomenon, almost exclusively university educated in law, rhetoric or the classics. Criticisms were made of the unrepresentative nature of the lower house, but to little effect.[36] Governments were short-lived. They lasted for less than a year on average, and their composition was always based on considerations of patronage and personal relations. They were rarely brought to an end by an unfavourable vote in parliament and ministers often went on from one government to another as they did in the French Third Republic. Unlike France, where the president exercised little power, the king's voice was often heard in the choice of ministers, parliament's seldom. Political principles never entered the lists, indeed principles were a handicap to an ambitious politician. Political leaders ran their areas as personal fiefs, with lesser, dependent MPs around them. The upper house or Senate, significant initially, declined in influence, stuffed as it was with ex-government has-beens. The system did not encourage opposition within parliament, but in the 1890s the formation of the Socialist Party attracted middle-class critics, and by the turn of the century the growth of industry in the north provided mass support for the PSI. A few years later, a slight softening of papal attitudes on parliamentary elections allowed a radical Catholic party to emerge. The hold of the old élites began to disintegrate, although the mutual hostility of the two new mass parties and the total negativism of the PSI, the larger of the two, prevented the development of an alternative to the notables before 1914. With the introduction of complete male suffrage in 1919 Italian politics reached an impossible stalemate. The notables never succeeded in working with the new parties and by 1919 were themselves a minority in parliament.

In the German Empire, although the *reichstag* was elected by universal male suffrage, the *landtäge*, the assemblies of the individual states in the federal empire, did not all follow suit. Prussia retained the three-class franchise. The entirely disproportionate influence this gave to the rich can be gauged by the fact that in 1914 in 2200 of the 29 000 electoral districts there was only one first-class voter, as for example Krupp in Essen. The educated also received privileges within the system. Those who had attended university for three years, or had passed the relevant state examination or were officials or army or navy officers, were classified in the group above that in which their actual tax payment placed them. No rearrangement was made of electoral districts to take account of migration and urbanisation. Thus, by 1914, the *landtäge*, even more than in the 1860s, overrepresented rural and agrarian interests. In Prussia in 1913 140 (31 per cent) of the 440 members were landowners, while only 28 were in industry and 9 in commerce. In earlier years members of the industrial and commercial middle classes had shunned politics, tending to distrust the civil servants who played a substantial part. Only 7 per cent of the members of the Frankfurt Parliament were in industry and commerce, and in the Prussian *landtäge* and later the *reichstag* only between 4 and 9 per cent of members came from these groups. This was lower than in other countries; in Britain between 1832 and 1865 15–30 per cent of MPs were in business. By 1881 6 per cent of the *reichstag* were academics and teachers, 23 per cent were administrative or judicial officials (but very different from those who sought to limit royal power in 1848), 15 per cent were lawyers, doctors or theologians and 13 per cent were in business. The proportion of businessmen in the *reichstag* continued to grow; by 1887 there were 19 per cent. Nearly a quarter of electors voted socialist, but the SPD held only 1.4 per cent of the seats. Whether an assembly was elected by universal suffrage or the three-class suffrage, politics remained the preserve of the wealthy, who, through pressure groups, could exert a disproportionate influence. Even in the case of the *reichstag*, where by 1914 the SPD was the single largest party, the structure of national politics was such that their influence was smothered by the constitution. The *reichstag* exercised no control over the government, which was appointed entirely by the emperor. By 1914 resulting social tensions were beginning to pose a real threat to the predominance of the notables, sanctioned by the rest of the middle class but opposed by the SPD, which was far more an alternative working-class culture than an opposition political party. Universal suffrage did nothing to undermine upper-class dominance of German politics and middle-class liberals themselves had played a substantial role in rendering the German constitution effectively authoritarian and inflexible.

Thus the determination of liberals to retain politics as a game for the wealthy outlasted the control of 'liberal' groupings over political power. In Russia, where those of liberal views were mainly nobles and other urban middle-class intellectuals and had very little mass support, the tsar was able to limit the suffrage for elections to the new *duma* three times in the years before the outbreak of war in 1914. Finally in 1907 the number of peasant and worker voters was reduced by half. In subsequent elections the richest 1 per cent of the population selected two-thirds of the actual electors and had control of nearly 300 of the 442 seats in the *duma*. Franchise manipulation reduced the representation of liberal-style groups such as the Kadets (54 in 1907). They also lost all but one of the fifteen *zemstva* presidencies they had held. The aftermath of the 1905 revolution, and the determination of the tsar's supporters to create support for the autocracy in the *duma*, left those of liberal views in Russia, who had previously put their faith in an elected assembly, hopelessly divided, and, as we have noted, entirely separate from the small middle-class political formations in the *duma*.[37]

At the beginning of this chapter we set out to consider to what extent old élites remained in political control through the century and to compare liberalism in our four states. The composition of parliaments would indicate that landed élites gave way to traditional elements within the middle class, especially lawyers but also including other professionals like teachers and doctors, and that politics itself became increasingly 'professionalised'. How far the new professional politicians were the spokesmen for traditional notables is another question, beyond the compass of this already overlong chapter. Liberalism itself proved multifaceted, but a number of common features have been distinguished, particularly the impossibility of establishing a *juste milieu* in a period when there was both economic change and marked developments in the role and function of the state. Liberals were essentially defensive conservatives, anxious to avoid democracy, combat socialist ideas and preserve private property, while striving to create political systems run by and for the benefit of traditional middle-class groups. In terms of norms and attitudes, it was members of the traditional professions who did most to shape the élitism of liberalism.

Conclusion

SOME signposts are needed if man is to pursue the ever-entrancing dissection of human society. When 'orders' or 'estates' determined by birth and corporate institutions no longer seemed adequate to describe societies beginning to be transformed by commercial and industrial developments, mid-eighteenth-century commentators adopted very vague financial and economic criteria. These were elaborated, with the tools of moral indignation but with no greater precision, by early-nineteenth-century socialists and social reformers, appalled at the great disparity of wealth and heart-rending poverty so visible in expanding cities. To such writers class distinctions were immoral and unjust features of social change, and various ideas, utopian, reformist and revolutionary, were aired by which the poverty and oppression of industrialisation could be ameliorated. Marx went the furthest and produced a comprehensive analysis of economic development in which class antagonisms were the vital ingredients of both economic and political change. He argued that traditional feudal landed aristocracies would be replaced by the entrepreneurial bourgeoisie. This process he believed to be a compound of the economic imperatives of entrepreneurial competition, only too apparent in the repeated financial and industrial cyclical depressions of the nineteenth century, and the united political awareness and aggression of a new middle class, manifest in repeated political upheavals in developed countries like France, which experienced revolution in 1789, 1830, 1848 and 1871. Marx's own analysis of this entrepreneurial bourgeoisie was far from simplistic; for him 1830 in France represented a takeover by the financial bourgeoisie, strongly backed by newer landed interests, while 1848 was a further stage in the establishment of middle-class power and the Commune of 1871 the beginning of what he believed would be the inevitable workers' revolt against self-destructive capitalism. However Marx was not principally an analyst of class and his distinctions between financial and industrial interests in 1830 do not bear detailed scrutiny, nor does his definition of the Commune as a modern 'workers' revolt', since the majority of Parisian workers were still artisans. He was attempting a total explanation of modern economic, social and political change and was also both a prophet and judge. Above all his name and his ideas were crucial to the development of modern socialism, not in an abstract academic sense, but as a revolutionary movement committed to the overthrow of capitalism. His followers often simplified the analysis of class into something resembling two opposing teams in a football match, making the economic imperative the only determinant of class. From being a rough guide to economic status, class thus became a principal component in the struggle to control society. Marx himself made predictions about the development of capitalism which did not materialise and both the political groups which owed allegiance to him and their 'capitalist' antagonists made it very difficult for even the most objective researcher to escape categorisation as either 'Marxist' or 'anti-Marxist'.

The concentration of the Marxist, though not Marx, on economic factors, especially the development of capitalism, as determinants of class have subsequently received considerable modification and no undergraduate today would dare to forget the many suggested ingredients in class, including the cultural and the psychological. This study began with a discussion of the complexities inherent in the term 'middle class' and, conscious of the impossibility of arriving at an objective definition of class itself, it has examined the components of the middle class, as defined by Marx and subsequent commentators in the context of the development of France, Germany, Italy and Russia in the nineteenth century. Class groupings, and the middle classes in particular, are above all the product of industrialisation. The achievements of the new industrial age, canals, railways, rapidly growing towns, were so tangible and had such an impact on the economy and the organisation of the state that contemporaries of all shades of opinion concurred that entrepreneurial capitalism was of great significance for the modern state and society. Indeed it has been observed that in Britain at least, contemporary writers put such a spotlight on the entrepreneur, at first in praise, later in blame, that they forgot the contribution of other elements within the traditional middle class. Marx stressed that the entrepreneur was set to inherit then lose the world, so our investigation of the middle classes began with this group. We noted the slow and gradual pattern of industrial change, even in Germany, where only in the last forty years of the century did factory-based industry begin to become the dominant element in the industrial economy. Far from being a cohesive, thrusting, politically united and aware new force, we found that entrepreneurs were a traditional element in society, often landowners especially in the first half of the century, cautious and concerned with the limited horizons of their own business. Very few were 'revolutionary'; quite the reverse in fact, for political unrest was singularly bad for trade as 1789 and subsequent upheavals showed. Many were noble, not bourgeois. Only in Russia was there evidence of substantial social mobility and evidence that the entrepreneurial class were occasionally 'new' men. Entrepreneurs, whatever their social origin, were united not by class interests, but by the needs of their individual enterprises, hence in France in the first half of the nineteenth century ironmasters co-operated to press for high tariffs on imported iron, and in the years of the great depression men with shared interests in tariffs, sometimes both landowners and industrialists, worked for the revival of a high tariff policy. Marx's impression that the state would be dominated by the capitalist entrepreneur is not evident in the composition of the parliamentary assemblies which existed in each of these states by 1914, for this group was comparatively underrepresented. It might be argued that adequate influence could be exercised through contacts with the bureaucracy and through pressure groups; yet the state was such a major customer for industry that one wonders who was calling the tune. For a variety of reasons, economic, racial and cultural, it seems unlikely that entrepreneurial groups could ever be politically cohesive. Entrepreneurial values, far from being predominant, were usually underplayed, even scorned. Rather than being the driving force within the bourgeoisie, entrepreneurs who were good at their calling often tried to act like members of the landed aristocracy, in their choice of schools and marriage partners, founding of art galleries and theatres, and buying of landed estates. Entrepreneurs did not confidently develop distinctive novel sets of norms, values and assumptions, but continued to add those of the aristocracy to traditional family attitudes, for entrepreneurs were not a new group. It is worthwhile stressing the importance of the acquisition of land to all wealthy elements within the bourgeoisie since, unlike Marx himself, many Marxists used the criterion of land to draw a sharp distinction between classes.

The growing importance of the professional middle class in parliaments underlined the significant role of the traditional bourgeoisie in the nineteenth century. Faced with the prospect of unwelcome social change, the professions themselves worked to maintain their own social exclusiveness. In defining educational prerequisites and standardised training, they effectively turned themselves more and more into closed shops. The two most prestigious careers, law and medicine, were increasingly dominated by the sons of lawyers and doctors. There was a well-defined ranking among professions, and families opted for a career which best matched their own social position. There were some exceptions. The notables lost their monopoly of engineering in France towards the end of the century as industry developed and engineers were unable to set their profession in the same protective aspic of 'professionalism' adopted by other occupations. But while sons of artisans gained the opportunity to train as engineers, the profession itself was downgraded. Although professions consciously sought a precise identity, asserted the moral virtues of 'professional' standards and took a very active role in politics, the growth in the power of the state actually reduced their independence.

While Marx stressed the dominant role of industrialisation and of the entrepreneurial bourgeoisie in society, later commentators like Max Weber were more inclined to observe the importance of the growth of state power and its attendant bureaucracies in shaping both classes and society. Perhaps less visible, and in many ways dependent on the expansion of the economy and urban society, the expanding function of the state and the unprecedented explosion in the numbers primarily of the middle class which it employed, undoubtedly had an enormous impact. The development of bureaucracies epitomised bourgeois cohesion and fragmentation, through the elaboration and sanctification of a hierarchical view of society, typified more by 'professionalism' and duty than economic competition as Marx had suggested. State service continued to be the pinnacle of professional ambition but, although the burgeoning state machinery offered far more employment by 1914, the senior reaches of the bureaucracy remained closed to all but the élite. Indeed standardised entry requirements and the apparent development of a more professional approach in the civil service actually led to a growth in noble dominance of the top jobs in Germany and the exclusion of the tiny minority who had previously risen to senior appointments from humble beginnings. State service provided many new jobs and types of employment for the middle class, but most were at the bottom, for instance as clerks, and in France as elsewhere there was an impassable ravine between *employé* and *fonctionnaire*. As one might anticipate, social stratification reached its most extreme in European armies. In Germany the nobility continued to control the senior posts, while in France there was a resurgence of interest shown by aristocratic families in army careers from around 1850. In all of these countries there were middle-class officers, but segregated into the more technical regiments, and thoroughly looked down on in a calling where it appeared that the further away from the days of the feudal levy one travelled in time, the nearer to that epoch were the officer corps in spirit. As for the lower-middle-class soldier an army career offered modest social advance, but no further than the rank of captain.

The philosophy of education and the schools themselves under-lined the differences within the class. Middle-class families chose a school which matched their own social milieu and had a curriculum which suited the assumed future role of their offspring. Very few parents anticipated that education would permit their son to rise socially. Even when a substantial proportion of the pupils in secondary schools were from the lower middle class, as in France in the 1860s, most parents assumed that their sons would take up their own type of job, or at best would move laterally into a cleaner, safer occupation, perhaps as a minor civil servant or elementary school teacher. Education actually reached a shrinking band of the social spectrum for most of the century. In Russia Nicholas I and his successors tried to exclude all but the nobility from secondary schools and universities. Elsewhere the process was more informal; a classical education was deemed unsuitable for the less well-off. There was some broadening of the social compass of education towards the end of the century, in direct response to the pace of economic change and the needs of expanding bureaucracies for basically educated employees. But the fare on offer was the less prestigious 'modern' or technical syllabus, and education still continued to be more intent on preserving the existing social fabric than satisfying the abilities of children regardless of their parents' social standing or wallets.

In trying to define the middle class of four of the major states of continental Europe, one is tempted to wonder whether Marx and his fellow socialists lived very isolated existences to believe in the cohesion of the bourgeoisie. Evidently the middle class was composed of very diverse elements; the nineteenth century saw no fundamental change in the component groups, but it witnessed distinct alterations in the proportions of each. The wealthier sections were increasingly unwilling to visualise themselves as part of the same class as the most humble. In Russia a separate category of honoured citizen was created; elsewhere ambitious bourgeois continued the well-established trend of marrying into the nobility, or at least living in as aristocratic a style as possible. The desire of the notables to set themselves apart intensified as the lower-middle-class artisans and shopkeepers drew a sharp distinction between themselves and the growing factory proletariat. One is forced to conclude that there was barely the semblance of homogeneity within that curious compound, the bourgeoisie, into which increasing numbers of citizens slotted themselves. In addition to the divisions within the class which were common to all four countries, there were unique circumstances in each state which gave the bourgeoisie of each distinct characteristics. Actual conflict within the Italian middle class echoed the gulf between the progressive, modernising, dominant north and the agrarian, semi-feudal, underdeveloped south. The Russian bourgeois groups were divided socially, politically and culturally; geographical and ethnic differences exacerbated the rift. Thus the failure of the revolutions of 1905 and 1917 related less to the tiny size of the middle class than to its internecine conflict. The fragmentation of the Russian bourgeoisie was intensified, sometimes created, by tsarist policies. Successive tsars cemented the survival of the autocracy more and more firmly to the aristocracy, fearful that the example of western Europe demonstrated the political radicalism of the bourgeois alternative. In our four states the middle classes graded themselves into a hierarchy. In France and Italy bureaucrats rated highly, while in Germany university professors, themselves a species of civil servant, also had a superior ranking. In Russia, however, senior merchants were accorded most respect, perhaps because the upper reaches of the Russian bureaucracy were filled with nobles.

Our analysis of the component elements within the middle class reveals diversity, the continued importance of traditional assumptions and attitudes, and the significant role of the bureaucratic and professional rather than the entrepreneurial elements. But Marx assumed that the entrepreneurial middle class was a force for change, the triumphant group in revolutionary upheaval. Thus finally we turned to consider the so-called 'bourgeois' revolutions of 1789 and 1830 and the nature of nineteenth-century liberalism, itself often included as a 'revolutionary' feature in politics. The revolutionary entrepreneurial bourgeoisie of popular legend is revealed as myth by the growing number of detailed studies undertaken in recent years. The revisionists offer a salutary reminder that social change was very gradual. Studies of the professions, of the army, the bureaucracy and education, all reveal the entrenched position of traditional attitudes of respect for old hierarchies, sometimes reinforced by the growing role of the state. In some respects the nineteenth century offered less opportunity for social mobility than before. We have been reminded of the major economic and social, and in some cases political, role of the old landed nobility. But revisionism often veers towards anti-Marxism and can tend to lose sight of the role of the traditional middle classes in politics and in transforming the basic institutions of the state. De Tocqueville rightly noted the strong lines of continuity between the centralisation of Napoleon and of the *ancien régime*; and while the revisionists may be right that many of the members of the old élites remained and survived to run new institutions, parliamentary, judicial, administrative, educational, they were joined by a proportion of newer, if equally rich, families.

The declarations of the Rights of Man in America and France defined a new equality in society based upon a codification of all laws relating to human social relationships and a new system of courts available to all to administer the laws. Privileges, fiscal, feudal, ecclesiastical, were abolished. There is no doubt that the declaration and the systematic preparation of codes of law was innovative and enormously influential in much of Europe. Freedom of religion was guaranteed, but the freedom of worship was seriously shackled by revolutionary policies which became blatantly anti-religious, and religious persecution and Church–State conflicts were rampant throughout the nineteenth century. Freedom never seriously included freedom of association: the Le Chapelier law of 1791 and the Napoleonic Civil Code banned associations of workers. Subsequently the terms of the Civil Code were also used to stifle any political club distasteful to the government of the day. Freedom of expression was idealised, but the censorship of the Empire, repeatedly re-enacted by all regimes in the years which followed, made a nonsense of the concept. Nevertheless the abolition of all feudal relationships and tenures, and the creation of common codes of law, were important guarantees of legal equality, for those who could afford to litigate. The Revolution and Empire were also seen to offer the beginnings of another freedom, to seek employment according to talent, a concept very much in embryo, but never still-born.

Such views on liberty and equality, however, did not make for a democratic, or even an open society, as reference to the political experiments of the 1790s onwards shows. Privilege does not need the sanction of law to be an elemental force in shaping society. Babeuf and others claimed that equality was a farce while economic inequality prevailed. The revolutionaries made the protection of economic inequality the cornerstone of their social order. The sanctity of private property was specifically guaranteed in the Declaration of Rights. The revolutionary and imperial years ultimately consolidated the power of ruling groups barely distinguishable from those of the *ancien régime*. Formal legal privilege, venal office, etc., were replaced by considerations of notability based on local influence, wealth, friendship and kinship, none of them new concepts, which quickly re-established élites of almost caste-like solidity. Privilege of birth was now additionally justified by income, education and professional training and by the illusion of a free society mirrored in documents like the Declaration of the Rights of Man and subsequent French and other written European constitutions. The dichotomy between the ideas and those who marketed them was nowhere more apparent than in nineteenth-century liberalism. Genuinely distressed and disadvantaged insurgent groups of artisans and peasants briefly believed during the revolutions of 1830 and 1848 that the wealthy bourgeois who were trying to share power with kings were forces of change. Ideas of liberalism and the rights of the nation based on those of the French Revolution were a veneer to justify the claims of a wealthy section of society to dominate the rest. The French liberals of the 1830s made few changes to the Restoration system and actually strengthened press censorship and laws on political association. The Prussian liberals of the 1850s abhorred democracy. Liberalism justified new paternalist hierarchies on the grounds of educational and financial criteria. Liberals were essentially defensive, believing that their ideas were the finger in the dyke, holding back violent, radical mass revolution. The emergence of socialism fuelled such fears. The middle class were on the defensive, protecting a citadel which they themselves had not yet stormed.

The nineteenth century was a 'bourgeois' century, not so much because of the development of industry but because of the growing role of the state. The new institutions set up were based on new assumptions, that society could be organised on logical, rational grounds, with written and predictable rules. The development of bureaucracies typified this ideal, Kafka notwithstanding. Although bureaucracies were dominated by a modified aristocratic ideal, and senior posts taken by nobles in some cases, the size and rapid growth of the civil service provided jobs for large numbers of the lesser bourgeoisie. Industrialisation created a veneer of innovation, deplored by many observers, but the development of the role of the state had a more permanent impact on the individual and his position in society.

Notes and References

1. WHO WERE THE MIDDLE CLASSES?

1. Quoted in A. Marwick, *Class, Image and Reality in Britain, France and the USA since 1930* (1980).
2. S. Ossowski, 'Different concepts of social class' in R. Bendix and S.M. Lipset, *Class, Status and Power: Social Stratification in Comparative Perspective* (1967), 87.
3. Alexis de Tocqueville, *The Old Regime and the French Revolution* (1955), 92, 115.
4. Alexis de Tocqueville, *Recollections* (1971), 92–3.
5. R. Robin, *La Société Française en 1789: Semur-en-Auxois* (1970), 342–3. M. Vovelle and D. Roche, 'Bourgeois, rentiers, propriétaires: elements pour la définition d'une catégorie sociale à la fin du XVIIIe siècle', *Actes du 84e Congrès National des Sociétés Savantes* (Dijon, 1959), *Section d'Histoire Moderne et Contemporaine* (Paris, 1962), 483–512. Tr. in J. Kaplow (ed.), *New Perspectives on the French Revolution: Readings in Historical Sociology* (1965), 25–46.
6. Babeuf, 'La Révolution n'est pas faite pour le peuple', *Le Tribun du Peuple*, no. 36 in A. Bayet and F. Albert, *Les Ecrivains Politiques du XIXe siècle* (1924), 101–2.
7. H. Perkins, *The Origins of Modern English Society, 1780–1880* (1969), 437–53.
8. Saint-Simon, 'Catéchisme des industriels' in Bayet and Albert, op. cit., 171–81.
9. K. Marx, *The Eighteenth Brumaire of Louis-Napoleon Bonaparte* (1926), 133.
10. Ossowski, op. cit., 89.
11. R. Dahrendorf, *Class and Class Conflict in Industrial Society* (1959), 16.
12. cf. *Eighteenth Brumaire*, op. cit.
13. L. Blanc, 'Organisation du travail' in J. A. R. Marriot, *The French Revolution of 1848 in its Economic Aspect* (1913).
14. F. Guizot, *Mémoires pour Servir à l'Histoire de Mon Temps* (1858).
15. F. Guizot, *History of Civilization in France*, I (tr.1887), 273.
16. F. Guizot in D. Johnson, *Guizot: Aspects of French History, 1787–1874* (1963), 74.
17. *Elementi di Scienza Politica* (1896) tr. as *The Ruling Class*.
18. *Trattato di Sociologia Generale*.
19. M. Weber, *The Protestant Ethic and the Spirit of Capitalism* (1904); M. Biddiss, *The Age of the Masses* (1977), 139–41.
20. W. J. Mommsen, *The Age of Bureaucracy: Perspectives on the Political Sociology of Max Weber* (1974), xv.
21. M. Weber, 'Class, status and party' in *Essays in Sociology* (1946) in Bendix and Lipset, op. cit., 27.
22. Mommsen, op. cit., 61–4.
23. Bendix and Lipset, op. cit., 44.
24. D. M. Smith, *The Making of Italy, 1796–1870* (1968), 9.
25. T. C. W. Blanning, *The French Revolution in Germany: Occupation and Resistance in the Rhineland, 1792–1802* (1983).

26. D. H. Pinkney, *Decisive Years in France, 1840–47* (1986), 23–49.

27. A. J. Tudesq, *Les Grands Notables en France (1840–1849): Etude Historique d'une Psychologie Sociale*, 2 vols (1964).

28. P. Higonnet, *Class, Ideology and the Rights of Nobles during the French Revolution* (1981), 54.

29. E. N. and P. R. Anderson, *Political Institutions and Social Change in Continental Europe in the Nineteenth Century* (1967), 103–5.

30. M. Walker, *German Home Towns: Community, State and General Estate, 1648–1871* (1971), 159.

31. M. Kitchen, *The German Officer Corps, 1890–1914* (1968), 22; J. R. Gillis, 'Aristocracy and bureaucracy in nineteenth-century Prussia', *Past and Present*, 40 (1963), 103–29.

32. G. Crossick and H-G. Haupt (eds), *Shopkeepers and Master Artisans in Nineteenth-Century Europe* (1984) gives a taste of the work of some of these writers.

33. D. Blackbourn, 'The *Mittelstand* in German society and politics, 1871–1914', *Social History*, 4, (1977), 421.

34. A. Faure, 'The grocery trade in nineteenth-century Paris: a fragmented corporation' in Crossick and Haupt, op. cit., 171.

35. R. H. Williams, *Dream Worlds: Mass Consumption in Late-Nineteenth-Century France* (1982); M. B. Miller, *The Bon Marché: Bourgeois Culture and the Department Store, 1869–1920* (1981).

36. P. G. Nord, *Paris Shopkeepers and the Politics of Resentment* (1986).

37. J. C. Farcy, 'Rural artisans in the Beauce during the nineteenth century' in Crossick and Haupt, op. cit., 220.

38. D. Blackbourn, 'Between resignation and volatility: the German petite bourgeoisie in the nineteenth century' in Crossick and Haupt, op. cit., 35–62.

39. R. A. Feldmesser, 'Social classes and political structure' in C.E. Black, *The Transformation of Russian Society* (1960).

40. V. T. Bill, *The Forgotten Class* (1959).

41. G. Fischer, 'The intelligentsia' in C. E. Black, op. cit.

42. J. Blum, 'Russia' in D. Spring, *European Landed Elites in the Nineteenth Century* (1977), 71.

43. A. J. Rieber, *Merchants and Entrepreneurs in Imperial Russia* (1982), 419.

2. ECONOMIC INTERESTS OF THE MIDDLE CLASSES: ENTREPRENEURS

1. J. A. Davis, *Merchants, Monopolists and Contractors: A Study of Economic Activity and Society in Bourbon Naples, 1815–1860* (1981), 1, quoting cereal producers from the Adriatic province.

2. H. Perkins, *The Origins of Modern English Society, 1780–1880* (1969), 221.

3. W. L. Blackwell in G. Guroff and F. V. Carstensen, *Entrepreneurship in Imperial Russia and the Soviet Union* (1984), 6.

4. G. Palmade, *French Capitalism in the Nineteenth Century*, transl. G. M. Holmes (1972), 35–6.

5. J. A. Davis, op. cit., 26–7.

6. P. Leon, *Histoire Economique et Sociale de la France*, t. III, *1789–1880* (1977); R. Price, *Economic History of Modern France, 1730–1914* (1981).

7. M. Levy-Leboyer, 'Innovation and business strategies in nineteenth- and twentieth-century France' in E. Carter *et al.*, *Enterprise and Entrepreneurs*, op. cit., 90.

8. J. A. Davis, *Conflict and Control: Law and Order in Nineteenth-Century Italy* (1988), 27–9.

9. S. J. Woolf, *The History of Italy, 1700–1860* (1979).

10. K. R. Greenfield, *Economics and Liberalism in the Risorgimento: A Study of Nationalism in Lombardy, 1814–48* (1965), 143.

11. V. Castronovo, 'The Italian take-off: a critical re-examination of the problem', *Journal of Italian History* (1978), 492–511; A. Gerschenkron, *Economic Backwardness in Historical Perspective* (1966); M. Clark, *Modern Italy, 1871–1982* (1984).

12. W. O. Henderson, *The Rise of German Industrial Power, 1834–1914* (1975); K. Borchardt, 'Germany 1870–1914' in C. Cipolla (ed.) *Fontana Economic History of Europe* 4(1), 1973.

13. W. L. Blackwell, *The Beginnings of Russian Industrialisation, 1800–60* (1966); M. E. Falkus, *The Industrialisation of Russia, 1700–1914* (1979).

14. L. Bergeron, *Les Capitalistes en France, 1780–1914* (1978); E. Carter *et al.*, *Enterprise and Entrepreneurs*, op. cit. Both of these provide a more comprehensible approach.

15. J. Blum, *The End of the Old Order in Rural Europe* (1978), 299.

16. W. L. Blackwell, *The Beginnings of Russian Industrialisation*, op. cit., 202–5.

17. T. C. Owen, *Capitalism and Politics in Russia: A Social History of the Moscow Merchants, 1855–1905* (1981), 1.

18. A. J. Rieber, *Merchants and Entrepreneurs in Imperial Russia* (1982).

19. G. Palmade, op. cit., 62.

20. J. A. Davis, *Merchants*, 154–5.

21. C. Morazé, *The Triumph of the Middle Classes* (transl.) (1966), 140.

22. H. Kaelble, *Social Mobility in the Nineteenth and Twentieth Centuries* (transl.) (1985), 94–118.

23. Ibid.

24. A. J. Rieber, op. cit.

25. F. Tipton, *Regional Variations in the Economic Development of Germany during the Nineteenth Century* (1976).

26. M. Levy-Leboyer in E. Carter, op. cit., 102–3.

27. V. T. Bill, *The Forgotten Class: The Russian Bourgeoisie from the Earliest Beginnings to 1900* (1959), 170.

28. E. Zola, *Au Bonheur des Dames* (1985).

29. H. Kaelble, op. cit., 98.

30. M. Levy-Leboyer, op. cit., 102.

31. R. Bezucha, *The Lyons Uprising of 1834* (1974).

32. A. J. Rieber, op. cit.

33. V. T. Bill, op. cit.

34. M. Levy-Leboyer, op. cit., 106.

35. C. P. Kindleberger, 'Technical education and the French entrepreneur' in E. Carter, op. cit., 3–39.

36. A. J. Rieber, op. cit.

37. P. J. Harrigan, 'Secondary education and the professions in France during the Second Empire', *Comparative Studies in Society and History*, 7 (1975), 349–71.

38. C. R. Day, 'The making of mechanical engineers in France: the École des Arts et Métiers, 1803–1914', *French Historical Studies*, 10 (1978), 439–60.

39. J. A. Davis, *Merchants*, 109.

40. K. R. Greenfield, op. cit.

41. W. L. Blackwell, op. cit., 194.

42. J. A. Davis, op. cit., 28.

43. A. Brandt, 'Une famille de fabricants mulhousiens au debut du XIXe siècle, J. Koechlin et ses fils', *Annales, Economies, Sociétés, Civilisations*, 6, 1951, 319–30.

44. P. Leuilliot, *L'Alsace au Debut du XIXe Siècle, 1815–30*, 3 vols (1959–60); R. Oberlé, 'La fortune de S. Koechlin, fondateur de l'industrie mulhousienne', *Revue*

d'Histoire Economique et Sociale, 46 (1969), 108–116; R. Oberlé, 'L'evolution des fortunes à Mulhouse et le financement de l'industrie au XVIIIe siècle', *Comité des Travaux Historiques et Scientifiques, Bulletin de la Section d'Histoire Moderne et Contemporaine*, 1971, 83–175.

45. D. Landes, 'Religion and enterprise: the case of the French textile industry' in E. Carter, op. cit., 41–86; J. Lambert-Dansette and J. A. Roy, 'Origines et evolution d'une bourgeoisie: le patronat textile du bassin lillois, 1789–1914', *Revue du Nord*, 37 (1955), 199–216.

46. C. P. Kindleberger, op. cit., 3–39.

47. F. Tipton, op. cit., 129–30.

48. J. A. Davis, *Conflicts*, 272.

49. J. A. Davis, *Merchants*, 311.

50. J. H. Bater, *St Petersburg: Industrialisation and Change* (1976).

51. J. A. Davis, *Merchants*, 114.

52. Ibid., 142–50.

53. Ibid., 246.

54. 'The Italian economy in the first decade after unification' in F. Crouzet, W. H. Chaloner and W. M. Stern (eds), *Essays in European Economic History, 1789–1914* (1969), 203–26.

55. M. Kitchen, *The Political Economy of Germany* (1978), 95.

56. M. Levy-Leboyer, 'Capital investment and economic growth in France, 1820–1930', *Cambridge Economic History of Europe* 7/1 (1978), 231–95.

57. M. Levy-Leboyer in Carter, op. cit., 103.

58. T. C. Owen, 'Entrepreneurship and the structure of enterprise in Russia, 1800–80' in G. Guroff and E. V. Carstensen, *Entrepreneurship*, op. cit., 77; T. C. Owen, *Capitalism and politics in Russia: A Social History of the Moscow Merchants, 1855–1905* (1981).

59. O. Crisp, *Studies in the Russian Economy before 1914* (1976), 111.

60. R. Cameron, *France and the Economic Development of Europe*, 65.

61. G. Palmade, *French Capitalism*, op. cit., 46.

62. Kitchen, op. cit., 134–5; H. Neuberger, *German Banks and German Economic Growth, 1871–1914* (1977).

63. T. Zeldin, 'Industrialists in France, 1848–1945', *Ambition and Love* (1979), 70.

64. E. Maschke, 'Outline of the history of German cartels from 1873 to 1914' in F. Crouzet et al., op. cit., 226–58.

65. J. A. Davis, *Merchants*, 338.

3. ECONOMIC INTERESTS OF THE MIDDLE CLASSES: BOURGEOIS LANDOWNERS

1. F. Engels, Preface to the third German edition of *The Eighteenth Brumaire of Louis Bonaparte* (1926), 22.

2. D. Beales, *The Risorgimento and the Unification of Italy* (1971).

3. D. Spring (ed.), *European Landed Elites in the Nineteenth Century* (1977), 3.

4. A. Young, *Travels in France During the Years 1787, 1788 and 1789* (1929).

5. S. Woolf, *The History of Italy, 1700–1860* (1979), 44.

6. J. A. Davis, *Conflict and Control: Law and Order in Nineteenth-Century Italy* (1988), 46.

7. H. Clout and K. Sutton, 'The cadastre as a source for French rural studies', *Agricultural History*, 43 (1969), 215–24.

8. A. J. Tudesq, *La Bourgeoisie de Béziers Sous la Monarchie de Juillet d'Après les Listes Electorales Censitaires* (1959). Extrait. Actes du 83e Congrèes des Sociétés Savantes, 1958.

9. A. Daumard, *Les Bourgeois de Paris au XIXe Siècle* (1970).
10. F. O. Sargent, 'Feudalism to family farms in France', *Agricultural History* (1961), 193–201.
11. M. Agulhon, *La République au Village*, 47. Also translated (1982).
12. F. O. Sargent, 'The persistence of communal tenure in French agriculture', *Agricultural History*, 32 (1958), 100–9.
13. D. C. Higgs, 'Social mobility and hereditary titles in France, 1814–30: the *majorats-sur-demande*', *Histoire Sociale–Social History* XIV, 27 (1981), 45.
14. D. C. Higgs, 'Politics and land ownership among the French nobility after the Revolution', *European Studies Review*, 1 (1971), 105–21.
15. M. Agulhon, op. cit.
16. F. O. Sargent, 'The persistence of communal tenure', op. cit., 106.
17. T. Zeldin, 'Peasants' in *France 1848–1945: Ambition and Love* (1979), 145.
18. Ibid., 160.
19. Enquiry of 1892 quoted by P. O'Brien and C. Keyder, *Economic Growth in Britain and France, 1780–1914* (1978), 127.
20. S. Woolf, op. cit., 44.
21. J. A. Davis, op. cit., 46.
22. S. Woolf, op. cit., 210–18.
23. J. A. Davis, op. cit., 46.
24. D. Beales, *The Risorgimento*, op. cit.
25. P. Ginsborg, *Daniele Manin and the Venetian Revolution of 1848–9* (1979).
26. J. A. Davis, *Merchants, Monopolists and Contractors*, op. cit., 298–312.
27. J. A. Davis, *Conflict and Control*, op. cit., 59–63.
28. G. Luzzatto, 'The Italian economy in the first decade after unification' in F. Crouzet *et al.* (eds), *Essays in European Economic History, 1789–1914* (1969), 218; S. Woolf, op. cit., 53.
29. A. Milward and S. Saul, *The Development of the Economies of Continental Europe, 1850–1914*, 232.
30. M. Kitchen, *The Political Economy of Germany*, op. cit., 10–12.
31. F. Stern in D. Spring, op. cit., 51.
32. F. Stern, *Gold and Iron: Bismarck, Bleichröder and the Building of the German Empire* (1977), 172.
33. F. Stern in D. Spring, op. cit., 56–64.
34. D. Spring, op. cit., 5.
35. J. Blum in D. Spring, op. cit., 68.
36. J. Blum, op. cit., 86.
37. A. Gerschenkron, 'Agricultural policies and industry in Russia, 1861–1917' in H. J. Habakkuk and M. Postan, *Cambridge Economic History of Europe*, vi, II (1966).
38. G. Stephenson, *History of Russia, 1812–1945* (1969).

4. THE MIDDLE CLASSES AND THE PROFESSIONS

1. G. Millerson, *The Qualifying Associations: A Study in Professionalisation* (1964), 3.
2. H. Perkins, *The Origins of Modern English Society, 1780–1880* (1969), 427–9.
3. J. A. Davis, *Conflict and Control*, op. cit., 116.
4. P. J. Harrigan, 'Secondary education and the professions in France during the Second Empire', *Comparative Studies in Society and History*, 7 (1975), 349–71.
5. R. Anderson, 'Secondary education in mid-nineteenth-century France: some social aspects', *Past and Present* (1971), 141.
6. J. Conrad, *The German Universities for the Last Fifty Years*, transl. (1885), 91.
7. M. Barbagli, *Educating for Unemployment: Politics, Labor Markets and the School System, Italy 1859–1973* (1982), 4.

8. T. Zeldin, 'Higher education in France, 1845–1945', *Journal of Contemporary History* (1967), 55.

9. M. Clark, *Modern Italy, 1871–1982* (1984).

10. M. Barbagli, *Educating for Unemployment*, op. cit., 18–20.

11. R. Anderson, *Education in France, 1848–70* (1975), 228.

12. F. Ringer, *Education and Society in Modern Europe* (1979), 60.

13. M. Barbagli, op. cit., 30.

14. H. Rogger, *Russia in the Age of Modernisation and Revolution, 1881–1917* (1983), 88–9, 93.

15. E. Acton, *Russia* (1986), 95.

16. T. Zeldin, 'Notaires', *France 1848–1945: Ambition and Love* (1981), 43–53.

17. L. Bergeron and G. Chaussinand-Nogaret, *Les Masses de Granit* (1979), 32.

18. P. Bastid, *Les Institutions Politiques de la Monarchie Parlementaire Francaise (1814–1848)* (1954), 344–5.

19. F. Ponteil, *Les Institutions de la France de 1814 à 1870* (1965), 173.

20. J. A. Davis, *Conflict and Control*, op. cit., 116, 247–9.

21. R. Anderson, *Education in France, 1848–70* (1975), 228; J. Leonard, 'Les études médicales en France entre 1815 et 1848', *Revue d'Histoire Moderne et Contemporaine*, 13 (1966), 87–94.

22. G. Weisz, 'Reform and conflict in French medical education, 1870–1914' in R. Fox and G. Weisz, *The Organisation of Science and Technology in France, 1808–1914* (1980), 61–94.

23. D. B. Weiner, *Raspail: Scientist and Reformer* (1968), 55–9.

24. P. J. Harrigan, op. cit.

25. J. Conrad, op. cit., 141.

26. M. Barbagli, op. cit., 27–36.

27. T. Zeldin, 'Doctors' in *Ambition and Love*, op. cit., 23–42.

28. M. Hughes, *Nationalism and Society: Germany 1800–1945* (1988), 71.

29. D. Pinkney, *Decisive Years in France, 1840–47* (1986), 70.

30. T. Shinn, 'From "corps" to "profession": the emergence and definition of industrial engineering in modern France' in Fox and Weisz, op. cit., 183–210.

31. C. P. Kindleberger, 'Technical education and the French entrepreneur' in E. Carter, R. Forster and J. Moody (eds), *Enterprise and Entrepreneurs in Nineteenth- and Twentieth-Century France* (1976), 3–39.

32. A. Daumard, 'Les élèves de l'école polytechnique de 1815 à 1848', *Revue d'Histoire Moderne et Contemporaine*, 5 (1958), 226–34.

33. F. B. Artz, *The Development of Technical Education in France, 1500–1850* (1966), 239.

34. Ibid., 146.

35. P. J. Harrigan, op. cit., 365.

36. M. Traugott, *Armies of the Poor* (1985).

37. D. Pinkney, op. cit., 77.

38. C. R. Day, 'The making of mechanical engineers in France: the *Ecole des Arts et Métiers*, 1803–1914', *French Historical Studies*, 10 (1978), 439–60.

39. Ibid. and C. R. Day, 'Education for the industrial world: technical and modern instruction in France under the Third Republic, 1870–1914' in Fox and Weisz, op. cit., 127.

40. M. Barbagli, op. cit., 367.

41. A. J. Rieber, *Merchants and Entrepreneurs in Imperial Russia* (1982).

42. N. Hans, *History of Russia's Educational Policy, 1701–1917* (1931).

43. M. Levy-Leboyer, 'Innovation and business strategies in nineteenth- and twentieth-century France' in E. Carter et al., *Enterprise and Entrepreneurs*, op. cit., 108–9.

44. N. Delefortrie-Soubeyroux, *Les Dirigéants de l'Industrie Française* (1961), 268.
45. T. Zeldin, 'Higher education', op. cit., 55.
46. C. Zwerling, 'The emergence of the *Ecole Normale Supérieure* as a centre of scientific education in the nineteenth century' in Fox and Weisz, op. cit., 31–60.
47. D. Johnson, *Guizot: Aspects of French History, 1787–1874* (1963), 118–22.
48. F. Ringer, *The Decline of the German Mandarins: The German Academic Community, 1890–1933* (1969); F. Ringer, 'Higher education in Germany in the nineteenth century', *Journal of Contemporary History*, 2 (1967), 123–38.
49. N. Hans, *History of Russia's Educational Policy*, op. cit.
50. R. Fox and G. Weisz, op. cit., 21–4.
51. *The Economist*, 26 December 1987, 28–9.

5. THE MIDDLE CLASSES AND THE BUREAUCRACY

1. C. Church, *Revolution and Red Tape: The French Ministerial Bureaucracy, 1770–1850* (1981).
2. A. de Tocqueville, *The Old Regime and the French Revolution*, transl. S. Gilbert (1955), 91–2.
3. T. Zeldin, *France 1848–1945: Ambition and Love* (1979), 113–31.
4. J. R. Gillis, 'Aristocracy and bureaucracy in nineteenth-century Prussia', *Past and Present*, 40 (1963), 103–29.
5. S. Woolf, *The History of Italy, 1700–1860* (1979); M. Fried, *The Italian Prefects* (1963).
6. E. Acton, *Russia* (1986), 57.
7. A. Cobban, *The Myth of the French Revolution* (1955), 23–5.
8. H. Rosenberg, *Bureaucracy, Aristocracy and Autocracy: The Prussian Experience, 1660–1815* (1958), 182.
9. J. R. Gillis, *The Prussian Bureaucracy in Crisis, 1840–60* (1971), 23.
10. J. Conrad, *The German Universities for the Last Fifty Years* (1885).
11. J. R. Gillis, 'Aristocracy and bureaucracy in nineteenth-century Prussia', *Past and Present*, 40 (1963), 103–29.
12. V. R. Berghahn, *Modern Germany* (1983), 13.
13. J. A. Armstrong, *The European Administrative Elite* (1973).
14. J. R. Gillis, 'Aristocracy and bureaucracy', op. cit.
15. J. A. Davis, *Conflict and Control: Law and Order in Nineteenth-Century Italy* (1988), 244.
16. Ibid., 118–19.
17. J. R. Gillis, 'Aristocracy and bureaucracy', op. cit.
18. De Montrémy in C. Church, *Revolution and Red Tape: The French Ministerial Bureaucracy, 1770–1850* (1981), 2.
19. C. Church, op. cit., 72.
20. Ibid., 278.
21. L. Bergeron and G. Chaussinand-Nogaret, *Les Masses de Granit* (1979), 32.
22. N. Richardson, *The French Prefectoral Corps, 1814–30* (1966), 7.
23. Ibid., 15.
24. Ibid., 16.
25. Ch. Pouthas, 'La reorganisation du ministère de l'intérieur et la reconstitution de l'administration préfectorale par Guizot en 1830', *Revue d'Histoire Moderne et Contemporaine*, ix, 1962, 241–63; D. Pinkney, *The French Revolution of 1830* (1972), 274–96.
26. Choppin d'Arnouville, *Dossier Personnel, Archives Nationales*, F1bI157.24; H. Faure, *Galérie Administrative ou Biographique des Préfets Depuis l'Organisation des Préfectures de nos Jours*, 2 vols (1839), 96–7.

27. Fargues, *Dossier Personnel, AN*, F1bI160.2; Viefville des Essarts, *Dossier Personnel*, AN, F1bI176.11.
28. Nau de Champlouis, *Dossier Personnel*, AN, F1bI168.1; P. Henry, *Histoire des Préfets* (1950), 147.
29. Siméon, *Dossier Personnel* and E. Bourloton, G. Cogny and A. Robert, *Dictionnaire des Parlementaires Français*, 5 vols (1889–91) v, 319–20.
30. B. Leclère and V. Wright, *Les Préfets du IIe Empire* (1973).
31. P. J. Harrigan, 'Secondary education and the professions in France during the Second Empire', *Comparative Studies in Society and History*, 7 (1975), 361.
32. E. A. Whitcomb, 'Napoleon's prefects', *American Historical Review* (1974), 1089–118.
33. R. Anderson, 'Secondary education in mid-nineteenth-century France: some social aspects', *Past and Present* (1971), 121–46; P. J. Harrison, *Mobility, Elites and Education in French Society of the Second Empire* (1980).
34. M. Vaughan, 'The Grandes Ecoles' in R. Wilkinson, *Governing Elites: Studies in Training and Selection* (1969), 74–107.
35. cf. *Dossiers Personnels, AN*, F1bI.
36. T. Zeldin, *France 1848–1945: Ambition and Love*, op. cit., 113–31.
37. D. Pinkney, *Decisive Years in France, 1840–47* (1986), 78.
38. J. A. Armstrong, *The European Administrative Elite* (1973).
39. *Dossier Personnel, AN*, F1bI158.14; *Archives Départementales*, Doubs M11, M711; J. Balteau, *Dictionnaire Biographie Française*, ix (1961), 984–5.
40. Laurent, *Dossier Personnel, AN*, F1BI166.16.
41. de Tremont, *Dossier Personnel, AN*, F1bI174.12.
42. T. Zeldin, op. cit.
43. D. Mack Smith, *The Making of Italy, 1796–1870* (1968), 6.
44. See *infra* ch. 8.
45. S. Woolf, op. cit., 200.
46. J. A. Davis, *Conflict and Control*, op. cit., 24–5.
47. S. Woolf, op. cit., 208–16.
48. J. A. Davis, op. cit., 25.
49. S. Woolf, op. cit., 208–16.
50. R. J. Rath, *The Provisional Austrian Administration in Lombardy–Venetia, 1814–15* (1969).
51. J. A. Davis, *Merchants, Monopolists and Contractors*, op. cit., 154–5.
52. J. A. Davis, *Conflict and Control*, op. cit., 165.
53. Ibid., 117.
54. J. A. Davis, *Conflict and Control*, op. cit., 245.
55. M. Barbagli, *Educating for Unemployment*, op. cit., 37–41.
56. J. A. Davis, *Conflict and Control*, op. cit., 267.
57. M. Clark, *Modern Italy, 1871–1982* (1984).
58. W. M. Pintner, 'The evolution of civil officialdom, 1755–1855' in W. M. Pintner and D. K. Rowney (eds), *Russian Officialdom: The Bureaucratisation of Russian society from the Seventeenth Century to the Twentieth Century* (1980), 191.
59. E. Strauss, *The Ruling Servant: Bureaucracy in France, Russia and Britain* (1961) 155.
60. Pintner, op. cit., 207.
61. *Home of the Gentry*, Penguin edn, 26.
62. Pintner, op. cit., 194–201.
63. J. Blum, 'Russia' in D. Spring, *European Landed Elites in the Nineteenth Century* (1977), 77.
64. W. M. Pintner, 'Civil officialdom and the nobility in the 1850s' in Pintner and Rowney, op. cit., 231–42.

65. Pintner, 'The evolution of civil officialdom, 1755–1855', op. cit., 192.
66. A. Edeen, 'The civil service, its composition and status' in C. E. Black, *The Transformation of Russian Society* (1960).
67. See *infra* ch. 7.
68. F. Guizot, *Mémoires pour Servir à l'Histoire de Mon Temps* (1859–64).

6. PROFESSIONAL ARMIES AND CIVILIAN MILITIAS

1. M. Kitchen, *The German Officer Corps, 1890–1914* (1968), xiv.
2. F. Ringer, *The Decline of the German Mandarins: The German Academic Community, 1890–1933* (1969), 47.
3. M. Kitchen, op. cit., 26–31.
4. Ibid., 35.
5. Ibid., See also K. Demeter, *The German Officer Corps in Society and State, 1650–1945* (1965).
6. J. Keep, *Soldiers of the Tsar: Army and Society in Russia, 1462–1874* (1986), 315. The commentator was a contemporary, Shcherbatov.
7. Ibid., 314.
8. Ibid., 282.
9. Ibid., 245.
10. J. Blum in D. Spring (ed.), *European Landed Elites in the Nineteenth Century* (1977), 83.
11. R. L. Garthoff, 'The military as a social force' in C. E. Black, *The Transformation of Russian Society* (1960), 323–38.
12. A. Solzhenitsyn, *August 1914*, transl. M. Glenny (1974), 527.
13. L. Girard, *La Garde Nationale, 1814–71* (1964), 205; see also E. Gigault de la Bedollière, *Histoire de la Garde Nationale* (1848).
14. P. M. Pilbeam, 'The "Three Glorious Days": the revolution of 1830 in provincial France', *Historical Journal*, 26, 4, (1983), 831–44.
15. L. Girard, op. cit., 340.
16. S. Edward, *Paris Commune 1871* (1971).
17. L. Girardet, *La Société Militaire dans la France Contemporaine* (1953), 17.
18. J. Bertaud, *La Révolution Armée: Les Soldats-Citoyens et la Révolution Française* (1979); S. F. Scott, *The Response of the Royal Army to the French Revolution, 1787–93* (1978).
19. T. Zeldin, 'The army' in *France 1848–1945: Anxiety and Hypocrisy* (1981), 113–5.
20. P. Chalmin, *L'Officier Française de 1815 à 1870* (1957), 69–73.
21. R. Holyrood, 'The Bourbon army, 1815–30', *Historical Journal*, xiv, 3 (1971), 540.
22. L. Girardet, op. cit.
23. P. Chalmin, op. cit., 63.
24. Ibid., 35.
25. J. A. Davis, *Conflict and Control*, op. cit., 77.
26. J. Whittam, *The Politics of the Italian Army* (1977), 28.
27. J. A. Davis, op. cit., 137–8.
28. P. Ginsborg, *Daniele Manin and the Venetian Revolution of 1848–9* (1979), 162–8.
29. J. Whittam, op. cit., 85.
30. M. Clark, *Modern Italy, 1871–1982* (1984), 69.
31. M. Clark, op cit., 49–50.
32. J. Whittam, op. cit., 151–2.

7. EDUCATION AND THE MIDDLE CLASSES

1. R. Dahrendorf, *Society and Democracy in Germany* (1967).
2. F. Guizot, *Mémoires pour Servir à l'Histoire de Mon Temps*, iii, 12.
3. P. J. Harrigan, *Mobility, Elites and Education in French Society of the Second Empire* (1980), 14.
4. M. J. A. N. de Condorcet, *Sketch for a Historical Picture of the Progress of the Human Mind*, transl. (1955), 183–4.
5. F. B. Artz, *The Development of Technical Education in France* (1966), 131.
6. T. Zeldin, *Intellect and Pride* (1980), 150.
7. R. Anderson, *Education in France, 1848–70* (1975), 192.
8. B. G. Smith, *Ladies of the Leisure Class: The Bourgeoisie of Northern France in the Nineteenth Century* (1981).
9. P. J. Harrigan, *Mobility, Elites and Education in French Society of the Second Empire* (1980), 14. Others, including T. Zeldin (op. cit.), would question claims that the social composition of secondary schools was broad.
10. R. Gildea, *Education in Provincial France, 1800–1914* (1983), 179–208.
11. P. J. Harrigan, 'Secondary education and the professions in France during the Second Empire', *Comparative Studies in Society and History*, 7 (1975), 349–71.
12. C. R. Day, 'Education for the industrial world: technical and modern instruction in France under the Third Republic, 1870–1914' in L. Fox and G. Weisz, *The Organisation of Science and Technology in France, 1800–1914* (1980), 127–55.
13. J. A. Davis, *Conflict and Control*, op. cit., 146–9.
14. M. Clark, *Modern Italy, 1871–1982* (1984), 169.
15. L. Minio-Paluello, *Education in Fascist Italy* (1946), 17–21.
16. M. Barbagli, *Educating for Unemployment*, op. cit., 2–12.
17. F. Ringer, *Education and Society in Modern Europe* (1979); J.C. Albisetti, *Secondary School Reform in Imperial Germany* (1983).
18. L. O'Boyle, 'The problem of an excess of educated men in Western Europe, 1800–50', *Journal of Modern History* (1970), 71–95.
19. R. H. Samuel and R. H. Thomas, *Education and Society in Modern Germany* (1949), 44.
20. J. Conrad, *The German Universities for the Last Fifty Years*, transl. (1885), 224. His detailed statistical assessments are the basis for most subsequent analyses, including recent ones.
21. F. Ringer, *Education and Society*, op. cit.
22. D. Blackbourn, 'Between resignation and volatility: the German petite bourgeoisie in the nineteenth century' in G. Crossick and H. G. Haupt, *Shopkeepers and Master Artisans in Nineteenth-Century Europe* (1984), 44–5.
23. Max Weber quoted by F. Ringer, *The Decline of the German Mandarins: The German Academic Community, 1890–1933* (1969), 32.
24. J. Conrad, op. cit., 21.
25. F. Ringer, *The Decline of the German Mandarins*, op. cit., 97.
26. J. Conrad, op. cit., presents an extensive statistical assessment with useful tables.
27. F. Ringer, 'Higher education in Germany', *Journal of Contemporary History* (1967), 135–8.
28. N. Hans, *History of Russia's Educational Policy, 1701–1917* (1931), 235.
29. N. Hans, op. cit., 56.
30. N. Hans, op. cit., 77.
31. J. Blum, 'Russia' in D. Spring (ed.), *European Landed Elites in the Nineteenth Century* (1977), 81.
32. See *supra* ch. 4, 148.

8. THE BOURGEOIS REVOLUTION, 1789–1815

1. A. Soboul, *La Révolution Française* (1965), 5.
2. A. Cobban, *Aspects of the French Revolution* (1968), 90–111; A. Cobban, 'The vocabulary of social history', *Political Science Quarterly*, lxxi (1956).
3. J. Lhomme, *La Grande Bourgeoisie au Pouvoir* (1960).
4. A. Soboul, *La Révolution Française*, op. cit., 8.
5. R. Forster, *The Nobility of Toulouse in the Eighteenth Century* (1960).
6. G. V. Taylor, 'Types of capitalism in eighteenth-century France', *English Historical Review*, lxxix (1964), 478–97; 'Non-capitalist wealth and the origins of the French Revolution', *American Historical Review*, lxxii (1967), 469–96.
7. C. Lucas, 'Nobles, bourgeois and the origins of the French Revolution', *Past and Present*, 60 (1973) and reprinted in D. Johnson (ed.), *French Society and the Revolution*, 88–131.
8. F. Furet and D. Richet, *La Révolution Française*, 2 vols (1965); F. Furet, *Interpreting the French Revolution* (1984), orig. *Penser la Révolution* (1978).
9. D. M. G. Sutherland, *France 1789–1815: Revolution and Counter-Revolution* (1985), 18.
10. G. Chaussinand-Nogaret, *Une Histoire des Elites, 1700–1848* (1975); G. Chaussinand-Nogaret, *La Noblesse* (1976).
11. A. Soboul, *Comprendre la Révolution: problèmes Politiques de la Révolution Française, 1789–97* (1981) provides a recent statement of this position; see also G. Ellis, 'The "Marxist Interpretation" of the French Revolution', *English Historical Review*, xciii (1978), 353–76.
12. W. Doyle, *Origins of the French Revolution* (1980) provides a recent succinct account of the subject.
13. A. Cobban, *Aspects of the French Revolution*, op. cit., 90–111.
14. K. Marx, *The Eighteenth Brumaire of Louis Bonaparte* (1926), 24–7.
15. L. Hunt, *Politics, Culture and Class in the French Revolution* (1986), 1–16; D. M. G. Sutherland, *France 1789–1815*, op. cit.
16. *Archives Départmentales, Haute-Marne: Série M, Listes Electorales.*
17. G. Chaussinand-Nogaret, L. Bergeron and R. Forster, 'Les notables du Grand Empire en 1810', *Annales, Economies, Sociétés, Civilisations* (1971), 1052–75.
18. L. Bergeron and G. Chaussinand-Nogaret, *Les Grands Notables du 1e Empire* (CRNS 1978).
19. M. Richard in Bergeron and Chaussinand-Nogaret, op cit., Bas-Rhin (1978), 7.
20. J. Tulard in G. Chaussinand-Nogaret, *Une Histoire des Elites*, op. cit., 218.
21. L. Bergeron, *Banquiers, Négociants et Manufacturiers Parisiens du à l'Empire* (1978), 12.
22. L. Bergeron and G. Chaussinand-Nogaret, *Les Masses de Granit* (1979), 32.
23. R. R. Palmer, *The Age of the Democratic Revolution*, 2 vols (1959, 1964); J. Godechot, *La Grande Nation: L'Expansion Révolutionnaire de la France dans le Monde, 1789–99* 2 vols (1956); J. Godechot, *Les Révolutions (1770–1799)* (1963), 258–74.
24. D. M. Smith, *Italy: A Modern History* (1969), 9.
25. T. C. W. Blanning, *The French Revolution in Germany: Occupation and Resistance in the Rhineland, 1792–1802* (1983); J. M. Diefendorf, *Businessmen and Politics in the Rhineland, 1789–1834*; K. Epstein, *The Genesis of German Conservatism* (1966); M. Walker, *German Home Towns: Community, State and General Estate, 1648–1871* (1971).
26. G. Ellis, *Napoleon's Continental Blockade: The Case of Alsace* (1981).
27. M. Hughes, *Nationalism and Society, 1800–1945* (1988), 44.
28. S. Woolf, *History of Italy*, op. cit., 168.
29. R. R. Palmer, op. cit., vol. 1, 263–91.

30. S. Woolf, op. cit., 164.
31. E. J. Hobsbawm, *The Age of Revolution, 1789–1848* (1962), 81.
32. S. Woolf, op. cit., 217.
33. R. J. Rath, *The Provisional Austrian Regime in Lombardy–Venetia 1814–15* (1969), 15.
34. S. Woolf, op. cit., 211–12.
35. H. Hearder, *Italy in the Age of the Risorgimento, 1790–1870* (1983), 52.

9. THE BOURGEOISIE AND LIBERALISM

1. A. J. Mayer, *The Persistence of the Old Regime: Europe to the Great War* (1981).
2. D. H. Pinkney, *The French Revolution of 1830* (1972), 290.
3. Mme de Stael in D. Johnson, *Guizot: Aspects of French History, 1787–1874* (1963), 28.
4. P. M. Pilbeam, 'The growth of liberalism and the crisis of the Bourbon Restoration', *Historical Journal*, 25 (1982), 351–66.
5. S. Kent, *The Election of 1827 in France* (1975).
6. P. M. Pilbeam, 'The economic crisis of 1827–32 and the French Revolution of 1830', *Historical Journal* (forthcoming).
7. J. Oeschlin, *Le Mouvement Ultra-Royaliste en France* (1960), 55.
8. P. M. Pilbeam, 'The "Three Glorious Days" ', *Historical Journal*, 26 (1983), 831–44.
9. L. Blanc, *Histoire de Dix Ans* (1841), ii, 33; E. Cabet, *La Révolution de 1830 et la Situation Présente* (1831), 108.
10. K. Marx, *The Class Struggles in France 1848 to 1850* (Moscow n.d. transl. fr. German edition 1895), 44.
11. J. Lhomme, *La Grande Bourgeoisie au Pouvoir*, quoted in G. Chaussinand-Nogaret, *Une Histoire des Elites, 1700–1848* (1975), 14.
12. P. Bastid, *Les Institutions Politiques de la Monarchie Parlementaire Française (1814–1848)* (1954), 244n. 1.
13. A. J. Tudesq, *Les Grands Notables en France (1840–1849)*; *Etude Historique d'une Psychologie Sociale* (1964) i, 211–36.
14. P.-B. Higonnet, 'La composition de la Chambre des Députés 1827 à 1831', *Revue Historique* (1968), 351–78; D. Pinkney, *The French Revolution of 1830* (1972), 279–80; figures for 1840 from Tudesq, *Les Grands Notables*, op. cit., vol i, 364–8.
15. T. D. Beck, *French Legislators 1800–34: A study in Quantitative History* (1975).
16. D. H. Pinkney, *Decisive Years in France, 1840–47* (1986), 23–50; Pinkney holds that these were real 'take-off' years for the French economy.
17. H. Kohn, *The Mind of Germany* (1961).
18. J. M. Diefendorf, *Businessmen and Politics in the Rhineland* (1980), 279–84.
19. J. J. Sheehan, *German Liberalism in the Nineteenth Century* (1982).
20. T. S. Hamerow, *The Social Foundations of German Unification, 1858–71: Ideas and Institutions* (1970), 38–45.
21. Ibid., 181–2.
22. Sheehan, op. cit., 108–9.
23. Hamerow, op. cit., 288.
24. R. J. Rath, *The Provisional Austrian Administration in Lombardy–Venetia, 1814–15* (1969), 30–1.
25. D. Ginsborg, *Daniele Manin and the Venetian Revolution of 1848–9* (1979).
26. S. Woolf, *History of Italy, 1700–1860* (1979), 259.
27. Ibid., 264.
28. Ibid., 322–8.

29. Ibid., 378.
30. J. A. Davis, *Conflict and Control: Law and Order in Nineteenth-Century Italy* (1988), 168.
31. R. W. Thurston, *Liberal City, Conservative State: Moscow and Russia's Urban Crisis, 1906–1914* (1987).
32. A. J. Rieber, *Merchants and Entrepreneuers in Imperial Russia* (1982).
33. F. A. de Luna, *The French Republic under Cavaignac* (1969), 107–15.
34. S. Elwitt, *The Making of the Third Republic* (1975).
35. R. Anderson, *France, 1870–1914* (1977), 66.
36. M. Clark, *Modern Italy, 1871–1982* (1984), 61–7.
37. H. Rogger, *Russia in the Age of Modernisation and Revolution, 1881–1917* (1983), 225, 234–5.

Bibliography

ARCHIVAL SOURCES

Archives Nationales.
Dossiers Personnels. Prefects. *Série* F1bI.
Archives Départementales.
Archives Départementales Doubs M11, M711; Haute-Marne, *Listes Electorales Série M.*

OTHER SOURCES

Albisetti, J.C. *Secondary School Reform in Imperial Germany* (Princeton, 1983).
Acton, E. *Russia* (London, 1986).
Agulhon, M. *La République au Village* (Paris, 1970). Also translated (1982).
Aminzade, R. *Class, Politics and Early Industrial Capitalism: A Study in Mid-Nineteenth-Century Toulouse* (Albany, N. York, 1981).
Anderson, E. N. and Anderson, P. R. *Political Institutions and Social Change in Continental Europe in the Nineteenth Century* (L. Angeles, 1967).
Anderson, R. *Education in France, 1848–70* (Oxford, 1975).
Anderson, R. 'Secondary school education in mid-nineteenth-century France: some social aspects', *Past and Present* (1971), 121–46.
Are, G. 'Economic liberalism in Italy, 1845–1915', *Journal of Italian History*, i (1978), 409–32.
Arlacchi, P. *Mafia, Peasants and the Great Estates: Society in Traditional Calabria* (Cambridge, 1983).
Armstrong, J. A. *The European Administrative Elite* (Princeton, 1973).
Artz, F. B. *The Development of Technical Education in France, 1500–1850* (MIT 1966).
Babeuf, 'La Révolution n'est pas faite pour le peuple', *Le Tribun du Peuple*, no. 36 in A. Bayet and F. Albert, *Les Ecrivains Politiques du XIXe Siècle* (1924), 101–2.
Baker, D. N. and Harrigan, P. J. (eds) *The Making of Frenchmen: Current Directions in the History of Education in France, 1679–1979* (Waterloo, Ont., 1980).
Balteau, J. *Dictionnaire Biographie Française*, ix (Paris, 1961).
Barbagli, M. *Educating for Unemployment: Politics, Labor Markets and the School System, Italy 1859–1973* (New York, 1982).
Barral, P. *Les Périers dans l'Isère au XIXe Siècle d'après leur Correspondance Familiale* (Paris, 1959).
Bastid, P. *Les Institutions Politiques de la Monarchie Parlementaire Francaise (1814–1848)* (Paris, 1954).
Bater, J. H. *St Petersburg: Industrialisation and Change* (London, 1976).
Baudelot, C. Establet, K, and Malemort, J. *La Petite Bourgeoisie en France* (Paris, 1974).
Beales, D. *The Risorgimento and the Unification of Italy* (London, 1971).
Beau de Lomenie, E. de *Les Responsabilitiés des Dynasties Bourgeoises*, 4 vols (Paris, 1943).

Bell, R. M. *Fate and Honour Family and Village: Demographic and Cultural Change in Rural Italy since 1800* (Chicago, 1980).

Bendix, R. and Lipset, S. M. *Class, Status and Power* (Glencoe, 1953).

Bergeron, L. *Banquiers, Negoçiants et Manufacturiers Parisiens du Directoire à l'Empire* (Paris, 1978).

Bergeron, L. *Les Capitalistes en France, 1780–1914* (Paris, 1978).

Bergeron, L. 'Negociants et manufacturiers français dans les premières décennies du dix-neuvième siècle: d'une approache typologique à une analyse sociologique', *Revue Historique*, cclxi (1979), 131–42.

Bergeron, L. and Chaussinand-Nogaret, G. *Grands Notables du 1e Empire* (Paris, 1978–   ).

Bergeron, L. and Chaussinand-Nogaret G. *Les Masses de Granit* (Paris, 1979).

Berghahn, V. R. *Modern Germany* (Cambridge, 1983).

Bertaud, J. *La Révolution Armée: Les Soldats-Citoyens et la Révolution Francaise* (Paris, 1979).

Beyrau, D. 'La formation du corps des officiers russes au XIXe siècle: de la "militarisation" à la "professionalisation" ', *Cahiers du Monde Russe et Soviétique*, 19 (1978), 309–10.

Bezucha, R. *The Lyon Uprising of 1834* (Harvard, 1974).

Biddiss, M. D. *The Age of the Masses: Ideas and Society in Europe since 1870* (London, 1977).

Bill, V. T. *The Forgotten Class: The Russian Bourgeoisie from the Earliest Beginnings to 1900* (N. York, 1959).

Black, C. E. (ed.) *The Transformation of Russian Society* (Camb. Mass., 1960).

Blackbourn, D. *Class, Religion and Local Politics in Whilhelmine Germany* (Yale, 1980).

Blackbourn, D. 'The mittelstand in German society and politics, 1871–1914', *Social History*, 4 (1977), 409–33.

Blackwell, W. L. *The Beginnings of Russian Industrialisation, 1800–60* (Princeton, 1968).

Blanc, L. *Histoire de Dix Ans*, 2 vols (Paris, 1841).

Blanc, L. *L'Organisation du Travail* in J. A. R. Marriott, *The French Revolution of 1848 in its Economic Aspects*, vol. 1 (Oxford, 1913).

Blanning, T. C. W. *The French Revolution in Germany: Occupation and Resistance in the Rhineland, 1792–1802* (Oxford, 1983).

Blum, J. *The End of the Old Order in Rural Europe* (Princeton, 1978).

Bohme, H. *An Introduction to the Social and Economic History of Germany* (Oxford, 1978).

Boltanski, L. *The Making of a Class: Cadres in French Society* (Cambridge, 1988).

Bond, B. and Roy, I. (eds), *War and Society* (London, 1975).

Bourgin, G. and Bourgin, H. *La Regime de l'Industrie en France du 1814 à 1830*, 3 vols (Paris, 1912–41).

Bourloton, E., Cogny G. and Robert, A. *Dictionnaire des Parlementaires Français*, 5 vols (Paris, 1889–91).

Bouvier, J. *Histoire Economique et Histoire Sociale: Recherches sur le Capitalisme Contemporain* (Paris, 1968).

Bouvier, J. *et al.* (ed.) *Conjuncture Economique, Structures Sociales: Hommage à E. Labrousse* (Paris, 1974).

Brandt, A. 'Une famille de fabricants Mulhousiens au début du XIXe siècle, Jean Koechlin et ses fils', *Annales, Economies, Sociétés, Civilisations*, 6 (1951), 319–30.

Braudel, F. *Civilisation Matérielle et Capitalisme* (Paris, 1967) transl. as *Capitalism and Material Life, 1400–1800* (1973).

Braudel, F. and Labrousse, E. *Histoire Economique et Sociale de la France (1660–1789)*, vol. 2 (Paris, 1970).

Briggs, A. 'The language of "class" in early-nineteenth-century England' in M. W. Flinn and T. C. Smouth (eds), *Essays in Social History* (Oxford, 1974).

Brower, D. R. 'Fathers, sons and grandfathers: social origins of radical intellectuals in nineteenth-century Russia', *Journal of Social History* (1969).

Cabet, E. *La Révolution de 1830 et la Situation Présente* (Paris, 1831).

Cameron, R. *France and the Economic Development of Europe* (Chicago, 1969).

Caron, F. *Economic History of Modern France*, transl. (London, 1978).

Carter, E. *et al. Enterprise and Entrepreneurs in Nineteenth- and Twentieth-Century France* (Baltimore, 1976).

Castronovo, V. 'The Italian take-off: a critical re-examination of the problem', *Journal of Italian History*, i (1978), 492–511.

Chalmin, P. *L'Officier Français de 1815 à 1870* (Paris, 1957).

Chaussinand-Nogaret, G. 'Capital et structure sociale sous l'ancien regime', *Annales, Economies, Sociétés, Civilisations* (1970), 463–76.

Chaussinand-Nogaret, G. *La Noblesse* (Paris, 1976).

Chaussinand-Nogaret, G. *Une Histoire des Elites* (Paris, 1975).

Chaussinand-Nogaret, G., Bergeron, L. and Forster, R. 'Les notables du Grand Empire en 1810', AESC (1971), 1052–75.

Church, C. H. *Revolution and Red Tape: The French Ministerial Bureaucracy, 1770–1850* (Oxford, 1981).

Church, C. H. 'The social basis of the French central bureaucracy under the Directory, 1785–1799', *Past and Present* (1967).

Cipolla, C. (ed.) *Fontana Economic History of Europe*, 4(1) (London, 1973).

Clark, M. *Modern Italy, 1871–1982* (London, 1984).

Clifford-Vaughan, M. 'Some French concepts of elites', *British Journal of Sociology*, (1960), 319–33.

Clout, H. *Agriculture in France on the Eve of the Railway Age* (London, 1980).

Clout, H. and Sutton, K. 'The cadastre as a source for French rural studies', *Agricultural History*, 43 (1969), 215–24.

Cobban, A. *Aspects of the French Revolution* (London, 1968).

Cobban, A. *The Myth of the French Revolution of 1789* (London, 1955).

Cobban, A. 'The vocabulary of social history', *Political Science Quarterly*, lxxi (1956).

Condorcet, M. J. A. N. de *Sketch for a Historical Picture of the Progress of the Human Mind*, transl. (London, 1955).

Conrad, J. *The German Universities for the Last Fifty Years*, transl. (1885).

Coppa, F. J. 'Economic and ethical liberalism in conflict: the extraordinary liberalism of Giovanni Giolitti', *Journal of Modern History*, 42 (1970).

Coppa, F. J. 'The Italian tariff and the conflict between agriculture and industry: the commercial policy of Liberal Italy, 1860–1922', *Journal of Economic History*, xxx (1970).

Crisp, O. *Studies in the Russian Economy before 1914* (London, 1976).

Crossick, G. and Haupt, H. G. (eds) *Shopkeepers and Master Artisans in Nineteenth-Century Europe* (London, 1984).

Crouzet, F., Chaloner, W. H. and Stern, W. M. *Essays in European Economic History, 1789–1914* (London, 1969).

Curtiss, J. S. *The Russian Army under Nicholas I, 1825–55* (London, 1965).

Dahrendorf, R. *Class and Class Conflict in Industrial Society* (London, 1959).

Dahrendorf, R. *Society and Democracy in Germany* (N. York, 1967).

Daumard, A. *Les Bourgeois de Paris au XIXe Siècle* (Paris, 1970).

Daumard, A. 'Les élèves de l'école polytechnique de 1815 à 1848', *Revue d'Histoire Moderne et Contemporaine*, 5 (1958), 226–34.

Daumard, A. 'L'evolution des structures sociales en France à l'époque de l'industrialisation.' *Revue Historique* (1972), 325–46.

Daumard, A. (ed.) *Les Fortunes Françaises au XIXe Siècle* (Paris, 1973).

Daumard, A. *Maisons de Paris et Propriètaires Parisiens au XIXe Siècle, 1809–1880* (Paris, 1965).

Davis, J. A. *Conflict and Control: Law and Order in Nineteenth-Century Italy* (London, 1988).

Davis, J. A. *Merchants, Monopolists and Contractors: A Study of Economic Activity and Society in Bourbon Naples 1815–1860* (N. York, 1981).

Day, C. R. 'The making of mechanical engineers in France: the Ecoles d'Arts et Métiers, 1803–1914', *French Historical Studies*, 10 (1978), 439–60.

Delefortrie-Soubeyroux, N. *Les Dirigéants de l'Industrie Française* (Paris, 1961).

Demeter, K. *The German Officer Corps in Society and State, 1650–1945* (London, 1965).

Diefendorf, J. M. *Businessmen and Politics in the Rhineland, 1789–1834* (Princeton, 1980).

Doyle, W. *Origins of the French Revolution* (Oxford, 1980).

Edwards, S. *The Paris Commune 1871* (London, 1971).

Ellis, G. *Napoleon's Continental Blockade: The Case of Alsace* (Oxford, 1981).

Ellis, G. 'The Marxist interpretation of the French Revolution', *English Historical Review*, xciii (1978), 353–76.

Elwitt, S. *The Making of the Third Republic: Class and Politics in France, 1868–1884* (Baton Rouge, 1975).

Epstein, K. *The Genesis of German Conservatism* (Princeton, 1966).

Eyck, F. *The Frankfurt Parliament, 1848–9* (London, 1968).

Falkus, M. E. *The Industrialisation of Russia, 1700–1914* (London, 1979).

Faure, H. *Galérie Administrative ou Biographique des Préfets Depuis l'Organisation des Préfectures de nos Jours*, 2 vols (Paris, 1839).

Fedor, T. S. *Patterns of Urban Growth in the Russian Empire during the Nineteenth Century* (Chicago, 1975).

Fohlen, C. *L'Industrie Textile au Temps du Second Empire* (Paris, 1956).

Fohlen, C. *Une Affaire de Famille au XIXe Siècle: Méquillet-Noblot* (Paris, 1955).

Forster, R. *The House of Saulx-Tavannes: Versailles and Burgundy, 1700–1830* (Baltimore, 1971).

Fox, R. and Weisz, G. *The Organisation of Science and Technology in France, 1800–1914* (Cambridge, 1980).

Frieden, N. *Russian Physicians in an Era of Reform and Revolution* (Princeton, 1982).

Frijhoff, W. and Julia, D. 'Ecole et société dans la France de l'ancien régime', *Cahiers des Annales*, 35 (1975).

Furet, F. *Interpreting the French Revolution*, transl. (Cambridge, 1984).

Furet, F. 'Le Catéchisme Révolutionnaire', *Annales, Economies, Sociétées, Civilisations* (1971), 255–89.

Furet, F. and Richet, D. *La Révolution Française*, 2 vols (Paris, 1965).

Garthoff, R. L. 'The military as a social force' in C.E. Black, *The Transformation of Russian Society* (Camb., Mass., 1960), 323–38.

Gelately, R. *The Politics of Economic Despair: Shopkeepers and German Politics, 1890–1914* (London, 1974).

Gerschenkron, A. 'Agricultural policies and industry in Russia, 1861–1917' in H. J. Habakkuk and M. Postan, *Cambridge Economic History of Europe*, VI, Part II, (Cambridge, 1966).

Gerschenkron, A. *Economic Backwardness in Historical Perspective* (N. York, 1965).

Giddens, A. *Capitalism and Modern Social Theory: An analysis of the Writings of Marx, Durkheim and Max Weber* (Cambridge, 1971).

Gigault de la Bedollière, E. *Histoire de la Garde Nationale* (Paris, 1848).

Gildea, R. *Education in Provincial France, 1800–1914* (Oxford, 1983).

Gille, B. *Les Origines de la Grande Industrie Métallurgique en France* (Paris, 1947).

Gille, B. *Recherches sur la Formation de la Grande Enterprise Capitaliste (1815–48)* (Paris, 1959).

Gillis, J. R. *The Prussian Bureaucracy in Crisis, 1840–60* (Stanford, 1971).

Gillis, J. R. 'Aristocracy and bureaucracy in nineteenth-century Prussia', *Past and Present*, 40 (1963), 103–29.

Ginsborg, P. *Daniele Manin and the Venetian Revolution of 1848–9* (Cambridge, 1979).
Girard, L. *La Garde Nationale, 1814–71* (Paris, 1964).
Girardet, R. *La Société Militaire dans la France Contemporaine, 1815–1939* (Paris, 1953).
Girault, R. 'Existe-t-il une bourgeoisie d'affaires dynamique en France avant 1914?' *Bulletin de la Société d'Histoire Moderne* (1969).
Godechot, J. *La Grande Nation: L'Expansion Révolutionnaire de la France dans le Monde, 1789–99*, 2 vols (Paris, 1956).
Godechot, J. *Les Révolutions (1770–1799)* (Paris, 1963).
Gray, M, 'Government by property owners: Prussian plans for constitutional reform on county, provincial and national levels', *Journal of Modern History* (1976).
Greenfield, K. R. *Economics and Liberalism in the Risorgimento: A Study of Nationalism in Lombardy 1814–48* (Baltimore, 1965).
Grew, R., Harrigan, P. J. and Whitney J. B. 'The availability of schooling in nineteenth-century France', *Journal of Interdisciplinary History*, xiv (1983), 25–63.
Gruner, S. 'The revolution of July 1830 and the expression "bourgeoisie" ', *Historical Journal*, 11 (1968).
Guillaume, M. P. 'Essai sur la composition et la repartition de la fortune bordelaise au milieu du XIXe siècle d'après les déclarations de mutations par décès de 1873', *Revue de l'Histoire Economique et Sociale* (1965), 321–62.
Guizot, F. *History of Civilisation in France*, transl. (London, 1887).
Guizot, F. *Mémoires pour Servir à l'Histoire de Mon Temps*, 8 vols (Paris, 1856–64).
Guroff, G. and Carstensen, F. V. *Entrepreneurship in Imperial Russia and the Soviet Union* (Princeton, 1984).
Hamerow, T. S. *Restoration, Revolution, Reaction: Economics and Politics in Germany, 1815–71* (Princeton, 1958).
Hamerow, T. S. *Social Foundations of German Unification, 1858–71: Ideas and Institutions* (Princeton, 1970).
Hamm, M. F. *The City in Late Imperial Russia* (Bloomington, 1986).
Hans, N. *History of Russia's Educational Policy, 1701–1917* (London, 1931).
Harrigan, P. J. *Mobility, Elites and Education in French Society of the Second Empire* (Waterloo, Ont., 1980).
Harrigan, P. J. 'Secondary education and the professions in France during the Second Empire', *Comparative Studies in Society and History*, 7 (1975), 349–71.
Hearder, H. *Italy in the Age of the Risorgimento, 1790–1870* (London, 1983).
Henderson, W. O. *The Rise of German Industrial Power, 1834–1914* (London, 1975).
Henry, P. *Histoire des Préfets* (Paris, 1950).
Heywood, C. *The Cotton Industry in France, 1740–1850* (Loughborough, 1977).
Higgs, D. C. 'Politics and land ownership among the French nobility after the Revolution', *European Studies Review*, I (1971), 105–21.
Higgs, D. C. 'Social mobility and hereditary titles in France, 1814–30: the majorats-sur-demande', *Histoire Sociale: Social History* VIV, 27 (1981), 29–47.
Higgs, D. C. *Ultra-Royalism in Toulouse from its Origins to the Revolution of 1830* (Baltimore, 1973).
Higonnet, P. *Class, Ideology and the Rights of Nobles during the French Revolution* (Oxford, 1981).
Higonnet, P.-B. 'La composition de la Chambre des Députés 1827 à 1831', *Revue Historique* (1968).
Hobsbawm, E. J. *The Age of Capital, 1848–1875* (London, 1975).
Hobsbawm, E. J. *The Age of Revolution, 1789–1848* (London, 1962).
Holyroyd, R. 'The Bourbon army, 1815–30', *Historical Journal* (1971), 529–52.
Howarth, J. and Cerny, P. G. *Elites in France: Origins, Reproduction and Power* (London, 1981).
Hughes, M. *Nationalism and Society: Germany 1800–1945* (London, 1988).

Hunt, L. *Politics, Culture and Class in the French Revolution* (Berkley; London, 1986).
Ibarrola, J. *Structure Sociale et Fortune Mobilière à Grenoble en 1847* (Paris, 1965).
Jardin, A. and Tudesq, A. J. *La France des Notables*, 2 vols (Paris, 1973) transl. as *Revolution and Reaction, 1815–48* (Cambridge, 1983).
Johnson, D. (ed.) *French Society and the Revolution* (Cambridge, 1976).
Johnson, D. *Guizot: Aspects of French History, 1787–1874* (London, 1963).
Jones, P. M. *Politics and Rural Society: The Southern Massif Central, c. 1750–1880* (Cambridge, 1985).
Kaelble, H. *Historical Research on Social Mobility in Western Europe and the USA in the Nineteenth and Twentieth Centuries* (London, 1981).
Kaelble, H. *Social Mobility in the Nineteenth and Twentieth Centuries: Europe and the USA in Comparative Perspective* (Leamington Spa, 1985).
Keep, J. *Soldiers of the Tsar: Army and Society in Russia, 1462–1874* (Oxford, 1985).
Kemp, T. *Industrialization in Nineteenth-Century Europe* (London, 1985).
Kent, S. *The Election of 1827 in France* (Camb., Mass., 1975).
Kisch, H. 'The impact of the French Revolution on the lower Rhine textile districts', *Economic History Review*, 2nd series xv (1962), 304–27.
Kitchen, M. *The German Officer Corps, 1890–1914* (London, 1968).
Kitchen, M. *The Political Economy of Germany* (London, 1978).
Kohn, K. *The Mind of Germany* (London, 1961).
Labrousse, E. 'Voies nouvelles vers une histoire de la bourgeoisie occidentale aux XVIIIe et XIXe siècles', *Comitato Internationale di Scienze Storiche*, Rome (1955), *Relazioni*, iv.
Lambert-Dansette, J. and Roy, J. A. 'Origines et évolution d'une bourgeoisie: le patronat textile du bassin lillois (1789–1914)', *Revue du Nord*, 37 (1955), 199–216.
Leclère, B. and Wright, V. *Les Préfets du IIe Empire* (Paris, 1973).
Lee, W. R. *Industrialisation and Industrial Growth in Germany* (London, 1986).
Leonard, J. 'Les études médicales en France entre 1815 et 1848', *Revue d'Histoire Moderne et Contemporaine*, 13 (1966), 87–94.
Léon, P. et al. *Histoire Economique et Sociale de la France, 1789–1880*, vol. 3 (Paris, 1977).
Leuilliot, P. *L'Alsace au Début du XIXe Siècle: Essai d'Histoire Politique, Economique et Religieuse, 1815–30* (Paris, 1958).
Levy-Leboyer, C. 'Capital investment and economic growth in France, 1820–1930' in P. Mathias and M. Postan, *Cambridge Economic History of Europe* VII, Part I (Cambridge, 1978), 231–95.
Levy-Leboyer, C. *L'Ambition Professionnelle et la Mobilité Sociale* (Paris, 1971).
Lhomme, J. *La Grande Bourgeoisie au Pouvoir, 1830–70* (Paris, 1960).
Lincoln, W. B. *In the Vanguard of Reform: Russia's Enlightened Bureaucrats, 1825–61* (De Kalb, 1982).
Lipset, S. and Bendix, R. *Social Mobility in Industrial Society* (California, 1959).
Lovett, C. M. *The Democratic Movement in Italy, 1830–1876* (Harvard, 1982).
Lowe, D. M. *The History of Bourgeois Perception* (London, 1982).
Lucas, C. 'Nobles, bourgeois and the origins of the French Revolution', *Past and Present*, 60 (1973).
Luna, F. A. de *The French Republic under Cavaignac* (Princeton, 1969).
Magraw, R. *France 1815–1914: The Bourgeois Century* (London, 1983).
Marcuse, H. *One-Dimensional Man: The Ideology of Industrial Society* (London, 1969).
Margadant, T. W. 'Tradition and modernity in rural France during the nineteenth century', *Journal of Modern History*, lvi (1984), 667–97.
Marwick, A. *Class, Image and Reality in Britain, France and the USA since 1930* (London, 1980).
Marx, K. *The Class Struggles in France 1848 to 1850* (Moscow n.d., transl. fr. German edition 1895).

Marx, K. *The Eighteenth Brumaire of Louis Bonaparte* (London, 1926).

Massafra, A. 'La crise du baronage napoletain à la fin du 18e siècle', *Annales Historiques de la Révolution Francaise*, xli (1969), 212–26.

Mayer, A. 'The lower middle class as a historical problem', *Journal of Modern History*, 47 (1975), 409–36.

Mayer, A. *The Persistence of the Ancien Regime* (London, 1981).

McBride, T. 'A woman's world: department stores and the evolution of women's employment, 1870–1920', *French Historical Studies* (1978).

Merriman, J. (ed.) *Consciousness and Class Experience in Nineteenth-Century Europe* (N. York, 1979).

Miller, M. B. *The Bon Marché: Bourgeois Culture and the Department Store, 1869–1920* (London, 1981).

Millerson, G. *The Qualifying Associations: A Study in Professionalisation* (London, 1964).

Milward, A. and Saul, S. *The Development of the Economies of Continental Europe, 1850–1914* (London, 1978).

Minio-Paluello, L. *Education in Fascist Italy* (London, 1946).

Mommsen, W. J. *The Age of Bureaucracy: Perspectives on the Political Sociology of Max Weber* (Oxford, 1974).

Monteilhet, J. *Les Institutions Militaire de la France (1814–1924): De l'Armée Permanente à la Nation Armeée* (Paris, 1926).

Morazé, C. *The Triumph of the Middle Classes: A Study of European Values in the Nineteenth Century*, transl. (London, 1966).

Mousnier, R. 'Le concept de classe sociale et l'histoire', *Revue d'Histoire Economique et Sociale*, 48 (1970), 449–59.

Nassau Senior, W. *Journals Kept in France and Italy, 1848–1852* (London, 1973).

Neale, R. S. *Class and Ideology in the Nineteenth Century* (London, 1972).

Newell, W. H. 'The agricultural revolution in nineteenth-century France', *Journal of Economic History*, 33 (1973), 697–731.

Nord, P. G. *Paris Shopkeepers and the Politics of Resentment* (Princeton, 1986).

Oberlé, R. 'La fortune de S. Koechlin, fondateur de l'industrie mulhousienne', *Revue d'Histoire Economique et Sociale*, 46 (1969), 108–16.

Oberlé, R. 'L'évolution des fortunes à Mulhouse et le financement de l'industrialisation au XVIIIe siècle', *Comité des Travaux Historiques et Scientifiques, Bulletin de la Section d'Histoire Moderne et Contemporaine* (1971), 83–175.

O'Boyle, L. 'Liberal political leadership in Germany, 1867–84', *Journal of Modern History*, 28 (1956).

O'Boyle, L. 'The middle class in Western Europe, 1815–48', *American Historical Review*, 71 (1966).

O'Boyle, L. 'The problem of an excess of educated men in Western Europe, 1800–1850', *Journal of Modern History* (1970), 471–95.

O'Brien, P. *Railways and the Economic Development of Western Europe, 1830–1914* (London, 1983).

O'Brien, P., Heath, D. and Keyder, C. 'Agricultural efficiency in Britain and France, 1815–1914', *Journal of European Economic History*, vi (1977).

Oeschlin, J. *Le Mouvement Ultra-Royaliste en France* (Paris, 1960).

Ossowski, S. 'Different concepts of social class' in R. Bendix and S. M. Lipset, *Class, Status and Power: Social Stratification in Comparative Perspective* (London, 1967).

Owen, T. C. *Capitalism and Politics in Russia: A Social History of the Moscow Merchants, 1855–1905* (N. York and Cambridge, 1981).

Palmade, G. *French Capitalism in the Nineteenth Century*, transl. (Newton Abbot, 1972).

Palmer, R. R. *The Age of the Democratic Revolution*, 2 vols (Princeton, 1959, 1964).

Paul, H. W. 'The issue of decline in nineteenth-century French science', *French Historical Studies*, 7 (1972), 416–50.

Perkins, H. *The Origins of Modern English Society, 1780–1880* (London, 1969).

Perkins, J. 'What is social history?' *Bulletin of the John Rylands Library*, xxxvi (1953), 56–75.

Perrot, M. *Le Mode de Vie des Familles Bourgeoises, 1873–1953* (Paris, 1961).

Pilbeam, P. M. 'The economic crisis of 1827–32 and the French Revolution of 1830', *Historical Journal* (forthcoming).

Pilbeam, P. M. 'The growth of liberalism and the crisis of the Bourbon Restoration', *Historical Journal*, 25 (1982), 351–66.

Pilbeam, P. M. 'The "Three Glorious Days": the revolution of 1830 in provincial France', *Historical Journal*, 26 (1983), 831–44.

Pinkney, D. H. *Decisive Years in France, 1840–47* (Princeton, 1986).

Pinkney, D. H. *The French Revolution of 1830* (Princeton, 1972).

Pintner, W. Mck. *Russian Economic Policy under Nicholas I* (Itacha, 1967).

Pintner, W. Mck. and Rowney, D. K. *Russian Officialdom: The Bureaucratisation of Russian Society from the Seventeenth Century to the Twentieth Century* (London, 1980).

Ponteil, F. *Histoire de l'Enseignement, 1789–1965* (Paris, 1965).

Ponteil, F. *Les Institutions de la France de 1814 à 1870* (Paris, 1965).

Porch, D. *Army and Revolution: France 1815–58* (London, 1973).

Portal, R. 'Origines d'une bourgeoisie industrielle en Russie', *Revue d'Histoire Moderne et Contemporaine*, viii (1961), 35–60.

Pouthas, C. H. 'La réorganisation du ministère de l'intérieur et la reconstitution de l'administration préfectorale par Guizot en 1830', *Revue d'Histoire Moderne et Contemporaine*, ix (1962), 241–63.

Price, R. *Economic History of Modern France, 1730–1914* (London, 1981).

Price, R. *A Social History of Nineteeth-Century France* (London, 1987).

Prost, A. *L'Enseignement en France, 1800–67* (Paris, 1968).

Raeff, M. *Understanding Imperial Russia: State and Society in the Ancien Regime*, transl. (N. York, 1984).

Raeff, M. 'The Russian autocracy and its officials' in H. Mclean, M. Mahia and G. Fischer, *Russian Thought and Politics* (Cambridge, 1957).

Ralston, D. *The Army of the Republic: The Place of the Military in the Political Evolution of France, 1871–1914* (London, 1967).

Rath, R. J. *The Provisional Austrian Administration in Lombardy–Venetia, 1814–15*. (Austin, Texas, 1969).

Richard, G. 'Du moulin banal au tissage mécanique: la noblesse dans l'industrie textile en Haute-Normandie dans le première moitié du XIXe siècle', *Revue d'Histoire Economique et Sociale*, xlvi (1968), 305–38, 506–49.

Richardson, N. *The French Prefectoral Corps, 1814–30* (Cambridge, 1966).

Rieber, A. J. *Merchants and Entrepreneurs in Imperial Russia* (Chapel Hill, N. Carolina, 1982).

Ringer, F. *Education and Society in Modern Europe* (Indiana, 1979).

Ringer, F. 'Higher education in Germany in the nineteenth century', *Journal of Contemporary History* (1967), 123–38.

Ringer, F. *The Decline of the German Mandarins: The German Academic Community, 1890–1933* (Harvard, 1969).

Ritter, G. *Sword and Sceptre*, 2 vols (London, 1970–3).

Robin, R. *La Société Francaise en 1789: Semur-en-Auxois* (Paris, 1970).

Roche, D. and Labrousse, C. E. *Ordres et Classes: Colloque d'Histoire Sociale.* (St Cloud, 1967).

Rogger, H. *Russia in the Age of Modernisation and Revolution, 1881–1917* (London, 1983).

Rosenberg, H. *Bureaucracy, Aristocracy and Autocracy: The Prussian Experience, 1660–1815* (Camb., Mass., 1958).

Samuel, R. H. and Thomas, R. H. *Education and Society in Modern Germany* (London, 1949).

Sargent, F. O. 'Feudalism to family farms in France', *Agricultural History* (1961), 193–201.

Sargent, F. O. 'The persistence of communal tenure in French agriculture', *Agricultural History*, 32 (1958), 100–9.

Scott, S. F. *The Response of the Royal Army to the French Revolution, 1787–1793* (London, 1978).

Seton-Watson, H. 'Russia: army and autocracy' in M. Howard (ed.), *Soldiers and Governments* (London, 1957), 101–14.

Sheehan, J. J. *German Liberalism in the Nineteenth Century* (Cambridge, 1982).

Smith, B. G. *Ladies of the Leisure Class: The Bourgeoisie of Northern France in the Nineteenth Century* (Princeton, 1981).

Smith, D. M. *Italy: A Modern History* (Ann Arbor, 1969).

Smith, D. M. *The Making of Italy, 1796–1870* (N. York, 1968).

Soboul, A. *Comprendre la Révolution: Problèmes Politiques de la Révolution Française, 1789–97* (Paris, 1981).

Soboul, A. *La Révolution Française* (Paris, 1965).

Spring, D. (ed.) *European Landed Elites in the Nineteenth Century* (Baltimore, 1977).

Starr, S. F. *Decentralisation and Self-Government in Russia, 1830–70* (Princeton, 1972).

Stern, F. *Gold and Iron: Bismarck, Bleichröder and the Building of the German Empire* (Knopf, 1977).

Strachan, H. *European Armies and the Conduct of War* (London, 1983).

Strauss, E. *The Ruling Servant: Bureaucracy in France, Russia and Britain* (London, 1961).

Suleiman, E. N. *Elites in French Society: The Politics of Survival* (Princeton, 1978).

Sussman, G. D. 'The glut of doctors in mid-nineteenth-century France', *Comparative Studies in Society and History* (1977), 287–304.

Sutherland, D. M. G. *France 1789–1815: Revolution and Counter-Revolution* (London, 1985).

Taylor, G. V. 'Noncapitalist wealth and the origins of the French Revolution', *American Historical Review*, lxxii (1967), 469–96.

Taylor, G. V. 'Types of capitalism in eighteenth-century France', *English Historical Review*, lxxix (1964), 478–97.

Thompson, F. M. L. *English Landed Society in the Nineteenth Century* (London, 1963).

Thurston, R. W. *Liberal City, Conservative State: Moscow and Russia's Urban Crisis, 1906–1914* (Oxford, 1987).

Tilly, R. *Financial Institutions and Industrialisation in the Rhineland, 1815–70* (Kingsport, Tenn., 1966).

Tipton, F. *Regional Variations in the Economic Development of Germany during the Nineteenth Century* (Middletown, 1976).

Tocqueville, A. de *Recollections*, transl. (N. York, 1971).

Tocqueville, A. de *The Old Regime and the French Revolution*, transl. (N. York, 1955).

Traugott, M. *Armies of the Poor* (Princeton, 1985).

Tudesq, A. J. *La Bourgeoisie de Béziers sous la Monarchie de Juillet d'après les Listes Electorales Censitaires* (1959). Extrait: *Actes du 83e Congrès des Sociétés Savantes, 1958.*

Tudesq, A. J. *Les Grands Notables en France (1840–1849): Etude Historique d'une Psychologie Sociale*, 2 vols (Paris, 1964).

Villani, P. 'Le royaume de Naples pendant la domination française (1806–1815)', *Annales Historiques de la Révolution Française*, xliv (1972), 66–81.

Volkov, S. *The Rise of Antimodernism in Germany: The Urban Master Artisans, 1873–1897* (Princeton, 1978).

Vovelle, M. and Roche, D. 'Bourgeois, rentiers, propriétaires: éléments pour la définition d'une catégorie sociale à la fin du XVIIIe siècle', *Actes du 84ème Congrès National des Sociétés Savantes* (Paris, 1959), 419–52. Tr. in J. Kaplow (ed.), *New Perspectives on the French Revolution: Readings in Historical Sociology* (1965), 25–46.

Walker, Mack *German Home Towns: Community, State and General Estate, 1648–1871* (Ithaca, 1971).

Walker, Mack 'Home towns and state administrators: South German politics, 1815–30', *Political Science Quarterly*, 82 (1967).

Walker, Mack 'Napoleonic Germany and the Hometown Communities', *Central European History*, 2 (1969).

Weber, M. *The Protestant Ethic and the Spirit of Capitalism*, transl. (N. York, 1957).

Weiner, D. B. *Raspail: Scientist and Reformer* (Columbia, 1968).

Weisz, G. *The Emergence of Modern Universities in France, 1863–1914* (Princeton, 1983).

Weisz, G. 'The politics of medical professionalization in France, 1845–8', *Journal of Social History*, 12 (1978), 3–30.

Index